EDUCATION AND
SOCIETY IN
MODERN EUROPE

EDUCATION AND SOCIETY IN MODERN EUROPE

Fritz K. Ringer

Indiana University Press
BLOOMINGTON AND LONDON

This book would not have been possible without the gracious assistance of the Department of West European Studies, Indiana University.

Manufactured in the United States of America

Library of Congress Cataloging in Publication Data
Ringer, Fritz K., 1934–
  Education and society in modern Europe.
  Bibliography: p. 349
  Includes index.
  1. Comparative education. 2. Educational sociology—Germany. 3. Educational sociology—France. 4. Education, Higher—Germany—History. 5. Education, Higher—France—History. I. Title.
LA126.R56 1978   370.19'5   77–9865
ISBN 0–253–31929–3   1 2 3 4 5 83 82 81 80 79

CONTENTS

Appendix

ACKNOWLEDGMENTS

This study was begun several years ago in two graduate seminars sponsored by the West European Studies Program at Indiana University. Grants from that program paid for photocopying of source materials and for other research assistance. More recently, Boston University has helped to defray the costs of preparing the manuscript. The concluding chapters and final revisions were done under a research fellowship from the National Endowment for the Humanities.

Several participants in those early seminars at Indiana contributed in important ways to the development of the analysis and text. Preliminary drafts were written by David Justice for Germany, Paul Vogt for France, and Susanna Barrows for England. Valuable criticisms were offered by Dan Graham and David Justice. Paul Vogt's thoughtful readings of successive drafts helped in decisive ways to clarify the argument and clean up the prose. Unfortunately, the difficulty of the subject has demanded so many revisions and taken so much time that I have had to drop my initial intention to make this a collaborative volume.

Among the many friends and colleagues I have to thank for comments on earlier drafts and papers are Edward Averill, Rudolph Binion, Jean-Michel Chapoulie, Christopher Greene, David Landes, Lenore O'Boyle, Carol Pryor, Laurence Veysey, and Hans-Ulrich Wehler. Robert R. Palmer was particularly constructive in his advice on two important occasions.

I am grateful to all my good colleagues, and especially to my former collaborators, students and now friends. I hope they will forgive any opinions in this final version that still fall short of their own best judgments.

Fritz K. Ringer

EDUCATION AND
SOCIETY IN
MODERN EUROPE

Introduction:

Concepts and Hypotheses

This book is to serve as a temporary foundation for a young field of study: the comparative social history of national systems of secondary and higher education. The word *systems* is important in this connection; the time has come to move beyond monographic studies of individual institutions, valuable though they may be. For educational systems are true systems; their parts are interlinked. No history of the German technical institutes can neglect the nonclassical secondary schools. The decline of the old special secondary program in France after 1880 coincided, not at all accidentally, with the rise of the higher primary and vocational schools. Faced with the apparent disappearance of certain curricula or groups of pupils after some new piece of legislation, the careful historian is bound to rediscover them under another name or in a neighboring compartment, within a nearly unchanged overall structure. Upper middle-class parents who are denied an accustomed enclave for their children in the public schools will make every effort to find a substitute in the private sector. Thus a kind of inertia, the consequence of accustomed expectations, distinguishes the underlying reality of an educational system from the unstable surface visible in ordinary political narratives or in accounts of individual institutions. Much remains to be said about this element of inertia. Among other things, it demands that educational systems be studied historically.

Equally obvious is the need for the comparative approach. There is simply no other means of arriving at explanations, and not just descriptions, of change in education. One must be able to separate characteristics unique to this or that national system from traits shared by several systems. This sort of discrimination, in which the generality of causes is related to the generality of their effects, is an indispensable step in the construction of adequate explanations. True, the vantage

1

point from which three educational systems can be compared lies at some distance from the qualitative variety and detail of experienced history. Granted also that little is known about many of the subject areas encompassed in the following chapters, since much basic research remains to be done. Still, the need for a systematic and comparative work is great enough even now to outweigh these objections. The time may not be ripe for a synthesis in a field that is just being opened up; but the laying of a temporary foundation should not be postponed.[1]

Education and Industrialization

One of the central themes in the pages to come will be that an educational system is at least partly an autonomous element in the total society, not just an adjunct of more decisive processes or institutions. Thus the relationship between education and the economy, though significant, has not been nearly as close as is often assumed. Certainly there have been parallels between the development of higher education and the advance of industry and technology since the eighteenth century, but the correspondence has been far from perfect, especially before 1870. In fact, it is possible to distinguish three major phases in the evolution of modern European secondary schools and universities. The first extended from the eighteenth through the middle of the nineteenth century and may be called the *early industrial phase*. It was followed by a *high industrial phase* that began in the 1860s and ended around 1930. The third period, or *late industrial phase,* is with us today.

During the early industrial phase, there was in fact little connection between higher education and economic life. University enrollments per population stagnated or declined, even while the industrial revolution overtook England and then spread to the Continent. When young men entered the more distinguished European institutions of secondary and higher education during this period, they almost never meant to prepare for industrial or commercial occupations. Education above the primary level had practically nothing to do with business. The system catered to the landowning classes, and it prepared future clergymen, lawyers, doctors, and secondary teachers. In France and Germany, to be sure, the educational system also served the needs of growing government bureaucracies, and these did take an interest in technological

---

1. My own particular interest in education is that of the intellectual historian. I see the history of higher education as a step toward an historical sociology of knowledge and of culture. My present concern, however, is with foundations.

progress and economic development. The fact that the bureaucracies recruited on the basis of academic merit, moveover, may well have helped to challenge the ascribed status system of traditional society. But even so, industrialization as such was nowhere a major concern of the leading educational institutions. On the contrary, during the early industrial phase, there was a clear conflict between the traditional academic culture—that of the preindustrial elites—and the emerging business civilization.[2]

During the second, high industrial, phase in the history of European educational systems, the situation started to change. From the 1860s and '70s on, new educational institutions and curricular options began to play a significant role as "modern" alternatives to the traditional forms of secondary and higher education. Nonclassical secondary schools and programs emerged to challenge the traditional dominance of Latin and Greek at the secondary level; and in higher education, the older university faculties were joined by younger foundations, or by academies and institutions that stressed technical and other applied studies. Almost invariably, however, the newer programs failed to attain the prestige of the older ones, and their status inferiority was associated precisely with their practical bent, their positive orientation toward commerce and technology.

Altogether, the defining characteristic of the second, high industrial, phase was a kind of dualism, a tension-ridden split in the educational system. Superimposed upon the ancient divide between secondary and primary schooling, a further barrier now separated traditional learning from its modern rivals. Secondary and university enrollments per population, we shall find, increased at a moderate pace between 1860 and 1930. But most of the increases were concentrated in the modern curricular tracks. Thus, while a new, positive relationship between higher education and the economy had certainly been established, it played a really decisive role only within certain specific sectors of the educational systems.

During the third, late industrial, phase in the history of European higher education, the curricular divisions of the second phase have begun to lose some of their sharpness. At the same time, unprecedented increases in enrollments per population have altered the whole significance of advanced schooling. Secondary and even university-level education has come to be sought in preparation for a greatly increased

2. The English case is particularly clear in this respect; see Halsey, "Changing Functions." (Short form of titles will be used in footnotes, with full titles available in the Bibliography.)

variety of occupations. The nonclassical options at the secondary level have gained in standing and popularity, and so have the newer, more technically oriented university-level institutions. Certainly, the demand for technical specialists and other white-collar workers appears to have played a role in the expansion of enrollments since the interwar period. In all, these changes would seem to signal the convergence of education and the economy, an adjustment of educational systems to the manpower requirements of the late industrial era.

Yet even in this latest phase in their history, systems of education have retained a notable degree of independence from the economy. Thus in a systematic survey of twentieth-century educational systems, C. Arnold Anderson found no clear correlation between enrollments per population and either per capita income or the proportion of the work force in agriculture and other "primary" employment. University attendance has apparently tended to increase over time. But there have also been remarkable contrasts between nations at apparently comparable stages of economic development, and Anderson traces these contrasts to differing "values, customs, and public educational policies."[3]

Some sociologists have, understandably, been tempted to regard specific levels of higher education as functional necessities of advanced technological societies. Indeed, there may be some truth in their contentions. Yet what Collins calls the "technical function" model of educational development can never do full justice to the national differences observed by Anderson.[4] Some kind of conflict theory is required, if only to deal with value questions and policy issues. During the third phase in the evolution of European educational systems, for example, political and civic reform has certainly been an important autonomous impulse for change. Even the arrival of women in higher education during the 1920s, a major cause of rising attendance levels, can scarcely be traced to the state of the economy. Indeed, the progress of women in education from the 1880s on is almost totally unexplained, and the technical function theory is not likely to improve the situation.

It may help to consider just how education can contribute to economic development. Landes has distinguished four pertinent levels of training: (1) reading, writing, and arithmetic, the rudiments disseminated by the primary schools; (2) the vocational skills of the craftsman and mechanic, presumably available either through apprenticeship or from intermediate vocational schools; (3) the engineer's combina-

3. Anderson, "Access to Higher Education," p.255.
4. Collins, "Functional and Conflict Theories."

tion of scientific principle and applied training, which might be taught at the institutions of higher technical education; and (4) advanced scientific knowledge, both theoretical and applied.[5] Perhaps one could add the higher sort of literacy disseminated by general secondary schools, which could be helpful in some types of white-collar employment. Specialized financial and business schooling might also be mentioned, along with the more indirectly relevant expertise of the lawyer and public administrator. Landes himself is particularly impressed with the importance of general attitudes that can be inculcated by educational systems, such as the emphasis upon achievement, rationality, and opportunity.

But one need not extend the list to recognize that the specific contribution of education to economic development could not have been as great in 1850 as in 1900 or in 1950. The needs of the early industrial economy differed from those of its high industrial successor, for there were dramatic changes in the technological and scientific "contents" of industry. These contents were not related simply to the degree of economic development; they were dictated, rather, by what Lundgreen calls the "absolute chronology" of technological and scientific innovation.[6] This is important because it helps to explain how societies at different stages of industrialization could nonetheless develop comparable systems of education, at least after 1860. In short, a clear and direct relationship between higher education and the economy probably did not emerge until the high industrial phase in the history of European education, when certain forms of scientific and technical instruction became at least contributing causes of further economic growth.

Before that time, the primary schools may well have played a vital role, along with a handful of advanced vocational schools that flourished chiefly on the Continent. Moreover, one should not underrate the significance of meritocratic attitudes associated with the educational reforms in France and Germany at the beginning of the nineteenth century. Nor should one neglect the role of technically educated civil servants, and of administrative rationalization more generally. The growth of government bureaucracies may be considered a secondary effect, if not a precondition, of industrialization and urbanization. Indeed, the expansion of the legal and medical professions can be regarded partly in this light. *In an indirect and long-range way,* therefore, some of the oldest academic programs may well have owed their

5. Landes, *Unbound Prometheus*, p.340.
6. Lundgreen, *Bildung und Wirtschaftswachstum*, p.131.

nineteenth-century growth to economic development and prosperity.

Yet purely functional theories of professionalization, too, are likely to prove inadequate. There is a large element of convention—and therefore of potential conflict—in any establishment of educational or professional "standards."[7] Custom must ultimately help to regulate what occupations are appropriate for university graduates. Certainly before 1860, and in the short run, the conventions surrounding the older learned professions—and the traditional ideal of the educated man—had much more to do with the history of university enrollments than any immediately functional requirement of the early industrial economy.

During much of the nineteenth century, as we shall shortly discover, periods of economic recession actually appear to have coincided with short-term enrollment increases in the traditional secondary schools and universities. The reflections of the last few paragraphs are not intended to demonstrate or to explain this curious phenomenon. They *are* meant to put the reader on his guard against the easy assumption that such things *could not* have happened.

Education as Tradition

Higher education can never be truly understood apart from its special relationship to tradition. Of course, secondary schools and universities do prepare and certify students for entry into various professions. But this training function is certainly not their only role; for systems of higher education also transmit a cultural heritage. This is true, to begin with, in the broad and obvious sense in which any curriculum embodies tradition. Even scientific innovation must take place in a framework of inherited truths; neither logic nor language is reinvented afresh by every generation, and the boldest utopian visions are informed by values that have a history.

More specifically, institutions of higher education have often concentrated on the perpetuation of especially prized elements in the traditional culture. They have taught the ancient languages, for example, or they have stressed the virtues of the "classics," whether narrowly or broadly defined. More or less consciously, they have also transmitted particular lifestyles and norms of conduct derived from the past. Today's modern English "gentleman" is largely the heir of the aristocratic and gentry culture preserved at Oxford and Cambridge throughout the nineteenth century. The ideal of the broadly cultivated amateur is a further example, with French and German variants in addition to the

7. For a French example, see Weisz, "Politics of the Medical Profession."

English one. (There was at least a family resemblance between German *Bildung* and French *culture générale*.) In all the major European countries, at any rate, the older secondary schools stubbornly adhered to the classical humanist curriculum as the most adequate source of "cultivation"; this was a sharply defined tradition and an almost universal one. Surely it derived at least part of its vitality from the aristocratic connotations of classical learning, from its place in the culture of the preindustrial elites.

Obviously, the traditions and values transmitted by higher education can conflict—and have often conflicted—with the contemporary hierarchy of social norms and purposes. At the height of the industrial revolution Oxford and Cambridge held fast to the older culture of the gentry and of the Anglican Church. It was as though these ancient universities really meant to sustain an alliance between Matthew Arnold's "barbarians" and Coleridge's "clerisy," and this in conscious opposition to the emerging industrial and liberal civilization.

In the name of a partly idealized past, higher education has thus repeatedly found itself in conflict with its present. Incompletely adjusted to the prevailing manner of life, it has perpetuated outlooks that were more or less explicitly at variance with its time. "Indeed," as Halsey writes, "the history of European and American universities in the age of coal and steam industrialism is one of successful resistance, by ideological and other elements in the 'superstructure,' to the pressures set up by economic change."[8]

As vehicles of a kind of cultural lag, European secondary schools and universities thus contributed to one of the most fascinating and difficult problems in modern European social and cultural history: the survival of preindustrial social roles and attitudes into the industrial era. The point is not only that European aristocracies retained much influence and prestige until the twentieth century. Large segments of the middle class also refused to identify fully with the new world of industry and commerce. A few tried to imitate the aristocracy in their outward manner of life. Many more were captivated by more or less frankly anticapitalist or antibourgeois mentalities and social norms. They preferred old wealth and gentility to new wealth and efficiency. They wanted to be gentlemen or cultivated amateurs, not entrepreneurs or technical specialists. They flocked to the liberal professions because they felt the stigma traditionally attached to commerce. They were attracted to government offices and to the ideal of communal service because they feared and despised plutocracy and the politics of undis-

8. Halsey, "Changing Functions," p.458.

guised class conflict. We are not talking merely about the "alienation" of middle-class intellectuals who castigated the philistine materialism of the bourgeoisie. The tensions involved were much more deep-seated than that, for the European middle classes of the nineteenth century were in some ways divided against themselves.

There is an already well-established approach to the analytical problem posed by these tensions, an approach that seems promising, if not entirely free of difficulties. Some of the great European social theorists have suggested the idea of an incomplete adjustment to industrialization, or to "modernization" more generally. Marx himself was perpetually alert to the reactionary longings of social groups that were soon to be eliminated by the forward march of history. And Schumpeter constructed his model of the singleminded entrepreneur partly to show that such a man would have had little interest in the chauvinism that emerged on the eve of the First World War, especially in the incompletely modernized societies of Central Europe.[9] "Atavistic" was Schumpeter's word for the influence of military castes and irrational sentiments that struck him as relics of the past. More recently, Dahrendorf has written about "faults" in the German social structure of the nineteenth and twentieth centuries and about "unmodern men in a modern world."[10] These examples could easily be multiplied. The very idea of aristocratic values assimilated by the middle class implies the survival of traditions that have become incongruent in their modern settings.

The possible objections to this approach have been most sharply stated by Schwartz.[11] No single sequence can be posited as a norm for modernization wherever and whenever it has occurred. Moreover, the most divergent outlooks are actually present in modern societies—and in traditional ones as well. Thus neither modernity nor tradition is nearly as homogeneous as one implies when one identifies some particular element within a modern culture as an "incongruent survival" from a traditional one.

Fortunately, there is an escape from these objections, though it leads along a narrow path. Suppose we take the particular case of the Ecole Polytechnique.[12] As a creation of the French Revolution, it was suspected of Jacobin leanings under the Restoration, and not entirely without justification. Partly as a result of its active role in the Revolution of 1830, it enjoyed a degree of official favor under the July Mon-

9. Schumpeter, *Imperialism and Social Classes*, p.65, for example.
10. Dahrendorf, *Society and Democracy*, esp. pp.49–64, 105–19.
11. B. Schwartz, "The Limits of 'Tradition versus Modernity'."
12. Shinn, *Dawning of a Bourgeois Elite*.

archy. In 1848, despite the socially reformist outlook of some of its students, it ultimately sided with the forces of order in the June Days. By 1880, it was a moderate republican institution, though with a strong Orleanist bent that brought it into conflict with the more democratic leadership of the Radical republic. This is a simple instance of cultural lag; the politics of the school did not keep step with national politics, even though national politics certainly affected the institution in the long run. At any rate, both its Jacobinism before 1830 and its Orleanism after 1880 were incongruent survivals.

One needs no monolithic concept of modernity to recognize that tensions may arise among more or less rapidly changing elements within a social and cultural system. Educational institutions are administered by bureaucracies which develop an interest in the status quo. The holders of academic degrees do not like to see their certificates devalued. Teachers do sometimes identify with the power and prestige of their students and therefore often become attached to curricula clearly linked with entry into elite positions.[13] This can also aggravate their distrust of any "lowering of standards" that might produce entering classes of diminished potential distinction.[14]

Of course other professional and social groups also resist some types of change, as all bureaucracies probably do. It is not difficult to imagine all sorts of attitudes and practices outliving the conditions in which they arose. The agrarian capitalist with a patriarchal image of his role is only one instance of backward-looking "ideology" in Mannheim's sense. What reason is there to suppose that education is particularly relevant to the apparently inexhaustible variety of cultural lag?

The answer lies in the special relationship between education and tradition. True, some sort of inertia can be found in other institutions as well; education certainly does not account for all the conflicts between past and present. On the other hand, no other set of institutions has been as centrally concerned as the educational system with the transmission of the cultural heritage. At least until the present century, the perpetuation of tradition took a particularly conscious and elaborate form in the secondary schools and universities. In a way, the system of higher education was conceived principally as a vehicle of tradition, which is why we ought to know more about it. Too often, we fail to ask just how the past survives. We may recognize that certain nineteenth-century societies were what they were because they had once been decisively shaped by aristocracies, but we do not ask exactly how

13. O'Boyle, "Klassische Bildung."
14. Chapoulie, "Le corps professoral."

the aristocratic influence survived as long as it did. The history of education may eventually help to fill this gap.

In the meantime, tradition should also be understood in its immediate impact upon the behavior of students and parents. In the chapters that follow, we shall repeatedly face questions about the causes of enrollment fluctuation, about changes in students' social origins, and the like. These questions will force us to interpret the behavior of pupils and parents, or better, of groups of pupils and parents. To set a framework for the interpretation of such behavior and of the role of tradition within it, we need a tentative model of the context in which specific curricular paths are chosen.

Following Raymond Boudon, we may suppose that the potential clients of a classical or other academic secondary program, for example, would normally engage in an informal analysis of the costs and benefits associated with it.[15] The benefits would vary with the demand for graduates in the job market, though prestige could also be a consideration, especially for the more prosperous classes. The most obvious costs would be tuition and related expenses. These might be offset by scholarships, although the really poor families would find it difficult to respond to aid that could not be anticipated well in advance. Of course, it would also have to be decided whether the pupil's parents could afford to have him defer earning his own living for a number of years. The indirect cost of advanced education may well have been more important than the direct cost, though the indirect cost could be lowered by a rise in the legal school-leaving age.

Boudon is particularly interested in another kind of cost, and his approach is helpful—as far as it goes. The working-class youngster who chooses to enter an "academic" secondary program may well be forced to separate from many of his friends; he may even threaten the solidarity of his family. If he chooses a vocational course, on the other hand, no one will think the worse of him. The offspring of an upper middle-class family faces the opposite situation. The choice of the vocational over the academic course would impose a considerable psychic cost; naturally, he will do his utmost to avoid this form of social demotion and isolation. Thus two students from different class backgrounds would probably choose different educational paths, even if they did not differ in ability, in cultural background, or even in their values. The advantage of Boudon's analysis is that it accurately predicts inequalities in

15. Boudon, *Education, Opportunity, and Social Inequality.* Further comments on this book will be found in note 1 to the Conclusion.

the distribution of education beyond those based on "merit," and that it does this on the basis of an elegantly simple model of rational choice.

The disadvantage of Boudon's analysis is that it stops short of asking the most vital questions. What characteristics of an educational system —and of a society—actually shape the context in which students and parents weigh the psychological consequences of attending this or that school? Obviously, reduced distances between social strata would diminish the psychic costs of mobility. But more immediately and directly: Does the perceived social character and "style" of a school make a difference? How alien does a university look to a working-class student and to his family? These questions call attention to the importance of the communications network that may or may not inform all social groups about all sectors of the educational system.

The same questions also point up the role of the noneconomic factors that affect educational paths. These include institutional and curricular barriers between schools and between curricular tracks, the attitudes of educators, and—inevitably—the traditions of the schools and universities themselves. Any educational institution does, after all, develop a more or less distinctive style. This style may be partly defined by the views of a founder or influential teacher. But in the long run, the institution's social role, the origins and career choices of its students, really molds its character. And once again, the process involved is not immediate but historical. The past as well as the present clients of a school define its "spirit." In turn, a school's spirit not only helps to shape the outlook of its graduates, but also confronts the new or potential student as a more or less unalterable given, a reality to be reckoned with.

This is the main point to be made about the role of tradition in the distribution of advanced schooling: the social character of an individual institution—and of the whole system of higher education—is a Durkheimian "social fact," something external to the individual student, a constraint upon his choice and a condition *sui generis* that cannot be reduced to individual actions and beliefs. Indeed, it is often nearly impossible to distinguish the characteristics of an educational institution from the opinions commonly held about it. Why, for example, did few businessmen send their sons to Oxford or Cambridge during the later nineteenth century? And why did so few graduates of these institutions enter careers in business? Has the reason something to do with the outlook of the English business community or with a certain animus against commerce at the universities themselves? The question cannot really be answered in an unequivocal fashion because such antagonisms are inevitably mutual to some degree. As is so often the case in the history of higher education, we are dealing with a social distance that has become a tradition and therefore a fact, not merely someone's opinion.

Class, Status, and Education

The most widely accepted theory of the relationship between education and social stratification is uncomplicated, plausible, and largely adequate to the available evidence, at least for the contemporary period. It construes the educational system as a more or less important intermediary between the social standing of fathers and that of their sons. On the one hand, inequalities among parents lead to inequalities in their children's access to advanced schooling. On the other hand, the schooling obtained by members of the younger generation helps to determine their subsequent occupations and positions in society.

It is not clear to what extent education actually enhances professional competence. Modern schools and universities may be screening and certifying agencies as much as educational institutions, and present-day employers may be tending to compensate for generally rising educational levels by demanding "credentials" that bear no clear relationship to the jobs they are offering.[16] It has even been doubted whether education—or scholastic certification—independently affects social mobility much at all. C. A. Anderson questioned some time ago whether, with social origins factored out, the remaining effects were far from random.[17] More recently, Jencks and his associates observed a substantial link between family background and educational attainment, but a much weaker connection between educational attainment and occupational success.[18]

On the other hand, these questions of degree and emphasis have not fundamentally altered the conclusions reached by Glass and his colleagues for postwar Britain and then by Blau and Duncan for the United States. According to Blau and Duncan, an individual's social background does have a degree of continuing influence upon his career, regardless of his education. But "most of the influence of social origins on occupational achievements is mediated by education and early experience," and "education exerts the strongest direct effect on occupa-

16. Jencks and Riesman, *Academic Revolution*, pp.61–64, discuss certification versus education in present-day American colleges and universities. With the French baccalaureate in mind, I cannot agree that the situation would be improved if the testing were done outside the colleges by a national agency.

17. Anderson, "Skeptical Note."

18. Jencks et al., *Inequality*.

tional achievements."[19] Here we see education as an intermediate term between the social position of fathers and that of their sons.

In its mediating role, the educational system is not only conditioned by the existing social hierarchy on the "input side," it also experiences the "pull" of the occupational structure on the "output" side. As long as schooling helps to determine access to various occupations, the attractiveness of a school to potential students is bound to depend largely upon the jobs to which it leads, regardless of whether it truly provides the pertinent skills. The prestige of various institutions and their curricular programs are thus likely to reflect the occupational and social positions reached by their graduates. As Banks put it,

> The high prestige of the grammar school [in England since the late nineteenth century], far from conferring prestige on the professional and clerical occupations, derives its own prestige from the occupations for which it prepares.[20]

Carried to its logical conclusions, this view makes education a strictly dependent variable in the social process, an essentially mute link in a circular sequence that begins and ends in the independently established hierarchy of occupations and social ranks. Education becomes an epiphenomenon. To be sure, schooling—or certification—may today be acquiring an increasing importance in the assigning of people to occupations. The uneducated or self-taught may no longer be able to rise in society. In the late industrial context, education may become a necessary, though not sufficient, condition for occupational success. Upward social mobility may thus be increasingly channelled *through* the institutions of higher education rather than *around* them. It is not clear whether present-day trends actually lie in this direction, though it does seem likely that scholastically self-made men have become rarer in the twentieth century than they were in the nineteenth. But none of this detracts from the view of education as a dependent variable. An educational system can perfectly well enlarge its role in

19. Blau and Duncan, *American Occupational Structure*, pp.402–3. The emphasis is somewhat more upon the effect of family background, apart from schooling, in Glass, ed., *Social Mobility*, esp. pp.306–7. This emphasis is further increased in Anderson, "Skeptical Note," which is based on the pertinent data in Glass, especially on Floud, "Educational Experience." The difference between Jencks and Blau/Duncan is partly a matter of degree and partly a difference of emphasis. Jencks wants primarily to show that schooling does not enhance competence and success *within* a profession, whereas Blau and Duncan in effect stress the role of educational certificates in providing *access* to desirable posts.

20. Banks, *Parity and Prestige*, p.190.

the selection and certification of individuals while simultaneously becoming more dependent upon the collective pull of the occupational
structure. Indeed, a system totally adjusted to the existing economic
system would be most functional as a mechanism for the screening
and training of future professionals.

Altogether then, the theory of education as an essentially passive
intermediary is highly plausible, and yet it ought to be modified in
several respects. It accords well with some of the evidence; it is partly
adequate to all major phases in the evolution of modern European
educational systems; and it may well be particularly appropriate to
the late industrial era. The revisions that will be suggested are designed to make the model more responsive to certain aspects of the
contemporary scene, but their main purpose is to increase the model's
historical range, to make it relevant to the nineteenth century as well
as to the present. For this purpose the emphasis will be shifted somewhat away from the training function of the schools and toward their
role in the perpetuation of the cultural heritage. It will be proposed
that tradition has often added an element of indirection to the relationship between education and society and that the relationship has
typically been more complicated and less one-sided than the unrefined
theory would have it.

Crucial to the argument that will be made is the historical role of
status. As defined by Max Weber, *status* is the social honor associated
with certain styles of life.[21] Status is "subjective" in the sense that it is
an attributed quality, though not in the sense that it is ephemeral or
merely individual opinion. Even a large group cannot unilaterally or
quickly alter the status of a given occupation, religious affiliation, or
the like. Weber distinguished status from *class*, which he defined in
terms of objective place in the system or production, that is, in terms
of wealth and leverage in the labor and commodity markets. High
class position entails the ability to command goods and services,
whether for consumption or for further production. A favorable status
situation, on the other hand, is sustained by the conventional respect
of others. It is expressed in patterns of behavior, including modes of
consumption. Power was another independent factor in Weber's analysis of social place. What he meant by power was the chance to affect social outcomes and the behavior of others, even against their will. He
also considered the power to resist the commands of others, but he did

21. Weber, *From Max Weber*, esp. pp.192–94. Weber's German for *status* is
Stand, the word used by Othmar Spann and other neoromantic sociologists to evoke
its original sense of *estate.* But Weber's own meaning is best rendered by *status.*

not make as much of this sort of autonomy as he might have. For our present purposes, antonomy is a particularly important form of power since it was often associated with the practice of a liberal profession and even with the educated man in general.

Runciman has cogently argued that class, status, and power are indeed the three irreducible dimensions of social stratification, even though they may be found to overlap or converge in specific empirical instances.[22] That is exactly how Weber saw the matter. He knew that status might, in some circumstances, be used to gain economic advantages. He thought it even more typical for power or class advantages to produce status gains, at least in the long run. Wealthy families do tend to become "good" families as well, particularly if they use their money properly, to acquire education and other signs of a high-status style of life. Weber was very much aware, in short, that class, status, and power were interrelated and partly interchangeable.

Nevertheless, Weber persistently emphasized the possibility of tension between the hierarchies of class and status. He lived in an age and society that felt this tension deeply. Against the background of an experienced dichotomy between industrial and preindustrial values and rank orders, some of Weber's colleagues confronted Marxist class analysis with a romantic or idealist sociology of "estates," which were defined in terms of traditional social roles and common consciousness. Weber clarified the controversy—and undercut obscurantist intentions that had become involved in it—by responding with his distinction between the objective class situation and the residual and subjective attribution of status honor. He could acknowledge the possibility of conflict between class and status rankings without having to deny the centrality of objective class divisions in modern capitalist society.

Weber's whole approach was based on a strong sense of history. Indeed, he was one of the subtlest of the theoreticians who have dealt with the survival of incongruent tradition. He saw class and status ranks as tending to converge, prevented from doing so only, or particularly, during periods of abrupt economic and technological change. Rapid development in the economy, he thought, would tend to make the "naked" class situation more visible, presumably by way of its disequilibrium with more slowly evolving, more traditional status conceptions. His own time was clearly characterized by such a disjunction between the historic attributions and the contemporary realities of social place. During an age of stability, on the other hand, the status hierarchy might be expected gradually to align itself with the class

22. Runciman, "Class, Status, and Power?"

pattern, which would thus come to seem less naked and more conventional. In any case, the phenomenon of class/status tension had to be understood in a chronological framework. It implied a contrast between more or less rapidly changeable elements of social life, a sense of historical inertia, and tradition.

Weber considered advanced education a centrally important source of status, though not the only one. This is particularly clear in some of his comments on the social significance of the German secondary schools, universities, and state examinations. Interestingly enough, he had his eye less on specialized training than on general education or "cultivation" (*Bildung*), as in the following passage from a 1917 essay:

> Differences of "cultivation" are nowadays undoubtedly the most important specific source of *status group* differentiation, as contrasted with property and differentiation of economic function, the sources of *class* formation. . . . Differences of "cultivation" are . . . one of the very strongest purely psychological barriers within society. Especially in Germany, where almost all privileged positions inside and outside the civil service are tied to qualifications involving not only specialized knowledge but also "general *cultivation*". . . . All our diplomas also— and principally—certify the possession of this important *status* qualification.[23]

Thus Weber's concept of status was closely linked to tradition on the one hand and to education on the other.

Many contemporary sociologists appear to have abandoned not only the polarity but also the sense of history that gave Weber's analysis its dynamic quality. Apparently, *status* has become a general term for social rank, no matter what its basis. Distinctions are made between economic status, occupational status, and status associated with a whole series of other characteristics, including education, sex, race, and religion. Some attention is given to the possibility of status "incongruity" or "inconsistency," which obtains when individuals or groups rank higher on one than on another of the various status scales.[24] Still, the emphasis is on the interactive and convergent character of these scales and on the conventional or reputational nature of all social rank. It appears to be generally held that status incongruities are neither marked nor consequential, and/or that the predominant trend in ad-

---

23. Weber, *Gesammelte politische Schriften*, pp.247–48. The original article on "Wahlrecht und Demokratie in Deutschland" was written in December 1917. Italics and quotation marks are Weber's.

24. Runciman reports that *incongruity* is the term generally used in this connection, while S. M. Lipset prefers *inconsistency*.

vanced industrial societies is one of "convergence" toward status consistency.[25]

Methodological considerations, too, seem to speak against the attempt to pursue Weber's distinctions. Social honor is nearly as hard to measure as power. Income and years of schooling are more accessible, but it is occupational status that has emerged as the most commonly used empirical index of social rank. To establish a scale of occupational status, one simply asks test populations to compare and grade specific occupations. The results make up an "objective" measure of conventional prestige that can be applied to independently collected data on occupational distribution and mobility. The Hall-Jones scale used by Glass and his associates in England is a leading example of this procedure, as is the work of Blau and Duncan in the United States.[26] Duncan has found a very high correlation between occupational status and a combined measure of income and education.[27] This has greatly strengthened the empirical case for occupational status as a general index of social rank in all its dimensions.

Still, two objections remain. First, a combined index cannot be used to assess the relationship among the constituents it joins together. Occupational status may correlate highly with a *compound* of education and income, but that tells us little about the degree of congruence between the distributions of income and of education. Jencks and Riesman discuss the inequalities of income, occupational status, and education in the United States, but they first combine income with occupational status under the heading of "social class." Then they consider the relationship between social stratification and "cultural stratification," which they identify essentially with schooling. They conclude, cautiously enough, that there is "considerable overlap" between social and cultural classes but that "it is by no means complete."[28] Might not a more differentiated set of measures have reduced the overlap?

The second objection is specifically historical, and it brings us back to our main theme. A unilinear approach to social stratification in terms of occupational status might indeed be fairly adequate to the contemporary situation, but it is too unrefined a tool for the analysis of

25. On industrial convergence theory, see Archer and Giner, "Social Stratification in Europe," pp.2–9.

26. See note 19 above. The Hall-Jones scale is used in Floud's survey of the English educational system.

27. Duncan's finding, a correlation of 0.91, is reported by Runciman, who considers it very significant. See his "Class, Status, and Power?"

28. Jencks and Riesman, *Academic Revolution*, p.85.

early industrial societies. It neglects the incongruities that complicated European social hierarchies during the nineteenth century, especially at the intermediate and upper levels. Deeply felt differences existed between old and new wealth, gentility and plutocracy, the cultivated man and the specialist. Neither social prestige nor education was distributed as income was. In this context, Weber's conceptual framework is absolutely indispensable. There was a tension between the surviving status conventions and the emerging industrial class society, and the educational systems were deeply involved in the antithesis.

Such, at any rate, will be a working hypothesis in the chapters that follow. At least until 1930, European secondary schools and universities mediated not only between the social positions of fathers and sons but also between past and present. As vehicles of tradition, they perpetuated social norms and status conceptions that came into conflict with the economic foundations of stratification, foundations which were changing rapidly—and which ultimately proved more powerful than the past. Particularly the older and more prestigious educational institutions transmitted a heritage that was derived from the culture of the aristocracy and clergy, though it later also took on some of the values of the civil service and the liberal professions.

A system of education that is not actively incongruent can be either "functionally adjusted" or simply marginal and irrelevant. American colleges of the early nineteenth century were probably irrelevant. They trained clergymen and schoolmasters, had little prestige, and were scarcely involved in the main business of the nation. Contemporary systems of education may be moving toward functional adjustment, concentrating on the training and certification of white-collar personnel. The prestige of present-day curricular programs may indeed be defined by the occupations for which they prepare. But European educational systems during the early and high industrial phases in their history were rich in prestige and yet very incompletely adjusted to the existing economic system and class structure. They complicated or skewed the prevailing class structures by reinjecting incongruent elements of inherited status. This made them actively incongruent forces within their societies.

The leading European secondary schools and universities of the nineteenth century certainly conferred status beyond that of the professions for which they prepared. Only part of their graduates' prestige was anticipated occupational status. Some of it may have been meritocratic—the graduates were thought to have demonstrated superior intelligence—but much of the social honor associated with advanced education was traditional and cultural. Respect was inspired by the historic importance of distinguished schools, by the eminence and power of former graduates, and also by the cultural heritage embodied in the curriculum. There has always been a sound conviction that the general, nonvocational aspect of education is enriching, that any contact with the inherited culture has a humanizing effect. But even this conviction does not fully account for the status significance acquired by *specific* aspects of the nineteenth-century curriculum, such as Latin.

In 1879, German civil engineers protested against the proposal that graduates of nonclassical secondary schools should, after completing advanced studies, be admitted to their branch of the civil service. They were afraid that the standing of their profession would be lowered if Latin were dropped as a prerequisite.[29] Here is an instance in which the utility of Latin in occupational practice was not seriously alleged. The status of a curriculum defined the status of a profession, rather than the other way around. The whole situation cannot be understood without the idea of active incongruence in education. But *how* did Latin become so powerful a source of social honor?

Part of the answer lies in the pedagogical views held, whether explicitly or not, by nineteenth-century supporters of the classical curriculum. From the late nineteenth century on, Latin was often recommended as a good exercise for the mind and an ideal test of intellectual prowess. But this argument was clearly defensive; it could as easily have been used in behalf of mathematics, modern European foreign languages, or Chinese. It probably took much of its force from an older, more forthright neohumanism that lost its good conscience during the course of the nineteenth century. This older neohumanism held, quite simply, that the study of classical antiquity was a great moral and spiritual experience, and that it totally transformed those who engaged in it. Even in today's pale version, the American college student's involvement with the "Classics of Western Civilization" is thought to be more than merely intellectual. But the "classics" of nineteenth-century secondary education were much more sharply defined than those of today's general education curriculum and so were the benefits to be derived from studying them. Contact with the revered sources of classical antiquity was thought capable of affecting the whole person of the learner. Such contact was by no means analytical only; the building of character was quite naturally an integral part of secondary education.

29. Paulsen, *Geschichte des Unterrichts*, vol. 2, p.571.

In German neoidealist theories of "cultivation," for example, the pupil's potential individuality was thought to develop through total engagement with the "contents" or values of the "objective culture."[30] The emphasis upon the unique potential of the individual student was here interestingly (dialectically) related to a sense of his being shaped by the values embodied in the curriculum. Education was at once a source of diversity and a transmission of grace. Max Weber most clearly characterized the whole conception in his remarks on the Chinese literati.

> For twelve centuries social rank in China has been determined more by qualification for office than by wealth. This qualification, in turn, has been determined by education, and especially by examinations. China has made literary education the yardstick of social prestige in the most exclusive fashion, far more exclusively than did Europe during the period of the humanists, or than Germany has done.
>
> The examinations of China tested whether or not the candidate's mind was thoroughly steeped in literature and whether or not he possessed the *ways of thought* suitable to a cultured man and resulting from cultivation in literature. These qualifications held far more specifically with China than with the German humanist *Gymnasium*. . . . As far as one may judge from the assignments given to the pupils of the lower grades in China, they were rather similar to the essay topics assigned to the top grades of a German *Gymnasium*.
>
> The dualism of the *shen* and *kwei*, of good and evil spirits, of heavenly *yang* substance as over against earthly *yin* substance . . . [suggested that the task of education was] the unfolding of the *yang* substance in the soul of man. For the man in whom *yang* substance has completely gained the upper hand . . . also has power over the spirits; that is, according to the ancient notion, he has magical powers.[31]

Weber may well have transferred to the Chinese context a set of observations and concerns that originated closer to home. In any case, one begins to see how he conceived the relationship between education and status.

Another way to understand that relationship is to consider the contrasts that actually prevailed among subsectors of European educational systems during the high industrial phase. Typically, for the

30. An elaboration of this point will be found in Ringer, *Decline of the German Mandarins*, esp. pp.86–87.

31. Weber, *From Max Weber*, pp.416, 428, 436. A more complete account of Weber's views on education would have to deal with his response to the antithesis between the expert and the cultivated man, which was not free of ambiguity.

large majority of the population, there was primary and higher primary schooling, designed to be as narrowly practical as possible, to produce a maximum of usable skills with a minimum of personal or social reflection, aspiration, or consciousness. For the nonentrepreneurial middle and upper strata, classical secondary education led via the traditionally most prestigious university-level institutions to the church, the high civil service, and the liberal professions. Modern secondary schools and certain younger university-level institutions held an intermediate place and catered primarily to the commercial and industrial/technical middle class. The sons of businessmen thus typically followed somewhat different educational paths than the offspring of lawyers and officials, although these groups would have to be ranked about equally high on a unilinear scale of occupational status. There was a visible separation between the traditionally learned professions and the new commercial and industrial occupations. The status hierarchy of education was not identical with the class hierarchy of the emerging industrial society, even though the top positions in both hierarchies were sometimes held jointly.

In any case, the traditional forms of secondary and university-level education were experienced as socially elevating. It was continually stressed for example, that Latin was useless from a vocational standpoint. (Not everyone noticed that the classical curriculum had itself become a routine professional qualification.) What mattered, apparently, was precisely that Latin was not a practical skill, a specialized expertise. For the ability to do without any particular competence was clearly honorific. It suggested the power to direct others, as against having to be useful and usable oneself. It evoked aristocratic leisure, as against the need to work. It demonstrated a certain independence from market considerations, a quality shared by most members of the preindustrial and nonentrepreneurial elites: gentlemen, officials, clergymen, teachers, and members of the liberal professions. These groups possessed a substantial degree of social autonomy, if not of power generally. This social advantage became associated with the cultural ideal of the educated man as rationally autonomous, self-directed, unspecialized, fully human.

Obviously, the concept of the cultivated man was profoundly ambiguous in its implications. On the one hand, it implied an ideal alternative to commerce, utility, narrow self-interest, and exploitation. The status incongruity associated with education can thus be understood as a value conflict, as a culturally productive dissonance. It can even be considered a clue to the persistence with which certain criticisms of industrial capitalism arose within the middle class itself. On the other hand, the concept of the cultivated man was used again and again to justify the exploitation and spiritual deprivation of the uncultivated. Even political and pedagogical reformers often insisted on the sharpest possible separation between "pure" learning for the elite and rigorously practical training for the rest of mankind. Nothing was more frightening, apparently, than the idea of a primary school with a secondary school outlook or of general education for workers.[32] Stephen Cotgrove nicely epitomized the catastrophic muddles about theory and practice that resulted from these obsessions. "The objection to educating the labouring classes above their station," he wrote, "did not apply to teaching them science."[33]

With that, however, we have passed well beyond the bounds of this study. We should note that this happened gradually; we encountered no natural frontiers between the social and the intellectual history of higher education. Even so, it will be prudent to return now to a narrower view of our subject and to focus upon a clear set of empirical questions.

Statistical Properties of Educational Systems

In addition to brief studies of major institutions, the following chapters will present the most important statistical information currently available on the educational systems of Germany, France, and England.[34] The three national systems will be described and compared *as systems*, along three basic dimensions: they will be characterized as more or less *inclusive*, *progressive*, and *segmented* or *tracked*.

An *inclusive* system is one that schools a relatively large proportion of the population or of the relevant age group. Total secondary and university enrollments per population are very general measures of inclusiveness, and the only ones that can be constructed for some countries and periods. To find out what fraction of a nation's youth is being educated at a particular level, of course, one should relate en-

32. Two very good examples are found in Prost, *L'Enseignement en France*, pp.346–47.

33. Cotgrove, *Technical Education*, p.18.

34. Much of the data for Germany and France is more formally presented in the annotated tables of the Appendix (Roman numerals, to be distinguished from text tables in Arabic numerals). Specialists will want to consult the detailed notes to these appended tables. For the general reader, specific references to the Appendix are kept to a minimum and take the form of Roman numerals in brackets that designate tables *and* associated notes.

rollments to the school-age population. There are several ways of doing this, and none of them is entirely satisfactory. The difficulty stems from the fact that secondary schools and universities differ, both over time and from country to country, in the age at which they are entered, in the number of grades or years they encompass, and in the rate at which pupils drop out before completing their courses of study.

Suppose that, as of 1840, exactly 100,000 students were distributed over the five grades of a lower secondary school as shown in the pyramid below,

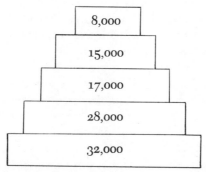

which is a typical pyramid of decreasing enrollments in ascending grades. There was a particularly marked loss of pupils after the second and after the fourth grade. The whole pyramid narrows rather sharply toward the top, which is only one-fourth as wide as the base. Suppose we also know that around 1840, the average pupil entered the lowest grade at age 10. There happened to be exactly one million ten-year-olds in the country at the time, and practically the same number in each of the age years 11 through 14. We are thus able to calculate enrollments per age group of 3.2 percent for the lowest grade, 2.8 percent for the second grade, and so on up to 0.8 percent for the highest grade. We could not be much better informed about this school's inclusiveness in 1840.[35]

For 1860, however, nothing is known about the distribution of students over the five grades. All that can be established, let us suppose,

35. One further refinement would be to determine the mean age of entry more exactly and to relate first-year enrollments (for example) to those aged 10 years and 4 months through 11 years and 3 months. The experts who worked on the *Robbins Report* used an even more perfect formula. They defined the percentage of "the age group" in a specified grade (first year of university) as the *sum of percentages* obtained after the students were grouped according to age (years), and the number of students in each year-group was divided by the total membership of that age year within the population.

is that total attendance reached 125,000. The mean age of entry and the size of the age years 10 through 14 did not change, fortunately, between 1840 and 1860. To obtain a common index of inclusiveness for 1840 *and* 1860, one can only describe total enrollments as percentages of the five-year age group 10 through 14. For 1840, one arrives at 100,000 : 5,000,000 or 2.0 percent; for 1860, the ratio comes to 2.5 percent. What these two results describe, clearly, is a kind of average, the *mean width* of the enrollments pyramid at an intermediate "altitude" that probably lies closer to the base than to the apex. This *average enrollment* turns out in practice to be the best single measure of inclusiveness in European secondary education, though it needs to be supplemented by occasional information about the base and top of the pyramid and about its general shape.

Above the secondary level things get a little more difficult, because there was no clear limit to the number of years a student spent at a European university. He might be required to register for a minimum number of semesters in order to earn a degree, but the stated minima varied over time, from faculty to faculty, and of course from country to country. One way to deal with the problem is to estimate informally the typical length of study. If it was just under four years, one divides total enrollments by the appropriate four-year age group, thus obtaining the mean width of the university pyramid and correcting as best one can for the overstated duration of studies.

An alternate method is possible where first-year enrollments can be discovered or accurately estimated, if only for an occasional year. Dividing total enrollments by the first-year figure, one obtains a somewhat specialized index of duration that may be allowed to dictate whether total enrollments for other years should be stated as percentages of a three-year or a four-year age group, for example. But a duration determined by the first-year method is a peculiar quantity. It really describes what the length of study would be if it were equal for everyone or if students were no more numerous in the first than in the later years of university attendance. It thus transforms the pyramid of enrollments into an imaginary rectangle of equal volume and equal width *at the base*. Therefore, when the result is used to calculate enrollments per age group, it produces a measure of the pyramid's base, not of its width at an intermediate altitude. Though it all sounds a bit complicated, it is really quite simple. The first-year method must eventually lead to a report on first-year enrollments and not to an average. If this is understood, and if precautions are taken against certain possible distortions, the first-year method is a reliable and highly practical approach to the issue of inclusiveness in European university education.[36]

It should be mentioned here that several careful scholars have seriously questioned the whole point of relating enrollments to total population or age groups at all.[37] They note that there has in fact been no clear correlation between enrollment trends and demographic changes. They also point out that the universities have been patronized by very narrow social groups, which might well have expanded or contracted independently of the general population. Even the demand for certain educated professionals, according to these observers, is dictated less by the size of the population than by the distribution of wealth and by other specific characteristics of the society.

This is true enough, and yet the objections based on it are ill advised. If a society grows *without changing its character,* there will be more potential university students, as well as an increase in openings for graduates. Of course societies do change, and enrollments per age groups can certainly be altered by a shift in the distribution of wealth, for example. But such alterations are a separate problem. The questions they raise could be ignored if enrollments merely kept step with the population; one must distinguish what needs to be explained from what does not. No historical or cross-national comparison makes much sense unless enrollments are stated in relative terms. It is a question of strategy.

A *progressive* educational system is one that draws a large proportion of its advanced students from the lower middle and lower classes. One way to measure progressiveness is to begin with what will be called an *access percentage.* If 10 percent of all workers' children in

36. First-year enrollments can sometimes be estimated from matriculations, as in Eulenburg, *Frequenz,* and Stone, "Size and Composition." Distortions must be guarded against during periods of rapid enrollment increase or decrease, when first-year enrollments might be misleadingly high or low. Here is another way to describe the consequences of the method. Let D be the duration defined by the method; E_t and E_1 are total and first-year enrollments; N is the population aged 20, 21, 22, etc. (these numbers being assumed equal to simplify the illustration.) Then, since D is E_t/E_1, and since the ratio of enrollments per age group (R) is calculated as $\frac{E_t}{D \times N}$, R must be $\frac{E_t}{\frac{E_t}{E_1} \times N}$ or $\frac{E_1}{N}$, i.e., first-year enrollments per age group. See V for additional details.

37. Parts of the argument are most explicit in Stone, "Size and Composition," p.9. The general position is implied in Maillet, "L'Evolution des effectifs," p.135, and it was informally stated at a conference by the formidable Victor Karady.

a given age cohort eventually reach the universities, the university access percentage for workers is 10. This figure can also be read as a probability; the working-class child has a 10 percent chance of a university education. To judge whether that is progressive or not, one needs to know the access percentages for other social groups or for the age cohort as a whole. If 20 percent is the access percentage for the whole age group, then the *comparative access chance* of a working-class youth is 0.5, or half that of the average member of his generation. Progressiveness, obviously, is a relative matter.

The other empirical approach to progressiveness is much more common, because it accords better with most of the available evidence. It involves *distribution percentages,* that is, the percentages of all university students whose fathers are workers, farmers, clerks, and so on. Distribution percentages ought to be related, where possible, to the social and occupational composition of the whole population, which is usually available in the form of a census. Consider a situation in which 8 percent of university students come from working-class backgrounds. This would be a rather progressive share if no more than 10 percent of the country's gainfully employed were workers. If one divides the university distribution percentage for workers by their share of the occupational census, one obtains an *educational opportunity ratio* that is very similar to the comparative access chance discussed above. The two would be identical, in fact, if mortality and fertility rates did not vary for different social or occupational groups. As it is, the opportunity ratio is a slightly more abstract quantity than the comparative access chance, but both are perfectly adequate measures of progressiveness in education.[38]

In practice it is seldom possible to calculate either comparative access chances or opportunity ratios with any degree of accuracy, because most occupational censuses are not fully comparable with the data available on students' social origins. In much of what follows,

38. Karady, "Normaliens et autres enseignants," develops the notion of access chances and the problems involved in moving from distribution to access percentages. C. A. Anderson, "Access to Higher Education," works with a "selectivity index" that is identical with the opportunity ratio described above. Kaelble, "Chancenungleichheit," calls the same ratio an "index of association"; he thus transfers to the analysis of academic recruitment a term initially used (by Glass et al., I think) in the study of intergenerational social mobility. I prefer "opportunity ratio" because it evokes the right intuitive interpretation *for the field of education* and because it helps join the two lines of analysis that begin with access and distribution percentages. To obtain a clear view of the relationship between an opportunity ratio and a relative access chance, suppose wCu and wCp are the numbers of workers' children of university age in the university and the general population respectively. Cu and Cp are all children of that age in the university

therefore, the censuses function as intermittent and informal standards of comparison only. Nevertheless, everything said about progressiveness derives its significance, in principle, from the concepts that have been defined.

How progressive can a system of education be? A progressive shift in an educational system is essentially a movement toward a more nearly proportional distribution of educational places.[39] At a statistically perfect level of progressiveness, the access percentages would be equal for all groups, and all opportunity ratios would stand at 1. But this abstract condition cannot be attained in practice, partly because measured academic "merit" is unequally distributed over the various social strata. Some fraction of such merit may be inherited; much of it is culturally conditioned. The test scores of parents correlate only imperfectly with those of their children. Differences in test scores are generally greater *within* a given social stratum than between any two of them. In any case, academic merit is more equally distributed over the range of social ranks than are wealth and other privileges. Efforts to make education more progressive have therefore traditionally been conceived as efforts to reward "merit" rather than wealth and influ-

---

and in the population, and W and A are all workers and all adults in the active population (occupational census). Then the relative access chance or ratio Ra is

$$\frac{\dfrac{wCu}{wCp}}{\dfrac{Cu}{Cp}} \quad \text{or} \quad \frac{wCu}{Cu} \times \frac{Cp}{wCp}$$

The opportunity ratio Ro is

$$\frac{\dfrac{wCu}{Cu}}{\dfrac{W}{A}} \quad \text{or} \quad \frac{wCu}{Cu} \times \frac{A}{W}$$

Obviously, Ra equals Ro if Cp/wCp equals A/W, i.e., if wCp/Cp equals W/A. But if $wCp/Cp > W/A$, then $Cp/wCp < A/W$ and $Ra < Ro$. In other words, to the extent that workers have more children surviving to university age than the rest of the population, one may expect the opportunity ratio for working-class students to come out higher than their relative access chance, or to overstate that chance.

39. There are exceptions. An increase in the opportunity ratio for the children of lower officials at the expense of the offspring of high officials would be progressive even if the relative access chance for lower officials already exceeded 1 (e.g., in a largely agricultural and poorly educated society). The notion of opportunity ratios should not be taken to imply a unilinear social scale on which educational opportunities are distributed in proportion to other social advantages. The educational opportunity ratio for the sons of poorly paid primary teachers, for example, might well exceed the ratio for the offspring of wealthy entrepreneurs in some circumstances.

ence. Such efforts have generally failed to attain their goal, partly because there are class differences in the costs and benefits associated with advanced education. In any case, the "meritocratic" level of progressiveness, if it were ever attained, would itself fall short of the statistically perfect progressiveness defined above.[40]

What is the connection between progressiveness and inclusiveness in education? Historically, the two have been intimately linked. Efforts to improve access percentages for the lower and lower middle classes have typically been coupled with attempts to make secondary and university-level education more inclusive. Jencks and Riesman have suggested a definition of equality in education.[41] They picture a situation in which the best-educated and the worst-educated fractions of the population do not differ very much in the years of schooling they obtain. Egalitarian effects in education might be achieved by raising the legal school leaving age, introducing secondary education for all, and making at least the lower levels of post-secondary education more inclusive as well. Obviously, such measures would simultaneously transform the affected sectors of the educational system in a progressive direction. Yet it is important to recognize that there is no *necessary* connection between progressiveness and inclusiveness in education. For example, there could be highly progressive recruitment within a system that restricted advanced schooling to a small fraction of the population and that trained this fraction much more thoroughly than the rest.

Does progressive education increase social mobility? Again, the relationship is far less clear than it seems at first glance. To begin with, a progressive educational system merely *recruits* a goodly portion of its students from among the lower strata. But social mobility through education also requires that these students end up in desirable positions after graduation. Whether or not that happens depends in part upon the demand for graduates, that is, upon the society's greater or lesser tendency to expect high educational qualifications from those it admits to its upper ranks. The placement of graduates will also be

---

40. By academic merit I mean what is measured either by so-called aptitude tests or by grades achieved in school. I gather that the old distinction between aptitude and achievement tests has not found much empirical support, but I am not sure about that. Moreover, I do not know (1) to what extent measured academic merit conceals a more basic, biological characteristic that could be called intelligence, and (2) whether *individual* differences of intelligence (thus defined) have anything to do with the observed inequality in the distribution of academic merit over the various social *classes*. The present essay simply takes that inequality as given; it contains no evidence that would bear upon its causes.

41. Jencks and Riesman, *The Academic Revolution*, pp.146–54, where the authors pose the alternative of mobility versus equality.

strongly affected by their number: if educational systems have become simultaneously more inclusive and more progressive, the net gain in social mobility through education may be insignificant, since the value of advanced schooling in the job market can be deflated as rapidly as lower-class access is increased. One must also remember that social mobility through education is not at all identical with social mobility in general. Advanced schooling may have been less of a prerequisite for social success in the nineteenth century than it is today. Thus it is possible to increase social mobility *through* the educational system at the expense of social mobility *outside* or *around* it.

A *segmented* or *tracked* system of education, finally, is one in which parallel courses of study are separated by institutional or curricular barriers, as well as by differences in the social origins of their students. The divide between the vocational and the college-preparatory stream in many American high schools is an example of tracking, and so is the traditional line between classical (or grammar) and non-classical (or modern) secondary schools in Europe. Several distinctive streams can be housed within a single institution, as in the American high school, or the segments can be physically separated, as in the case of the classical *Gymnasium* and the *Realschule* in nineteenth-century Germany. The channeling of pupils into specialized tracks can be undertaken on various grounds, including meritocratic ones. It may come early or late in the sequence of grades. But curricular specializations alone do not constitute segmentation, nor do status differences among people who have spent unequal amounts of time in school. Segmentation requires *simultaneous* differences between curricular paths and the social origins of students who travel them.

In most instances of tracking, one of the streams stands out as the social preserve of the higher strata. This common form of socially *vertical segmentation* should be distinguished from a *horizontal* variant, in which *some part* of the social difference between tracks *cannot* be described in terms of social altitude. One school might cater to the offspring of entrepreneurs and technicians; the other, to those of lawyers and high officials. At a different social level, one might attract the sons of shopkeepers and artisans; the other, those of petty civil servants and elementary teachers. In both cases, one would be dealing with divergent social clusterings at roughly comparable levels in the social hierarchy, i.e., with socially horizontal segmentation.

It is important to recognize that the divide between those members of an age group who attend educational institutions and those who do not is an instance of segmentation. Indeed, that particular divide

is the limiting case of segmentation, and it can be socially horizontal
as well as vertical. Take a society in which workers' children hardly
ever attend school beyond the age of twelve. The introduction of
popular postprimary schools for ages twelve to fourteen in such a
society must not be regarded as an increase of segmentation, even if
the postprimary stream is sharply separated from the secondary schools.
One could say, to be sure, that the postprimary schools served to absorb
into the educational system a divide that had lain outside it, but that
would be rather too cumbersome. If the postprimary schools subsequently became a branch of secondary schooling, one would want to
say that the segmentation of the system as a whole had been further
reduced, not that an older form of segmentation had been newly intruded into the secondary stream. In the same way, it is best to regard
any decisive extension of an educational system as a movement away
from segmentation.

Obviously, it is educational segmentation that tends to legitimize
and to perpetuate social distances. More specifically, much of the case
for an actively incongruent role of European education rests on the
evidence for socially horizontal segmentation. Vertical tracking is com-
patible with functional adjustment in an educational system; it can be
described, too, on a unilinear scale of occupational status. But horizontal segmentation suggests a disjunction between the hierarchies of
education and of class. This is clearest in the limiting case, where business is practically unrepresented in higher education, as in England
during the industrial revolution of the eighteenth century.

Unfortunately, there is no single statistical index of horizontal segmentation in nineteenth-century education. One can discover the occupations of students' fathers, but one cannot determine their income or
their status, not to mention the possibility of separating the two. At an
informal level, nonetheless, one cannot miss the evidence of horizontal
segmentation, for entrepreneurs and shopkeepers really did differ
demonstrably from lawyers and lower officials in their relationship to
the educational system.

Thus, while statistical data are certainly pertinent to all the questions
that have been raised, they do not provide direct numerical answers to
them all. Perhaps statistics are constitutionally evasive in this way.
They seem most comfortable in a purely negative role, forbidding
otherwise attractive hypotheses and thus limiting interpretive choices.
They do not positively dictate theories. Even at their best, they offer
us correlations in the place of explanations. That is no reason to reject
comparative statistical approaches in the history of education. It is
certainly much better to generalize with the numbers than without

them. Even so, one should never forget that statistics, like other evidence, must be interpreted.

A perfect example is provided by the data on the social origins of students. What do the sources *mean* when they describe people as "workers" or "merchants," not to speak of "property owners" or "private officials"? We are dependent upon schemes of occupational classification used in university records or by government and private statisticians, and these schemes are seldom fully comparable. They reflect conventions that changed over time and from country to country. It is therefore best to admit that a history of occupational distributions is in some measure a history of ideas. The way in which professional and social groups are named and clustered is important in its own right: it reveals how social roles and relations were experienced. Of course one should attempt to penetrate the realities behind the categories one encounters, but at the same time, one cannot neglect the independent significance of social *perceptions*. The border between social and intellectual history, we notice again, is nowhere clearly defined.

1. The German System:
Institutions and Enrollments

The Institutional Framework

Except during the National Socialist regime, schools and universities in Germany have been administered by the governments of the several German states (*Länder*).[1] Nonetheless, a fairly homogeneous national system of education emerged even before 1870, especially at the secondary and university levels. German students often crossed state lines, attending more than one university before completing their studies; in conjunction with an expanding network of standardized examinations, this freedom of movement encouraged a certain homogeneity in matters of curriculum. The political predominance of Prussia also made for uniformity, for it lent great weight to the precedents set in that state.

In Prussia, as in other German states, education has been essentially a government enterprise. Private associations and religious groups have run few schools of their own, though local authorities have participated in the maintenance of the middle and lower schools. Until the 1920s, the clergy inspected the public primary schools, many of which were denominational in character, but all decisive initiatives came from the state, particularly at secondary and university levels. Secondary teachers and university faculty above the rank of instructor have been members of the higher civil service, and the universities, though theoretically autonomous in scholarly matters, have been financed and controlled directly by the state ministries of culture.

1. The main sources for this chapter are Paulsen, *Geschichte des Unterrichts,* vol. 2; Lexis, *Unterrichtswesen;* Ringer, *Decline of the Mandarins;* and sources mentioned in the notes to appended Tables I–VIII. See the Bibliography for complete titles.

The elementary levels of primary schooling had become practically universal before the middle of the nineteenth century, largely due to the efforts of modernizing princes and officials. The full primary school (*Volksschule*) normally encompassed eight grades for ages six through thirteen. The overwhelming majority of children never advanced beyond this institution, which concentrated on the rudiments of literacy and on religious instruction. While it was possible to enter a secondary school after completing the fourth grade of a *Volksschule,* such transfers were not frequent in most states. Many pupils entered secondary schools at age nine or ten from three-year presecondary schools (*Vorschulen*) or from private elementary institutions. Primary teachers were trained, after graduation from the *Volksschule,* in special preparatory courses and did not, like prospective secondary teachers, attend secondary schools and universities. The primary system as a whole was thus largely isolated from all forms of "higher" education. This kind of segmentation was characteristic of all European systems at that time. The primary and secondary schools did not, as the names seem to indicate, follow one another sequentially. From age six, or from age ten at the latest, they functioned as separate educational tracks.

Throughout the first half of the nineteenth century, the Prussian authorities were primarily interested in the preparation of candidates for the higher civil service and the "learned professions." Mercantilist or cameralist principles might dictate a certain amount of attention to intermediate vocational and technical schooling, but it was the university-educated official who became the chief example of middle-class merit in an essentially preindustrial society. Among the pedagogical ideals that played so great a role in the Reform Period after 1806, one does find the vision of an integrated school system. A draft law of 1819 proposed a linear sequence of elementary, intermediate, and secondary education in which "middle schools" would take their pupils from common elementary institutions, teach some Latin along with other subjects, and send the best of their graduates to humanistic secondary schools. This linear scheme, however, was never made law. Instead, the aspirations of the German neohumanists and Idealists were realized only in the secondary schools and universities, and then only in a spirit of rigid formality.[2]

Indeed, the whole institutional history of German secondary and higher education during the early nineteenth century must be conceived as a process of bureaucratic rationalization. The relatively di-

---

2. Jeismann, *Das preussische Gymnasium,* is an excellent new history of that institution.

verse patterns of an earlier age were simplified and standardized. Among the results were the elevation of the classical *Gymnasium* above all other schools, the creation of a distinctive corps of philologically oriented secondary teachers, and the proliferation of state examinations and official prerequisites for professional accreditation.

In Prussia, the elevation of the *Gymnasium* can be dated from a regulation of 1812 [I]. While leaving examinations had been given at leading Prussian secondary schools since 1788, the stipulations were made much more specific in 1812. Greek and Latin became the most important elements in the test. The certificate of maturity (*Reifezeugnis* or *Abitur*) earned by successful candidates made them eligible to enroll for university study, to take various higher state examinations, or directly to enter the middle ranks of the civil service. The name *Gymnasium* had been used to describe humanistic secondary schools for some time, but it was now reserved for nine-year institutions empowered to confer the *Abitur*. So-called Latin schools that failed to achieve accreditations were in effect demoted to a lower category of secondary institutions that also included various "higher burgher" or "modern" schools (*Realschulen*). In the *Gymnasium,* according to a definitive instruction of 1837, Latin and Greek were to take up some 46 percent of the total nine-year curriculum and French an additional 4 percent, as against 17.5 percent for mathematics, physics, and natural history and 32.5 percent for history and geography, German, religion, singing, calligraphy, drawing, and philosophy.[3]

In 1810, rigorous state examinations raised the standing of secondary teachers, separating them from their colleagues in the primary schools and bringing them closer to their mentors in the universities. The university arts faculty had begun its career as a preparatory school for the theological and professional faculties. Under the influence of this tradition, the faculty continued even after 1812 to take in students without the *Abitur* [V]. These students could then earn full academic rights by passing the faculty's own maturity examination, which was relatively easy. Complaints about these laxities led to some minor restrictions in 1831. Then, in 1834, the Prussian universities were essentially closed to anyone who had not earned the *Abitur* from a *Gymnasium*. In the eighteenth century, private tutors had prepared many well-to-do pupils for the universities, and a few so-called knight's academies had still been available to young aristocrats. But all these earlier patterns were replaced, as the *Gymnasium* became the only avenue to higher education, the liberal professions, and the higher civil service.

3. Paulsen, *Geschichte des Unterrichts,* vol. 2, p.354.

From 1818 to 1914, there were twenty-two universities in the German states (excluding Austria), half of them in Prussia.[4] The four typical faculties at each university were those of theology (Catholic and/or Protestant), law, medicine, and "philosophy" (arts and sciences). In the reform plans of the German Idealists, the faculty of philosophy had been conceived as the heart of a philosophically and philologically oriented system of higher education. Embodying the theoretical unity of knowledge, it was to devote itself to pure scholarship and to general education or "cultivation" (*Bildung*), defined as the full development of the student's mind, spirit, and character. In practice, the examination introduced in 1810 also gave the faculty the more specific task of preparing teachers for the classical secondary schools. In a way, it thus became a professional faculty in its own right. During the early decades of the nineteenth century, some students continued to regard the faculty of theology as the higher humanistic faculty, a path to the teaching and scholarly professions as well as to the church. Some research and training in the natural sciences similarly continued under the auspices of the medical faculty. Gradually, however, the faculty of philosophy transcended its initial philological emphasis and teacher-preparatory function. It was eventually to emerge as the most general of the German faculties and by far the largest as well.

When a student arrived at a German university of the mid-nineteenth century at about age nineteen, he generally had behind him three years in a presecondary school, or four in a private or public elementary school, along with nine years in a *Gymnasium* and an *Abitur*. He was now almost totally free in his approach to higher learning; he faced no fixed or supervised curriculum. His first academic objective was generally to prepare for a state examination in his field. To that end, he did have to enroll in a few obligatory courses, but he might wait from two to six years before taking the test. Both the required minimum and the normal duration of study varied from subject to subject [V]. In most fields, including law and secondary teaching, two or more years of apprenticeship followed upon the passing of the state examination, and candidates faced further examinations on their "practical" experience before being fully accredited.

It is impossible to understand German higher education apart from the complex system of state examinations and academic privileges (*Berechtigungen*) that evolved during the early decades of the nineteenth century. This system had its roots in the transformation of the

---

4. This includes the University of Strassburg, opened in 1872, and two specialized university-level institutions at Braunsberg and Münster that were commonly counted among the universities.

civil service on merit principles. Tenure and seniority certainly played a role in the German bureaucracy throughout the nineteenth century, but the widening of middle-class access to it from the eighteenth century was achieved by way of increased emphasis on educational qualifications. The various ministries tended to set their own standards and administer their own tests for the several branches and grades of the service, though the universities were consulted in the process. Of course a student's certified training for a public post could help him obtain private employment as well. Governments needed not only trained jurists but also health officials, chemistry teachers, and mining engineers. They were interested, moreover, in maintaining standards in such fields as pharmacy and construction. As a result, there was hardly a discipline in which one or more state, or "diploma," examinations were not eventually established. Even exemption from ordinary military conscription was a privilege earned on the basis of six years of secondary schooling. The *Abitur* was a prerequisite for admission to the higher state examinations, so that university attendance without the secondary certificate was of little practical use.

There were two purely academic degrees conferred by the university faculties without reference to the state examination system—the doctorate and the *venia legendi*. The doctorate was generally, though not invariably, a more advanced degree than the state examination or diploma. It called for independent research and a doctoral thesis. The highest German scholarly degree was the *venia legendi* or *Habilitation*. Earned on the basis of a second dissertation, it entitled its holder to begin teaching at a German university as an instructor (*Privatdozent*).[5] The doctorate became a fairly common academic objective, taken even by students who did not intend to enter scholarly careers. In its effect on the structure of the educational system as a whole, however, it was certainly less important than the state examinations.

Almost totally excluded from the network of official examinations and academic privileges were the postprimary and lower secondary schools left behind by the Prussian *Abitur* regulation of 1812. One must think of them as an initially very heterogeneous cluster of institutions [I]. So-called burgher or middle schools were essentially senior elementary institutions designed to carry their pupils a little beyond the level of the public primary schools. Some of the provincial Latin schools that had failed to qualify as full *Gymnasien* managed to serve

5. Though most beginning university teachers held the *venia legendi* even in 1850–69, it was only toward the end of the nineteenth century that this second degree became the normal prerequisite for the right to lecture in a university faculty. See Busch, *Geschichte des Privatdozenten,* p.106.

as six or seven-year lower *Gymnasien* or *Progymnasien;* they were able to place their graduates in the upper grades of a *Gymnasium*. That left a group of "higher burgher" and "modern secondary" schools (*Realschulen*) which emphasized nonclassical subjects, though rarely to the total exclusion of Latin. Loosely related to the *Realschulen,* finally, were the intermediate provincial trade schools (*Provinzial-Gewerbeschulen*) that emerged in Prussia after 1817. Their pupils came from *Realschulen* or from primary schools, and some of them went on to more advanced vocational and technical academies. But little is known about the *Gewerbeschulen,* and they were not considered secondary schools [I].

In 1832, some of the Prussian *Realschulen* were empowered to confer leaving certificates of their own, but these were of little academic value. A reorganization in 1859 was more decisive. It distinguished nine-year *Realschulen* of the first order, later renamed *Realgymnasien,* from six-year *Realschulen* of the second order, which continued to be called *Realschulen* into the twentieth century. The later *Realgymnasium* taught almost as much Latin as the *Gymnasium* but replaced Greek with a modern foreign language, and it made a little more room than did the *Gymnasium* for the natural sciences. The ordinary *Realschule* emphasized modern languages, German, and the sciences, to the total exclusion of Latin and Greek.

Important curricular divisions between secondary schools were thus added to the sharper divide between primary and secondary education. As of 1860, there were three distinctive secondary streams: (1) Only the fully classical *Gymnasium* and *Progymnasium* led to the universities and learned professions. (2) The six-year *Realschule* did rank as a secondary school, but since it was terminal in character, there was little to distinguish it from the surviving burgher or middle schools. (3) The emerging nine-year *Realgymnasium* was a little more distinguished, academically, since it represented a compromise between the classical and the nonclassical curriculum. Some of the six or seven-year higher burgher schools came to serve as lower *Realgymnasien* or *Realprogymnasien,* officially acquiring that name in 1882. The graduates of the whole *Realgymnasium* stream, however, earned few academic privileges before 1870. Even in name, therefore, the *Realgymnasium* long continued to be grouped with the ordinary *Realschulen*. The most important divide *within* the secondary system, in other words, was that between the classical and the modern track.

As a matter of fact, a very similar division took place in higher education as well. By the late nineteenth century, various nonuniversity institutions of higher education existed in Germany, chief among them the technical institutes (*technische Hochschulen*) and the academies of mining, forestry, veterinary medicine, and agriculture. Most of these were higher vocational and technical schools. (The first business school [*Handelshochschule*] was not founded until 1898.) Lundgreen has emphasized the state's early and active encouragement of technical education in the continental successor countries, which needed to compensate for the English lead in the industrial revolution.[6] In Prussia, academies of mining and of civil engineering (*Bauakademie*) were created during the later eighteenth century, and an advanced institute of trades (*Gewerbeinstitut*) was added in 1827, partly to top off the network of provincial trade schools established since 1817. From the 1820s on, various higher vocational schools existed in other German states also. They differed a good deal in their organization and standards during the early nineteenth century; but partly under the influence of foreign models, a number of them evolved into "polytechnical" schools by mid-century and into predominantly postsecondary "technical institutes" by the 1870s. In 1879, the Prussian institute of trades and the academy of civil engineering were combined and reorganized as a technical institute.

Though separate academies continued to exist in such fields as mining, forestry, veterinary medicine, and agriculture, the technical institutes became the most important nonuniversity institutions of higher education in Germany. By 1914 there were ten technical institutes, their rapid expansion after 1860 closely paralleling that of the modern secondary schools from which they apparently took many of their students. Devoted chiefly to the applied sciences and to engineering, the institutes greatly strengthened the German chemical and electrical industries during the closing decades of the nineteenth century. Their main problem was that they could not equal the universities in academic standing and prestige.

The four decades between the reclassification of the Prussian secondary schools in 1859 and the turn of the century were filled with heated controversies over the accreditation of the nonclassical secondary curriculum. In the face of fierce resistance from traditionalists, the modern secondary schools gradually improved their legal position. Already in 1859, graduates of Prussian *Realgymnasien* (first-order *Realschulen*) had been admitted as auditors to the university faculties of arts and sciences. By 1870, they could enter as fully accredited stu-

---

6. On German scientific and technical education: Lundgreen, *Bildung und Wirtschaftswachstum*, pp. 128–49, 157; Manegold, *Technische Hochschule*; Pfetsch, *Zur Entwicklung der Wissenschaftspolitik*.

dents and were allowed to prepare for the teachers' state examinations in nonclassical subjects. (From 1879 to 1886, however, they were excluded from teaching even those subjects in a *Gymnasium*.) In 1878, the old provincial trade school was replaced by a nine-year general secondary school with a completely nonclassical curriculum [I]. Named upper modern school (*Oberrealschule*), it was meant to extend the curriculum of the existing six-year *Realschulen* for three more years. A further reclassification of 1882 would thus complete a tripartite scheme of nine-year institutions, each of which was complemented by a six-year lower school. What the *Gymnasium* was to the *Progymnasium*, and the newly renamed *Realgymnasium* to the *Realprogymnasium*, the *Oberrealschule* was to be to the *Realschule*. Graduates of the new *Oberrealschule* were to be admitted to the state examinations in certain specialized fields at the technical institutes. But that privilege was briefly withdrawn in 1886, just as the restrictions upon *Realgymnasium* graduates in secondary teaching were slightly eased. Shortly thereafter, a Prussian school conference of 1890 produced a tactical alliance between the supporters of the *Gymnasium* and those of the *Oberrealschule*, an alliance directed against the *Realgymnasium*. The curriculum of the *Gymnasium* was adjusted to resemble that of the *Realgymnasium* more closely. Graduates of the *Oberrealschule* were admitted to the universities under the severely restricted terms that had previously been granted only to students of the *Realgymnasium*. Some of the *Gymnasium* men clearly meant to eliminate the *Realgymnasium*, their most threatening rival. Others were dissatisfied with the tactic, however, because it included a dilution of the *Gymnasium*'s own curriculum.

The battle of the schools was finally ended by a Prussian decree of 1900, the provisions of which were accepted in all other German states by 1908. In theory, graduates of all three secondary streams were henceforth to be admitted to all institutions of higher education on equal terms. In practice, modern school students long continued to face a variety of specific obstacles: they were still excluded from the faculties of theology, and special examinations in Latin and even in Greek survived as preconditions for admission to various state examinations and professions.

In 1899, the Prussian technical institutes were granted the right to confer doctorates. This was the outcome of a long and bitter conflict in which the German Association of Engineers and the faculty of the technical institutes faced stubborn resistance from university professors and traditionalist officials. Despite the universities' own rapidly increasing involvement in applied research, the defenders of the status quo presented their case as a defense of pure learning against mere utility.

So deep-seated was the status inferiority of applied science that only the Emperor's intervention finally led to a solution. By the turn of the century, nonetheless, the modern curriculum had clearly asserted itself in secondary and higher education. What remained of the curricular conflicts of the nineteenth century was a difference in status between the traditional and the modern streams that has not been entirely bridged even today.

The period between 1870 and 1914 also witnessed important developments in higher primary education. In Germany, as in other European countries, the whole sector of higher primary and vocational schooling was socially very significant in ways that deserve spelling out. First, higher primary instruction was far cheaper to obtain than secondary and higher education. Tuition and fees in German secondary schools and universities were a significant element in de facto academic recruitment until after the Second World War.[7] If one also considers the indirect costs of withholding pupils from the labor market, one begins to appreciate what it meant to pass through the secondary schools, the state examinations, and the years of practical apprenticeship that were required even of secondary teachers, not to mention university instructors. Higher primary schools were economically attractive not only because they charged relatively low fees but also because they led rather quickly to earnings from partly skilled jobs.

A second important characteristic of the higher primary sector resulted simply from its place in the whole institutional structure of German education. Though separated from the secondary system, it could provide some further training for pupils from the public schools. As has been noted, transfers from public primary to full secondary schools at age ten were not common in most states. Graduates of the public primary schools did have the choice of becoming primary or higher primary teachers. They could enter a three-year preparatory course, move on to a teachers' seminary for another three years, and spend a final year or two as candidates in practical training. This was

---

7. Around 1900, secondary tuitions ranged from 110 to 150 Marks per year; university lecture fees and related expenses (but not including medical, examination, and registration fees) were 120–140 Marks per year in theology, philology, mathematics, and law, and 230–240 Marks in chemistry and medicine. The total cost of university study was estimated as from 1,000 to over 2,000 Marks per year. Around 1885, German primary teachers earned 1,500 Marks per year; secondary teachers earned 3,000–7,000 Marks (Beier, *Die höheren Schulen*, p.1170; Lexis, *Die deutschen Universitäten*, vol. 1, pp.162–64; Lexis, *Unterrichtswesen*, vol. 3, p.170). But these are occasional bits of information. There is an urgent need for systematic and comparative work on all costs of education in relation to incomes and standards of living.

certainly a path of upward mobility for youngsters from the lower classes, but it was a relatively narrow path because there were limits to the demand for primary teachers. Higher primary schools provided important further options.

The last two points to be made about the higher primary sector are that it interacted to some degree with the lower secondary schools and that it provided an environment for the emergence of girls' secondary education. Prussian developments will provide some examples.

During the early decades of the nineteenth century, enrollments in Prussian burgher, or middle, schools were sometimes grouped with enrollments in higher burgher schools and *Realschulen* [I]. In all likelihood, the middle schools were only a little more advanced and distinguished than the primary schools. On the other hand, the position of the nonclassical secondary schools was still somewhat unclear as well. This gradually changed as many higher burgher schools became de facto *Realprogymnasien*, and as even the entirely nonclassical *Realschulen* were more precisely defined. The six-year *Realschulen* could confer exemption from ordinary conscription and probably drew students away from the higher primary sector.

In 1872, Prussia grouped the remaining senior elementary institutions under the now official title of middle schools (*Mittelschulen*). Apparently, these took in most of their pupils at age nine or ten and moved them a year or two beyond the eight-year run of the primary schools. Some middle schools were public; others were private. They were distinguished from a few advanced classes attached to elementary schools and also from the *Realschulen*. Though a foreign language might be taught, the emphasis in the *Mittelschulen* was on practical and vocational subjects.

It is surely significant that the first official enrollment statistics for the Prussian *Mittelschulen* date from 1878. That was the year in which the six-year *Realschulen* acquired a "big sister" in the form of the nine-year *Oberrealschule*, itself the heir of the provincial trade school. Thus, as one form of vocational schooling became secondary, another took its place, though at a lower level. And as the nonclassical secondary stream improved its standing by being extended to nine years, it was sharply separated from the higher primary sector.

Even after 1878, however, expanding enrollments at Prussian middle schools are not easy to interpret [I]. The difficulty stems chiefly from the fact that a category of "higher girls' schools" was grouped with the middle schools until just before the turn of the century. As a matter of fact, girls were more numerous than boys even in the ordinary middle schools, especially in the private ones. In other words, secondary education for girls slowly developed within the middle school system during the 1880s and after. A Prussian regulation of 1910 may be regarded as the completion of the process; it raised some of the higher girls' schools to full secondary status. Similar to the *Realgymnasien* in their curriculum, the new girls' secondary schools clearly benefited from the improved status of modern secondary education after the turn of the century. Just on the eve of the First World War a few women began to appear at German universities.

Between 1918 and 1933, under the Weimar Republic, a series of reforms reduced the institutional barriers that separated German primary from secondary and higher education. Ever since the 1890s, determined reformers had been proposing the so-called common school (*Einheitsschule*), a single institution of primary and secondary schooling with a diversified curriculum in the upper grades. During the year or two of revolutionary optimism immediately after the war, it looked as though the republican parties might actually achieve something like the common school, along with other decisive changes in an educational system that had been thoroughly identified with the old regime. These hopes were considerably reduced during the 1920s as the parties of reform were weakened and divided. Nonetheless, a few moderate but not insignificant innovations survived the process of political attrition and retrenchment.

Despite determined resistance from conservatives and unfortunate entanglements in confessional conflicts, presecondary and private primary schools were gradually abolished during the 1920s. All pupils were henceforth to receive four years of common elementary schooling in the so-called *Grundschule*, the lower division of the public *Volksschule*. After leaving the *Grundschule*, the student had three options: he could enter the upper division of the primary school, as most continued to do; he could go to a middle school; or he could transfer to the secondary sector.

That sector, in turn, was enlarged through the addition of two new schools [I]. The German high school (*Deutsche Oberschule*) was a nine-year institution that offered neither classical nor modern foreign languages. It was primarily intended to provide secondary education for elementary teachers. Among its supporters, some had socially progressive motives, but many also liked the nationalistic curricular emphasis on all things German. The other new secondary school was the continuation school (*Aufbauschule*). It took promising pupils after seven years of primary or middle schooling, and it prepared them for the *Abitur* in a six-year program. Perhaps it was intended to keep rural or provincial youngsters on the farm, but it had a progressive dimension as well. Potential access to the *Abitur* was further increased by the establishment of a substitute maturity examination for non-secondary students (*Ersatzreifeprüfung*) in 1923. As we shall see, the practical effect of these innovations was not very great. Supplementary tests in the classical languages continued to obstruct the path to the state examinations in certain fields. Still, new passages were now at least available across the divide between primary and secondary education. And since graduates of modern and girls' secondary schools were also arriving at the universities in growing numbers, the old *Gymnasium* monopoly was broken.

At the same time, important steps were taken in the direction of universal, compulsory vocational schooling [1]. Part-time vocational schools were established for graduates of the primary schools. The vocational schools usually provided six to ten hours of instruction per week. Employers were required to give their employees time off to attend. In theory, all males aged fourteen to eighteen had to enroll, unless they were engaged in some sort of full-time schooling; but, unfortunately, this provision was not strictly enforced, primarily because of the financial crises that beset the government and the country.

The full-time middle schools continued to function. Institutionally, they were strengthened by the right to confer the certificate of intermediate maturity (*Zeugnis der mittleren Reife*), which replaced the old military exemption after completion of six years of secondary schooling. Nonetheless, the middle schools lost enrollments to the secondary system, which had become nearly as easy to enter.

Three new universities appeared on the interwar scene. Founded between 1914 and 1919 at Hamburg, Frankfurt, and Cologne, they represented a new urban atmosphere for higher learning. They were also particularly open to new developments in economic and social studies. Beyond that, the 1920s witnessed a series of conflicts between the universities and the republican parties. Efforts to reform university governance were not very successful, and the academic community as a whole remained hostile to the Weimar regime.

Still, the reforms of the Weimar period reduced some of the obstacles that had hindered the movement of students from one compartment of the educational system to another. Above all, the choosing of an educational path was postponed from age six to age ten for all students by the establishment of the *Grundschule*. Moreover, the choice was no longer irrevocable because one could transfer to the *Aufbauschule* at age thirteen or attempt a substitute maturity examination later on.

Though far from radical in its approach, the Republic had provided the basis for a new era in German education before it fell to Hitler in 1933.

As soon as the National Socialists came to power, they began to reorganize the schools and universities. For the first and only time, Germany was given a nationally centralized system of educational administration. Primary schooling was left much as it had been, but there were important alterations in secondary and higher education. In general, the National Socialists were quite hostile to the classical and humanistic elements in the traditional system, and by 1938 only three types of secondary institutions remained. A version of the German high school (*Deutsche Oberschule*) was favored because of its freedom from the taint of foreign influence. It thus became the most important of the secondary schools, accounting for over three-quarters of secondary enrollments. The *Gymnasium* was particularly distrusted; its share of the secondary population was little more than a tenth. The remaining secondary pupils (about 5 percent) attended variants of the *Aufbauschule*.[8]

In the field of higher education, the National Socialists dismissed hundreds of faculty members, mostly on "racial" grounds. They tried to divert students from large urban universities to small-town institutions and attempted to restrict women at the universities to 10 percent of the total academic population. They also introduced compulsory labor service as a prerequisite for university study. These and other techniques were meant not only to assure the students' ideological reliability but also to reduce a presumed oversupply of graduates stemming from the Weimar period.[9]

A small program existed to advance promising primary pupils to the universities. In addition, special party schools were designed to reward loyalty and create a new political and military elite. The "national political educational institutions" and the "Adolf Hitler schools" were to play this role at the secondary level, the *Ordensburgen* at the university level. But none of these National Socialist measures ever became very successful or significant, whether in numerical, academic, or social terms. The regime's most notable impact upon secondary

8. Samuel and Thomas, *Education and Society*, p.50.
9. On National Socialist education: Samuel and Thomas, *Education and Society* (general introduction in English); Hartshorne, *German Universities* (politics); Schoenbaum, *Hitler's Social Revolution* (issue of opportunity); Stephenson, "Girls' Higher Education in the 1930's" (broader than title, though a bit unsystematic on enrollment changes.)

and higher education was a dramatic cutback of enrollments in just about all fields of learning.

After the Second World War, West German education returned to the patterns established during the Weimar period. The centralization of the National Socialist system was abandoned, and each of the federal states again administered its own schools and universities. The three traditional groups of secondary schools were reinstated; but the curricular differences among them have been reduced, and all now carry some form of the name *Gymnasium*. Full-time vocational schools have become available at intermediate and advanced levels to graduates of the primary and middle schools [I]. In higher education, a whole cluster of new universities has been founded since 1945. The distinction between universities and technical institutes has become less sharp, and certain newer groups of academies have begun to be considered university-level institutions [V].

As of 1960, there was still an institutional barrier between the primary, middle and vocational schools on the one hand, and secondary and higher education on the other. Reforms of all kinds have been, and are, much debated. The most difficult practical problem faced by the Federal Republic, however, has been a rapidly rising demand for places within the existing system of secondary and higher education.[10]

Enrollments during the Early Industrial Phase

The three major phases in the history of modern European educational systems can be clearly discerned in the evolution of German enrollments. A first distinctive period, the early industrial phase, encompassed the early nineteenth century and ended around 1860 or 1870. The second, or high industrial phase, terminated during the Weimar period. The third, the late industrial phase, extends to the present, though we shall follow it only until the early 1960s. During the first phase, the German educational system adjusted, after a period of instability, to the early industrial society that surrounded it. The second phase was characterized by an expansion of modern secondary and technical university-level education. This process was at once a response to the technological character of Germany's belated industrialization and a challenge to the traditions that had been established earlier. During the last phase, curricular and institutional barriers among schools have gradually become less marked. At the same time,

10. Hess, *Die deutsche Universität.*

unprecedented enrollment increases have produced a new wealth of qualified white-collar personnel for the late-industrial economy.

Our approach to the three phases will necessarily reflect the quality of the information available, which is actually best for the period from 1870 to 1930. For the early nineteenth century, enrollments can be related only to the total population. From 1870 on, we can work with enrollments per age group, a better measure of inclusiveness. There is much evidence, besides, on the shape of the educational pyramid between 1870 and 1930, which can also be exploited retrospectively, to shed light on the decades before 1870. Therefore, this account will begin with a general report of the first phase, move on to an intensive and partly retrospective analysis of the German system in its second phase, and conclude with a brief look at recent developments.

To understand what happened in German education during the early nineteenth century, one has to begin by noting a surprising fact about the even more distant past. Students at German universities were apparently over 50 percent more numerous before 1750 than in 1800 [V]. From an absolute low around 1801–05, enrollments rose slowly until after the Napoleonic wars. They then doubled abruptly between 1817 and 1830. A peak reached in 1830 was followed by a sharp decline during the subsequent decade. German university enrollments per thousand population were 0.31 in 1817, 0.52 in 1831, 0.35 in 1840, and never far from 0.34 during the subsequent three decades. In other words, a low plateau was reached around 1840 that was maintained until 1870 and that closely approximated the level of 1817. (The forerunners of the technical institutes were numerically insignificant during the early decades of the century. They did not reach total enrollments around 1500 until the mid-1850s. Their more rapid expansion during the following two decades is best associated with the second phase in the history of the German system.)

The curve of enrollments in Prussian middle and secondary schools resembled the university pattern in several respects [I]. The *Gymnasium* stream reached a peak of just under 2.0 students per thousand population around 1830, dropped to 1.5 during the 1830s and early 1840s, and then began to recover. Similarly, the absolute number of yearly *Abitur* certificates nearly doubled, from just over one thousand to just under two thousand, between 1820 and 1830; it then fell back to the level of 1820 during the 1830s and early 1840s before reaching two thousand again around 1860. Since the population had grown in the meantime, maturity certificates, like university students, were *relatively* less numerous in 1860 than in 1830. Modern secondary education was about half as popular as the *Gymnasium* stream from 1830 to 1870. The middle schools, in turn, easily matched the whole secondary sector in enrollments. At all of the middle and secondary schools, however, the curve of enrollments dropped from a peak in 1830 to a low around 1840.

What chiefly distinguished the secondary schools from the universities during this period was their somewhat more complete and continuous recovery from the setback of the 1830s. By 1860, the ratios of secondary pupils to the population had, at 2.0 per thousand in the *Gymnasium* and 1.0 per thousand in the modern schools, regained and slightly surpassed their levels of 1830. The proportion then continued to advance to 2.7 per thousand in the *Gymnasium* and 1.8 in the modern schools by 1875. *Abitur* certificates lagged a little, but had certainly recovered by 1870.

One way to account for the movement of enrollments before 1870 is to trace them to specific changes in the organization of secondary and higher education. Thus, the eighteenth-century decline in university attendance may have been partly due to the increased role of the classical secondary schools. Together with the surviving knights' academies, the *Gymnasien* may have drawn students away from the university arts faculties, which had earlier prepared even rather young pupils for the professional faculties. The Prussian *Abitur* regulations of 1788 and 1812 may be associated with this trend, for they set firm standards in secondary education and also made it more difficult to reach the universities. This was true to an even greater extent of the Prussian restrictions of 1831 and 1834, which were consciously designed to decrease the flow of unqualified students into the faculties. Did they contribute to the sharp decline in enrollments during the 1830s?

The difficulty with this line of reasoning is that the causes it proposes are less general than the trends to be explained. The long-term decrease in university attendance after 1750, for example, affected the centrally important faculties of theology as well as the arts. Indeed, the German universities were not alone in the difficulties that beset them during the eighteenth century: in Castile, high enrollments during the early seventeenth century were followed by a long-term decline until about 1770 and by a very modest recovery thereafter;[11] French and English examples will concern us later. As for the Prussian restrictions of the 1830s, they could not have produced the contraction in attendance during that decade. The contraction occurred at all German universities, not just in Prussia. It was visible even in the middle and secondary schools. It was sharper, moreover, during the

11. Kagan, "Universities in Castile."

early than during the late 1830s: it thus preceded the more significant of the Prussian measures to reduce university access, which was that of 1834.

A better approach to the problem of German enrollments during the late eighteenth and early nineteenth centuries is based on the notion of a long-term shift in the demand for university graduates. As has been suggested, the need for highly educated men is never absolutely or objectively given. Economic and technological conditions will set certain bounds, but various conventions will be involved as well. Social roles and statuses must be defined before specific academic qualifications will seem appropriate for certain occupations and positions. Obviously, the definitions can be altered, although very rapid change will tend to disappoint expectations and produce social tensions. The whole idea of a specific demand for graduates must be taken with a grain of salt. Properly qualified, however, it is indispensable as an explanatory device.

A decline in the number of theological posts was probably a major cause of the shrinking demand for university graduates after 1750. Students of theology used to enter all sorts of learned professions, including teaching, and the temporary revival in the fortunes of the German theological faculties during the early nineteenth century was almost certainly stimulated by opportunities in secondary teaching. It is possible, conversely, that the decline of the private tutor and secretary had as much to do with the eighteenth-century contraction in the theological studies as the more general phenomenon of secularization. Certainly the old aristocratic society outstripped its successor in the number of livings it offered to educated men, many of whom were "clerics."

The other major demand for graduates during the decades around 1800, of course, came from the civil service, which played an extremely active role in defining the learned occupations and their academic prerequisites. In Prussia, civil service reform and educational reform went hand in hand. "Merit" asserted itself within the bureaucracy, and the ranks of officials were graded according to specified qualifications. At the same time, the *Gymnasium* and the *Abitur* were created, along with a corps of professional *Gymnasium* teachers, the faculty of philosophy that trained them, and the whole system of state examinations and privileges that came to dominate German education for over a century. Taken together, these institutions defined the demand not only for high officials but for all members of the learned professions. Apparently, they defined it at a level of inclusiveness below that of the decades around 1700.

Strong empirical support for this account of the demand for education may be found in the attendance statistics themselves. The long plateau in enrollments per population during the three decades after 1840 is particularly striking. It testifies to the existence of an equilibrium between the supply and demand for educated men. The level of inclusiveness reached in 1817, and again between 1840 and 1870, must have been normal for early industrial Germany. The dip in the attendance curve around 1800 and the high between 1817 and 1840 can only be considered irregularities in the long-term transition from the characteristic demand levels of the early eighteenth century to those of the nineteenth. The political and military disturbances of the Napoleonic era may have helped to produce the dip around 1800. The increasing university populations that followed the Napoleonic wars probably included students who had postponed their studies. Some of them may also have been encouraged by new opportunities in the civil service after the Prussian Reform Period. In any case, the gradual recovery of enrollments after about 1805 became a veritable boom by the 1820s, until it ended in the abrupt decline of the 1830s.

There is nothing surprising, incidentally, about the appearance of a cyclical pattern in university attendance curves. We shall encounter such patterns again in other contexts. One has to remember that increasing student numbers will create a demand for teachers that will tend further to accelerate the influx of students, and this is just one of the ways in which enrollment growth is likely to become self-accelerating to some degree. Moreover, while enrollments rise and fall partly in response to reported opportunities for graduates, there is bound to be a time lag involved. Expectations and plans cannot be instantly adjusted when the reported opportunities begin to shrink. In a kind of momentum effect, enrollment booms are thus likely to overshoot the limits of normal demand and produce an "excess" of university graduates.

As a matter of fact, there were intermittent complaints throughout the eighteenth and early nineteenth centuries about an oversupply of educated candidates, especially for public office. O'Boyle has found such complaints especially frequent and agitated in Germany from the 1820s into the 1840s.[12] The complainers were often established officials; but several of the leading German statisticians of the day also documented the shortage of openings in the learned professions in relation

12. O'Boyle, "Excess of Educated Men," makes a solid case for a perceived excess, especially in Germany. She recognizes the conventional element in the idea of an overproduction of educated men, and she makes the important distinction between short-range and long-range effects.

to the number of graduates.[13] A kind of intellectual proletariat was apparently created by the abnormally high enrollments that extended about a decade in each direction from the peak at 1830. Once created, the excess of educated men was hard to absorb, even after normal levels of inclusiveness were reattained around 1840, and consequent dissatisfaction among junior civil servants and young intellectuals may well have contributed to the ferment of 1848.[14]

It should be noted, however, that an oversupply of graduates was occasionally registered well before 1820, and with characteristic social biases and anxieties. A memorandum of 1708 regretted that "even artisans and farmers" were sending their sons to the universities, regardless of ability, although they could be much more useful to the community in "manufacturing, crafts, the military, and even in agriculture." In 1769, again, the objection was that too many children from poor families were seeking advanced schooling, rather than preparing early enough to earn their living in an "honest trade or profession."[15] Less than twenty years later, the Prussian *Abitur* regulation of 1788 was introduced in response to widespread sentiments that too many unqualified students were reaching the universities. The feeling was that these young men would end up being a "totally useless class of people for the state." At the University of Königsberg, a warning that poor youths should enter practical employments was signed by Immanuel Kant as Dean.[16] Since these views were expressed during a period of declining enrollments, they testify to a long-term reduction in the demand for graduates during the eighteenth century; this in contrast with the concerns of the 1830s and 40s, which reflected the short-term difficulties raised by the enrollment boom around 1830.

It should be emphasized that there was no positive correlation between enrollments and the state of the economy during the early industrial phase in the history of the German system. On the contrary, the relationship was antithetical; attendance at the classical secondary schools and universities varied *inversely* with the degree of prosperity.

According to Rosenberg, a cycle of very moderate expansion in the German economy from 1770 to 1806 was followed by a setback until the early 1830s.[17] A renewed upswing thereafter was checked around

13. Dieterici, *Geschichtliche und statistische Nachrichten;* Hoffman, *Sammlung,* pp.187–226. See also Conrad, *Universitätsstudium.* It was Conrad who first suggested that high enrollments might have been due in part to economic difficulties.

14. Gillis, *Prussian Bureaucracy.*

15. Eulenberg, *Frequenz,* pp.136–38.

16. Jeismann, *Das preussische Gymnasium,* pp.102–4. See also P. Schwartz, *Gelehrtenschulen Preussens,* vol. 1, pp.70–71.

17. Rosenberg, *Grosse Depression,* esp. pp.32–37.

1840 and again around 1846–48, until sustained growth began in the 1850s. Thus, the university expansion of the 1820s partly coincided with a mild recession while the decline from the enrollment peak at 1830 was accompanied and probably facilitated by expanding opportunities outside the learned professions. The next major period of growth in the German economy, according to Rosenberg, extended from the 1850s to the long-term depression of 1873–96. University enrollments per population remained stable between 1840 and 1870. Their renewed upswing thereafter thus fell into the recession that began in 1873. True, there was some growth in attendance at the secondary schools between 1860 and 1875, but it was most pronounced at the nonclassical schools, which increased their share of all secondary enrollments from 31 to 39 percent during this period [I]. The technical institutes also prospered markedly from the 1850s to the mid-1870s. In contrast to the *Gymnasien* and the universities, they responded directly and positively to increased opportunities in the economy.

Apparently, then, the traditional and the modern segments of the German educational system stood in almost diametrically opposed relationships to the early industrial economy. As we shall see a little later, graduates of the German *Gymnasien* and universities hardly ever sought employment in commerce or industry during the early nineteenth century. This circumstance can help to explain the excess of educated men around 1830. The German economy was as yet relatively undeveloped. More important, the technology on which the economy depended was comparatively simple—at least it did not absolutely call for large numbers of technicians and scientists with formal training at advanced levels. Higher education, conceived essentially as theoretical learning, could therefore be considered irrelevant to the realm of business and of practice. Ambitious young men chose to prepare either "practically," for careers in commerce and industry, or "academically," for the learned professions and government posts. Which of the two alternatives they chose depended partly upon the state of the economy, but the *worse* opportunities looked in that sector, the *more* likely were they to enter the *Gymnasien* and the universities and, thus, to swell the ranks of aspirants to appropriate positions in the "academic" professions. At the same time, students already in the secondary schools and universities probably prolonged their studies during periods of economic recession and shortened them during periods of economic opportunity. Particularly students from the lower middle classes may well have altered their career strategies in accordance with the business climate and the advice of their teachers. Taken together, the changing choices of students and parents thus engendered a negative correlation between enrollments and economic cycles. Of course all this applied particularly in the short run, to the traditional sector of the German system, and during the first phase in its history.

The High Industrial Pattern

The expansion of the nonclassical secondary schools and technical institutes in the 1860s really marked the beginning of a new stage in the evolution of the German educational system. This high industrial phase was characterized less by an overall increase in inclusiveness than by an almost one-sided growth in the modern sector. Thus, the *Gymnasium*'s share of Prussian secondary enrollments fell from 69 to 61 percent between 1860 and 1875 [I], and, after a brief recovery to 63 percent in the 1880s, continued to decline to under 50 percent of Prussian secondary students in 1911. By the early 1920s less than 33 percent of students in German boys' secondary schools were enrolled in *Gymnasien*. The *Gymnasium* did continue to award some 80 to 90 percent of graduate certificates until the turn of the century, but by 1911 its portion had declined to 66 percent. Until the 1870s, the *Realgymnasium* had been larger by far than the *Realschule,* the other modern school, but the establishment of the *Oberrealschule* in 1878 and the administrative measures taken against the *Realgymnasium* in 1879 and during the 1890s altered this. From 1880 on, the *Oberrealschule* grew very rapidly. Outstripping the *Realgymnasium* around 1895, it was by 1926 easily the largest of the three main secondary schools.[18]

In higher education, the technical institutes had almost a third as many students as the universities by 1875 [V]. During the 1880s, however, they suffered a very sharp decline. The *Realgymnasium* was also having difficulties during this period, while the *Gymnasium* experienced a brief but remarkable revival, which may have been partly due to the temporary exclusion of modern school graduates from the state examinations in certain technical subjects. But the great depression of 1873–96 certainly played a role as well. Although its impact was not felt immediately, it eventually produced a sharp contraction of enrollments at the technical institutes from about 1876 to the mid-1880s [V].

18. Lundgreen, *Bildung und Wirtschaftswachstum,* estimates enrollments near one thousand for the Prussian provincial trade schools that were replaced by the *Oberrealschule* in 1878, but he does not elaborate on the basis for this judgment [I]. Despite some interesting regional variations, incidentally, the distribution of pupils over the school types was nearly identical for Prussia and for Germany as a whole in 1902 [I].

At the universities, it had the opposite effect; student numbers there rose especially fast between 1877 and 1885. So pronounced was this upswing that it gave rise, once again, to official concern about over-crowding in the learned professions and about the rise of an academic proletariat.[19] Together with the temporary revival of the *Gymnasium,* the whole sequence points up the diametrically opposed relationship of the two main curricular branches to the German economy.

In 1899, the technical institutes earned the right to confer the doc-torate, but their share of university-level enrollments did not increase. Having recovered from the setback of the 1880s well before the end of the century, they entered a period of relative quiescence that ex-tended into the Weimar period. Indeed, from 1900 to 1931 they consistently accounted for around 20 percent of all German university-level enrollments. (The considerably smaller academies were not gen-erally regarded as university-level institutions until the Weimar period, when their share of enrollments in higher education was about 6 to 9 percent.)

The most interesting enrollment ratios for the period 1870–1931 are summarized in Table 1.1. The figures make plain how little growth there really was in German secondary education before the First World War. Over the entire period from 1870 to 1914, the ratios of secondary enrollments and certificates to the age group increased by roughly 50 percent. Certificates, to be sure, declined from 0.8 to 0.6 percent of the age group during the decade after 1870, but they made up for it by doubling between 1880 and 1911. The entire secondary system did not expand with any consistency until after 1880, and then the increases were confined almost exclusively to the modern secondary schools. *Gymnasium* enrollments and certificates per age group re-mained essentially unchanged into the 1920s [I].

This is all the more striking in view of the fact that the *Gymnasium* figures for 1870 rank little above the level that had already been reached in 1830. The traditionally academic track in German sec-ondary education was, therefore, almost a fixed quantity for nearly a century after 1830. The modern stream was simply added on. The consequent enlargement of the secondary system as a whole took place principally during periods of increased economic opportunity, from the 1850s to the early 1870s, and again from the 1890s to the First World

19. Pfetsch, *Zur Entwicklung der Wissenschaftspolitik,* pp.173–78, for these concerns and for a detailed and sophisticated analysis of enrollments at the uni-versities and technical institutes in relation to the economy. Pfetsch writes of the "counter-cyclical" character of university enrollments, and he suggests that ex-penditures for certain types of scientific research were counter-cyclical as well.

Table 1.1
German Enrollments and Certificates, 1870–1931
(As Percentages of Age Groups)

Year	Secondary enrollments	Abitur certificates	University enrollments
1870	2.3	0.8	0.5
1875	2.5	0.7	0.6
1880	2.6	0.6	0.7
1885	2.6	0.8	0.9
1890	2.5	0.9	0.8
1900	2.7	0.9	1.1
1905	3.0	1.0	—
1911	3.2	1.2	1.5
1921	6.0	1.3	2.7
1926	7.1	1.7	1.9
1931	8.8	3.3	2.7

Secondary enrollments and *Abitur* data through 1911 are for Prussia; the rest of the figures pertain to Germany as a whole. See I and V for details.

War. It was the second, and more significant, expansion of the modern sector after 1890 that accounted for most of the 50 percent increase in German secondary education between 1870 and 1911.

The figures for the secondary schools of the Weimar period, to be sure, look much more dramatic; by 1931, both enrollments and certificates per age group were almost three times as high as they were in 1911. The *Grundschule* really seems to have made a difference. Unfortunately, there is little exact information on the role of the pre-secondary schools before 1920. Between 1885 and 1911 in Prussia, they apparently supplied about a third of the entrants to each of the main secondary streams [I]. Conrad, a contemporary observer, thought that most of the remaining pupils in Prussian *Gymnasien* during the 1880s had begun their schooling in private elementary institutions. However, conditions varied from state to state, so that no firm conclusions can be drawn for Germany as a whole. Nonetheless, the data for the Weimar period would suggest that the common school to age ten did considerably increase the flow of children into the secondary branch.

The augmented secondary enrollments of the Weimar period also included girls, who had previously been counted among middle school pupils [I]. As noted earlier, middle school students were somewhat more numerous than secondary pupils in Prussia until the 1860s. The development of the middle schools during the following two decades is not well documented. They probably lost some pupils to the *Realschulen* before the 1880s, but then they were enlarged by the rapid growth of postelementary education for girls. From 1885 to 1905, total enrollments were actually around 50 percent greater at the middle than at the secondary schools in Prussia. On the other hand, in 1886, two-thirds of Prussian middle school pupils were girls, chiefly because the higher girls' schools were still counted with the middle schools. As fully accredited girls' secondary schools emerged and expanded, on the eve of the First World War and during the 1920s, the middle schools shrank in size. Apparently, they also lost boys to various nonclassical secondary schools during the Weimar period. In Prussia, the middle schools were only marginally larger than the secondary schools by 1911. In all of Germany between 1921 and 1931, they then continued to contract, from 5.2 to 3.5 students per thousand population, while secondary enrollments hovered around 12 per thousand population. Thus, part of the growth in German secondary education after 1911 was due to the arrival of girls at the secondary level, and part to a more general shift away from the middle schools.

The results are described in Table 1.2, which also reports on the new schools of the Weimar period—the German high school (*Deutsche Oberschule*) and the continuation school (*Aufbauschule*). Obviously, neither had made much progress by 1926, when the sources ceased to distinguish among boys' secondary institutions. The *Gymnasien* actually contracted a little, in relation to the age group. The more than two-fold increase in German secondary enrollments per age group between 1911 and 1931 was thus due entirely to the girls' schools and to

Table 1.2
German Secondary Enrollments, 1911–1931
(As Percentages of Age Groups 11–19)

Year	Gym-nasien	Modern schools	New schools[a]	Girls' schools	All schools
1911	1.5	1.7	–	–	3.2
1921	1.3	2.5	0.2	2.1	6.0
1926	1.4	3.1	0.3	2.3	7.1
1931		5.6		3.2[b]	8.8

See I for details.

  [a] The German high school (*Deutsche Oberschule*), the continuation school (*Aufbauschule*), and other equivalent institutions.

  [b] Counts girls attending boys' secondary schools.

the modern secondary sector. By 1931, girls were 36 percent of German secondary pupils and earned 23 percent of the *Abitur* certificates [I].

This brings up the internal structure of the secondary schools, and of German higher education as a whole. To begin with, over the entire period from 1870 to 1931, *Abiturs* were much less numerous than enrollments, in relation to the age group. The indicative figures for certificates of maturity in Table 1.1 are generally just under a third as large as the numbers for secondary students in general. Certificates per age group fell to around 23 percent of enrollments per age group only during the early 1920s, when many girls and other new arrivals in the secondary sector had not yet reached the *Abitur*. Conversely, the ratio of certificates to enrollments per age group rose to around 37 or 38 percent only in 1911 and 1931; these were periods when preceding waves of expansion had been fully assimilated even at the level of the *Abitur*. It is fascinating to observe this process of assimiliation. As the system digested the sporadic additions of new schools or classes of students, the ratio of certificates to enrollments tended to reestablish itself at roughly 33 percent.

That figure does not mean, however, that one of three entrants into secondary schools reached the *Abitur*. The inclusiveness of German secondary education has so far been described in terms of average enrollments per age group. Total secondary enrollments have been divided by the appropriate nine-year age cohort. It is the mean width of the enrollment pyramid that has thus been measured and found to be just under three times as wide as its top at the *Abitur*. Since the base must have been wider than the mean width, there were certainly more than three entrants for every graduate.

One way to describe the situation more exactly is to indicate what percentages of all pupils attended the lowest, the middle, and the highest three grades of the secondary sequence [I]. In Prussian *Gymnasien* as of 1832, about 57 percent of the students were enrolled in the lowest three grades. The proportion had declined only slightly, to 53 percent, by 1865; but it then fell to 46 percent in 1885 and 43 or 44 percent in 1911 and 1931. In the meantime, the top three grades expanded from 18 percent in 1885 to 21 percent in 1911 and 26 percent in 1931. In the *Realgymnasium* stream from the 1880s to 1911 just over half of all pupils were enrolled in the lowest three grades, while the highest three grades accounted for 14 percent. By 1931, these ratios had changed to 47 percent for the lowest three and 23 percent for the highest three grades. The *Oberrealschule*, of course, was not created until 1878. Its highest three grades enrolled only 1 percent of its pupils in 1885, though the proportion had advanced to 4 percent by 1900, 8 percent by 1911, and 20 percent by 1931. The lowest three grades of the *Realschule–Oberrealschule* stream accounted for about two-thirds of its students in 1865 and 1885, for 61 percent in 1900, 52 percent in 1911, and 49 percent in 1931.

The real surprise, in view of all this, is that the secondary pyramid as a whole changed its shape so little between 1870 and 1930. Beginning pupils in all Prussian secondary schools were about 3.2 percent of their age group in 1870, ranged between 3.2 and 3.8 percent until the turn of the century, and then climbed to over 4 percent before 1914 and to over 11 percent by 1931 [I]. In other words, new entrants essentially kept pace with the increase in *Abitur* certificates. Again the image of successive assimilations will make it easiest to grasp how this could happen. As more *Gymnasium* students completed their studies, the two modern streams compensated with an enlarged supply of early leavers. The whole evolution of the secondary sector is summarized in the following percentages of the age group.

	Beginning pupils	Mean enrollments	Abitur certificates
1870	3% plus	2.3%	0.8%
1911	4% plus	3.2%	1.2%
1931	11% plus	8.8%	3.3%

The ratio of graduates to entrants remained nearly constant at one to four, though it was probably on the increase by the end of the high industrial phase around 1930.

Characteristic of the German system, as compared with the French, was a substantial degree of meritocratic weeding out well before the level of the *Abitur*. In 1931/32, roughly one-tenth of all pupils in all grades of public boys' secondary schools were barred from advancing to the next grade at the end of the year; about one-third of these students chose to repeat a class while two-thirds left school [I]. Non-academic factors also contributed to high rates of attrition, especially after the fourth and sixth years of secondary schooling. On the other hand, among students who reached the highest grade, more than 90 percent passed the *Abitur* examination.

The proportion of secondary graduates who went on to higher education was generally high [II]. Among recipients of the classical *Abitur* in Prussia, 98 percent planned to enter universities in 1832, 82 percent in 1860, 88 percent in 1880, and 73 percent in 1900. The *Realgymnasium* had just begun to award a few certificates in 1860, and the *Oberrealschule* followed with a few hundred per year by the turn of the century; however, graduates from these two modern schools were much less likely to attend universities than were their colleagues from the *Gymnasium*. Over the whole period from 1875 to 1899, prospective university students comprised 77 percent of *Gymnasium* graduates, 30 percent of *Realgymnasium* graduates, and 20 percent of *Oberrealschule* graduates. For all recipients of Prussian certificates, classical and modern combined, the figures were 76 percent in 1860, 80 percent in 1880, 64 percent in 1900, and 69 percent over the whole interval between 1875 and 1899. For all German secondary graduates in 1931, the comparable figure was 67 percent [I].

Secondary graduates who did not intend to continue their studies at the universities generally opted for one of four alternate paths. Some entered directly into the middle grades of the civil service. Others chose military careers, which usually required additional training at specialized institutions. A few went into agriculture or business, with or without advanced schooling at agricultural academies or schools of commerce. Finally, a significant portion prepared for various technical professions or for the technical branches of the public service.

Obviously, most of this last contingent passed through the technical institutes. The numbers involved do not suffice to account for all enrollments at these institutions, which must have accepted some students without the *Abitur* until late in the century. But another consideration is more important: among Prussian graduates who planned to enter the technical fields between 1875 and 1899, nearly half came from the nonclassical streams. Clearly, the modern secondary sector was always an important recruiting ground for the technical institutes. When the institutes were elevated to university standing around the turn of the century, there was an abrupt increase in the proportion of secondary graduates who continued their studies at the university level, and of course the change affected the modern schools much more radically than the *Gymnasium*. By 1911, at any rate, just under 80 percent of secondary graduates were registered as prospective "university" students once again. Even for the modern schools alone, the proportion came close to 75 percent. The ratio fell again during the Weimar period, but for reasons that were partly temporary: girls had begun to reach the Abitur in considerable numbers, but many of them still hesitated to go on to higher education. Also from the 1920s on, future primary teachers passed through the secondary schools on the way to academies that were not considered of university level.

Another way to consider the links between secondary and higher education is to inquire into the previous schooling of university students [IV]. Even after 1834, there were always a few among them who had no secondary certificates at all. They generally enrolled in what may be called the "minor" fields within the faculty of arts and sciences: pharmacy and dentistry, agriculture, and "cameralia," an ancient combination of agricultural, economic, and administrative studies. The professional faculties never admitted uncertified students, and they also excluded graduates of modern schools until the end of the nineteenth century. As a result, the nonclassical graduates were channeled almost exclusively into the faculty of philosophy, and particularly into the natural sciences. As of 1887, some 85 percent of Prussian university students held the *Abitur* from a *Gymnasium*. Only 8 percent came from the *Realgymnasium*, and an almost equal fraction had no valid certificates. The *Gymnasium* graduates made up all the enrollments in the professional faculties but constituted only half the students in the faculty of arts and sciences. Within that faculty, two-thirds of those without certificates studied the "minor fields," while the *Realgymnasium* supplied over one-fifth of the humanists and almost half the scientists.

Table 1.3 follows these patterns to 1911 and then to 1931. It shows that the traditionally privileged position of the *Gymnasium* was thoroughly undermined during the Weimar period. Even the professional faculties were no longer dominated by classical graduates. The old distinctions among curricular compartments were beginning to fade. What specializations remained are best described as positive correlations between nonclassical secondary schooling and certain subject groupings within the faculty of philosophy. The modern secondary schools supplied two-thirds of the students in the natural sciences, while also holding their own in the humanities. As the preferred training ground for future secondary teachers, the humanities were especially attractive to women, as well as to the new categories of secondary graduates created during the 1920s. This last group was also particularly well represented in the minor fields, which now included education for a few prospective primary teachers along with a rapidly growing area of economics and business studies. At the technical institutes in 1931, almost 70 percent of students came from the modern secondary schools, while just over 20 percent came from a *Gymnasium* [IV].

In the meantime, the internal structure of higher education had changed as well. Table 1.4 provides a rough sketch of long-term trends in the distribution of university students over the various faculties and fields of study. Law (with government) and theology clearly dominated the German university of the early nineteenth century. In 1831,

Table 1.3

Secondary Preparation of German University Students, 1911 and 1931
(Percentages by Column)

Year: Sec. Prep.	All students	Law, theol.	Medi- cine	Humani- ties	Sciences	Minor fields[a]
1911: Gymnasium	65	85	75	65	44	29
Modern schools	25	15	25	28	50	14
None	9	–	–	8	6	57
1931: Gymnasium	34	48	38	27	20	22
Modern schools	53	47	53	49	65	56
Girls' schools	6[b]	1	5	13	8	5
New schools[c]	4	2	2	5	4	7
Other[d]	4	1	2	6	3	10

See IV for details.

[a] Encompasses such subjects as pharmacy, dentistry, agriculture, and "cameralia" (economic, agricultural, and administrative studies). For 1931, enlarged to include education for prospective primary or middle school teachers (few universities offered this option). Economics and business administration, also counted here, were much more established and popular subjects in 1931 than in 1911.

[b] Since 16% of German university students in 1931 were women, some of them must have prepared at boys' secondary schools.

[c] The German high school and the continuation school.

[d] Covers a whole range of alternatives; only a fraction can be traced to the substitute maturity certificates of the 1920s or to transfers from the old teachers' seminaries.

Table 1.4

Distribution of German University Students
over the Fields of Study, 1830–1930
(Rounded Percentages by Row)

Period	The- ology	Law, Govt.	Medi- cine	Humani- ties	Sci- ences	Minor fields[a]
1830–60	30	30	15	15	5	5
1860–90	20	25	20	15	10	10
ca. 1911	10	20	20	25	15	10
ca. 1931	10	20	20	20	15	15

The distributions are approximate, indicative of long-term trends. The last three columns jointly represent the faculty of arts and sciences ("philosophy"). See V for details.

[a] Chiefly pharmacy, dentistry and agriculture; considerably enlarged by 1931 with the appearance of education as a subject for a few prospective primary and middle school teachers and with the rapid expansion of economics and business administration.

theology actually accounted for nearly 40 percent of all students [V]. It then lost ground quite rapidly throughout the nineteenth century. The more gradual decline of law was compensated by the advance of the medical sciences, but only for a while. Thus, the most important and consistent change was the growth of the arts and sciences, which took place at the expense of the professional faculties in general, and of theology in particular.

It must also be remembered that the technical institutes accounted for roughly 20 percent of German university-level enrollments from their accreditation in 1899 to the end of the Weimar period [V]. As of 1931, over one-quarter of students at the technical institutes were in architecture and construction, nearly half specialized in the various branches of engineering, while most of the rest prepared to be chemists, applied mathematicians and physicists, vocational or middle school teachers, economists, and business school instructors. The academies were numerically less significant. Until the First World War, most of their matriculations were in agriculture, forestry, and veterinary medicine, though there were a few students of mining as well. A new group of business schools (*Handelshochschulen*) acquired some importance on the eve of the First World War. They have been added to the category of academies from 1921 on. By 1931, according to this classification, nearly half the students at academies were actually engaged in business studies; less than a quarter were prospective theologians, and about a third remained in the more traditional specialties of agriculture, forestry, veterinary medicine, and mining.

A closer examination of university-level enrollments in Table 1.5 initially raises several problems. To begin with, there is the numerical relationship between secondary certificates and university enrollments per age group. On the one hand, not all secondary graduates went on to the universities or to other institutions considered equivalent. On the other hand, some 7–9 percent of Prussian university students had no secondary certificates in 1887 and 1911. At the technical institutes, the share of nongraduates may well have been higher than that, even after 1900. A fair conclusion would seem to be that *beginning* university students should have been just slightly less numerous than secondary graduates in most age groups and periods between 1860 and 1911. Much depends, of course, on which institutions are counted with the universities, and on how many students at technical institutes and academies really had no certificates. Besides, large numbers of *Abiturs* do not have to produce an immediate rise in the university population; they can be cancelled by lower rates of graduation during subsequent years. The figures for the 1870s suggest that possibility. University

Table 1.5

German Secondary Certificates and University-Level
Enrollments, 1870–1931
(As Percentages of Age Groups)

Year	Abitur certificates (age 19)	University Enrollments[a] (ages 20–23)		
1870	0.8		0.5	(0.6)
1875	0.7		0.6	(0.8)
1880	0.6		0.7	(0.8)
1885	0.8		0.9	(1.0)
1890	0.9		0.8	(1.0)
1900	0.9	(0.8)	1.1	(1.2)
1911	1.2	(1.2)	1.5	(1.5)
1921	1.3	(2.0)	2.7	
1926	1.7	(1.3)	1.9	
1931	3.3	(2.1)	2.7	

The table merely elaborates upon portions of Table 1.1. See I and V for details.

[a] In the central column, the technical institutes are counted beginning in 1900 and the academies beginning in 1921. The figures in parentheses to the right of the main column include technical institutes and academies from the beginning. The numbers to the left cover universities alone from 1900 on. Without female students, the percentages in the central column would be 1.4 for 1911, 2.5 for 1921, 1.7 for 1926, and 2.3 for 1931. The university figures for 1921 and 1926 look particularly high, and may actually be too high, because they were calculated in relation to age groups depleted by the casualties of the First World War and because uncertain estimates of those age groups almost certainly make at least the result for 1926 somewhat higher than it should be.

enrollments per population remained essentially stable between 1840 and 1870, while secondary pupils per population increased, especially at the modern schools. The result may have been a partly erratic peak in certificates per age group around 1870 that affected the universities less than the temporary resurgence of the *Gymnasium* during the 1880s.

A further difficulty in the interpretation of Table 1.5 has to do with the duration of university study. This has been estimated by way of the first-year method [V]. The tabulated figures are therefore not averages; it is not the mean width but the base of the enrollment pyramid that is measured in this case. The ratios really report on first-year university access, on beginning students as percentages of their one-year age group. This may be awkward; but it is less serious than the fact that the duration of study differed over time, as well as from field to field, and that we know only roughly what it was. Around 1886–1911, students who finished their preparation for the major state examinations took about 4 years to do so in theology, 3.3 years in law, 6.3 years in medicine, and 5.8 years in the humanities and natural sciences [V]. On the other hand, programs may have been shorter in some of the minor fields, and a number of students presumably left without completing their work. The first-year method and related considerations suggest that *average* durations of study for *all* university students were about 3.5 years into the 1860s, 4 years by the 1870s, and roughly 4.5 years for universities and technical institutes from the eve of the First World War into the 1920s. Even for all university-level institutions, the duration probably exceeded 4 years during the Weimar period and reached 4.5 years after the Second World War. The enrollment ratios in Table 1.5, which assume a four-year duration, are therefore in need of correction. They probably understate first-year access to the universities by up to 15 percent before 1870, and they overstate it by up to the same amount during the twentieth century.

The unusual enrollment fluctuations of the Weimar period may be somewhat exaggerated by the poor quality of the demographic data for a time when successive age years differed dramatically in size. Unfortunately, the methods of calculation that had to be used were too rough to yield more than approximate results [V].

On the other hand, the curve of university attendance really did move up and down sharply during the Weimar period, in the aftermath of war and in response to two major economic crises. Secondary graduates who had interrupted their studies before 1918 streamed back into the universities with the return of peace. During the inflation of the early 1920s, employment was hard to find, a student could as cheaply prolong his stay at a university as starve at home. The currency stabilization of November 1923 triggered a sharp decline in university attendance until 1926, when a gradual recovery began. By 1931, huge university populations again coincided with unemployment, which this time grew out of the Great Depression.

To understand the high attendance figures around 1931, one has to distinguish between short-run and long-run causes of enrollment growth. In the short run, there were the usual consequences of reduced business opportunities—one could speak of disguised unemployment in this case. Moreover, the momentum effects that had accompanied the enrollment boom around 1830 were at work once again. World War I and the violent fluctuations in the size of successive age groups must have disturbed the balance between the supply and the demand for graduates, loosening the conventional sense of what jobs were appropriate for the highly educated. At the same time, more long-term changes were under way. Various higher-level white-collar positions were becoming more numerous. A wave of increased enrollments was advancing toward the universities from the secondary schools, and much of this wave was made up of women. Sooner or later, levels of inclusiveness would have had to increase in German higher education. Even so, the high enrollments before 1924 and around 1931 certainly were as abnormal as those around 1830. They rose like peaks above the gradually rising slope of normal university attendance, and they were certainly *experienced* as social problems.[20] Once again, an "intellectual proletariat" contributed to a pervasive sense of social and cultural crisis.

The overall development of German university enrollments between 1840 and 1930 can be established from Table 1.5, once all necessary corrections have been made for shortcomings in the data and methods of calculation. The level of inclusiveness at university entry for the German system probably hovered around 0.6 percent of the age group between 1840 and 1870. Around 1885, it reattained the position initially reached in 1830 [V]. By 1911, it had advanced to around 1 percent at the universities, and to somewhat below 1.5 percent at the universities and technical institutes combined. Before the end of the Weimar period, it rose to just under 2 percent at the universities and to about 2.5 percent at all university level institutions. The access percentages fell just short of doubling between 1870 and the First World War and doubling again, more quickly, between 1911 and 1931. The arrival of women at the universities contributed to the expansion of the interwar period, but only slightly. Women were about a third of German secondary pupils during the Weimar period. Their share of university-level enrollments, however, was confined to 9 percent in 1926, and 16 percent in 1931. This helps to explain why secondary certificates per age group increased so much more rapidly than university access after 1911. Eventually, as has been suggested, the arrival of women would probably have occasioned significantly higher university enrollments, if the National Socialists had not interrupted the established trends.

Of course, the German university of 1931 differed markedly from its ancestor of the mid-nineteenth century. As in secondary education, if to a lesser degree, growth during the high industrial phase was a kind of superimposition. As enrollments increased, several of the tradi-

20. Ringer, *Decline of the German Mandarins,* esp. pp.65, 77–80; Stephenson, "Girls' Higher Education."

tional subject areas shrank in relative importance. Expansion was concentrated in fields that were characteristically most open to graduates of modern secondary schools. If it made sense to speak of "modern" areas of study, one could say that the "modern" university was simply added to the traditional one. Thus, the German educational system became partially adjusted to a new environment. Needless to say, the adjustment was painful; it took place in an atmosphere of tension and conflict. The older curricular streams retained their special prestige long after they had been forced to share their legal privileges. The result was a dichotomy at the heart of the system, a set of status differences and value conflicts in which the high industrial present was opposed to the early industrial past.

The Late Industrial Phase

Some of the tensions of the high industrial phase have survived to the present day; but they have become increasingly marginal and artificial. During the late industrial phase in the history of the German system, the nineteenth-century distinctions among curricular streams have lost much of their sharpness. At the same time, there have been unprecedented increases in levels of inclusiveness, and the traditional university subjects have lost even more ground to the newer specialties. If one tries to locate a point of departure for all these developments, one ends by looking to the interwar years. The common school to age ten was introduced during that time, and secondary pupils per age group did nearly triple in the two decades before 1931. This represented a rate of change that exceeded anything known before 1911.

Unfortunately, there is some difficulty in the dating of the late industrial phase, and it stems entirely from the intervention of the National Socialists. The problem is illustrated in Table 1.6, which describes the evolving pattern of enrollments between 1931 and 1960. It has been surmised that the increase in secondary certificates per age group before 1931 had not yet fully affected the universities when Hitler came to power. An improvement in the employment situation apparently occasioned a slight decrease in university enrollments in 1932–33, just before the National Socialists launched their policy of restricting university access.[21] But that policy itself was certainly responsible for drastic reductions at all postelementary levels and particularly at the universities. In this area at least, the National Socialists did manage to turn the clock back to 1911. It is unclear how long they

21. Stephenson, "Girls' Higher Education."

Table 1.6
German Enrollments and Certificates, 1931–1960
(As Percentages of Age Groups)

Year	Secondary enrollments (ages 11–19)	Abitur certificates (age 19)	University enrollments (age 20–23)
1931	8.9	3.3	2.7
1937/38	6.9	?	1.5
1950/51	9.1	4.5	3.8
1955	10.8	4.1	4.3
1960	12.4	5.4	5.4

See I and V for details.

succeeded in maintaining their restrictive policies. Manpower needs may have forced enrollments back up after 1938, especially at the practically vital technical institutes.[22] But wartime conditions would pose special problems of interpretation in any case.

Developments after 1945, however, are fairly clear. The postwar reorganization of the German educational system was clearly based on the precedents of the Weimar period. As students flocked back into the higher schools after the financial and political stabilization of 1948 and 1949, secondary enrollments per age group recovered their 1931 level by 1950. The figures are really quite striking, for they make it seem that developments resumed in 1949 exactly where they had left off in 1931. The decade of the 1950s witnessed further growth in all sectors, but at relatively moderate rates. It is best to think of a period of adjustment, which has been followed since 1960 by explosive enrollment increases that lie beyond the bounds of this study.

The development of secondary education after 1950 requires little additional comment. As noted earlier, the National Socialists reduced the *Gymnasium*'s share of the secondary population to little more than a tenth. One may assume that the classical stream has regained some of the lost ground since 1949. But all full secondary schools are now called *Gymnasien*, and the sources fail to report precise breakdowns, presumably because they are losing much of their former significance. Girls, who were about one-third of secondary students in the 1920s and a bit less than that in 1938, constituted over 40 percent of sec-

22. Schoenbaum, *Hitler's Social Revolution*, p.274. The quick change between 1938 and 1939 looks a little suspicious. A book on education under National Socialism is still needed, with a more detailed and systematic analysis of enrollments *per age group* than we have been offered so far.

ondary students in 1955 and 1960. The middle schools, having declined during the Weimar period, recovered somewhat during the early 1950s. Together with the new full-time vocational schools, they enrolled about four-fifths as many pupils as the secondary schools by 1960.

In the meantime, the shape of the secondary pyramid has probably changed a little. Certificates used to be around one-third as numerous as average total enrollments in relation to the age group; but they were only slightly more than half as numerous between 1950 and 1960. More secondary pupils apparently stayed in school until the *Abitur,* and the ratio of new entrants to graduates must have shrunk accordingly. Beginning secondary pupils were probably not much more than 15 percent of their age group in 1960.

At the universities, the proportion of women—reduced by the National Socialists from 16 percent in 1931 to 11 percent in 1938—climbed back to 16 percent in 1951 and reached 22 percent in 1960. The tabulated figures for the university-level institutions since 1945 do not cover the pedagogical academies for primary teachers, which enrolled about one-eighth as many students as are counted in the total by 1960. Along with the traditional complement of academies and technical institutes, several art and music schools are newly included among university-level institutions after 1945. Without them, the ratio of students to the age group would have been slightly smaller in 1955, and the figure for 1951 would have been that much closer to its equivalent for 1931.

The only other caution to be raised about the university data since 1945 has to do, once again, with the average duration of study. It apparently continued to lengthen, at least at the universities. For all university-level institutions combined, however, it probably remained fairly close to 4.5 years around 1960. This means that Table 1.6 continues to overstate the level of inclusiveness at university entry by some 10 to 12 percent. In reality, the university access rate must have stood very near 5 percent of the age group in 1960, or at roughly four times what it had been in 1911.

In the meantime, the older university faculties and subjects have continued to lose ground, more rapidly than ever, to newer areas of study [V]. As Table 1.7 makes clear, the three giants of the new university are the natural sciences, the social sciences and business studies, and the technical specialties. Among the older fields, only the pedagogically oriented humanities have kept pace with the three new clusters. The old professional faculties, taken together, accounted for scarcely more than a quarter of total enrollments in 1955.

As late as 1960, little more than 15 percent of German children reached secondary schools, about a third of these eventually earned

Table 1.7
Distribution of German University-Level Students
over Various Institutions and Fields of Study, 1955
(As Percentages of All University-Level Enrollments)

Field of study	Univer- sities	Technical institutes	Acade- mies	All institutions
Theology	4	—	2	5
Law, government	12	—	—	12
General medicine	9	—	—	9
Humanities	16	—	—	16
Natural sciences	10	4	—	14
Pharmacy, dentistry, veterinary medicine	4	—	—	5
Economics, business administration, social sciences	14	1	2	16
Architecture, engineering, mining	—	16	1	17
Agriculture, forestry	1	1	—	2
Music, arts, etc.	—	—	4	4
All fields	70	21	9	100

See V for details.

the *Abitur*, and 5 percent entered university-level institutions. One can hardly call this a case of "mass" higher education. Yet it is hard to avoid the impression of a major transformation since the 1920s. Levels of inclusiveness in secondary and university-level education had changed so little during the nineteenth century that their four-fold increase since the First World War does seem striking. Besides, there is every indication that enrollments would have grown much more decisively without the intervention of the National Socialists.

Thus from the 1920s on, German society has apparently been engaged, once again, in redefining its demand for highly educated men and women. The rapidly growing importance of certain newer subject areas at the universities would tend to support this hypothesis. If the experience of the early nineteenth century is any indication, however, such redefinitions can be painful. Social roles must be specified, along with their statuses. Expectations must be reoriented as academic qualifications are matched with appropriate positions. The importance of the skilled white-collar worker does appear to be an objective characteristic of contemporary societies; it would be difficult to imagine a system of education that did not respond to this reality in one way or another. The predominance of the older professional faculties at the nineteenth-century universities would seem impossible today. The common school, at least to age ten, along with the muting of curricular distinctions at the secondary level, appears to fit naturally into the late industrial era. Yet no comparative historian can miss the conventional and attitudinal element that enters into any specification of academic demand.

It is not surprising, therefore, that the kind of redefinition that has been suggested should be accompanied by a certain instability in enrollment patterns, by periods of academic "overproduction," by disappointed expectations and related anxieties. An "academic proletariat" may be created in part by misinterpretations during periods of transition, as during the Weimar period, for example. But the same pattern of academic "overproduction" and "proletarization" can also aid the emergence of new and wider role definitions for the highly educated. These considerations may shed light on the sense of crisis that overtook the German academic community between the wars and again from the 1960s.

2. The German System: Education and Society

The Social Role of the Secondary Schools

The best introduction to the role of higher education in nineteenth-century Germany is a report on the social origins and career plans of the roughly 85 thousand pupils who earned the *Abitur* at all Prussian secondary schools between 1875 and 1899 [II]. The period is particularly interesting because it covers the early stages of the second phase in the history of the German system and can thus suggest some of the characteristics of the first phase as well. Moreover, since most German secondary graduates went on to advanced studies, the report also reflects something of the situation at the university level.

Table 2.1 summarizes the results of the survey. Like all other tables in this chapter, it deals with distribution percentages, not access percentages. It describes what fractions of students' fathers were in given occupations and what portions of graduates intended to enter specified professions. It does not indicate how high a percentage of lawyers' sons reached the classical *Abitur* as distinct from the modern *Abitur* or none at all. Nor does it reveal what share of those intending to enter the commercial occupations came from the *Gymnasium* rather than from a modern school, or without any secondary certificate. The distinction is by no means academic; some 71 thousand of the 85 thousand graduates in the group received the *Abitur* from a *Gymnasium,* whereas less than 13 thousand came from a *Realgymnasium* and just over a thousand from an *Oberrealschule.* One consequence is that the distribution for all secondary schools closely resembles that for the *Gymnasium,* which dominates the sample with its numbers. The other effect is more important, since it can lead to misunderstandings. The table indicates, for example, that 17 percent of graduates from the

70

Oberrealschule were the offspring of artisans as against only 7 percent of *Gymnasium* graduates. This is revealing, but it does not alter the fact that most artisans' sons who completed any form of secondary

Table 2.1
Social Origins and Career Plans
of Prussian Secondary Graduates, 1875–1899
(Percentages by Column)

Professional Category	Gymnasium		Realgym-nasium		Oberreal-schule		All schools	
	IN	OUT	IN	OUT	IN	OUT	IN	OUT
1. Law, high officials	5	23	1	2	–	–	5	20
2. Secondary and university teaching	5	10	3	18	3	11	4	12
3. Clergy/theology	7	22	1	2	1	–	6	19
4. Medicine	4	20	2	4	1	1	4	18
1–4. Learned professions	21	75	7	26	5	12	19	68
5. Officers/military	3	7	2	7	2	3	3	7
6. Middle and lower civil service[a]	12	5	15	19	13	13	13	7
7. Lower teachers	7	–	4	–	2	–	6	–
8. Tech. professions	4	7	7	30	9	56	5	11
9. Landowners[b]	2 } 2		1 } 4		1 } 2		2} 3	
10. Farmers[b]	11 }		8 }		4 }		10}	
11. Industrialists[c]	5 } 4		9 } 10		13 } 11		6} 4	
12. Merchants, innkeepers/commerce[c]	20 }		26 }		27 }		21}	
13. Artisans	7	–	13	–	17	–	8	–
11–13. Commerce and industry	32	4	48	10	57	11	35	4
14. Rentiers, others, unknown	8	–	8	4	7	3	7	–

The table reports on the roughly 85 thousand students who received the *Abitur* certificate at all Prussian secondary schools between 1875 and 1899. The percentage distibutions shown are those for the occupations of students' fathers (IN) and those for the intended professions of the graduates (OUT). See II for details.

[a] Lower civil service includes a few fathers who were "private officials" and a few graduates who merely listed "administration" or "office service."

[b] Under OUT, combined figures given for agriculture and forestry.

[c] Under OUT, combined figures given for commerce and industry (merchants, banking, bookselling, and "other subjects of trade and commerce").

education did so at a classical school. Even 7 percent of the *Gymnasium* contingent represents many more individuals than does 17 percent of the small group from the *Oberrealschule*. Similarly, a large majority of the students who meant to take positions in commerce and industry came from a *Gymnasium,* even though the business world was decidedly a more common goal among modern school graduates than it was among classical graduates.

Over the last quarter of the nineteenth century, the table indicates, less than 13 thousand Prussian secondary graduates intended to enter business and the technical professions. During the same interval, the *Gymnasium* alone produced about 62 thousand aspiring judges, lawyers, officials, theologians, doctors, officers, and secondary or university teachers. Of course, three out of four secondary pupils left school before earning a certificate. Most of the nongraduates came from the modern sector and many of them probably entered commerce or industry. Moreover, some of the graduates may eventually have failed to attain the professions they were aiming at. While almost all of them presumably reached the advanced educational programs of their choice (since the *Abitur* served as a universal entrance examination and certificate), at least a few of them may subsequently have abandoned their university-level studies before passing the obligatory state examinations. They would then have had to settle for careers in the middle ranks of the bureaucracy, in the military, or even in business. The table tells us nothing about the nongraduates, and it deals with stated intentions, not with eventual achievements. At the level of the *Abitur* and of intentions, however, the Prussian secondary system clearly was designed to prepare for the "learned," noncommercial professions, including the high civil service.

This was especially true of the *Gymnasium,* which still awarded over five times as many certificates as the two modern schools combined. Nearly a fourth of the *Gymnasium* graduates planned to take higher positions in law or government. Another 42 percent expected to study medicine or theology, while 10 percent hoped to become secondary teachers or university professors. Thus, no less than three-fourths anticipated employment in high public administration and the liberal professions. Most of the rest selected careers in the military or in the middle ranks of the bureaucracy. Only 7 percent chose any of the technical professions, and a mere 4 percent opted for commerce, banking, and related occupations.

At the *Oberrealschule,* the situation was almost reversed. Practically none of its graduates headed for high government posts or the liberal professions. About a quarter were attracted by teaching or by immediate employment in the civil service, but well over half selected positions in engineering, mining, architecture and the like, while another 11 percent chose commerce and industry.

The *Realgymnasium* stood somewhere between the *Gymnasium* and the *Oberrealschule*, though clearly nearer the *Oberrealschule*. Only 8 percent of its graduates went into the liberal professions and high civil service. The technical professions drew 30 percent and the commercial occupations another 10 percent. That left a sizable share of *Realgymnasium* graduates for the military, teaching, and the middle grades of the bureaucracy.

Obviously, differences among the German secondary schools were not merely curricular. The *Realgymnasium* might have been a natural training ground for future physicians, but even in this field it was totally overshadowed by the *Gymnasium*. Traditional prestige and the assurance of university access determined the character and role of the schools, and eloquent debates over the intrinsic merits of classical and modern studies did little to change that situation. As noted, the *Gymnasium* long controlled entry to the learned or "academic" professions, while graduates of the *Realgymnasium* found it difficult to reach the universities and state examinations. They did have a chance to become military officers, generally after further training at special academies (*Kadettenanstalten*); but most of them were deflected toward the less prestigious positions in the civil service, which did not require university study in law, or toward the technical institutes and professions. In many ways, the *Realgymnasium* functioned as a second-rate *Gymnasium*.

The *Oberrealschule* clearly stood lowest on the ladder of academic prestige. It lost most of its students well before graduation, and it was also most closely identified with the world of business and technology. Among *Oberrealschule* students who stayed on for the *Abitur*, the majority apparently meant to take up such vocations as construction, mechanical engineering, chemistry, mining, general and electrical engineering, shipbuilding, surveying, railway transport, and metallurgy. All of these specialties were taught at the technical institutes, which did not rank as universities yet. A smaller number of graduates from the *Oberrealschule* intended to enter the business world, with or without further study at business schools. The specific occupations they indicated suggest that commerce and banking, rather than industry, were typical goals.

Among the fathers of graduates from all three schools, about one-fifth were educated jurists, Protestant theologians, physicians and other medical professionals, secondary and university teachers. A slightly larger contingent were officers or lower-ranking officials and teachers. Agriculture accounted for only an eighth of students' fathers. That left 5 percent for the technical professions and 35 percent for all the commercial and industrial occupations from the level of large manufacturers or wholesale merchants to that of the artisans or petty tradesmen.

Altogether, late nineteenth-century German secondary education was really rather progressive for its time. Aristocrats among the fathers would presumably have registered as juridically trained officials, landowners or officers, but none of those groups were particularly large. While the industrial working class was practically unrepresented at the secondary schools, the pattern of recruitment was dominated by the middle class.

Needless to say, the German middle class of those days was not a collection of corporate executives and factory owners. It is best to think of the relatively prosperous shopkeeper or independent artisan, the postal inspector and the primary teacher. One should picture an early industrial middle and lower middle class of provincial townsmen or burghers. True, German society was changing very rapidly during the closing decades of the nineteenth century. Industrialization came late; but it took place with extraordinary speed, in an environment that favored the immediate emergence of huge combines and trusts. Thus many a German burgher became a bourgeois, in Thomas Mann's phrase, while the remaining members of the old middle stratum (*Mittelstand*) experienced increasing economic insecurity. Yet Table 2.1 really reflects a transitional stage in this process. The early industrial society remains at least as visible in it as its high industrial successor. It is worth noting that commerce was much more strongly represented than industry among students' fathers, as well as in the specific career choices of future businessmen among the graduates [II]. Even more striking are the large numbers of students who came from the families of lower-ranking civil servants and teachers. The high representation of this noncommercial wing of the old burgher class was out of all proportion to its relative size in the total population.

The most distinguished elements among the fathers of graduates were chiefly members of the liberal professions, clergymen, and high civil servants. To understand the role of this elite, one again has to imagine an early industrial social system, in which the economic upper middle class was not yet very strong and the aristocracy was no longer solely dominant either. In this transitional context, the notables of the educated upper middle class stood out as a kind of substitute nobility, an aristocracy of mind. Rising above the burgher milieu from which many of them initially came, the members of the "academic" professions formed a distinctive learned or cultivated stratum (*Bildungsschicht*). Their high status was based primarily upon educational qualifications, though many of them were also closely identified with the power of the state. Among the fathers of Prussian graduates, about 20 percent had academic degrees themselves [II]. The educated elite thus recruited about one-fifth of its members from among its own offspring. That is not a particularly high rate of self-recruitment; we shall encounter higher proportions when we turn to the universities themselves. Nonetheless, the leading role of the learned and high public professions remains clearly discernible in the data on secondary graduates, particularly against the background of an otherwise predominantly burgher, not bourgeois, recruitment.

With this background clear, the differences in the social origins of students at the three types of school are easily described. The sons of officers and landowners favored the *Gymnasium* over the modern schools. So did the offspring of farmers, many of whom were probably destined for the Catholic priesthood, and the sons of lower teachers, who presumably meant to become secondary teachers. No clear trend is visible in the choices of young men from the families of middle and lower-ranking officials. The offspring of artisans, or petty tradesmen, however, were much more numerous at the *Oberrealschule* than at the *Gymnasium*. The same is true, to a slightly lesser degree, of the sons of technical professionals, industrialists, and merchants, shopkeepers, and innkeepers. Thus commerce, industry, and technology jointly accounted for two-thirds of graduates at the *Oberrealschule,* as against little more than half that share at the *Gymnasium*. On the other hand, some 22 percent of fathers had university educations in the case of the *Gymnasium*, as against only 7 and 4 percent, respectively, in the cases of the *Realgymnasium* and the *Oberrealschule*. In short, the proportion of "academic" parents at the three schools varied inversely with the share of the economic middle and lower middle classes.

Several characteristic ambiguities in the occupational categories used in Table 2.1 involve the relationship between secondary education and the state. Among fathers listed with the middle and lower civil service, a few were reported as "private officials," a term often used to describe higher white-collar personnel in banking, insurance, and other parts of the private sector; on the other hand, many technical professionals were in fact civil servants—the source specified railroad officials, mining officials, civil engineers, and surveyors [II]. Because the state was extensively involved in various economic enterprises, including the railroads, mining, and public construction, there was always a large technical branch of the civil service. Officials of all ranks therefore made

up a much larger share of graduates' fathers than the table would indicate. Among parents of Bavarian *Gymnasien* and Latin schools
around 1870, no less than 40 percent were state officials and another
8 percent were lower teachers [II].

In the same way, government service was an even more common
goal of secondary students than the table would suggest. On the one
hand, a few of the graduates listed as prospective lower officials had
merely indicated "administration" or "office service." They might have
meant to become "private officials." On the other hand, the majority
of future landowners and farmers really intended to study forestry,
very often in preparation for state employment. More important, a
large share of those opting for the technical specialties must have had
their eye on the technical branches of the civil service. Thus well over
half the graduates would eventually be working for the state, and that
is a conservative estimate. The labels used in the original survey are
too vague to permit an exact determination, which is itself highly revealing. Such categories as "administration" (*Verwaltungsfach*), "office service" (*Bureaudienst*), and "private official" were popular precisely because they blurred the distinction between the public and the
private sector. They made ordinary private and even commercial occupations sound as public and official as possible. The belatedly growing entrepreneurial middle class was so unsure of itself that it yearned
to imitate the role and feign the status of the civil servant. The traditional connection between higher education and the bureaucracy
helped to foster this kind of false consciousness.

Obviously, the differences of recruitment to the three main secondary
streams cannot be described on a unilinear scale of social rank, not to
mention a class scale that would make wealth and economic power the
chief criteria. German secondary education during the late nineteenth
century provides a perfect example of segmentation, and of socially
horizontal segmentation in particular. The classical and modern tracks
differed in their clients, as well as in their curricula. Since educational
routes were chosen for most children at age six, only their family backgrounds could really affect the decisions made in their behalf; their
interests and abilities were scarcely known. The *Gymnasium* was certainly the most prestigious of the secondary schools: it was the path
of theoretical learning and disinterested cultivation; it represented
tradition; and it led more surely to status than to wealth. It was favored
by parents in the liberal professions and the high civil service, by landowners, and by officers. The modern schools stood for the more "practical" social roles: they *sometimes* brought wealth, but rarely much
social esteem. Artisans and small businessmen often sent their sons to

the *Oberrealschule*. At the same time, the *Gymnasium* particularly attracted the offspring of lower officials, teachers, and farmers, while the modern schools were favored by entrepreneurs and engineers, not only by petty tradesmen. This is the socially horizontal aspect of segmentation, and it cannot be overlooked.

To grasp the role of the secondary schools in German society around 1890, one should look simultaneously at their recruitment and at the careers for which they prepared. Taking seriously the metaphor of tracking, one can imagine students coming into the schools from certain sectors of society and being channeled out again to others. In those terms, the net flows within the *Gymnasium* and indeed the system as a whole were oriented almost exclusively toward the learned professions and the high civil service. As we noted, there was a certain amount of "academic" self-recruitment at the *Gymnasium*. This was supplemented by a quite substantial rate of upward mobility through education from the lower to the higher grades of the civil service and of other noncommercial occupations. The *Gymnasium* or the system as a whole served, finally, to direct young men away from the early industrial business community toward the bureaucracy and the learned professions. It is not surprising that it did this most effectively during periods of reduced opportunity in the economy.

Against this overall pattern, the modern schools stood out in three respects. First, they recruited with particular vigor from the commercial, industrial, and technical occupations. Second, they rather specialized in staffing the middle and technical grades of the civil service. Third, they alone sent any significant portion of their graduates back to the "practical" realm from which most of them came. More specifically, they routed a share of their pupils from the artisanal occupations toward commerce and banking, as well as into the technical specialties. Thus mobility through education *within* the business world, what little there was of it, was confined to the less prestigious modern schools, particularly the *Oberrealschule*. The emerging entrepreneurial-technical elite was just beginning to assert its need for advanced schooling. That is how the modern track developed and extended upward toward the technical institutes during the later nineteenth century, and especially during periods of economic prosperity.

The *Gymnasium* of the late nineteenth century was itself in a state of transition. Its ancestor of the period around 1800 had been even more exclusively dominated by the bureaucracy and the educated elite. At a representative group of Prussian secondary schools between 1784 and 1808, for example, some 40 percent of students' fathers were officials, officers, and members of various academic professions; another

33 percent were clergymen and secondary teachers, and 2 percent were landowners. That left 14 percent for noncommissioned officers, soldiers, primary teachers, artisans, and workers, 6 percent for merchants and manufacturers, and 5 percent for peasants and day laborers [II]. In comparison with their English counterparts these schools were certainly middle-class in composition; they counted few noblemen among their students. What really stands out about them, however, is their close alliance with the civil service and the highly specialized character of their recruitment *within* the middle class. As of about 1800, no more than 15 percent of their pupils came from the world of commerce and industry, and the lower classes were almost totally excluded as well. Upward mobility through education was not only comparatively rare; it was also oriented largely toward the church and the bureaucracy.

This began to change during the nineteenth century, and probably at an increasing rate after 1860. Recruitment patterns may have become slightly more progressive, although this cannot be established with certainty.[1] Much more pronounced was a shift in favor of the entrepreneurial and technical middle class. By the late nineteenth century, this group not only accounted for about one-third of secondary graduates; it had also opened its own channel of upward mobility through the modern secondary schools.

Table 2.2 describes developments since 1900, but it must be approached with caution. The higher secondary grades, one has to realize, were socially as well as scholastically more select than the lower ones. The representations of certain social groups shrank on the way up the academic ladder. Particularly affected by this process were the economic middle and lower classes: the tradesmen, nonexecutive employees, and workers. Some of the proportional representation lost by these groups in the higher grades was taken over by the economic upper middle class; but most of it was occupied by the high officials and learned professions. This characteristic form of attrition must not be confused with genuine change over time.

To relate the social origins' patterns of 1931 to those of the late nineteenth century, one must compare the distribution for all secondary graduates before 1900 (Table 2.1) with that for the highest (13th) grade of all public boys' schools in 1931. The most obvious difference is an increase in the share of the middle and lower officials and teach-

---

1. Crew, "Definitions of Modernity," pp.63–64, finds few sons of workers among students at Bochum secondary schools (or even at a *Gewerbeschule*) during the later nineteenth century. However, his samples, where he indicates their size, are not large; his percentages do not add up to one hundred; and his categories and notes are not as clear and detailed as they might be.

ers, from under 20 percent before 1900 to over 30 percent in 1931. The representation of the commercial and industrial occupations, meanwhile, rose from 35 to 40 percent. Decreases of about 5 percentage

Table 2.2

Social Origins of German Secondary Students, 1931 and 1965

(Percentages by Column)

Father's Occupation	Boys' public, 1931				All, 1965	
	All grades[a]	5th grade	13th grade	Gym- nasium[b]	10th grade	13th grade
1. High officials[c]	7	5	10	13	5	7
2. Secondary and university teachers					3	4
3. Clergy					1	1
4. Medicine					5	7
5. Other lib. professions with univ. educ.	4	4	6	7	3	4
1–5. Learned professions	11	9	16	20	17	24
6. Other lib. professions without univ. educ.	3	3	3	3	2	2
7. Military	1	1	2	2	1	2
8. Middle and lower officials	30	29	31	30	12	10
9. Lower teachers[c]					3	3
10. Agriculture	6	4	6	9	4	3
11. Entrepreneurs[d]	8	8	9	7	21	21
12. Tradesmen	21	24	19	17	13	11
13. Employees	10	12	7	6	15	12
14. Workers	7	7	5	4	12	8
11–14. Commerce and industry	46	51	40	34	60	52
15. Others, unknown, without occupation	3	2	2	2	2	3

See III for details.

  [a] Very similar to distribution for the 10th grade.

  [b] All institutions of that type, not just boys' public schools.

  [c] 'High officials' in 1931 presumably included university professors and clergy but not secondary or primary teachers, who must have been included with a large contingent (21–25 percent) of middle officials.

  [d] Includes executive employees (3–5 percent in 1931, 14 percent in 1965) and, for 1965 only, engineers and architects who were employees rather than independent.

points each came in the figures for agriculture, the technical professions, and for "rentiers, others, unknown." The decline of agriculture probably reflected changes in the German occupational structure. The case of the technical professions is more complex, since they were separately listed in the earlier of the two samples but not in the later one. Some of the technologists of the decades before 1900 were undoubtedly officials; others might later have been grouped with the liberal professions or with the industrial occupations.

Altogether, these changes suggest at most a mild increase in progressiveness between 1900 and 1931. They also make it seem likely that the representation of commerce and industry in German secondary education continued to grow during this period, but at a much reduced rate. This could seem puzzling in view of the persistent expansion of the modern schools at the expense of the *Gymnasium*, which accounted for only 25 percent of boys' secondary enrollments by 1931 [I], but the riddle is solved by a comparison between the 1931 distribution of parental occupations for the *Gymnasium* and that for all grades of all boys' schools. Although, as a group, the boys' schools still attracted substantially more offspring of tradesmen, lower white-collar employees, and workers, and fewer of high officials and learned professionals, the extent of this segmentation was no longer as great in 1931 as it had been some three to five decades earlier. The modern schools clearly became less specialized in their recruitment as they gained in size and standing after the turn of the century. That is why they did not enlarge the share of business in German secondary schooling as much as might have been expected. The figures for 1931, at any rate, testify less to the continued advance of commerce and industry than to the revived importance of middle and lower-ranking officials and teachers among the fathers of German students.

The distributions for 1965, however, create a very different impression. No distinctions among secondary streams were made in 1965; segmentation was no longer a major issue. But one can compare the 10th grade in 1965 with all grades in 1931; or one can contrast the two columns for the 13th grade instead. The major shift that emerges in either case is a sharp reduction in the share of parents who were middle and lower officials and teachers, and a corresponding increase in the percentages for commerce and industry. There is a problem of categorization, in that secondary teachers and other intermediate officials were handled somewhat differently in 1965 than in 1931. The further decline in the figure for agriculture presumably accompanied a continuing trend in the German occupational structure. But neither of these subordinate developments accounts for much of the change in the overall pattern, so that the major shift is confirmed—the increase in the representation of commerce and industry, which had begun before 1900 but had slowed around 1931, continued swiftly after 1945. It took place largely at the expense of the middle and lower officials and teachers, who had been a mainstay of German secondary education throughout the nineteenth century and again during the Weimar period. Around 1800, at most 15 percent of Prussian secondary students had had fathers in commerce and industry. By 1965, the comparable proportion had reached 60 percent in the 10th grade and 52 percent in the highest grade of all German secondary schools.

One of the most remarkable characteristics of this long-term transformation in recruitment patterns is that it came about without significant increases in the progressiveness of German secondary education. In the columns for 1965, for example, about half the sharply augmented percentages for commerce and industry were due to the arrival of the executive employees as a strong new element within the entrepreneurial bourgeoisie. Workers and nonexecutive employees also improved their representation, but they did so partly at the expense of the older categories of shopkeepers, artisans, and small independent producers. Similarly, among the nonbusiness groups some of the newer learned or liberal professions expanded their shares, while the high officials held their position much better than the middle and lower ranks. Changes in nomenclature call for caution, and the long-term decline in agriculture is hard to locate on a unilinear scale. Nonetheless, there is a strong suggestion that during much of the nineteenth and twentieth centuries, levels of progressiveness in German secondary education remained approximately stable, and this in spite of expanding enrollments per age group. This is a startling generalization, to say the least; but it has enough evidence behind it even now to serve as a major working hypothesis for the study of university recruitment in the remainder of this chapter.

Social Origins of
University Students during the Early Industrial Phase

One of the most useful sources on the first phase in the history of German higher education, summarized in Table 2.3, deals with the social origins of students at the University of Halle from approximately 1770 to 1880. If one ignores the unusual pattern of 1852, the long-term trends are quickly described. Relatively few of the students came from aristocratic families. Even around 1770, landowners, officers, and high officials accounted for less than one-quarter of students' fathers,

Table 2.3
Social Origins of Students
at the University of Halle, 1770–1880
(Percentages by Column)

Father's Occupation	1770	1821	1834	1852	1874	1879
1. High officials, lawyers	19	13	12	12	11	6
2. Secondary and univer- sity teachers	3	3	2	4	2	5
3. Clergy	28	26	19	28	19	16
4. Medicine	5	4	5	5	5	5
1–4. Learned professions	55	46	38	49	37	33
5. Officers	1	2	1	2	1	1
6. Lower officials[a]	9	9	13	11	10	12
7. Lower teachers[a]	5	8	8	8	12	11
8. Landowners, large farmers	4	4	4	5	7	6
9. Smaller farmers	4	7	8	6	6	7
10. Industrialists	–	2	2	2	3	3
11. Merchants, innkeepers	8	8	11	7	10	11
12. Artisans	12	14	12	8	8	11
13. Workers, servants	1	1	2	1	1	1
10–13. Commerce and industry	21	25	26	18	23	27
14. Rentiers	1	1	1	1	4	4

Years listed at head of columns are median dates for samples covering 1768–71, 1820–22, 1832–36, 1850–54, 1872–76, and 1877–81. Students of pharmacy and agriculture are excluded. As of 1850–54, about half of enrollments at Halle were in theology, 31 percent were in law, 11 percent in medicine, and 7 percent in arts and sciences. See VI for details.

[a] Those without university education.

and that total certainly included many commoners. Thus the dominant element at Halle during the late eighteenth and early nineteenth centuries was not the old nobility of birth, but the newer aristocracy of learning. Around 1770, well over half of the students were descended from this educated and public elite, which included high officials and other jurists with university education, clergymen, doctors, and other members of the liberal professions, along with secondary and university teachers. The rate of self-recruitment for the "academic" occupations was almost three times as high at Halle around 1770 as at Prussian *Gymnasien* around 1890.

The most important change over the whole period from 1770 to 1880 was the gradual erosion of the learned elite's representation, from 55 to 33 percent of students' fathers. The reductions came chiefly among high officials and other jurists, who fell from 19 to 6 percent of the total, and among clergymen, whose share declined from 28 to 16 percent. Most of the places thus "vacated" at the university were taken up by lower officials and, more particularly, by primary teachers. Characteristically, it was their lack of educational qualifications that distinguished these two groups from the "academic" high officials and other jurists, secondary teachers, and university professors. Many of the lower officials probably served in the intermediate grades and technical branches of the bureaucracy; they might well have attended secondary schools, and even technical institutes or their forerunners. Altogether, the lower officials and teachers were an extremely important source of recruits for German higher education during the nineteenth century. At Halle, they increased their joint representation among students' fathers from 14 to 23 percent between 1770 and 1880. Here again, social mobility through higher education was a kind of internal movement from the middle to the higher grades of the public service and of related professions.

The agricultural sector increased its representation among fathers of students at Halle from 8 to 13 percent during the century after 1770, and about half of that contingent were large landowners. The whole group of industrial, commercial, and artisanal occupations accounted for just over one-fifth of students' fathers in 1770, and for just over one-quarter by 1880. Obviously, this was a remarkably small share. Only some 2 to 3 percent of students were the sons of industrialists, and only 1 percent were the offspring of workers and domestic servants. The bulk of what representation there was for the nonagricultural economy was thus taken up by merchants, shopkeepers, small-scale producers, and independent artisans. Throughout the first phase in the history of German higher education, students from this economic wing of the old burgher class were only slightly more numerous at Halle than the sons of lower officials and teachers. As has been suggested, their entry into the universities was almost always a choice to leave the business world for more secure and more honored positions in the learned professions and the high civil service.

This brings up some of the short-range changes in distribution percentages and particularly the unusual figures for 1852, which have been neglected so far. It will be recalled that German university enrollments per population expanded very rapidly between 1817 and 1830, fell sharply during the subsequent decade, and then remained relatively stable between 1840 and 1870. Overcrowding in the learned professions was apparently severe during the 1830s and 40s. In the meantime, opportunities in the economy improved, particularly from the 1850s on. At the University of Halle, absolute enrollments were in fact lower during the early 1850s than they had been two decades earlier [VI]. Taken together, these circumstances will help explain why the long-term changes in distributions that have been discussed were particularly rapid around 1821 and 1834, before being temporarily reversed about 1852. As enrollments declined absolutely, and as prospects looked better in the economy than in the learned professions around 1850, clergymen and jurists temporarily recovered their relative predominance among students' fathers at the expense of ordinary burghers, lower officials, and primary teachers. Social mobility through education was probably replaced, briefly and partially, by social mobility outside or around the universities. During the decades after 1850, as absolute enrollments moved steadily upward once again, this regressive effect was erased. The trends of the 1820s and 30s reasserted themselves, though at a more moderate pace.[2]

Of course, Halle was only one among a score of German universities, and an unusual one at that—it should not stand without qualification for the German universities in general. It was traditionally known for its close ties to the Prussian bureaucracy and to the Protestant religion. As of 1852, about half of its students were prospective pastors and theologians, whereas very few were enrolled in medicine or the arts and sciences. In fact, the emphasis on theology and law may help to explain the regressive movement of the early 1850s.

Fortunately, additional surveys of students' fathers are available for the University of Leipzig and for students from the state of Württemberg at German universities. In Table 2.4, the most interesting distribution percentages are listed under approximate dates for Württemberg and Leipzig, and the figures for Halle around 1874 are repeated to facilitate comparison. Obviously, differences in occupational classification must be taken into account. Up to now, "high officials" have

2. For three samples of *Gymnasium* graduates at the University of Tübingen, Conrad, *Universitätsstudium*, estimated the percentages of fathers with university education at some 52–53 percent around 1825 and again around 1875, but at 57 percent in 1845. The figures may be a little high, because only students with secondary certificates are considered; but the regressive effect and the recovery from it are clearly visible (VI).

essentially been "academic" officials, men with university education. In the case of Leipzig, however, the category also covers nonacademic officials in the higher grades (*höhere Beamte*). The treatment of the commercial and industrial occupations near the bottom of the table represents a likely interpretation of vague and changing terminologies encountered in the sources.

Quite apart from any peculiarities of categorization, there were clear differences in the social composition of the three groups of samples. In Württemberg, small or medium-sized but independent farmers took the place of the large landowners and economically dependent peasants who predominated in some of the Prussian provinces (Halle figures). The overwhelming emphasis upon theology at Halle was character-istic neither of Leipzig nor of students from Württemberg. Leipzig, a much larger town than Halle and a commercial center, was also lo-cated in a relatively industrial area. A large faculty of law there was supplemented by unusually high enrollments in the arts and sciences. Of course these differences are reflected in the social origins of stu-dents. Clergymen among the fathers were particularly numerous at Halle, while jurists were more prominent at Leipzig. Agriculture was about equally weak in all three cases, but within the farm contingent the landowners stood out at Halle. At Leipzig, the commercial, indus-trial, and artisanal occupations were particularly strong, at 30 percent of all fathers in the 1870s as against some 23–24 percent in the cases of Halle and Württemberg.

Nevertheless, the general conclusions established for Halle are not invalidated by the variations for Leipzig and Württemberg—they are qualified, but also broadened in scope. In all three cases, the learned and public professions still accounted for nearly 40 percent of stu-dents' fathers in the 1870s. In all cases also, these professions had declined in representation from around 50 percent during the early nineteenth century, and they were continuing to fall after the 1870s, to around 30–33 percent by the 1880s. In Württemberg as at Halle, some of the ground thus vacated was taken up by the lower officials and teachers, whose share of students' fathers stood slightly above 20 percent in the 1870s. The reduced significance of this group at Leipzig is partly a matter of terminology, but it also reflects the somewhat greater prominence of the economic middle and lower middle classes in an urban setting. As of the 1870s, the commercial and industrial occupations accounted for 30 percent of enrollments at Leipzig; but even there, small merchants and artisanal producers were much more numerous among the fathers than industrialists, high-level "private officials," or wholesale merchants. The French would speak of *petit*

Table 2.4

Social Origins of German University Students, 1837–1886
(Percentages by Column)

Father's Occupation	at Halle	from Württemberg[a]			at Leipzig[b]		
	1874	1837	1875	1885	1866	1876	1886
1. High(er) officials,[c] lawyers	11	17	12	10	17	14	12
2. Secondary and university teachers (scholars)[d]	2	4	5	4	6	4	4
3. Clergy	19	14	14	12	16	10	9
4. Medicine	5	8	7	5	7	6	6
5. Other liberal professions[e]	–	–	1	1	2	3	4
1–5. Learned professions	37	43	38	32	48	37	34
6. Officers (nobility)[f]	1	2	1	1	1	1	2
7. Lower officials	10	14	11	12	9	7	7
8. Lower teachers[g]	12	7	10	11	7	6	5
9. Landowners (and large farmers)[h]	7	1	1	1	2	4	3
10. Other farmers	6	7	14	10	7	10	9
11. Large(r) industrialists (and executive employees)[i]	3	3	2	11	3	5	6
12. Large merchants	10		4				
13. Smaller merchants, innkeepers			5		13	19	21
14. Small-scale producers	8	23	19				
15. Artisans			12				
16. Skilled workers	1				9	7	7
17. Unskilled, servants		–	–	1			
11–17. Commerce and industry[i]	23	26	24	30	25	30	33
18. Rentiers	4	–	2	3	3	5	7

Parentheses used in descriptions of occupations indicate variations in the scope of the categories involved. See VI for details.

[a] Fathers of students *from* the state of Württemberg (at all German universities) in 1835–40, 1871–81, 1881–91.

continued next page

commerce. In German terms, it was just the economic wing of the old burgher stratum that joined the lower officials and teachers in supplying new recruits to the universities. In all three samples, the economic middle and lower middle class can be seen to have increased its representation at the universities over the course of the nineteenth century. It was to play an increased role during the second, high industrial, phase in the history of German higher education.

A final characteristic of the first phase is described in Table 2.5, which compares the distribution of students' fathers for the university as a whole with the distributions for the major faculties and fields of study. The variations clearly indicate that a considerable number of students were preparing to take up their fathers' careers. The result was a high rate of self-recruitment, especially in theology and law. At the same time, sons of jurists who did not study law tended to make a sort of second choice for medicine, rather than for the arts and sciences or for theology. The offspring of landowners and officers also showed a clear preference for the law, presumably on the way to positions in the high civil service. Students from the families of lower officials, teachers, and artisans, by contrast, most often opted for the humanities or for theology. Their choices were undoubtedly affected by the long duration and high cost of medical studies and by the extended practical apprenticeships that similarly raised the expense of entry into the juridical professions. But certain affinities of outlook may also have helped to propel the sons of the early industrial lower middle class toward careers in the church and secondary teaching. The industrialists and merchants represented a slightly more worldly and mobile outlook. Their sons showed a preference for medicine and for the sciences. At Leipzig by the 1870s, they had also begun to turn to the law, the favored training ground of the governing elite.

----

[b] Fathers of students at the University of Leipzig in 1864–68, 1874–78, 1884–88. At Leipzig around 1876, about 11 percent of enrollments were in theology, 10 percent in medicine, 41 percent in law, and 37 percent in arts and sciences.

[c] All "higher officials" are counted as such in the columns for Leipzig; only those with university education are covered in the other two cases, with the inclusion of a few state foresters for Württemberg.

[d] Includes a small group of private scholars for Württemberg.

[e] Artists and writers, with the addition of engineers and architects for Leipzig.

[f] Some high noblemen counted for Württemberg.

[g] Those without university education for Halle and Württemberg; primary teachers only in the case of Leipzig.

[h] Large farmers grouped with landowners in the case of Halle only.

[i] Brackets around figures for the commercial and industrial occupations reflect our interpretation of changing and partly vague terms in our sources.

Table 2.5
Social Origins of German University Students
by Faculty or Field of Study, 1850–1880
(Percentages by Column)

	University of Halle,[a] 1850–1854				
Father's Occupation	All Faculties	Theology	Law	Medicine	Arts and sciences
High officials, lawyers	12	3	28	12	8
Clergy	28	41	14	19	15
Medicine	5	2	5	16	6
All learned professions	49	50	50	50	33
Officers	2	1	5	1	2
Lower officials and teachers	19	24	11	13	29
Landowners, large farmers	5	2	10	6	2
Smaller farmers	6	7	5	7	4
Industrialists, merchants	9	6	9	17	13
Artisans, workers, servants	9	10	6	6	17

	University of Leipzig, 1874–1878				
	All Faculties	Theology	Law	Medicine	Humanities	Sciences[b]
Higher officials, lawyers	14	3	24	11	8	8
Clergy	10	40	5	6	11	6
Medicine	6	2	5	16	4	8
All learned professions	37	50	39	40	30	27
Officers	1	—	2	1	1	1
Lower officials and teachers	13	19	9	10	20	13
Landowners	4	1	6	1	2	5
Other farmers	10	9	8	9	10	15
Larger industrialists, commerce	24	11	27	29	20	25
Artisans, workers	7	9	3	4	12	9

Secondary and university teachers are included only in the subtotals for the learned professions, and rentiers are left out entirely, so that columns do not add up to 100 percent. See VI for details.

[a] Students of pharmacy and agriculture were excluded by source.

[b] Students of pharmacy and agriculture probably counted under Sciences by source, which helps to account for the high percentage of farmers' sons in that field.

The combined effect of these predilections was a milder version of the segmentation that played so great a role at the secondary level. The most prestigious professions were obviously those that recruited the largest proportions of students from the learned professions and from the ranks of officers and landowners. This was most consistently true of law, but it also raised Protestant theology and medicine above the arts and sciences. The faculty of philosophy was the first to admit graduates of modern secondary schools, and it also drew the greatest share of enrollments from the two main wings, economic and noneconomic, of the early industrial middle and lower middle classes. Lower officials and teachers were particularly well represented in the humanities, while the larger industrialists and merchants were oriented more toward the sciences. The differences involved are not very large, but they suffice to indicate that the bifurcation of secondary education produced an echo even within the universities, and that it was a social as well as a curricular divide. Of course much of the social differentiation that took place in German education was accomplished long before a remnant of students reached the universities. From age six on, pupils whose background suggested a practical career were channeled away from the path that led to the universities, particularly from the professional faculties. What one sees in Table 2.5 is only the final specialization among the few students who nonetheless arrived at the universities.

The real surprise, in view of the circumstances, is that German higher education was socially as progressive as it was, even during the early nineteenth century. The only way to account for it is to refer again to the crucial role of the lower officials and teachers. A look at the German occupational census of 1882 will underline the importance of this noncommercial wing of the old burgher class.

Despite the advance of industrialization since the 1850s, some 43 percent of the German working population were still engaged in agriculture as of 1882 [VII]. Another 7 percent were in domestic service. Just under 30 percent were family helpers or workers in the nonagricultural sectors. That left 14 percent for all "independents" (self-employed or of equivalent standing) in commerce and industry, and only 5 percent for all officials and employees in government, the professions, nonprofit organizations, and other service occupations. Recall that only about 0.6 percent of the age group reached universities between 1840 and 1870. This means that little more than 1 percent of all males in the work force were fully qualified members of the "academic" professions.

The rate of self-recruitment in these professions stood very near 50 percent during the early nineteenth century, especially before 1820 and again around 1850. It sank below that level during and shortly after the enrollment boom of the 1820s, and it then declined to some 30–33 percent by the 1880s. Among the replacements that entered the

universities, however, a remarkably large contingent was drawn from
the middle and lower-ranking public professions. The lower officials
and teachers accounted for roughly 15 percent of German university
students near the beginning of the nineteenth century and for about
20 percent by the 1870s. Almost two-thirds of those who reached higher
education thus continued to come from the 5 percent of the work force
in government, the professions, and services. Much of the specialization in the patterns of academic recruitment took place at the expense
of the agricultural population, for only some 10–15 percent of university students came from the land. But the segmentation of the educational system also made for relatively low rates of access from the
commercial and industrial occupations. The economic wing of the
burgher stratum accounted for roughly 20 percent of German university students near the beginning of the nineteenth century, for some
25–30 percent by the 1870s, and for 30–35 percent a decade later. This
was not a large representation for a group that made up about 45 percent of the occupational census in 1882, even if only 14 of those 45
percentage points represented independents rather than helping family
members or workers. Industrial labor, of course, was practically unrepresented at the German universities of the nineteenth century, but
even the more fortunate members of the commercial and industrial
classes fell far short of matching the access rate achieved by the lower
officials and teachers. This circumstance essentially defines the social
character of the German universities during the early industrial period.

Problems of the Second Phase

Needless to say, the situation changed considerably during the high
industrial phase. Around 1910, a German historian tried to describe
the social origins of students at the University of Berlin since its foundation a century earlier [VI]. Among the three categories he used to
group his data, one essentially covered the learned professions; a
second was designed to represent the propertied elements in society,
from landowners and rentiers to industrialists and merchants of all
sizes; his third and last grouping included the lower officials and
teachers, along with artisans and farmers. This was a way of isolating
the burgher element, though it did so at the cost of ranking even
modest shopkeepers with the propertied classes. For that reason, the
scheme is not very useful. It does, however, throw light on the changing balance between the learned and the propertied sectors of the
middle class among students' fathers. The representation of the burgher
group, as he (somewhat narrowly) defined it, fluctuated unsteadily

between 20 and 30 percent during the century after 1810. The share of the learned classes stood at 50 percent in 1815, declined slightly during the 1820s, recovered to 48 percent in 1840 and 1850, and then fell to some 30–33 percent during the period from 1880 to 1910. The representation of the propertied and commercial classes rose from 25 percent in 1810 to some 30–33 percent between 1820 and 1870 and to 40 percent or slightly above thereafter. The increasingly competitive role of property as a client of higher education was one of the hallmarks of the second phase.

A more precise account of changing distribution percentages from the late 1880s to 1931 is provided in Table 2.6. The samples involved are now much larger and more representative than any discussed so far: they cover all Prussian universities through 1925, and all German universities thereafter. The emphasis upon Protestant theology was peculiar to Halle. High officials were narrowly defined as officials with university education in the Prussian figures for 1889–1911. But these changes in samples and terms merely exaggerate a trend that was real in itself. The representation of the learned professions, according to our previous estimates, was roughly 37 percent in the 1870s and 30–33 percent in the 1880s. In all of Prussia, it still stood at 23 percent in 1889, but it then fell to 20 percent by 1911. Even if part of the change was nominal, this was a dramatic decline in the rate of self-recruitment into the learned elite. Among fathers of German students at Prussian universities, some 26–28 percent had university educations from the late 1880s to around 1902, but the proportion then declined to 22 percent by 1911 [VII].

The other trends registered in Table 2.6 through 1911 are even less ambiguous. The presence of agriculture at the universities fell to 11 percent by 1911, and 5 percent by 1931. The figure for lower officials and teachers, according to our earlier calculations, had reached 20 percent by the 1870s, and it now continued to rise to over 25 percent by 1911. The commercial and industrial occupations accounted for some 25–30 percent of students by the 1870s, and for 30–35 percent by the 1880s; their share advanced to 38 percent by 1889 and to 40 percent by the turn of the century.

There was an important change in the categorization of the economic middle class between 1900 and 1911 in Table 2.6. Through 1900, the term *entrepreneur* is used loosely to refer to all independents in industry and insurance, down to the level of the small producer or independent artisan. *Tradesmen* similarly covers all independents in commerce, grouping large merchants with innkeepers and shopkeepers. From 1911 on, however, the sources finally permit a clear and consistent distinction

Table 2.6
Social Origins of German University Students, 1887–1931
(Percentages by Column)

Father's Occupation	All Prussian universities				All German universities
	1889[a]	1900	1911	1925	1931
1. High (er) officials (and lawyers)[b]	7	6	6	14	15
2. Secondary and university teachers	3	5	4	14	15
3. Clergy	7	6	5	14	15
4. Medicine	5	5	4	7	7
5. Other lib. professions[c] (with univ. educ.)	1	1	1	7	7
1–5. Learned professions	23	23	20	21	22
6. Officers	1	2	2	1	1
7. Oth. lib. professions (without univ. educ.)	–	–	–	1	2
8. Lower officials[d]	12	13	16	27	32
9. Lower teachers	8	8	11	27	32
10. Landowners[e]	2	2	5	3	1
11. Farmers	12	11	6	5	4
12. Entrepreneurs[f]	16	15	12	9	11
13. Tradesmen[g]	19	22	23	22	18
14. Employees	3	3	3	6	6
15. Workers	1	1	2	1	3
12–15. Commerce and industry	38	40	40	38	37
16. Others, without profession, unknown	4	1	2	4	1

For continuity through the 1880s, see especially Halle 1884 (Table 2.2) and Württemberg 1885 (Table 2.3); but note some of the changes in categorization, as well as the particular prominence of clergymen's sons at Halle. See VII and VIII for details.

[a] An averaged sample for the period 1887–91.

[b] All "higher officials" are counted as such in 1925 and 1931; only those with university education are covered through 1911. Lawyers are moved to the combined figures for medicine and the other liberal professions for 1925 and 1931.

[c] Chiefly artists and writers through 1911; thereafter a distinction made between those with university education and those without. See also note b.

[d] Some middle-level officials *with* university education appear for the first time in 1931.

continued next page

between big business and the rest of the commercial and industrial occupations. The word *entrepreneur* is henceforth used in a more appropriate sense; it describes owners, directors, and executive employees of the larger concerns in all sectors of the nonagricultural economy. The small independents in these sectors are regrouped under the category of tradesmen, while nonexecutive employees and workers each retain a heading of their own.

Here is a classic example of a phenomenon one encounters again and again: a shift in vocabulary belatedly registers real changes in the society is it used to describe. The two decades before the First World War may in fact be regarded as a turning point in the history of the German social structure and of the German university as well. This was a period of renewed prosperity, of rapid industrial growth and concentration. Many burghers became "bourgeois," while others began to feel the insecurity of the "old middle stratum." The line between the entrepreneur and the tradesman thus became more visible, while the white-collar employee emerged to form a problematic "new middle stratum" (*neuer Mittelstand*). Socially and politically, big business was made a partner in the precarious synthesis of the bureaucratic monarchy. In education, the modern secondary schools and technical institutes greatly improved their academic standing. Secondary and university-level education became gradually more inclusive, as newer subject areas were superimposed upon the traditional curriculum. As a consequence, the economic middle class ultimately captured an important place even at the universities themselves. It is not easy to recognize the German academic world of the early nineteenth century in a distribution of students' social origins that includes 40 percent for the commercial and industrial occupations as against 20 percent for the traditional learned professions.

All the more surprising are the figures for the Weimar period shown in Table 2.6. The only important changes in terminology involve the civil service. All higher officials, regardless of education, are counted in the combined percentages that also cover clergymen and higher teachers. This might help to account for the apparent recovery in the representation of the learned professions after the First World War,

---

e Owners of noble estates, but with the inclusion of lessees and stewards of domain lands from 1911 on.

f "Independents" (self-employed or equivalent) in industry and insurance through 1900; thereafter, owners, directors, and executive-level employees of large concerns in all sectors of the economy.

g All independents in commerce, transport, and innkeeping through 1900; small-scale independents in all sectors thereafter.

except that there were probably not many high-ranking civil servants without university education by 1925. Their transfer from the category of the lower to that of the higher officials apparently did little to reduce the figure for the lower officials, since the joint percentage for the lower officials and teachers also continued to grow from about 25 percent in 1911 to 32 percent by 1931. The share of the commercial and industrial occupations, on the other hand, was reduced for the first time in almost a century.

Table 2.7 compares the Prussian situation in 1911 with the distributions for Württemberg, Leipzig, and Bavaria at about the same time. Bavaria was more Catholic than Prussia, and Württemberg was more Protestant; hence the variations in the proportion of clergymen among students' fathers. Nevertheless, if one also discounts the obvious differences in the categorization of the civil service and of certain liberal professions, one discerns a substratum of common trends. The representation of the learned professions continued to decrease in all samples until the World War, but the decline was arrested or even reversed during the Weimar period. The share of agriculture fell off as rapidly in Bavaria as in Prussia. The commercial and industrial groups everywhere gained in strength on the eve of the First World War; but then they suffered a mild setback in Bavaria as in Prussia during the 1920s. Beyond that, one notices a change in the character of the business representation, particularly if one compares the breakdowns in Table 2.7 with those for the period 1837–86 in Table 2.4. Large owners, managers, and executive employees, on the one hand, and lower white-collar personnel, on the other, were coming to take the place of smaller independents in all sectors. At the same time, a few working-class students were beginning to appear at the universities.

The German occupational census of 1933 will help in the analysis of these trends [VIII]. As of 1933, just under 30 percent of the German work force was still engaged in agriculture, including 7 percent who were independents. The comparable figure in 1882 had been 43 percent, with 12 percent independents. Because of territorial changes at the end of the First World War, large landowners were no longer as significant a component of the German agricultural population in 1933 as they had been in 1882. This may explain why the farm sector as a whole declined even faster in its university representation than in its share of the census. In any case, rural Germany continued to be grossly underrepresented, as it had always been, in the nation's institutions of higher learning.

Commerce and industry accounted for nearly 60 percent of the German working population by 1933 as against 45 percent in 1882, but independents in this sector declined from 14 to 9 percent during the

Table 2.7
Social Origins of German University Students, 1891–1925
(Percentages by Column)

Father's Occupation	Prussia 1911	Württemberg[a] 1895	Württemberg[a] 1905	Leipzig[b] 1896	Leipzig[b] 1906	Bavaria[c] 1914	Bavaria[c] 1925
1. High(er) officials and lawyers[d]	6	9	9	9	8	8	13
2. Secondary and university teachers	4	6	5	5	6	4	5
3. Clergy	5	12	10	8	7	3	3
4. Medicine	4	6	5	6	5	7	7
5. Other lib. professions[e]	1	–	–	4	4	1	1
1–5. Learned professions	20	34	29	32	31	23	28
6. Officers (and nobility[f])	2	1	1	2	2	1	1
7. Lower officials	16	13	13	8	9	10	12
8. Lower teachers	11	12	12	7	7	8	7
9. Landowners[g]	5	1	1	3	2	–	–
10. Farmers	6	9	10	8	8	10	6
11. Large owners and directors: industry	8	12	5	6	8	5	9
12. Executive employees			1			3	
13. Large owners and directors: commerce	4		5			18	25
14. Smaller independents: commerce, innkeeps.	18	16	6	23	23		
15. Nonexecutive employees	3		3			2	
16. Smaller producers to artisans	6		11			6	
17. Skilled workers	2	1	1	5	5	3	3
18. Unskilled, servants							
11–18. Commerce and industry	40	29	32	35	36	37	36
19. Others (and rentiers)[h]	2	2	2	7	6	11	9

continued next page

period. White-collar employees in commerce and industry, an almost negligible quantity in 1882, now made up about 10 percent of the work force. Helping family members were no longer significant numerically except in agriculture, and domestic servants had fallen from 7 to 4 percent of the census. However, workers in commerce and industry had increased to nearly 40 percent of the active population, which must be compared with less than 30 percent for workers and family helpers in this sector as of 1882. Obviously, the working class had expanded in size without significantly improving its share of enrollments. White-collar workers below the executive level were a little more successful in that respect. Yet it was ultimately the shrinking group of business independents that accounted for most of the increase in the university representation of commerce and industry before 1911: owners and executives of large firms, a small elite, were at least a tenth of students' fathers on the eve of the First World War, and the offspring of the smaller independents accounted for almost another quarter of enrollments.

As for the learned, liberal, and public professions, they apparently added up to a larger share of the German work force in 1933 than in 1882. As of 1882, a single figure of 5 percent covered all independents, officials and employees in government, the liberal professions, nonprofit organizations, and other services. In 1933, about 1 percent were independents in the professions and services; 3 percent were officials in government, nonprofit organizations, and services; 3 percent were employees in the same sector; and a further 2 percent were civil servants in commerce, transportation, industry, forestry, and agriculture. In other words, the liberal and public professions were still very

---

Brackets around figures for some of the commercial and industrial occupations reflect our interpretations of changing and partly vague terms in our sources. See VII for details.

a Fathers of students *from* Württemberg (at all German universities) in 1891–1901 and 1901–1911.

b Fathers of students at Leipzig in 1894–98 and 1904–1908.

c Fathers of students at the Bavarian universities in 1913–14 and 1924–25.

d All "higher officials" counted as such for Leipzig and Bavaria; only those with university education covered in the other two cases, plus a few state foresters for Württemberg.

e Only those with university education for Bavaria. Artists, writers, and scholars for Prussia; the same with the addition of a strong contingent (3 percent) of engineers and architects for Leipzig.

f A few high noblemen included for Württemberg.

g Prussian landowners include lessees and stewards of domain lands.

h Men without profession and "unknowns" for Prussia; rentiers (retired, pensioned, living on income) for the other samples, with the addition of a few members of minor health professions in the case of Bavaria.

significantly overrepresented among fathers of German university students on the eve of the First World War, but the truly staggering disproportions of the early nineteenth century had been much reduced nonetheless. The entrepreneurial elite was clearly drawing closer to the educated elite in its patronage of higher education.

The really difficult question, under the circumstances, remains whether German university recruitment was socially more progressive, in any unambiguous sense, around 1911 than it had been before 1870. The rate of self-recruitment into the "academic" occupations had certainly been reduced. The proportion of students from the families of lower officials and teachers had grown almost without interruption. Gradual advances in the inclusiveness of secondary and university education after 1870 also establish a presumption in favor of a progressive effect. The difficulty lies in the interpretation of the increased access from the commercial and industrial sector.

During the early nineteenth century, an enlargement in the share of enrollments from burgher families was undoubtedly progressive. The academic proletariat of the decades around 1830 must have included many students from the early industrial lower middle class of artisans and shopkeepers. The demand of the nonclassical schools for equality with the *Gymnasium*, too, was generally regarded as a democratic aspiration during the nineteenth century. Yet the ultimately successful entry of the economic middle classes into higher education came at a time when the burgher had been extensively replaced by the bourgeois and the independent artisan by the proletarian worker. The universities ended by recruiting to a large extent from the shrinking upper and middle strata of the commercial and industrial hierarchy, at the expense of the widening base of industrial labor. It is therefore entirely possible that neither the moderate increase in inclusiveness nor the more marked change in students' social origins during the three decades before the First World War brought any clear advance in a socially progressive direction. This general conclusion has already been suggested for the secondary schools. The transformation of German higher education during the three decades was real enough, but it should be conceived less as a democratization than as an encroachment of the high industrial class society upon the early industrial status system.

That brings us back once more to the remarkable patterns for the Weimar period, particularly those for 1931. They were accompanied, as we know, by equally remarkable developments in secondary education, and they seem to require an entirely separate explanation. The decline in the university representation of the learned professions was

arrested or even reversed; the share of commerce and industry decreased for the first time in nearly a century; and only the proportion of
students from the families of lower officials and teachers continued its
advance to a staggering 32 percent of enrollments. Workers and white-
collar employees below the executive level, moreover, jointly accounted
for almost a tenth of the university population by 1931. Changes in
the occupational census will explain some of these developments, but
not all of them. How are we to understand the rest?

In connection with the recovery of the learned professions, one ought
to consider the arrival of women in higher education. There is good
evidence that the members of the educated elite were somewhat
quicker to send their daughters to the university than the propertied
elements of society; they were decidedly quicker, of course, than the
lower and lower middle classes [VI, VIII]. This circumstance is highly
interesting in its consequences, since it suggests a kind of second life
for the status system in the environment of the class society.

Another factor in the recovery of the "academic" occupations has
become really important only in recent years, but it probably began to
play a role even before the Second World War. This was a gradual
expansion of the professional and educated sector of the population.
As a greater percentage of a given generation gained access to the
universities, the pool of educated parents for the following generation
was enlarged. In a kind of feed-back effect, the number of offspring of
"academic" fathers reaching higher education could thus increase, even
while the rate of self-recruitment declined or remained unchanged. At
the same time, new specialties were added to the traditionally liberal
professions. Self-employed engineers and architects, for example, joined
lawyers and doctors. The state bureaucracy took up a growing share
of the occupational census, and so did various independent service
professions, which were often classed with the older learned occupations. One can detect the effects of this process not only in the census
itself, but also in the unstable definitions of the liberal and educated
professions that appear in the sources for Tables 2.6 and 2.7. In the
nineteenth century, the educated elite essentially encompassed the
civil service and the clearly "academic" occupations. But this traditional identity began to dissolve even before 1930. Toward the beginning of the third phase in the history of the German system, the
society was drifting toward a new and wider set of role definitions
for the highly educated.

Meanwhile, an "academic proletariat" populated the German universities of the Weimar period. During the 1920s and 30s, levels of in-

clusiveness in German secondary and higher education increased more decisively than ever before. It seems reasonable to suppose that university recruitment also became somewhat more progressive at this point, and probably for the first time since the decades around 1830. Among the commercial and industrial groups, nonexecutive employees replaced the smaller independents to some degree, and the representation of the working class finally reached 3 percent, but this shift was certainly no more than marginally progressive. The further increase in the share of lower officials and teachers therefore emerges as the critical element in the situation. The economic crises of the 1920s and 30s may have done as much as the institutional reforms of the Weimar period to steer more young people from this sector of society toward the academic world. In short, what progressive effect was achieved really followed a well-established pattern. The lower classes, properly speaking, were scarcely affected. The bulk of the new wave of students came from the lower middle classes and specifically from the noncommercial groups that had supplied a disproportionate share of recruits to the German universities throughout the nineteenth century. Given the simultaneous check to the long-term decline in the representation of the learned professions, the academic proletariat of the Weimar period was actually rather traditional in character. At a somewhat more progressive level, it temporarily revived the old link between the universities and the nonindustrial status hierarchy of the educated and public occupations. Like its predecessor of the early nineteenth century, however, the academic proletariat of the period around 1930 faced a lack of clearly appropriate positions in a context of social change and economic dislocation.

There is some evidence that for the first time substantial numbers of "overly educated" young people sought jobs as ordinary business employees during the Weimar period.[3] Their employers were apparently fascinated with the status implied by their credentials, yet anxious to keep them in their place nonetheless. One can imagine the tensions that accompanied such situations, which were essentially unprecedented in the German tradition. The whole phenomenon raises that ever troublesome question about the effects of increased progressiveness in higher education. Just as university recruitment became somewhat more progressive in Germany around 1930, some "academic proletarians" took posts "beneath their station." The net gain in social mobility through education may have been negligible. The figures

3. Dreyfuss, *Occupation and Ideology*, pp.292–98.

suggest the possibility, but they permit no firm conclusions. All one can say, really, is that the age of the "academic" white-collar worker had opened in Germany before the end of the Weimar period.

In the meantime, the main faculties and fields of study continued to differ in the social origins of their students. The old segmentations survived even at the university level, though in forms partly softened and altered. The distributions for 1900 in Table 2.8 point up a sharp contrast between Protestant and Catholic theology that has been neglected so far. Among fathers of students of Protestant theology, a remarkable 30 percent were clergymen themselves, another 8 percent were in other "academic" occupations, and 33 percent were lower officials and teachers. Thus over 70 percent can be assigned to the learned and public professions. In Catholic theology, the comparable figure was only 26 percent. Of course there were no sons here to follow their fathers' careers; but that was not the only difference between the two faculties. Prospective priests were also less likely than future pastors to come from the families of other learned professionals or of lower officials and teachers. Instead, the Catholic faculty recruited predominantly among the sons of farmers, of workers, and even of the smaller independent producers that are still included among "entrepreneurs" in 1900. In Germany and elsewhere, this close tie between Catholicism and the lower or lower middle classes was a decisive characteristic of the early industrial social system. The relevant figures in Table 2.8, including those for lower officials and teachers, help to explain some of the social and political differences between the Catholic and Protestant churches in Germany before 1933.

The professional faculties clearly continued to outrank the faculty of philosophy in the social standing of their students. The humanities and natural sciences, as usual, were particularly attractive to children of lower officials and teachers. An important change in the prestige of the professional faculties apparently took place between 1900 and 1931. By 1931, medicine attracted the largest proportion of students from the educated classes; law ranked second in this respect; and Protestant theology had fallen, rather abruptly, to third place. The faculty of law also drew substantially upon the offspring of "entrepreneurs," now accurately defined as owners, directors, and executive employees of the larger business concerns.

Still, one's overall impression of the pattern for 1931 would be one of generally muted contrasts were it not for the two newly introduced headings. In economics and business studies, a rapidly growing specialty within the faculty of arts and sciences, some 53 percent of students came from the families of entrepreneurs, tradesmen, employees, and workers. And at the technical institutes these groups reached a

Table 2.8
Social Origins of German University-Level Students
in Selected Faculties and Fields of Study, 1900 and 1931
(Percentages by Column)

Prussian Universities, 1900[a]

Father's Occupation	All faculties	Prot. theol.	Cath. theol.	Law	Medicine	Humanities	Sciences
High officials, lawyers	6	2	2	12	4	4	5
Clergy	6	30	–	4	5	5	3
Medicine	5	1	1	5	11	3	5
All learned professions	23	38	4	27	25	20	19
Lower officials and lower teachers	21	33	22	17	20	28	22
Farmers	11	8	26	9	10	8	8
Entrepreneurs[b]	15	8	22	14	14	17	21
Tradesmen[c]	22	9	15	24	26	19	22
Employees	3	2	4	2	2	3	4
Workers	1	1	4	–	1	2	1

German Universities and Technical Institutes, 1931[d]

	All univ. faculties	Law	Medicine	Humanities	Sciences	Economics Business	Tech. inst.
Learned professions	22	26	31	19	16	13	17
Lower officials and lower teachers	32	27	25	37	38	26	28
Entrepreneurs[b]	11	13	11	9	11	17	18
Tradesmen[c]	18	19	19	17	16	25	17
Employees	6	5	4	7	8	7	8
Workers	3	2	1	4	4	4	3

A number of occupations are excluded from the table, so that columns do not add up to 100 percent. See VII and VIII for details.

[a] Unreported are distributions for "Cameralia" (agricultural and administrative subjects, in which sons of high officials, officers, and farmers were strongly represented), and for Pharmacy (high representations: medicine and tradesmen).

[b] It should be particularly noted that in 1900, "entrepreneurs" are still all independents in industry and insurance; in 1931, they are owners, directors, and executive employees of large concerns in all sectors of the economy.

[c] All independents in commerce, transportation, and innkeeping as of 1900, but smaller independents in all sectors as of 1931.

[d] Unreported are distributions for Protestant Theology (learned professions represented at 24 percent), Catholic Theology (learned professions represented at 4 percent), and a small field in Education for lower teachers (high representations: lower teachers, employees, workers).

representation of 46 percent. This was the counterpart, for the commercial and industrial occupations, of the special link between the older professional faculties and the learned professions.

Table 2.9 provides a more detailed report on the contrasting roles of the German universities and technical institutes in 1931. Students' social origins are placed beside the occupations they proposed to enter, so that the net flows through the two institutions can be observed. The method of tabulation matches that applied in Table 2.1 to Prussian secondary graduates between 1875 and 1899. Of course, Table 2.9 deals not only with a later stage in the evolution of German education but also with a more specialized and rarefied level in the channelling of students through the system. Still, the two tables can be usefully compared, for a number of common elements stand out clearly enough.

Like the *Gymnasium* of the late nineteenth century, the German universities of 1931 still sent the vast majority of their graduates into the learned and public professions. The church was a far less common objective in 1931 than it had been before 1900, but medicine and secondary teaching made up for the decline of theology. To be sure, prospective secondary teachers were so numerous at the overcrowded universities of the Weimar period that one wonders how many of them had merely specified the state examinations they intended to take, knowing or suspecting that they might end up as ordinary white-collar employees. That fate was probably in store for a portion of those who listed the other learned professions as well. The percentage of students willingly choosing business careers was a little greater at the universities in 1931 than at the *Gymnasium* before 1900, and the difference was almost certainly increased when hopes were replaced by realities. Yet German university students in 1931 were still almost as convinced as *Gymnasium* graduates some three to five decades earlier that commerce and industry offered few appropriate places for the highly educated.

Thus the universities of 1931, like the *Gymnasien* of the late nineteenth century, fulfilled three main functions. First, they provided for self-recruitment into the learned professions at the rate of some 20–25 percent. Second, they were a path from the lower to the upper-ranking noncommercial occupations, a path taken by almost a third of the students by 1931. Finally, they routed a portion of their students from the commercial and industrial to the learned and public professions, leaving only about 8 percent to return to the business world.

The technical institutes of 1931 were to the universities of that time what the modern secondary schools had been to the *Gymnasien* of an earlier day. Only about a third of their students proposed to enter the learned professions, typically as officials in the technical branches of

Table 2.9
Social Origins and Career Plans of Students
at German Universities and Technical Institutes, 1931
(Percentages by Column)

Professional Category	Universities IN	Universities OUT	Technical institutes IN	Technical institutes OUT
1. Higher officials[a]/civil service	}	12	}	18
2. University professors, archivists, librarians	} 15	1	} 13	–
3. Secondary teachers	}	24	}	6
4. Clergy/theology	}	9	}	–
5. Law, including patent law	}	7	}	1
6. Medicine	} 7	28	} 4	–
7. Other lib. professions with univ. educ.	}	3	}	9
1–7. Learned professions	22	83	17	34
8. Officers	1	–	2	–
9. Other lib. professions without univ. educ.	2	–	3	–
10. Lower officials	}	–	}	–
11. Lower teachers	} 32	6	} 28	9
12. Agriculture	5 }		4 }	
13. Entrepreneurs	11 }	8[b]	18 }	52[b]
14. Tradesmen, employees, workers	27	–	27	–
15. Others, unknown	1	3	1	5

IN columns deal with social origins; OUT columns, with career plans. See VIII for details.

[a] IN columns: higher officials not restricted to those with university education. OUT columns: all students specifying government service listed with the higher officials.

[b] We are given only lumped figures for students proposing to enter agriculture, commerce, and industry, though it is specified that 1 percent at the universities and 4 percent at the technical institutes expected to be owners or independents.

the civil service, as teachers at modern secondary schools, or as independent architects, engineers, and the like. Over half of the students at technical institutes in 1931 willingly took positions in industry and commerce, and nearly that many actually came from the families of businessmen. Thus the old curricular and social divides were extended upward into the higher reaches of the German system during the early twentieth century, though they lost some of their former sharpness in the process. Around 1875–99, after all, only 4 percent of *all* secondary graduates had expressed an interest in industry or commerce, and only an additional 11 percent had chosen the technical specialties. Most of this small number of students, moreover, had been forced to finish their schooling with the *Abitur* or at institutions not considered of university rank. By 1931, the business world attracted half the graduates of the university-level technical institutes, along with a smaller share of students from the universities themselves. That change really sums up the second phase in the history of German higher education.

The Late Industrial Phase and the Issue of Progressiveness

Table 2.10 pursues the story of German university recruitment into its most recent phase, up to the chronological limits of this study in the early 1960s. The first column in the table covers all fields at all university-level institutions, including the academies. Perhaps the most interesting trend it reveals is the continued recovery of the learned professions. The distribution percentage for this group declined steadily throughout the nineteenth century; it reached a low near 20 percent, at Prussian universities, on the eve of the First World War. But the downward drift was arrested or reversed during the Weimar period, at a level of some 20–22 percent, and by 1963, the representation of the educated elite had climbed back up to 29 percent at all German university-level institutions. A further decrease in the share of the clergy was quantitatively insignificant in the face of increased proportions for higher officials, for medicine, for secondary teachers, and especially for the newer liberal and "academic" professions.

A closer examination of this trend confirms two explanations that have already been suggested; they have to do with the arrival of women at the universities and with certain changes in the German occupational census. Women made up more than one-fifth of German university-level enrollments in 1960. Among the fathers of female students alone some 37 percent were members of the learned professions [VIII]. The comparable figure for male students must have been 26–27 percent, since the joint percentage for the two sexes was 29. Obviously, the educated classes were notably quicker than other groups to send their daughters to the universities. The influx of women into German higher education therefore accounts for part of the rise in the university representation of the learned professions between 1911 and 1963.

The German occupational structure was thoroughly transformed during the three decades between the censuses of 1933 and 1961 [VIII]. The share of agriculture dropped from 29 to 15 percent. Independents in commerce, industry, and related sectors also decreased, from 9 to

6 percent of the active population. The percentage of nonagricultural workers advanced from 38 to 46, while the proportion of white-collar employees in commerce, industry and agriculture also continued to rise, very rapidly, from 10 to 15 percent of the census. But the most remarkable changes took place precisely in the figures for the learned and public professions. Independents in the professions and services

Table 2.10

Social Origins of German University-Level Students
and of Students in Selected Fields of Study, 1963
(Percentages by Column)

Father's Occupation[a]	All fields	Law	Medi-cine	Hum.	Sci.	Econ. Bus.	Tech-nology
1. Higher officials	9	16	10	9	8	6	8
2. Secondary and university teachers	6	5	6	8	7	3	4
3. Clergy	2	1	2	2	1	1	1
4. Medicine	7	5	26	4	3	3	3
5. Other lib professions with univ. educ.	5	11	5	4	4	5	6
1–5. Learned professions	29	38	49	27	22	18	22
6. Other lib. professions without univ. educ.	2	2	1	2	1	2	2
7. Lower officials, military	13	17	14	21	20	16	17
8. Lower teachers	5						
9. Agriculture	4	3	3	4	3	4	3
10. Entrepreneurs	23	22	17	20	24	32	28
11. Tradesmen	8	6	5	7	8	11	9
12. Employees	9	7	5	10	12	10	10
13. Skilled workers	5	4	3	7	7	6	6
14. Unskilled	1						
10–14. Commerce and industry	45	37	30	44	51	58	54
15. Others, unknown	3	3	3	3	2	3	2

Not included in table are distributions for Protestant theology (learned professions 35 percent), Catholic theology (learned professions 10 percent, workers 21 percent), education (for lower teachers, a small group with workers at 10 per-
continued next page

were 1 percent of the German work force in 1933, but 2 percent in 1961. Officials in government, nonprofit organizations, and various services raised their share from 3 to 4 percent over the same interval, while officials in other sectors were 2 percent in 1961 as in 1933. At the same time, the proportion of employees in government and the services doubled, from 3 percent around 1930 to 6 percent three decades later. There were thus not only many more civil servants in 1961 than in 1933; there had also been a great increase among independent professionals and in the so-called tertiary sector of the service occupations generally. The representation of the learned professions at the universities could increase even at stable or declining rates of self-recruitment.

Among fathers of Prussian university students in 1911, some 22 percent had themselves been educated at the university level. The comparable figure for all German university-level institutions in 1963, however, reached 29 percent, which is about what it had been during the last two decades of the nineteenth century [VI, VII]. This sort of reversal can be considered a feedback effect, for it was a delayed consequence of increased university access among parental generations after 1900 and especially after 1920.

Two related phenomena were the increase of highly educated men in occupations that had not formerly attracted university graduates and the addition of certain newer independent and educated professions to the traditionally academic contingents of jurists, doctors, theologians, and higher teachers. These twentieth-century learned professions were often located in the growing sector of the service occupations. They accounted for 5 percent of German students' fathers in 1963, as against 1 percent of Prussian enrollments in 1911. At the same time, about 8 percent of students' fathers in 1963 had higher education but no jobs that normally required it. Some of them had probably belonged to the academic proletariat of the Weimar period. At any rate, the distribution for 1963 points to an enlargement of the nineteenth-century circle of the educated professions, an enlargement that was partly linked to the rise of the white-collar specialist and the service occupations. Altogether, the recovery of the learned professions among students' fathers between 1911 and 1963 seems a characteristic symp-

---

cent), and a large collection of other subjects (social sciences, philosophy, art, journalism, pharmacy, mining, etc., with a collective distribution resembling that for all fields). See VIII for details.

a Categories are essentially those used since 1925, except that some officers and other military personnel are included with the lower officials and that 'Skilled Workers' explicitly covers dependent artisans as well.

tom of the transition from the high industrial to the late industrial context.

Much more surprising is the sharp decline in the university representation of the lower officials and teachers, from 27 percent in 1925 and 32 percent in 1931 to 18 percent in 1963. The inclusion of the technical institutes and academies may have reduced the figures for the lower officials and teachers, who were always particularly strong in the university arts and sciences. The source for 1963 might also have reclassified a few workers in state enterprises as ordinary workers, reducing the number of lower officials in this way. On the other hand, a few officers and other military men were counted among the lower officials for 1963; percentages for the workers did not rise very much; and the share of the lower teachers fell at least as sharply as that of the lower officials. Thus most of the change must have been real, not nominal. The noncommercial lower middle class really did lose ground, relatively, as levels of inclusiveness increased for the society as a whole and as the economic middle and upper middle classes became full partners in German higher education.

Certainly the share of students from families in the commercial and industrial occupations was greater in 1963 than ever before. From 37–38 percent during the Weimar period, it rose to 45 percent, nearly half of all university-level enrollments. But which specific occupations contributed most to this collective advance?

The representation of the working class climbed from 3 to 6 percent between 1931 and 1963. Some of this change was due, however, to a widening in the definition of "workers" and to an increase in labor's share of the German occupational census. Under the circumstances, the gain of three percentage points can hardly be called significant, especially in relation to the considerable increase in inclusiveness that helped to bring it about.

Retail merchants, innkeepers, independent artisans, and other small businessmen declined even faster in their university representation than in their share of the occupational census. They accounted for 23 percent of Prussian students in 1911, for 18 percent of the German university population in 1931, and for 8 percent of all enrollments in German higher education as of 1963. These were certainly drastic reductions, and they were not balanced by increases in the representation of the lower white-collar workers. The pertinent figures for nonexecutive employees among students' fathers were 3 percent in 1911, 6 percent in 1931, and 9 percent in 1963. It seems very much as though the new middle stratum was unable fully to take over the role of the old burgher class.

Much depends, of course, on the interpretation of the percentages for entrepreneurs, which increased more radically than those for any other group. "Entrepreneurs" accounted for some 11–12 percent of students' fathers in 1911 and in 1931, and for 23 percent, nearly a quarter, in 1963. The overall figure for 1963 can be broken down into 4 percent manufacturers and wholesale merchants, 4 percent architects, engineers, and accountants who were not independent, 2 percent other employees with university education, and 13 percent executive employees without university education [VIII]. The dominant elements within the general category were thus not the owners of large or middle-sized enterprises, but the technical specialists and other higher grades in the white-collar hierarchy. Together with their independent colleagues, who were counted with the learned professions, these leaders of the late industrial economy had become the outstanding clients of German higher education by 1963. In relation to the occupational census, they were probably as well represented among students' fathers as the high officials, lawyers, clergymen, doctors, and higher teachers. They can be regarded as the real successors of the nineteenth-century learned elite.

Given the growing importance of the high white-collar groups, German higher education was almost certainly no more progressive in 1963 than it had been in 1931. Despite markedly increased university-level enrollments per age group, the only clear sign of improved access chances for the lower and lower middle classes was the advance of the working class from 3 to 6 percent. On the other side of the balance sheet, both the learned professions and the entrepreneurs increased their representation, whereas smaller business independents, along with the lower officials and teachers, lost ground.

One can arrive at joint percentages for university-level enrollments from the upper and upper middle classes by adding up the shares of the learned and other liberal professions, and of the officers, landowners, and entrepreneurs. The totals can be compared to similar sums for lower officials and teachers, tradesmen, nonexecutive employees, and workers. The results, for 1911, 1931, and 1963, are as follows.

	1911	1931	1963
Upper and upper middle classes	39%	37%	54%
Lower and lower middle classes	55%	59%	41%

The impression of a mildly progressive effect during the Weimar period remains intact, but developments between 1931 and 1963 look decidedly regressive. The sums for 1963 are affected, to be sure, by changes in the census figures for the "learned professions," by other aspects of feedback, and possibly by a somewhat widened definition of the "executive employee." Yet no reasonable corrections for these factors in the equation would suffice to produce a progressive result.

All this solidifies the general conclusion that levels of progressiveness in German higher education have remained essentially stable since the First World War, and indeed since the early nineteenth century. For the period 1910–60, the point has been forcibly made by Kaelble.[4] Relating selected university distribution percentages to estimates of corresponding percentages in the German occupational census, he has calculated opportunity ratios of about 1.2–1.6 for independent artisans, shopkeepers and innkeepers, 0.4–0.8 for nonexecutive employees, and roughly 0.1 for workers. The upper middle class, according to Kaelble, accounted for some 32–42 percent of students, and there was no consistent upward or downward trend in any of these figures between 1911 and 1960.[5] Kaelble feels that economic growth did increase the available positions for higher officials, for secondary and university teachers, and for members of other learned professions.[6] Enrollments per age group rose as a result of industrialization, but the change was not great or rapid enough to improve access chances for the lower middle and lower classes. Real incomes rose no faster than the costs of schooling, and the educational reforms of the Weimar period were simply too mild to transform the established social patterns.

While Kaelble's arguments are generally convincing, he may be exaggerating or simplifying the relationship between education and industrialization. Particularly if one looks at the nineteenth century as well, one has to recognize that the economic upper middle class only gradually came to patronize the secondary schools and universities. Much of what increase there was in levels of inclusiveness, therefore, represented additional access from the upper ranks of the commercial and industrial hierarchy, rather than improved opportunities for the

---

4. Kaelble, "Chancenungleichheit."

5. The opportunity ratios (indexes of association, in Kaelble's terms) for agriculture (*Landwirte*) fluctuated widely, between 0.4 and 1.2; those for middle-level officials, between 4.3 and 12.0. The distribution percentage for the lower classes was unstable as well. But this has to do with the inevitable difficulties involved in relating (changing) university distributions to (changing) census categories, and/or in estimating the sizes of various occupational groups. When these difficulties surpass a certain level, it may be best to abstain from calculations that can create a false air of precision.

6. In 1907, according to Kaelble's estimates, about 1 in 800 Germans was a high official; in 1960, the corresponding ratio was 1 in 370. Academically educated teachers per population increased by over 50 percent between 1910 and 1960, and the number of university professors doubled.

less privileged strata. During the early nineteenth century, roughly half of German university students had fathers in the learned professions. In 1963, about the same proportion came from the families of a now amalgamated upper middle class, within which entrepreneurs and members of certain service occupations had become as important as the traditionally academic professions.

Only two periods of mildly increased progressiveness stand out in the whole history of modern German university recruitment, one around 1830 and the other about a century later. It is fascinating that, in both cases, enrollments per population were abnormally high, so that an "excess" of graduates caused widespread concern. Almost by definition, this type of excess or "intellectual proletariat" includes students who must take undesirable jobs. Their academic qualifications are "devalued" in the sense that they do not open the way to appropriate positions. Where increased progressiveness in recruitment is accompanied by such conditions, as around 1830 and again during the Weimar period, the net gain in upward mobility through education is likely to be minimal.

Additional clues to the long-term trends in German higher education are provided by the columns for selected areas of study in Table 2.10. Because all university-level enrollments are taken into account for the first time in 1963, one would expect to find increased differences among the distributions for the various fields. Actually, the variations in the percentages for the learned professions were no greater in 1963 than they had been in 1931. Medicine was decidedly the most prestigious subject by 1963, drawing almost half of its students from the educated elite. Law came next, but at some distance, with 38 percent, and Protestant theology continued to hold third place with 35 percent. The percentage for the humanities stood little below that for all of higher education; science and technology held equal positions somewhat lower on the scale; economics and business studies followed close behind; and even in Catholic theology the learned professions now accounted for one-tenth of enrollments. In short, segmentation remained a characteristic of the system, though the variations were relatively mild given the broader scope of the sample.

More important, the remaining social differences among fields of study had little left in common with the characteristic patterns of the nineteenth century. The old antithesis between the traditionally learned occupations and the business classes had lost much of its former force. By 1963, the learned professions themselves had changed in character. Moreover, the new entrepreneureal elite had outgrown the special relationship it had once had with the technical institutes. As noted earlier, the sons of businessmen began to study law and medicine in increasing numbers on the eve of the First World War. In the meantime, the faculty of Protestant theology lost some of its earlier prestige, and even law was increasingly surpassed by medicine in the social standing of its students.

Together with the decline in the significance of lower officials and teachers after the 1930s, these converging developments really produced a new pattern in German higher education. At the new university, to put it in summary terms, the surviving variations among fields of study were as much a matter of class as of status. The old line between the academic and the commercial sectors of society was fading. The segmentations that remained were more vertical than horizontal. A unilinear scale of social rankings could therefore give an increasingly adequate account of prevailing conditions. Medicine was not only most favored by the somewhat altered successor of the old learned elite; it also attracted by far the largest share of students from the upper middle classes generally. The same was true of law, as compared with the arts and sciences, and of the universities, as compared with the technical institutes.

There are two different indexes that can be used to summarize the social standing of German educational institutions. One is the distribution percentage for the learned professions; the other is the *sum* of the percentages for the learned professions *and* for the entrepreneurs —the upper middle class as a whole. In the little scheme below, both measures are applied to the universities and technical institutes in 1931 and to all university-level institutions and then to technical institutes alone in 1963.

	1931		1963	
	% Learned professions	% Upper middle	% Learned professions	% Upper middle
Universities, or all university-level	22	33	29	54
Technical institutes	17	35	22	52

What is interesting is how the position of the technical institutes is described. Every student of German education knows that the universities far outranked the technical institutes in prestige around 1930 and, to a lesser extent, around 1960 as well. Thus the situation in 1931 is correctly described by only one of the two indexes, the one based exclusively on the learned professions. For 1963, however, both indexes point in the same direction. The consolidated percentage for the upper middle class has finally become an adequate measure of social realities in German higher education.

By the early 1960s, in other words, the hierarchy of status through education was no longer sharply separated from the class hierarchy of the commercial and industrial world. The remnants of the old status system were losing their separate existence, superseded by the convergent, integrated rank order of the late industrial society. The unilinear social scale of contemporary sociologists had become largely adequate as an analytical tool. The old separation of academic from practical higher education certainly survived, but not with its former rigor. Education had lost some of its autonomous or active role in the social process, some of its capacity to skew the prevailing class hierarchy by confronting it with a partly incongruent scale of social esteem. More nearly passive than formerly, the secondary schools and universities were less likely than in the past to complicate the rank order of social advantages they transmitted from one generation to the next. Even while functioning as a more general prerequisite for entry into *all* positions of leadership within the society, higher education increasingly took on the character of an ordinary investment. The honor it conferred was the prestige of the professions for which it prepared, or it was seen as a reward for, and sign of, "merit." The old tension between class and status, commerce and learning, began to fade in the socially unilinear environment of the late industrial society.

3. The French System Compared: Institutions and Enrollments

The Institutional Framework

The system of secondary and higher education that existed in France just before 1789 certainly stood in need of reform, but it was not without its virtues. The twenty-two established universities generally encompassed the professional faculties of theology, law, and medicine, along with a faculty of arts that prepared many of its students for entry into the professional faculties. Much of the teaching in the arts faculties was actually done in affiliated *collèges*, which served as secondary and even elementary schools, not just as university-level institutions. Indeed, many of the *collèges* did not encompass the higher grades at all. Some of them were municipal foundations, but most were run by secular clergy or by one of the Catholic teaching orders. Before their expulsion in the early 1760s, the Jesuits were the most influential and independent of these orders; their rigorous version of the classical curriculum was imitated at all the *collèges*.[1]

The *philosophes* and the educated public generally had a low opinion of the universities and *collèges* of the eighteenth century. Critics could point to flagrant abuses in the awarding of professional degrees and to empty lecture halls in the courses that supposedly prepared for them. The Jesuits were heartily disliked not only by deists but also

---

1. The best survey of French secondary and higher education is Prost, *L'Enseignement en France*, which largely replaces such earlier classics as Liard, *L'Enseignement supérieur*. Helpful in English are Farrington, *French Secondary Schools*, and Zeldin, "Higher Education." Artz, *Development of Technical Education*, is broader than its title and still a major quantity in the field. On the eighteenth century, see also Taton, ed., *Enseignement et diffusion des sciences*. Palmer, ed., *The School of the French Revolution* is an extremely enlightening case study of French secondary education before and during the Revolution.

by Jansenists and Gallicans. There were demands for a national and civic orientation in the schools. But the most prevalent objection was to the traditional curriculum. Because it incorporated too little of the new learning, it seemed useless, artificial, "scholastic." It was more likely to produce obscurantist theologians and contentious lawyers, the *philosophes* thought, than creative scientists, good craftsmen, and enlightened citizens.

Another standard of social utility, one not applied at the time, would have permitted a more positive judgment. Many of the *collèges* of the eighteenth century benefited from endowments, some of which dated back to the Middle Ages. Most of the funds from these sources were used to provide free instruction, or even residential scholarships, for pupils who qualified under the provisions of the endowments.[2]

The French Revolution swept away not only the old universities and *collèges* but also their endowments, which were treated as church property. The revolutionaries intended to create an integrated educational system centrally administered by the state. Their pedagogical preferences came to expression in the central schools, advanced secondary schools that emphasized the sciences, French, modern languages, and history, all in the context of a relatively unstructured system of elective courses. The famous Ecole Normale Supérieure has its antecedents in a spectacular but ultimately unsuccessful experiment of 1795, in which leading scholars were called together to instruct the new nation's future teachers. The Ecole Polytechnique of 1795 was a more enduring foundation of the revolutionary Convention. It attracted some of the foremost scientists of the day, and it became the most distinguished higher school of military and civil engineering in France and, for a time, in the world.

Still, the basic framework of secondary and higher education for nineteenth-century France was established by Napoleon, rather than by any of the revolutionary regimes, and Napoleon had a passion for rationality and hierarchy in administration. The so-called University he created in 1808 was not an advanced institution of learning; it was a hierarchically organized public corporation that henceforth encompassed all public secondary and higher education and its personnel. Since 1808, intense centralization and state control have been salient characteristics of the French educational system. The country has been divided into regional "academies" (seventeen of them during most of our period), and each of these has been headed by a "rector." But all

2. For this and the following, see Palmer, "Free Secondary Education," but also Julia and Pressly, "La population scolaire."

important decisions have come from the center. Indeed, the state has generally asserted effective control even over Catholic and other private schools through its standardized examinations and certificates.

Napoleon's conception of higher education was much narrower than that of the Encyclopedists or of their disciples among the legislators of the revolutionary period. The Emperor saw the need for advanced professional training in law and medicine, which might be done at the appropriate "faculties" or "special schools." The Ecole Polytechnique enjoyed Napoleon's favor, and he reopened the Ecole Normale in 1808, since he needed secondary teachers. But for most of the nineteenth century, France had no universities in the commonly accepted sense of that term. Even in those of the academies that possessed a full roster of faculties, the faculties were not interrelated enough to form coherent larger units. In secondary education, Napoleon distrusted the unsystematic quality of the instruction offered at the central schools; he believed in order and discipline. He also favored the classical curriculum of the Jesuits, although he wanted it enriched in the natural sciences and especially in mathematics. These preferences shaped the state *lycées*, which replaced the central schools in 1802. Napoleon allotted funds for a cluster of full scholarships in each of the *lycées*. These were to put the new institutions on their feet financially, while also rewarding loyalty to the Empire and providing opportunities for youngsters from the poorer classes. In education as in other fields, Bonaparte converted the revolutionary passion for equality into a practical emphasis upon opportunity and mobility.

It is worth noting how much the Napoleonic reforms in French education resembled the innovations of the Reform Period in Prussia after 1806. The state's need for trained personnel and its determination to maintain standards in the liberal professions seem to have been primary considerations in France as in Prussia. In both cases, a professional corps of lay secondary teachers emerged at the beginning of the nineteenth century. In 1808, Napoleon instituted the so-called baccalaureate examination and certificate, which was nearly identical with the German *Abitur*. A difficult secondary leaving examination, it also became the prerequisite for access to higher education and to the higher civil service.

Like the German *Gymnasien*, the Napoleonic *lycées* remained the key institutions in French secondary education until well into the present century [IX]. Called *collèges royaux* under the monarchical regimes of the early nineteenth century, they were reoriented under the Restoration toward an almost exclusively classical curriculum. Although mathematics always retained a secure place in the program of studies, especially in the higher grades, *culture générale* in France, like *Bildung* in Germany, came to be largely identified with Latin, grammar, and rhetoric. The *lycées* (*collèges royaux*) were generally established in the larger cities and were financed directly by the central government. The more numerous public *collèges* (*collèges municipaux*) were more likely to be found in the smaller towns. Though integral parts of the state university, they were partly supported by the municipalities. Their curriculum was that of the *lycées*, but many of them lacked the higher grades, and the teachers were generally more poorly paid than their colleagues at the *lycées*.

In competition with the public *lycées* and *collèges*, various private secondary schools attracted—and still attract—large numbers of French pupils [IX]. During the early nineteenth century, many of these private schools were run by laymen; some were simply supervised boarding houses for youngsters who took courses at public *lycées* or *collèges*. Increasingly over the course of the century, however, private secondary schools were essentially Catholic *collèges*. Run by the Jesuits, by other teaching orders, or by the regular clergy, they varied in their academic and social standing, as well as in the tuitions they charged.[3] Some of the Jesuit institutions came close to matching the prestige of the famous Parisian *lycées;* but they did this at the cost of shamelessly drilling their charges in the art of passing the baccalaureate examination, which of course reflected the curriculum of the *lycées*. Apparently, there were also relatively cheap Catholic schools, which catered to a humble clientele in the French countryside. In addition to the ordinary private secondary schools, lower seminaries (*petits séminaires*) provided intermediate schooling for boys who supposedly intended to enter the priesthood via the higher seminaries (*grands séminaires*), even though many of them were in fact headed for other careers [IX]. Such, at any rate, was the situation after the passage of the Falloux Law of 1850, a sort of charter of liberties for private and Catholic education in France.

Whether private or public, however, secondary education was as sharply separated from primary education in France as in Germany. Progress in the provision of elementary schooling was relatively slow in France. The Guizot Law of 1833 required all communities to establish primary schools. Their teachers were to be trained in primary normal schools to be created in every administrative district (department). Higher primary schools (*écoles primaires supérieures*) were to be provided in the more substantial towns. But these early higher

3. R. Anderson, "Conflict in Education"; Bush, "Education and Social Status."

primary schools were unsuccessful; attendance at the elementary schools was not enforced, and some tuition was charged. Thus it was not until the Ferry Laws of 1881–82 that primary schooling in France became free and compulsory for ages six through thirteen. As a result of the Ferry Laws, two types of higher primary education were successfully instituted: the complementary course (*cours complémentaire*) and the higher primary school proper (*école primaire supérieure*), which was typically the more prestigious of the two [IX]. Both provided a somewhat more specialized form of primary education for a year or two beyond the legal school leaving age, and both were free. A pupil might transfer to a higher primary school at age eleven or to a complementary course at thirteen. Few opportunities for further full time education were available to him from there on, but he could always enter a three-year primary normal school at age fifteen. In France as in Germany, primary teachers were graduates of the primary system; they had little contact with their colleagues in the secondary schools.

The barrier between primary and secondary education was not totally impassable. Students could enter *lycées* or *collèges* at age eleven, after five years in an ordinary primary school. In practice, such transfers were neither frequent nor easy before the First World War. Both public and private secondary schools ran "elementary classes" of their own [IX]. Like the German *Vorschulen,* these courses prepared children directly for the specialized curriculum of the secondary schools, and this put pupils from ordinary primary schools at a disadvantage. Until 1860, French *lycées* taught Latin to nine-year-olds. By age nine, and certainly by age eleven, it was difficult to transfer without supplementary instruction or loss of time.

Of course it was the economic obstacle that most immediately separated secondary and higher from primary education. The direct costs of advanced instruction were probably higher in France than in Germany during the nineteenth century. Estimates for the 1840s and 1860s, when primary teachers earned about 500 francs a year, place tuition near 100 francs for day pupils at an average *lycée.*[4] Resident students had to add roughly 700 francs for room and board. Municipal *collèges* and most Catholic schools were cheaper, but the best Parisian *lycées*

---

4. For this and the following, see Palmer, "Free Secondary Education"; R. Anderson, "Secondary Education"; Bush, "Education and Social Status." See also Talbott, *Politics of Educational Reform,* pp.18–19. The official statistical reports on secondary education (listed in the Bibliography) generally contained much detail on costs and scholarships. I did not pursue this subject, which still needs to be studied in a systematic way.

and Jesuit *collèges* were more expensive. Roughly half of French secondary pupils were boarders, though some of them saved a little money by living in supervised boarding houses rather than in the *lycées* themselves. Naturally, walking from home to a little *collège* was cheapest of all. But if one wanted to get very far in French higher education, one had to take at least the higher grades in a major *lycée*, preferably one of the more distinguished and expensive institutions in Paris.

As for scholarships, they were simply not numerous enough to make much difference.[5] The First Empire had fallen far short of its goal in the state scholarships it eventually made available to help launch the Napoleonic *lycées*. Subsequent regimes were even less generous, because less genuinely interested in social mobility through education. They also began to pay general subsidies to secondary schools, while reducing the funds paid directly to needy students. This tended to subsidize middle-class schooling at the expense of scholarship aid to the poor. By 1842, only about 13 percent of pupils in public secondary schools were exempted from tuition payments, as against 46 percent of students in the *collèges* of 1789. The proportion of scholarship holders continued to decline during the Second Empire, and even the efforts of the Third Republic after 1880 could not substantially improve the situation. It became general practice to give out partial tuition scholarships where possible. But these could be useful at best to the sons of loyal officials and teachers, who were traditionally favored in the distribution of scholarships even at the expense of needier groups. Thus, in 1911, only about 20 percent of all scholarship holders were the children of peasants, artisans, petty employees, and workers. Among working-class students who reached the baccalaureate examination in 1932, only 35 percent held public scholarships; the comparable proportion among sons of petty officials was 38 percent. Obviously, access to French secondary education was severely limited by purely economic obstacles.

Curricular differences *within* the secondary system, on the other hand, were probably a little less significant and controversial in France than in Germany. Perhaps the bitterness of the battle over the rights of Catholic schools in France took up some of the energy and concern that Germans brought to the value conflict between defenders of the *Gymnasium* and champions of the modern secondary schools. Perhaps the assured role of mathematics in the Napoleonic *lycée* somewhat reduced the differences between the two camps. In any case, the French created no new categories of secondary schools to teach modern

5. In addition to Palmer and Talbott, see Farrington, *French Secondary Schools,* p.402; Commission Carnegie, *Enquêtes,* p.71.

courses. Instead, they introduced nonclassical subjects through new programs of study within the existing *lycées* and *collèges*.

During the Restoration and the July Monarchy, the classicists were generally in control of French public secondary education. Even so, there were several temporary victories for the advocates of instruction in science in the higher grades, even before the curricular bifurcation of 1852 [IX]. The grades in French secondary schools are named Sixth, Fifth, Fourth, and so on, in *ascending* order, with the Second followed typically by a class of rhetoric and one of philosophy. The bifurcation mandated in 1852 came after the Fourth. The upper grades were divided into a scientific and a literary (essentially classical) branch. Though the two sections shared some courses, they terminated in separate baccalaureate examinations and certificates. Even after the formal bifurcation was dropped in 1864, the science baccalaureate was maintained. And secondary students preparing to take entrance examinations for the Ecole Polytechnique and for certain other university-level schools were permitted, both before 1852 and after 1864, to begin their preparation in general and applied mathematics after the Third. They could thus in effect bypass the concluding years of the classical program.

Much more radical than the bifurcation of 1852 was the "special secondary" curriculum (*enseignement spécial*) introduced by Napoleon III's reforming minister Victor Duruy between 1863 and 1865.[6] This had its antecedents in a few prevocational courses and programs attached to some of the municipal and private *collèges* since the 1830s and 40s. What Duruy had in mind was a clear alternative, at the secondary level and within the existing secondary schools, to the abstract and literary bent of the traditional curriculum. He was influenced by the example of the German *Realschule*. In a four-year course beginning with the Sixth and leading to a certificate, he emphasized the applied sciences, laboratory work, and even manual training [IX]. His scheme had a frankly vocational dimension—he wanted programs adjusted to the needs of local industries—yet he also insisted on courses in French literature. He sought a fully general education that nonetheless encompassed men's vocational lives in a technical and industrial society.

Duruy's "special secondary" education was very popular for over a decade and a half; it survived his fall from office and the defeat of the Second Empire. Nonetheless, one senses a certain fatality about the way it was transformed out of existence during the 1880s. In effect, it was gradually assimilated to the traditional form of secondary education. It became less vocational and more academic; its duration was

6. Day, "Technical and Professional Education."

extended beyond the original four years; the practical science courses
were replaced with more theoretical ones; French literature, taught in
the traditional manner, took on an ever greater role in the curriculum.
In 1891, the transformed version of "special" secondary education
officially became the "modern" stream (*enseignement moderne*) within
the French system. Needless to say, a controversy promptly ensued
over the accreditation of the new curriculum. Was *culture générale*
attainable without Latin? Or would the award of a full baccalaureate
for modern studies dilute the nation's intellectual standards and weaken
its future leaders?

While these questions were being fiercely debated, especially during
the 1880s and 90s, two forms of intermediate instruction developed at
the margin of the secondary system. The first, secondary education for
girls, grew out of another of Victor Duruy's reforms [IX]. In 1867,
Duruy created so-called secondary courses for girls (*cours secondaires
de jeunes filles*) in a number of towns, despite vigorous objections from
Catholics and conservatives.[7] Patterned after the special secondary
program, the three or four-year courses emphasized French language
and literature, history, geography, and the basic sciences. While the
"secondary courses" languished after Duruy's fall from office in 1869,
they clearly inspired the girls' *lycées* and *collèges* that began to be
established in the 1880s. These too initially offered short forms of postprimary instruction with a modern bent. But they gradually acquired
the character of ordinary secondary schools, and they were fully accredited as such by 1924.

The other form of intermediate schooling that appeared toward the
end of the nineteenth century was full-time vocational education [IX].
From the beginning, some of the higher primary schools created in the
early 1880s took a partly vocational or prevocational direction. In a
way, they filled a void created by the transformation of Duruy's special secondary into modern secondary education. The sponsors of the
new higher primary schools were determined, however, to keep them
from becoming secondary schools and thus encouraging inappropriate
ambitions to their students.[8] In any case, after a jurisdictional dispute
between the Ministry of Commerce and the Ministry of Education,
some of the more successful and vocationally oriented higher primary
schools became "practical schools of commerce and industry" (*écoles
pratiques de commerce et d'industrie*) in 1892. Like the somewhat more
advanced "national vocational schools" (*écoles nationales profession-*

---

7. Horvath, "Victor Duruy."
8. Gréard, *Education et instruction* describes the background and context in
which higher primary and vocational schools developed in Paris. Prost, *L'Enseignement en France*, p.346, cites a revealing passage from a report by Jules Ferry.

nelles), the practical schools increased public involvement in a sector that had attracted some private and Catholic initiatives even before 1880 and that was to be of increasing significance during the twentieth century.

In the meantime, the conflict between classicists and modernists in secondary education was resolved, in France as in Germany, around the turn of the century as the modern curriculum gained at least nominal parity with its older rival. After several earlier compromises, a 1902 law laid down the framework for all subsequent developments in French secondary education [IX]. The full seven-year course of secondary studies that began with the Sixth at age eleven was divided into two cycles, four and three years long. In the first cycle, the student opted for either a classical or a modern route. In the second cycle, he could choose among four sections labeled Latin and Greek, Latin and Modern Languages, Latin and Sciences, and Modern Languages and Sciences. Before entering the last year of the second cycle, he had to pass the first part of the baccalaureate examination. If successful, he then enrolled in either the philosophy or the mathematics section of the terminal year, which prepared him for the second part of the baccalaureate.

The baccalaureate examination itself, of course, was notorious for its difficulty. Over half the candidates might fail either the first or the second part of the test [IX], and some therefore repeated the concluding classes of the second cycle. The baccalaureate was a prerequisite for entry into the faculties and other university-level institutions. Such elite schools as the Ecole Polytechnique and the Ecole Normale Supérieure actually required more than the baccalaureate. They held their own highly competitive entrance examinations, accepting only a handful of the highest scorers [XI]. As a consequence, some of the most distinguished—and expensive—*lycées* and private schools ran special "preparatory classes" for advanced students who might already hold the baccalaureate, but who had to get ready for these entrance examinations. The preparatory classes too could be repeated. They formed a kind of intermediate region—and barrier—between secondary and higher education.

The chief peculiarity of French *higher* education during the nineteenth century was that it encompassed no universities in the ordinary sense of that term. Within each of the "academies," the Napoleonic faculties had no connection with each other. Prior to 1896, they were essentially professional schools, if not mere certifying agencies.[9] The

---

9. Basic for the following, in addition to Prost: Liard, *L'Enseignement supérieur;* Zeldin, "Higher Education."

faculties or "schools" of law, medicine, and pharmacy were much larger than the faculties of letters and of sciences [XI]. What advanced education there was in theology took place most often at the Catholic higher seminaries (*grands séminaires*). The faculties of letters and sciences, heirs to the old arts faculty, had practically no students until late in the nineteenth century. Their main task was the setting and grading of the secondary baccalaureate examinations. They also awarded a few "licenses" for secondary teachers, chiefly those preparing for positions at the *collèges*, but the examinations for these *licences* essentially covered the materials taught in the higher grades of the *lycées*. One could pass them without attending a faculty, as long as one registered as a student on the eve of the test itself. Professors who were not content with their examiner's role had only the choice of developing their "public" lectures into spirited high popularizations for fashionable audiences.

The first effective change in this situation was made, once again, by Duruy. He wanted to encourage specialized scholarship and research along with "practical" teaching by example, in small discussion groups or seminars of the German type. Failing to move the conservative faculties in that direction, he bypassed them to create the School of Advanced Studies (Ecole Pratique des Hautes Etudes) in 1868. Though primarily a source of research funds—and not a wealthy one at first—the Ecole Pratique did not disappoint Duruy's expectations. Today, of course, it is one of the largest and most distinguished clusters of research institutions in the world.

More direct attempts to transform the faculties followed during the late 1870s and early 1880s. Leading French scholars and administrators were partly motivated by the shock of defeat in the War of 1870. They also saw science and learning as the potential source of a secular, civic morality that could strengthen the newly secured republican regime. Like Duruy, they meant to encourage specialized scholarship and seminar teaching. In 1877, a beginning was made with the creation of three hundred fellowships for students preparing for the *licence* in letters or sciences. Three years later, two hundred additional fellowships were established for more advanced work. The fellowship holders actually attended courses and devoted themselves fully to their studies, and some of the other students followed suit. The public lectures were gradually replaced by "closed courses" and by a certain number of discussion courses or seminars (*conférences*).

A degree of specialization began to be permitted in the preparation for the *licence*. Beyond the *licence*, the "diploma of higher studies" was introduced to attest to the capacity for independent scholarship.

It became a normal step on the way to the highest honors in the letters and sciences system: the "state doctorate" and the *agrégation* [XI]. The state doctorate was much rarer and more difficult to obtain than German or American doctorates. Its two published theses might take ten years to prepare. It was sought by scholars who wished to become university professors. The *agrégation* was a competitive examination for teaching posts in the *lycées* or in the faculties. It was almost as high an accreditation as the state doctorate. The *lycée* professor who was *agrégé* taught the more advanced courses, had a lighter teaching load, earned a higher salary, and had a wider selection of teaching positions than his less fully accredited colleague.

Changes taking place in some of the other faculties toward the end of the nineteenth century were much less dramatic. Some older programs and certificates lost in popularity [XI]. In pharmacy, the degree most commonly sought was the "state diploma"; in law, it was the *licence;* in medicine, the medical doctorate. All these served as professional accreditations. In 1877, the law faculties began to teach some rudimentary economics. Some years later, a new sense of interdependence among the several faculties was manifested in a reform of medical studies. Beginning in 1893, medical students had to begin their university work with a year of basic studies in the science faculties, for which they earned a special certificate.

This movement toward a closer integration of the several faculties into a (preferably small) number of coherent units was one of the main concerns of reformers during the closing decades of the century. In 1885, interfaculty councils and assemblies were created to link the faculties within each academy. At the same time, the faculties were given the right to own and manage property and to receive financial support directly from private sources. Then, in 1896, the faculties in fifteen of the seventeen academies were officially drawn together as "universities." Some of the new units were too small to be effective, and the coordination among the faculties never became as close in France as in Germany, England, or the United States. The year 1896 is nonetheless commonly regarded as the birth date of genuine universities in France.

It remains true that the French faculties of the nineteenth century failed to fulfill roles that were taken up by the universities in other countries. The French faculties of letters and sciences moved away all too slowly—and never completely—from the task of examining and certifying secondary students and teachers. This inevitably tied them to the secondary curriculum to some extent. An emphasis upon the formal analysis of literary texts and something like a Latin requirement continued to be associated with the teaching *licence* and *agré-gation* into the interwar period, and this tended to restrict higher education generally. These circumstances may help to account for the singular importance of the *grandes écoles* in French higher education.

What exactly defines a *grande école* has never been specified.[10] During the mid-nineteenth century, there was reference to "special" or "government" schools. These were creations of the late eighteenth or early nineteenth century, and they were clearly designed to train specialists for the various branches of the government service. The traditionally so-called *grandes écoles* undoubtedly were the older and more distinguished among these public university-level institutions [XI]. They were generally small residential schools. The elite group of students they accepted on the basis of highly competitive entrance examinations (*concours*) were educated and boarded at the expense of the state, generally for a three-year course. The designation *grande école* has also (more recently) been used to encompass all public university-level institutions other than the traditional faculties, and it is in this larger sense that the term will be used in this study.

The archetypal *grande école*, surely, was and is the Ecole Polytechnique.[11] Founded in 1794 as a School of Public Works, it was transformed during the following year into the Polytechnic School. Its curriculum was kept relatively general and abstract, with a special emphasis on mathematics. It was meant to prepare military as well as civil engineers for government service. Many of its graduates went on to complete their training in such older "applied schools" as the artillery and naval schools, the School of Mines, and the School of Bridges and Roads. Especially during the early nineteenth century, the Ecole Polytechnique had an international reputation in pure mathematics and science, as well as engineering; yet its graduates rarely entered academic life. A large majority ended up in the military. Among the rest, most went into the technical branches of the high civil service, though a few also worked in private industry.

The Ecole Polytechnique's most ancient and formidable rival has been the equally famous Ecole Normale Supérieure, refounded by Napoleon in 1808 after a false start under the Convention in 1795.[12]

10. On the *grandes écoles*, in addition to Prost and Zeldin, see Artz, *Development of Technical Education*; D'Ocagne, *Les grandes écoles*; Vaughan, "The Grandes Ecoles."

11. Shinn, *Dawning of a Bourgeois Elite*, should soon be available on the Ecole Polytechnique.

12. Basic on the Ecole Normale: Smith, "L'Atmosphère politique," and an as yet unpublished book by the same author.

Moved to its present location on the Rue d'Ulm (Paris) in 1847, it probably saw its greatest days during the later nineteenth century. Its graduates generally obtained the best posts not only in the *lycées,* as originally intended, but also in the faculties of letters and sciences. They far outstripped their competitors from the faculties in the examination for the *agrégation* [XI]. Some resentment at this state of affairs may have played a role in the decision to integrate the Ecole Normale into the University of Paris in 1903. The merger has not been total, however. With only some one hundred to one hundred twenty students at any one time, the Ecole Normale was able to play a pioneering role in the development of small-group instruction (the *conférence*); its faculty were all styled *maîtres de conférences.* Some of the atmosphere that grew out of this approach and out of the school's residential character has survived to the present day. Strictly speaking, there are now four *écoles normales supérieures.* During the early 1880s, one of these was created at Sèvres (on the outskirts of Paris) for girls' secondary teachers, and two more, at Saint-Cloud and Fontenay, for teachers in the primary normal schools. In addition, between 1865 and 1891, Duruy's "special" program had its own higher normal school at Cluny. Since 1934, there has been a higher normal school for vocational educators. But even today, the prestige of the Rue d'Ulm assures that it alone is simply called "the Ecole Normale."

The Ecole Centrale des Arts et Manufactures was privately founded in 1829 to train engineers, managers, and entrepreneurs for French industry.[13] Its entrance examination and curriculum were patterned after those of the Ecole Polytechnique, though the emphasis was somewhat more practical. Especially during its early years, it accepted candidates who had not been admitted to the Ecole Polytechnique. The government provided a few fellowships to the school in the 1830s, and the Ecole Centrale was fully absorbed into the system of state schools in 1857.

The Ecole Libre des Sciences Politiques also began, in 1872, as a private institution. Its emphasis was on politics and international affairs, public administration, economics, and financial affairs. Though it long remained in private hands, it acquired something close to a monopoly of access to key departments of the upper civil service. Immediately after the Second World War, it came under state control and was renamed Institut d'Etudes Politiques, and six new institutes in the provinces were added to the main one in Paris. All of these schools are now closely linked to the Ecole Nationale d'Administration (ENA),

13. Weiss, "Origins of a Technological Elite."

which was also founded immediately after the war. Not considered a *grande école*, the ENA was given the task of training and certifying all entrants into the higher civil service. It was to take a fraction of its candidates (after special examinations) directly from the lower ranks of the bureaucracy; but in practice, it has drawn heavily upon graduates of the Institut d'Etudes Politiques in Paris, which is still unofficially known as "Sciences Po."

Other notable *grandes écoles* or nonuniversity institutions of higher education include the Colonial School, several naval schools, and the famous Special Military School of Saint-Cyr. Among more purely scholarly or artistic higher schools in Paris, one must count the Ecole des Chartes, which trains archivists and paleographers, the Ecole des Langues Orientales Vivantes (Eastern Languages), the Ecole des Beaux-Arts (Fine Arts), and the various sections of the Ecole Pratique. The ancient Collège de France is an institute of advanced study; its tenured faculty do not formally teach students. The Museum of Natural History and the Conservatoire des Arts et Métiers, too, are not schools in the ordinary sense, though they have sponsored important public lectures.

At the side of these ancient and distinguished establishments, several clusters of younger institutions have sprung up since the later nineteenth century and especially since the First World War [XI]. Some have been oriented toward business administration, but the overwhelming majority have been specialized technical and engineering schools. Their ancestors are not the Ecole Polytechnique and the Ecole Centrale, but the *écoles d'arts et métiers*, now formally called *écoles nationales d'ingénieurs arts et métiers*.[14] These institutions have not normally been considered *grandes écoles*, except in the most inclusive sense of that term and since the Second World War. Two of them were founded by Napoleon on the model of certain highly interesting charitable and vocational institutes of the late eighteenth century, which had been called drafting or drawing schools (*écoles de dessin*). Napoleon was hoping to prepare "noncommissioned officers" for French industry. After a curricular reform in 1832, the strenuous program of instruction at the *écoles d'arts et métiers* included courses in applied sciences and mathematics, mechanics, and drafting, along with manual work in the machine shops and foundries of the schools. A third school was founded in 1843. Graduates of the schools made a reputation, during the industrial expansion of the mid-nineteenth century, not only as skilled foremen and technicians, but also as entrepreneurs in their own

14. Day, "Transformation of Technical Education."

behalf. With the rapid development of higher primary and vocational schooling during and after the 1880s, the *écoles nationales d'arts et métiers* could raise their standards. The place they had occupied was now taken over by the national vocational schools (*écoles nationales professionnelles*). These took students from the practically oriented higher primary schools and sent some of their graduates to the *écoles d'arts et métiers*. The latter were granted the right to confer an engineering diploma in 1907, and they were joined by three new sister institutions between 1900 and 1912. Further progress in vocational and "secondary technical" education, especially since 1945, has confirmed the *écoles nationales d'arts et métiers*—and many younger engineering schools—in their role as university-level technical institutions.

Clearly, the *grandes écoles* have played a decisive role in the education of France's intellectual, administrative, and technical elites. The older and more famous *grandes écoles* have outranked the faculties in several respects. They have attracted excellent students and professors. They have been free of constraints that have made the faculties slow to respond to developments in new disciplines. Their small enrollments have encouraged them to experiment with intensive teaching methods. Students have therefore often done their learning at a *grande école*, even while officially registered at a faculty for the sake of an examination. Some of the younger and less prestigious *grandes écoles* have come to the fore, particularly since the 1920s, in the environment created by the new technology.

In France as in Germany, the period between the two World Wars witnessed a series of hotly contested reforms in education.[15] On both sides of the Rhine, the leading reformers were inspired by the ideal of the common school (*école unique*), which was to reduce barriers among social groups by starting all children in the same school, and by having curricular specializations branch off from a "common trunk" as late as possible. The divergence of programs, when it did take place, was to reflect the pupils' interests and aptitudes rather than their family backgrounds. Progress toward this goal was in some ways slower and more painful in France than in Germany, at least until the 1930s. But while the National Socialists brought all reform to a standstill in Germany as of 1933, change accelerated in France after 1936 and continued almost uninterrupted into the postwar era.

In the mid-1920s, French reformers began by trying to change the teaching personnel and curriculum of the "elementary classes" attached

---

15. Excellent on the politics though less detailed on social contexts and consequences is Talbott, *Politics of Educational Reform.*

to public *lycées* and *collèges* [IX]. Their purpose was to make these classes so similar to the early grades of ordinary primary schools as to create something like the common school to age eleven. They made some progress in curricular matters, but they failed to remove the financial barrier in the path of common elementary education, for until 1945, pupils in the "elementary classes" paid tuition, whereas public primary school children did not.

Also during the mid-1920s, common courses began to reduce the differences not only among the several secondary branches, but also between higher primary and secondary education [IX]. Within the secondary system, the four baccalaureate options of 1902 were reduced to three. The combination Latin-Modern Languages was dropped, which left Latin-Greek and Latin-Sciences as the two classical options, and Modern Languages-Sciences as the modern route. The natural sciences were strengthened in all three branches; joint courses in French and in the sciences were introduced to good effect. At the same time, and partly for reasons of economy, common classes united pupils in certain higher primary schools with their age mates in those public *lycées* or *collèges* to which these nonsecondary programs were attached. While not numerically significant at first, this experiment eventually led to far-reaching innovations.

To begin with, it was utterly illogical to have secondary students in these common classes pay tuition while their classmates from the higher primary schools did not. In 1928, pupils in the Sixth through Third at the approximately one hundred fifty schools involved in the experiment were exempted from tuition. In 1929, the exemption was extended to the remaining grades at these selected schools. But this produced a situation in which some public secondary schools were free, while others were not. In 1930, tuition payments (not board) were abolished for the entire Sixth at all public secondary schools. After angry exchanges in the legislature, in which the moderate Socialists joined the middle-class Radicals in support of reform, free public secondary education was extended in steps to the Fifth and Fourth in 1931 and 1932 and to the rest of the upper grades in 1933. The continuation of tuition charges in the "elementary classes" now looked particularly anomalous. For relatively little money, it gave middle-class children a considerable advantage, at age eleven, in the competition for access to secondary schooling. The Vichy regime resolved the issue by reintroducing tuition for all secondary grades. At the Liberation, however, French public secondary education became free from the elementary classes on.

In the meantime, further steps had been taken to draw higher primary and lower secondary schooling closer together. Especially important in this development was the work of Jean Zay, Minister of Education in the Popular Front government of 1936. Zay began by advancing the school leaving age to fourteen. His larger plan was essentially to end all primary education at age eleven and to follow it up with at least one year of common intermediate schooling in which pupils could be observed and "oriented" toward appropriate specializations. He reorganized the educational administration to reflect his conception. With his common "orientation classes" at the level of the Sixth, however, he encountered a great deal of opposition from some of the parents and teachers. Even so, he broke through important barriers, and the logic of his overall scheme appears to have convinced his Vichy successor. Under Vichy, in any case, the higher primary schools (*écoles primaires supérieures*) and the practical schools (*écoles pratiques de commerce et d'industrie*) were brought into the secondary system as *collèges modernes* and *collèges techniques,* respectively [IX]. The new *collèges* lacked the highest grades; apparently, some of the older *collèges* renamed themselves *lycées* to show that they didn't, or that they were "real" secondary schools. Even so, it was henceforth difficult to distinguish the modern section of a traditional *lycée* or *collège* from a former higher primary school. The place formerly occupied by the higher primary schools was promptly taken over by the complementary courses (*cours complémentaires*).

In vocational education, too, important steps were taken during the 1930s [IX]. An earlier measure, the Astier Law of 1919, was not very significant. It stipulated that those not in full-time education were to receive part-time vocational instruction for three years beyond the legal school-leaving age. Employers were to release their young employees for the four hours per week that were involved. But as in Germany during the interwar period, the enforcement provisions were too weak and the funds too scarce to have much effect. More interesting and fruitful were the retraining centers opened in 1939 and 1940 to deal with unemployment and to prepare workers for skilled positions in the armaments industry. These initially temporary and marginal institutions became "apprenticeship centers" under the Vichy regime. Together with the existing full-time vocational schools, the practical schools, and the somewhat more advanced national vocational schools, these new centers gave France a complete and effective system of vocational education before the end of the Second World War.

Since 1945, a few further steps have been taken toward the ideal of the common school, although specific reforms have fallen short of the objectives initially set down in the famous Langevin-Wallon plan. Developed between 1944 and 1947, that plan proposed a common "orientation cycle" for all children aged 11 through 15. The old first cycle of secondary education was in effect to be replaced by a common middle school. A set of guidelines rather than a legislative proposal, the Langevin-Wallon plan ultimately aroused opposition from conservative parents as well as from secondary teachers, whose special position it threatened. Even the Billères bill of 1956 failed to carry, though it called for only two years of "orientation" and common schooling from age eleven. The optimistic and cooperative atmosphere of 1945 simply did not last very long. The "new" (later "pilot") classes instituted in 1945 to enlarge curricular options within a common lower secondary program never became very numerous. Similarly, the 1945 decision to abolish the elementary classes in public *lycées* and *collèges* was only very gradually carried out.

Nevertheless, a series of ad hoc measures did in fact produce an enlarged, diversified, and somewhat less rigidly segmented secondary system, especially at the level of the first cycle [IX]. In 1959, plans were made to encourage the "observation" of pupils aged eleven through thirteen at whatever schools they attended. The presumption was that transfers should remain possible at least until age thirteen. At the same time, the old complementary courses became four-year *collèges d'enseignement général*. A year later, the apprenticeship centers of 1940 were reorganized as *collèges d'enseignement technique*. In 1963, finally, the so-called *collèges d'enseignement secondaire* were created to offer a comprehensive form of lower secondary education. The joint result of these innovations was a whole system of "short" or first-cycle secondary schooling. At least in theory, students could transfer from this new cluster of institutions to a full ("long") secondary program.

While the French secondary pyramid was thus widened at the base, new baccalaureate options after 1946 altered its shape at the top as well [IX]. One important innovation was a technical *lycée* and baccalaureate that led principally to the younger technical *grandes écoles*. Further changes in nomenclature resulted when older full-program *collèges* restyled themselves *lycées*. In addition to the new short or first-cycle *collèges*, there were now essentially three types of *lycées* or *lycée* programs. The classical stream was still the oldest, most academic, and most prestigious; it joined either Greek or the natural sciences to the basic curricular emphasis upon Latin. The modern program was the successor not only of Duruy's "special secondary" education and of its "modern" offspring, but also of the former higher primary schools. The "technical" secondary course, finally, was a further stage in the evolution of the national vocational schools (*écoles nationales professionnelles*) and of the initially less advanced "practical schools" (*écoles pratiques de commerce et d'industrie*), which had become *collèges techniques* in the early 1940s.

Inevitably, the new secondary options increased the number of baccalaureates awarded. With that, a larger proportion of each age group became eligible to enter the universities. In 1948, a preparatory year (*année propédeutique*) was introduced as a sort of intermediate stage and sifting device between secondary and higher education. So-called university colleges in the smaller towns came to specialize in this first year of university instruction. According to one report, some 40 percent of students failed to advance beyond the preparatory year during the early 1960s [XI]. Problems of adjustment were particularly severe about that time, because the large birth cohorts of the immediate postwar years were beginning to reach the universities. Like other societies, France was entering a period of crisis in higher education that has not ended yet.

Enrollment Patterns in the Secondary Schools

It used to be thought that some 72–73 thousand pupils attended French *collèges* on the eve of the Revolution of 1789; this estimate was initially included in an official report on French secondary education published by the Ministry of Education under Villemain in 1843 [IX]. A recent critique of the Villemain report by Julia and Pressly, however, suggests that a rough estimate of 50 thousand pupils in the 1780s may be more realistic, at least for the *collèges* that offered a fairly complete course of studies.[16] This would exclude a scattering of small presecondary Latin schools, as well as an indeterminate number of private residential establishments, probably not equipped to do much teaching, that were beginning to emerge during the later eighteenth and early nineteenth centuries. If one relates Julia and Pressly's 50 thousand pupils to a roughly estimated total population of 25 million, one arrives at about two students per thousand population for full secondary teaching *collèges* on the eve of the French Revolution.

16. Palmer, "Free Secondary Education," has now been superseded, at least in the matter of total enrollment estimates, by Julia and Pressly, "La population scolaire." Julia and Pressly have effectively discredited the estimates included in the Villemain report, which stemmed essentially from Kilian, *Tableau historique de l'instruction secondaire en France* (1841).

Julia and Pressly are also somewhat skeptical of Villemain's figures for the years 1801–1815, but they suggest no alternative; and they do not question the data offered by Villemain for the years after 1815. As of 1809, according to Villemain's report, enrollments in French secondary schools, public and private, stood at about 1.8 students per thousand population [IX]. A recovery followed, but it was slow and rather specialized in character. Until 1842, the public *lycées* (*collèges royaux*) and *collèges* (*municipaux*) grew only marginally faster than the population. Baccalaureate awards actually fell below 3 thousand per year in 1842 after having slightly surpassed that level in 1820 and 1831. The private secondary schools, predominantly secular during this period, were nearly as popular as the public institutions in 1809; but they then declined in relative importance. In sum, the whole regular system of public and private secondary education probably shrank very slightly between 1789 and 1809, and then remained essentially static, in relation to the population, from 1809 to 1842.

What growth there was between 1809 and 1842 was due almost entirely to the Catholic lower seminaries. Though very little is known about them, they apparently expanded from nearly negligible proportions in 1812 to total enrollments around 15 thousand in 1830 and near 20 thousand in 1842 [IX]. Despite intermittent attempts to restrict them to their nominal function of preparing candidates for the higher seminaries, they were the most dynamic element in French secondary education during the early nineteenth century. Even so, enrollments at the lower seminaries and at ordinary public and private secondary schools, taken together, still fell short of three students per thousand population in 1842.

At public secondary schools in 1842, about 23 percent of all pupils were enrolled in "elementary secondary" grades below the Sixth, apparently in a Seventh and an Eighth for the most part. A further 36 percent of the total attendance was in the Sixth through Fourth, which left 28 percent for the highest four grades, and 14 percent for mathematics classes and other special programs [IX]. In other words, almost no net loss of enrollments occurred below the level of the Third. Even above that level, the enrollment pyramid narrowed less abruptly in France than in Germany, at least in the public sector and before the baccalaureate examination. The terrifying rate of failure on the "bac," on the other hand, was legendary throughout the nineteenth century. Between 1840 and 1842, according to Villemain, an average of over 5 thousand candidates per year attempted the examination; but less than 3 thousand, on the average, were passed [IX]. The weeding out came late, but it was drastic, not to say traumatic.

Among those who passed the baccalaureate between 1840 and 1842, about 47 percent had prepared at *collèges royaux*, 26 percent at *collèges municipaux*, 22 percent through "domestic studies," and less than 6 percent at any of the private schools [IX]. This suggests that most of the private institutions of the early nineteenth century specialized in the lower secondary grades. The same was probably true of the lower seminaries, which may have drawn the bulk of their students from the rural areas. A number of French youths thus began their education in private schools, only to switch later to a tutor or to one of the more distinguished and typically Parisian public schools, which specialized in preparing for the baccalaureate. As a result, the *net* reductions in enrollments for ascending grades were relatively small in the *public* schools, even though there was considerable attrition in the system as a whole.

As of 1842, pupils in all French public and private secondary schools were about 1.2 percent of French children aged 8 through 17, or 1.5 percent if the lower seminaries are counted as well. The figure is conservative, since it essentially relates nine grades to a ten-year age group. All the more striking is the fact that only about 0.5 percent of those aged 17 actually earned the baccalaureate in 1842 [IX]. The mean width of the whole enrollments pyramid was thus three times as great as its width at the top, after the passing of the baccalaureate. At the base, those entering the lower grades of all secondary schools and lower seminaries must have been some 3–4 percent of their age group. These patterns should be kept in mind when efforts are made to assess the movement of French secondary enrollments from the 1780s to the 1840s.

Unfortunately, there is no way of knowing how the 50 thousand pupils in French *collèges* before 1789 were distributed over the range of grades. As Frijhoff and Julia have shown for several *collèges* of the eighteenth century, they took in students of widely divergent ages and levels of preparation.[17] Especially for the beginners, there was no clear sequence of classes at all. The modern hierarchy of grades and age levels was only just beginning to emerge. Villemain's report on public secondary schools in 1809, on the other hand, made a distinction between "elementary secondary" and "elementary primary" pupils [IX]. Apparently, it considered the Eighth the first elementary secondary grade. It reported only a handful of elementary primary pupils, and it excluded these from the overall total for secondary education. Did

17. In addition to Julia and Pressly, "La population scolaire," see Frijhoff and Julia, *Ecole et société.*

the *collèges* of 1789 enroll and count their youngest pupils in a comparable way? The evidence suggests that they did, but we cannot be sure. We must therefore concede that what change there was in French secondary enrollments per population between 1789 and 1809 may have been partly or even wholly nominal. Indeed, as Julia and Pressly suggest, much the same may have been true of an apparent contraction in the French secondary system that began in the seventeenth century. All one can say, really, is that the total output of educated men per population in France in 1842 was no greater, and was perhaps a little smaller, than it had been around 1700, in the 1780s, and about 1809.

Yet, as both O'Boyle and Weisz have pointed out, an excess of educated men occasioned complaints in France as in Germany during the 1830s and 40s.[18] There were probably weaker objective grounds for such complaints to the west than to the east of the Rhine. France had experienced nothing like the enrollment boom at the German universities during the 1820s. Two competent French officials who commented on the situation saw no shortage of positions for secondary graduates. On the contrary, Villemain's report of 1843 explicitly called for 3 thousand baccalaureates per year to ensure replacements for retiring members of the high government service and the liberal professions.[19] O'Boyle therefore supposes that the complaints were occasioned by secondary students who did not earn the "bac." Though characteristically left out of Villemain's calculations, they might still have become disaffected placehunters, marginal Parisian literati, or radical journalists in a politically turbulent era.

The evidence clearly favors O'Boyle's contention. In France as in Germany, it seems, the rationalized form of early industrial society that emerged around 1800 had less room than its predecessor for educated and partly educated men. Various theological and clerical positions had almost certainly become less numerous than formerly. Centralization and reform may also have reduced the number of posts available in public administration and in the judiciary, or at the margins of these institutions. Opportunities in traditional "nonproductive" employments had shrunk; yet high industrialization had not yet created enough socially accepted "productive" alternatives. This imbalance arose, it should be remembered, in a context of largely legal and administrative, government-sponsored or bureaucratic modernization. In

18. O'Boyle, "Excess of Educated Men," pp.487–93; Weisz, "Politics of the Medical Profession," pp.14–17. O'Boyle recognizes that the case for an excess is weaker in the French than in the German context.

19. Villemain, *Rapport,* pp.57–59, 99–100.

any case, French critics of unemployed students around 1840 typically felt that they could be usefully engaged in private commerce, industry, or agriculture, if they would only deign to turn their attention in those directions. The perceived excess of educated men was thus thoroughly entangled with conflicting definitions of social roles. It was unclear, in an era of transition, what activities were appropriate for a student with a traditional secondary education.

In France as in Germany, complaints about an excess of educated men apparently ceased for at least a generation after 1850, just as the secondary system entered a period of expansion. Table 3.1 charts the development of French secondary schooling between 1842 and 1898. What it makes plain immediately is that total enrollments per age group

Table 3.1

French Secondary Enrollments, 1842–1898

(Thousands, per Thousand Population, and Percent of Age Group)

	1842	1854	1865	1876	1887	1898
Lycées and *collèges*:						
Elementary classes[a]	10.3		17.9	23.7	24.5	(22.0)
Lower classical[b]	16.2		14.8	14.3	18.7	13.6
Upper classical	12.5		12.2	12.4	14.7	16.5
Mathematics classes	6.3[c]		3.9	6.1	9.0	5.8
Lower special/modern[d]	–		13.4	19.5	19.3	18.3
Upper special/modern	–		3.5	3.2	3.6	9.7
Sum: public secondary	45.3	46.4	65.7	79.2	89.9	63.9
Private secondary	25.3	64.4	74.6	75.4	68.3	48.8
Sum: all secondary	70.5	110.8	140.3	154.7	158.2	112.7
Per thousand population	2.0	3.1	3.7	4.2	4.1	2.9
Percent of age group[e]	1.2	1.7	2.2	2.4	2.4	2.5
Lower seminaries (est.)	20.0	20.0	23.0	25.0	24.0	22.0
Per thousand population	0.6	0.6	0.6	0.7	0.6	0.6
Baccalaureates	2.8	4.3	5.9	5.4	6.6	7.8
Percent of age 17	0.5	0.7	0.9	0.8	1.0	1.2

See IX for details.

 [a] Those below the Sixth; excluded from the totals for public and private secondary education in 1898.

 [b] Sixth through Fourth.

 [c] Contains an unspecified number of students in other programs.

 [d] The lower "special" grades are the first three; their "modern" equivalents (Sixth through Fourth) are listed for 1898.

 [e] Through 1887, all secondary enrollments are related to the ten-year age group 8 through 17; enrollments in 1898 are related to the seven-year age group 11 through 17.

remained practically stationary, near 2.5 percent, from the 1870s to the end of the century. Before that plateau was reached, however, there was considerable growth between 1842 and 1876, and especially during the 1850s and 60s. More specifically, the expansion took place in three sectors of the system: in the elementary classes, in the private schools, and in the lower grades of special secondary education.

Attendance in the elementary classes of public *lycées* and *collèges* increased at a disproportionate rate between 1842 and 1876. The evidence suggests that this was due to a downward extension of presecondary schooling [IX]. Below the level of the Eighth, a Ninth and at least a Tenth were in effect added on. Enrollment in these lowest grades probably never matched those in the Eighth and Seventh; yet the Eighth clearly ceased to be the normal beginning of public secondary education. A new line between secondary and presecondary schooling began to be drawn in 1880, when the commencement of Latin instruction was postponed from the Eighth to the Sixth. A gradually increasing number of pupils henceforth transferred from public primary to public secondary schools at the level of the Sixth, which came to be considered the first true secondary grade. Enrollments in the elementary or "primary" classes below the Sixth of public secondary schools contracted during the 1880s and 90s. By the end of the century, some 25–50 percent of entrants into the public Sixth came either from public primary schools or from the primary classes of private secondary schools. But before 1880, between 1842 and 1876, the trend was in the opposite direction. Public presecondary enrollments *below the Eighth* were apparently rising, if slowly. This was a mild structural change, not a real increase in inclusiveness.

More genuine and significant was the dramatic advance of private secondary education between 1842 and 1865 [IX]. Much of this growth was concentrated in the years immediately after the Falloux Law of 1850. The liberties granted to Catholic and other private establishments became effective in the generally conservative climate that followed the Revolution of 1848.[20] It is worth noting that the Catholic share of all private education climbed only gradually from around 40 percent in 1854 to 60 percent in 1876. The Falloux Law thus encouraged more lay than religious institutions. Conversely, the intentionally anticlerical measures of the 1880s probably helped to destroy lay private education, even while failing to halt the absolute growth of the Catholic schools, which accounted for close to 90 percent of private enrollments by 1898.

Unfortunately, nothing is known about the distribution of private school pupils over the grades and curricular streams before 1898. It

20. R. Anderson, "Conflict in Education."

seems reasonable to assume that the presecondary course became at least as popular in the private as in the public system. Some of the private schools provided relatively cheap forms of lower secondary schooling; others offered a "protected" atmosphere for young children from middle-class families. By 1898, at any rate, the private schools had 1.4 thousand pupils more than the *lycées* and *collèges* in the elementary grades (below the Sixth), and over 15 thousand students less than their public rivals in the secondary grades (Sixth and above). We do know that some of the distinguished private schools of the late nineteenth century placed more emphasis than the state schools upon the classical curriculum. Thus the Jesuit schools refused to adopt the modern curriculum when the public schools did. Of course they made up only a small part of the Catholic system, but it was the most expensive, prestigious, and academically successful part. In 1896, the average national success rate on the baccalaureate examination was 45 percent; at the best Jesuit schools, which rivaled the leading Parisian *lycées*, the success rate was 86 percent.[21] That only underscores how much variety there was among the Catholic schools, however, for taken as a group, they clearly specialized in the elementary classes. Their rapid expansion during the 1850s was probably concentrated in the grades below the Third.

Indeed, this was true of the total growth in public secondary education between 1854 and 1876. Some of it took place in the elementary classes, and the rest was due entirely to the development of Duruy's special secondary education in the 1860s and early 70s [IX]. In 1865, the first year of the program, over 13 thousand pupils were enrolled in its lowest three grades. Some of these students probably came from higher primary and vocational sections that were already attached to *collèges* as nonsecondary courses in 1865; Duruy simply made it possible for these sections to reorganize themselves as special secondary classes. In any case, the very rapid advance of the special secondary branch that began in 1865 did not affect the highest secondary grades very much until "special" had become "modern" secondary schooling in 1898. In the meantime, there were decidedly more pupils in the special or modern than in the classical division of the lowest three secondary grades from 1876 to 1898.

Altogether, special secondary education affected the French system much as the *Realschulen* affected its German counterpart. Until late in the nineteenth century, it was a predominantly nondegree (nonbaccalaureate) form of secondary education. Simply added on to the existing classical program, it increased the mean width of the enroll-

21. Bush, "Education and Social Status."

ment pyramid primarily by widening its base. As a matter of fact, enrollments in the classical Sixth and higher grades of French public *lycées* and *collèges* actually declined in absolute terms between 1842 and 1876. The traditional sector thus had no share at all in the notable growth of French secondary schooling that extended from the 1840s or 50s to the new plateau reached in the 1870s. A greater number of students in the upper grades did seek and earn the baccalaureate after 1842; annual awards increased without notable interruption to the end of the century [IX]. Baccalaureates in mathematics were generally about one-third to one-half of all certificates. A further distinction in 1898 identified 22 percent of baccalaureate recipients as graduates of the modern stream, which was clearly advancing toward full secondary status. But again, all this happened after the expansion of the 1850s and 1860s. That expansion took place in the elementary classes, in private secondary education, and most notably in the special secondary branch.[22]

How were these enrollment changes related to fluctuations in the condition of the French economy during the nineteenth century? Compared to Germany, France experienced a much more gradual increase in the gross national product, along with business cycles that were less extreme in either direction.[23] A phase of relatively rapid growth occurred in the 1850s and 60s, while the most seriously recessionary period, the French version of an international crisis, extended from the early 1880s to around 1896. During the economic upswing of the 1850s and 60s, enrollments increased in private secondary and special secondary education. During the same period, there was an absolute drop in the numbers attending the classical segment of public secondary education. A modest recovery for that segment was reflected in the figures for 1887; that is, it probably took place during a severe recession.

It is thus possible to argue, for France as for Germany, that traditional secondary education stood in an antithetical relationship to the economy during the early industrial period. At least in the short run, prosperity tended to reduce enrollments. Special secondary education was a novelty in the 1860s not only in its curriculum and its nondegree character but also in its positive response to an improved business climate. Admittedly, the correlations involved were not nearly as clear

22. Maillet, "L'Evolution des effectifs," is the most sustained analysis to date of French secondary enrollments between 1809 and 1961. Unfortunately, Maillet does not consistently report enrollments as fractions of age groups, nor does he pay sufficient attention to the shape of the enrollment pyramid. He thus fails to identify the *specific location* of what growth there was during the nineteenth century. A further consequence is that he totally misconstrues the relationship between education and the economy.
23. Cameron, "Economic Growth."

in France as in Germany. Neither economic cycles nor enrollment fluctuations were as pronounced to the west as to the east of the Rhine. Moreover, the direct cost of secondary schooling was probably a more important factor in France than in Germany, which probably encouraged enrollments during periods of prosperity.

Whatever one thinks about these relationships, however, one has to recognize the arrival of the special secondary program during the 1860s as a major landmark in the history of the French system. Here was a practically oriented course that immediately attracted crowds of students, while the classical stream entered a period of stagnation and decline. Duruy's innovations of 1865, in other words, marked the opening of a new, high industrial, phase in the evolution of French education.

Unfortunately, the available information permits only the roughest sketch of the French secondary system between 1898 and 1936 [IX]. For girls' and boys' *lycées* and *collèges*, the sources make the basic distinction between secondary and primary classes, with the dividing line at the Sixth and age 11. For the private schools, however, presecondary and secondary enrollments are intermingled, so that usable figures for the Sixth and higher grades can be only roughly estimated. As it happened, the ratio of secondary to total enrollments (secondary and presecondary) for the private schools in 1936 was almost exactly what it had been in 1898. Why not assume that it remained approximately stable, despite the changing overall size of the private sector, during the intervening years as well? It is a very large assumption, but no clear arguments speak against it [IX]. In fact, the figure for private secondary enrollments in 1911 must be interpolated even more indirectly, yet educated guesses may be preferred to nothing at all. Several of the figures in Table 3.2, at any rate, are presented in that spirit.

The table reveals that there was little change in enrollments per population or age group at French boys' secondary schools between 1898 and 1921. There was some growth at girls' secondary schools; their accreditation in the 1920s significantly raised the overall measures of inclusiveness. Even so, one is left with a puzzling plateau in the boys' percentages that really extended from the 1870s to the early 1920s. How does one account for this long-term stagnation, which followed immediately upon a period of vigorous expansion during the 1850s and 60s?

The answer lies partly in the rapid development of the higher primary and vocational schools after 1880. Though their programs were much shorter than the secondary curriculum, they enrolled more pupils than the boys' *lycées* and *collèges* by 1911. To understand what hap-

Table 3.2

French Secondary Enrollments, 1898–1936

(Thousands, per Thousand Population, and Percent of Age Group)

	1898	1911	1921	1931	1936
Boys' public secondary	63.9	67.0	75.3	86.2	116.7
Per thousand population	1.7	1.7	1.9	2.1	2.8
Percent of age group	1.4	1.5	1.6	2.6	2.7
Girls' public secondary[a]	(9.0)	(22.0)	28.6	37.3	53.5
Per thousand population	(0.2)	(0.6)	0.7	0.9	1.3
Percent of age group	(0.2)	(0.5)	0.6	1.1	1.2
Boys' and girls' private secondary[b]	48.8	52.7	63.2	105.0	147.1
Per thousand population	1.3	1.3	1.6	2.5	3.5
Percent of age group	1.1	1.1	1.3	3.2	3.3
All secondary	112.7	119.7	167.1	228.5	317.3
Per thousand population	2.9	3.0	4.3	5.5	7.6
Percent of age group	2.5	2.6	3.5	6.9	7.2
Baccalaureates	7.8	7.2	9.8	15.6	15.4
Percent of age 17	1.2	1.1	1.4	2.3	3.9

Enrollments in the Sixth and higher grades are related to the seven-year age group 11 through 17. See IX for details.

[a] Formally recognized as equal to the boys' schools in 1924; students included in the tabulated totals for all secondary enrollments from 1921 on, but listed in parentheses before then.

[b] Rough estimates.

pened, one has to recall that special secondary education was initially a nondegree course with a practical orientation. It thus resembled the higher primary and vocational schools of the 1880s, except that it was called secondary and that it required tuition payments. The new schools of the 1880s were free and therefore attractive to lower income groups. They were designed to supply skilled workers, tradesmen, and clerks for commerce and industry without raising their expectations by way of the secondary label. In any case, they manifestly stepped into the place left vacant when the highly popular special secondary curriculum became the full-length modern secondary stream during the 1880s. Once again, the conclusion is that only the traditional secondary programs stagnated after the 1870s, and indeed before that time as well. The more practical schools, which were also academically and socially modest, continued to flourish.

Much more difficult to analyse is the movement of enrollments between 1921 and 1936. Average attendance in the seven-year program at public boys' secondary schools increased substantially but not over-whelmingly in relation to both the age group and the total population; the pertinent measures rose by about 50 percent between 1921 and 1936. Enrollments at public girls' schools expanded much more rapidly; the indicative percentages actually doubled. As in Germany, roughly one-third of all secondary pupils must have been girls by the 1930s. Finally, French private secondary schools apparently grew at a truly remarkable rate during the interwar period—they more than doubled their share of the age group. They prospered particularly during the 1920s, whereas the public schools made their gains later and more gradually. It is a bewildering pattern.

To see it in greater detail, one has to consider the effects of wildly fluctuating birth rates during and after the First World War. Fortunately there is fairly reliable evidence on the size of the Sixth or entering class at public boys' and girls' secondary schools between 1924 and 1936. Relating this information to the size of pertinent age years, one obtains a microscopic view of secondary access during that period [IX]. The sharply reduced birth cohorts of 1914–1918 reached the public Sixth at age eleven between 1925 and 1930. The result was a kind of "compromise" reaction in the enrollment pattern that is prob-ably quite characteristic in such circumstances. On the one hand, there was a decline in the absolute number of new secondary students —and therefore also in the ratio of entering students to the total popu-lation. On the other hand, there was an increase in the access percent-ages; a larger proportion of the reduced age group managed to enter the schools, presumably because parents and teachers encouraged young people to fill what would otherwise have been empty classrooms. Then, from 1931 on, the huge birth cohorts of the immediate postwar years approached the Sixth, and now the "compromise" reaction oc-curred in reverse, if only mildly and temporarily. The absolute num-ber of entrants to the public Sixth moved abruptly upward in 1930 and 1931, but it did not at first keep pace with the increased size of the age years involved. The access percentage therefore dipped slightly in 1931, although it then recovered to the level it had initially reached in the late 1920s and remained there throughout the early 1930s. These details are obscured by the summary ratios reported in Table 3.2, which deal with seven grades and age years at once.

Yet Table 3.2 is accurate enough in its way. It simply translates the short-range fluctuations of 1924–36 into their long-term consequences. It correctly reports a moderate increase in boys' public secondary en-rollments per age group, a more substantial advance in public secondary schooling for girls, and an equally significant enlargement of the private secondary sector. The question is how to account for these trends.

It will be recalled that minor curricular reforms in the presecondary and lower secondary grades were initiated during the mid-1920s. Initially limited in scope, they apparently led to no significant changes in the distribution and movement of students, at least until the later 1930s. Among all students entering the Sixth at public secondary schools in 1936, some 48 percent came from a public Seventh, 7 percent from a private Seventh, and 45 percent from a public primary school [IX]. If not especially notable, this probably represented a modest and recent increase in the number of transfers from the primary to the secondary system. More important, certainly, was the abolition of tuition in public secondary schools, which took place in steps between 1928 and 1933. In 1930, the Sixth became free in all public institutions. It is important that these reforms were undertaken after strenuous public debates that began even before 1918. This may explain the revived popularity of private secondary schools during the interwar period; they may have become refuges for middle-class parents who feared the "democratization" of the public sector.

Beyond that, however, it is hard to link the enrollment changes of the interwar period to specific institutional reforms. As Jaubert remarked some time ago, the access percentages for the public Sixth did not rise, as might have been expected, when tuition was abolished in 1928–30.[24] More girls reached the secondary schools, and a larger portion of the boys may have advanced into the higher grades.[25] But it is difficult to prove anything more precise than that, especially if one looks only at the years around 1930. To claim that free secondary education made a difference at all, one has to portray the high access percentages of the later 1920s as partly artificial, a temporary "compromise" reaction to the abnormally low birth rates during the War. One can then suggest that only the abolition of secondary tuitions in 1930 prevented a long-term *retrenchment* in the access percentages when the postwar baby boom reached the level of the Sixth in the early 1930s. I personally find this a plausible position.

24. Jaubert, *La Gratuité*.
25. J.-M. Chapoulie has privately suggested these explanations for what rise there was in total public secondary enrollments per age group. We shall know a good deal more about the whole question when J.-P. Briand, J.-M. Chapoulie, and H. Peretz publish their current work on French secondary and higher primary education between the wars.

Yet there were certainly other, more general causes of the long-term increase in French secondary enrollments during the interwar period. As in Germany at that time, the fluctuating sizes of age groups probably disturbed the conventional balance between the supply of educated persons and the positions they were expected to fill. Like other enrollment booms, the postwar increase in French secondary attendance may have become self-accelerating to some extent. Girls entered the secondary system in growing numbers. The world-wide Depression that began to affect France about 1932 almost certainly kept many pupils in the schools for want of jobs. Finally, a new demand for educated white-collar workers emerged in the late industrial era. There is no real way of choosing among these causes of change; it may in fact have been their convergence that finally ended the long stagnation of the decades before the First World War.[26]

The shape of the French secondary pyramid, incidentally, was remarkably similar to its German counterpart during these years. It also changed very little during, or before, the interwar period. From the 1840s to the 1930s, baccalaureates per age group were between one-third and one-half as numerous as total secondary enrollments per age group. Within that fairly narrow range, baccalaureates were least frequent, in relation to average enrollments, when new students or programs had recently entered the secondary system; they were most numerous when a wave of new clients had been fully assimilated, as in 1898 and 1936. Even the legendary rate of failure on the baccalaureate examination apparently remained fairly constant. In 1932, it was 63 percent on the first part and 51 percent on the second part of the test [IX].

Between 1854 and 1898, some 30–50 percent of baccalaureates were awarded in mathematics, rather than in philosophy [IX]. This proportion too remained fairly stable over time. In 1911–12 and in 1921–22, about 37–38 percent of baccalaureates were in mathematics, and about the same share of students chose the Science-Modern Language option on the first part of the baccalaureate exam in 1921–22. By the 1930s, the distinction between mathematics and philosophy baccalaureates had become essentially identical with the divide between the classical (Latin-Greek or Latin-Science) and the nonclassical (Science-Modern

26. On this general point I can agree with Maillèt, "L'Evolution des effectifs," although I am uncomfortable with Maillèt's references to a "takeoff" into "sustained growth" in education. Apart from the fact that it exaggerates the extent of the change that actually took place, such language reflects a dogmatic economism that has become an obstacle to thought.

Language) stream within the secondary curriculum. In 1931–32 and in 1936, some 30–31 percent of baccalaureates were awarded in mathematics. In short, about one-third of French secondary graduates came from the modern track by the 1930s, and roughly the same proportion had always taken their certificates in mathematics. This tradition was bound to mute the conflict between classicists and modernists in matters of curriculum.

In any case, that conflict was essentially over by the 1930s. After the institution of free public secondary schooling, the main issue in the social and political history of French education had to do with the barrier between the higher primary and the secondary schools. The abolition of secondary tuition was itself part of an effort to reduce that barrier, and so were the structural changes initiated by Jean Zay after 1936. A new phase in the evolution of the French system really began during the 1930s, and its guiding idea was that of the common secondary school. Though their intellectual antecedents date back at least to the 1920s, the institutional reforms of the 1930s did not come to fruition until after the Second World War. This is clear from Table 3.3, which follows the history of enrollments and structural reform from 1936 to 1961.

Traditional public and private secondary education appears to have grown at only a moderate pace until 1951. The figures tabulated for traditional public secondary schools in 1946 no longer include students in the modern secondary stream; the resulting shrinkage in this sector is nominal, not real. During the 1950s, relatively small age cohorts led to particularly sharp increases in enrollments per age group, while enrollments per population advanced at a slower pace. The reverse effect can be observed in the data for 1961. The private schools grew much less rapidly than the public ones between 1946 and 1961; the traditional Catholic presence in French secondary education thus lost some of its former weight. But all these are subordinate observations. The change most visible in Table 3.3 is the overall growth of the French secondary system between 1936 and 1961. Having doubled between 1921 and 1936, the indicators for the traditional sector alone nearly doubled again by 1956.

Still, the really significant development in the decade after 1936 was the entry of new schools into the secondary system. Vocational became technical secondary education, and the higher primary schools joined the modern secondary stream. One wonders how many of those already in that stream remained to mingle with the new arrivals. By 1946, at any rate, the heir of the old public classical track had nearly as many pupils as the whole public secondary system ten years earlier.

Table 3.3

French Secondary Enrollments, 1936–1961

(Thousands, per Thousand Population, and Percent of Age Group)

	1936	1946	1951	1956	1961
Private (traditional) secondary	147.1	195.7	186.6	225.9	317.3
Per thousand population	3.5	4.8	4.4	5.2	6.9
Percent of age group	3.3	4.3	4.6	5.9	6.2
Public (traditional) secondary	170.2	164.5	178.2	252.5→	823.4
Per thousand population	4.1	4.1	4.2	5.8	17.9
Percent of age group	3.9	3.7	4.3	6.6	16.1
Higher primary/modern secondary	100.3	159.7	171.0	249.0	
Per thousand population	2.4	3.9	4.1	5.7	
Percent of age group	2.3	3.5	4.2	6.6	
Vocational/technical secondary	60.9	137.5	173.1	208.4	245.4
Per thousand population	1.5	3.4	4.1	4.8	5.3
Percent of age group	1.4	3.1	4.2	5.5	4.8
Complementary/general secondary	149.2	217.5	278.6	387.5	769.1
Per thousand population	3.6	5.4	6.6	8.9	16.8
Percent of age group	3.4	4.8	6.8	10.2	15.1
All secondary[a]	317.3	657.4	708.9	935.8	2155.2
Per thousand population	7.6	16.2	16.9	21.5	47.0
Percent of age group	7.2	14.6	17.3	24.6	42.3
Baccalaureates	15.4	28.3	34.5	51.2	66.2
Percent of age 17	3.9	4.4	5.7	9.0	11.2

Enrollments in the Sixth and higher grades are related to the seven-year age group 11 through 17. No distinction is made between girls and boys (almost equally represented since the Second World War) or between public and private versions of vocational/technical secondary or of complementary/general secondary education. See IX for details.

[a] Only enrollments above the solid line in the table were in fully "secondary" institutions and are included here.

Nevertheless, the new modern secondary program made its way. It approximately matched the classical branch in overall enrollments. The rate of early leaving was doubtless higher in the modern than in the classical stream, but the difference was not as great as might have been expected. The upper modern and technical grades eventually attracted significant numbers of students. By 1961, with new options available on the baccalaureate, about 5 percent of certificates were in technical subjects, 25 percent each were in mathematics and in the experimental sciences, and the rest were in philosophy. This pattern cannot be taken to represent the popularity of the various secondary branches. Considered in conjunction with enrollments in the upper grades, however, it indicates at least that the newer streams eventually became full-length, baccalaureate programs.

That the structural reforms slowly led to real changes in the movement of pupils can be observed in the development of presecondary education after the Second World War [IX]. As of 1936, the primary classes still accounted for about a third of all enrollments in private secondary schools and for some 26–29 percent at boys' and girls' public *lycées* and *collèges*. The ratio at the public schools then fell to 17 percent in 1946 and to 6 percent by 1961. In the meantime, a characteristic reaction to the abolition of fees in public presecondary education drove enrollments at private primary classes up to around 45 percent of all private school enrollments during the 1950s. By 1961, however, the ratio had fallen back to about 35 percent even at the private schools. For public and private schools combined, it hovered around 27–29 percent from 1946 to 1956, before declining to 16 percent by 1961. Change was slow and clearly painful, but it asserted itself in the end.

The best summary approach to the distribution of students over the various secondary grades is to compare baccalaureates to average enrollments per age group, the top of the enrollment pyramid to its mean width. This interesting ratio, we know, fluctuated between 33 and 50 percent in the years from 1842 to 1931. In 1936, it actually reached 54 percent; but it then fell to 30 percent in 1946. The sharp decline was the initial effect of the redefinitions that brought the higher primary and vocational schools into the secondary system. Gradually, as this reorganization affected the higher grades, the ratio climbed back to 33 percent in 1951 and 37 percent in 1956. In 1961, it would have reached 41 percent, if the recent transformation of the complementary courses into lower secondary schools had not reduced it to an unprecedented low near 25 percent. Even so, the structural reforms after 1936 were in large part responsible for the almost threefold increase in baccalaureates per age group, from 3.9 to 11.2 percent, between 1936 and 1961. Any change that helped to produce such results at the level of the baccalaureate was certainly more than nominal. The reclassification of the higher primary and vocational schools after 1936 led to a genuine enlargement of the French secondary system.

University-Level Enrollments and Some Franco-German Comparisons

Part of the significance of the baccalaureate in France has been due to the late development of university-level institutions. For much of the nineteenth century, the "bac" was the highest academic honor normally sought by the nonspecialist. The *licence* in law may occasionally have been taken as a generalist's degree, but it never acquired the importance of the baccalaureate. In any case, little can be said about French university-level education before the reforms of the 1870s and 80s [XI]. During the 1850s and 60s, for a total population of some 36–38 million, the French faculties annually awarded some 800–1,100 *licences* in law, about 400–500 medical doctorates, 200–300 pharmacist's diplomas, and around 100 teaching *licences* each in letters and sciences. More important though smaller were the numbers of candidates admitted each year by the *grandes écoles* about this time. These ranged around 130–180 at the Ecole Polytechnique, 30–35 at the Ecole Normale, 100–150 at the Ecole Centrale, and 250–300 at Saint-Cyr. For postsecondary schooling during the early industrial phase of the French system, these are the only meaningful figures available.

It was only in the 1870s that enrollments in the faculties began to be officially counted and published by the Ministry of Education. While matriculation continued to be nominal, in some cases, until the 1890s or even later, it is worth looking at the data from the 1870s on. Table 3.4 reports total enrollments per population and age group from 1876 to 1961. The choice of a four-year age group as a point of reference tends to understate university access, at least during the nineteenth century [XI]; the average duration of university attendance has until recently been shorter in France than in Germany. Note also that baccalaureates per age group were a good deal more numerous than university enrollments per age group until the 1890s. Unlike the German *Abitur,* the French baccalaureate long retained a role as a terminal degree. At several points between 1911 and 1946, on the other hand, there would seem to have been fewer baccalaureate awards than university entrants. The discrepancy may be partly due to differences in the time scales involved, while particularly high enrollments in 1921 and 1946 probably included war veterans. Foreign and French Algerian students, too, were especially numerous at French universities during the interwar period. Still, it is certainly possible that some French students reached the faculties without the baccalaureate until the 1930s.

The share of women among university attendants advanced from 3 percent in 1901 and 10 percent in 1911 to 14 percent in 1921, 27 percent in 1936, and 40 percent in 1961 [XI]. This represents a sharp contrast with developments in Germany, where women were 9 percent of university students in 1926, 16 percent in 1931, 16 percent again in 1951, and still only 22 percent in 1960.

Altogether, the history of French faculty enrollments is one of moderate and steady expansion. There were no sharp fluctuations. Enrollments per age group took two decades to double after 1876 and only

Table 3.4

French Faculty Enrollments and Baccalaureates, 1876–1961

(Thousands, per Thousand Population, and Percent of Age Group)

Year	Enrollments in all faculties	Per thousand population	Percent of age 19–22[a]	Baccalaureates as percent age 17
1876	11.2	0.3	0.5	0.8
1881	12.0	0.3	0.5	
1886	16.3	0.4	0.6	1.0[b]
1891	20.7	0.5	0.8	
1896	26.9	0.7	1.0	1.2[c]
1901	29.9	0.8	1.2	
1906	35.7	0.9	1.4	
1911	41.2	1.0	1.7	1.1
1921	49.9	1.3	2.0	1.4
1926	58.5	1.4	2.2	
1931	78.7	1.9	2.9	2.3
1936	73.8	1.8	3.7	3.9
1946	123.3	3.0	4.9	4.4
1951	139.6	3.3	5.4	5.7
1956	157.5	3.6	6.6	9.0
1961	210.9	4.6	9.6	11.2

See IX and XI for details.

[a] Use of a four-year age group tends, at least for the nineteenth century, to understate access, though to a decreasing degree over time.

[b] Calculated for 1887.

[c] Calculated for 1898.

a little longer to double again by 1921. The leveling off in the curve of French secondary enrollments after the 1870s thus had no counterpart at the university level. The somewhat accelerated growth of the faculties between 1926 and 1936 was due largely to the influx of foreign students and of women. One would not be surprised to learn that an excess of university graduates was a concern in France as in Germany by the 1930s, yet the tempo of change did not rise enough to suggest a real break in the evolution of the system until after 1931 or 1936.

The long-term trends in the distribution of students over the various faculties are outlined in Table 3.5. It must be remembered that theology was never a numerically significant field of study at the French universities. Priests prepared at the higher seminaries, and there were few Protestant pastors. That accounts for much of the difference between the French and the German distributions of students during the nineteenth century. But the other divergence was really more consequential: around 1860–90, some 15 percent of German university enrollments were in the humanities, and 10 percent were in the sciences. The German faculty of philosophy thus began well before its French counterparts to educate scholars and generalists, rather than future secondary teachers alone.

In the twentieth century, the trend has been toward increasingly similar distributions of students over the various faculties and subject areas. Theology has gradually become a numerically marginal field even in Germany. The professional faculties of law and medicine have declined to a joint share of some 30–40 percent of enrollments about 1960. Especially with the arrival of the social studies, the arts and sciences have come to dominate the curriculum. The data for the 1950s suggest, as a matter of fact, that the natural sciences have come to play an even larger role at French than at German universities since World War Two. But a more detailed study would be required to confirm this special hypothesis against the background of generally convergent developments.

No comparison between French and German higher education would be complete in any case if it confined itself to the university faculties. The importance of the German technical institutes is generally recognized. The *grandes écoles*, however, are too often conceived as a tiny cluster of institutions for a few hundred students. That notion is inaccurate even for the nineteenth century [XI]. The Ecole Centrale alone graduated some 100–200 engineers per year. Most of the 130–250 students who annually left the Ecole Polytechnique went into the armed services; but a few ended up in the private sector. The *écoles d'arts et*

Table 3.5

Distribution of French Students over the Faculties, 1876–1956
(Rounded Percentages by Row)

	Law	Medicine	Pharmacy	Letters (Theology)[a]	Sciences
1876–91	40	35	10	3–13[b]	3–8[b]
ca. 1911	40	25	5	15	15
ca. 1931	25	25	5	25	20
ca. 1956	20	20	5	27	27

The percentages are approximate, indicating orders of magnitude around dates listed. The shares of Letters and of Sciences were still rising, at the expense of Law and Medicine, in 1961 (Law 16 percent, Medicine 15 percent, Letters 31 percent, Sciences 33 percent). See XI for details.

[a] Theology students included under Letters were never numerically significant.

[b] Indicates rise between 1876 and 1891.

métiers were not *grandes écoles*. But they may have been just as significant for the economy as the German technical institutes, which also failed to achieve recognition as university-level institutions until the turn of the century. Each of the *écoles d'arts et métiers* annually took in about 100 students for a three-year course. There were three of the schools by the 1840s, five by 1901. Particularly when related to the population, these figures pose a challenge to the old notion that the technical institutes helped Germany outstrip France in the industrial race of the nineteenth century.[27] Of course the German technical institutes expanded rapidly during the decades after 1860. Comparable developments in France have not been sufficiently studied. But we do know that three additional *écoles d'arts et métiers* were founded around the turn of the century, that other French engineering and business schools sprang up and expanded at an ever increasing rate from the late nineteenth century on, and that most are now considered university-level institutions. The higher commercial schools alone equalled the *écoles d'arts et métiers* in enrollments by the 1890s [XI].

French students have always been able to attend *grandes écoles* while registering and taking degrees at university faculties. According to one estimate, about 40 percent of students at the *grandes écoles* during the 1950s were doubly signed up in this way [XI]. But even allowing for this practice, the *grandes écoles* must be assigned a significant weight in calculations of inclusiveness in French higher education. In 1961, some 48.2 thousand French students attended public institutions of higher education other than the university faculties, and 6.2 thousand engineering diplomas were awarded that year. Properly to estimate French university-level enrollments per population and age group from the 1880s on, one therefore has to enlarge the figures for the public faculties by some 10–15 percent for the *grandes écoles* alone. An additional correction of 5–6 percent would be required to cover

27. The term *technical institutes* is used loosely in this discussion, so as to include the institutes' forerunners of the mid-nineteenth century. As a group, the German technical institutes probably graduated some 10–20 engineers per million population annually around 1860. The Ecole Centrale and the Ecole Polytechnique at that time jointly accounted for about 5–10 graduates per million population, and the existing *écoles d'arts et métiers* added another 5–10 per million. There is reason to believe that a significant portion of graduates from the German technical institutes entered the civil service during the nineteenth century. However, the Prussian provincial trade schools (*Gewerbeschulen*) before 1878 are left out of account. Together with the *Realschulen,* they may have been an important advantage for Germany industry, which was unusually well supplied with non-graduate modern secondary students. That, indeed, is a highly plausible *variant* upon the argument—or assumption—that is here being questioned. See V and XI for details.

private and religious institutions of higher education *other than* the higher seminaries.

As of 1961, for example, enrollments in French public university faculties amounted to 9.6 percent of the four-year age group 19 through 22. If the average duration of university attendance at that point had been four years, that 9.6 percent could be taken to measure the mean width of the pyramid of faculty enrollments. Actually, the average course of study had probably risen somewhat above four years by then, so that the 9.6 percent should be taken to represent the pyramid near its base. An official French source cited 7.3 percent of age 20 as the highest share of any age year in attendance at a public university faculty as of 1964–65 [XI]. However, since students in fact reached the universities at widely divergent ages, from 18 to 30, that 7.3 percent is certainly too low a measure of university access. Corrections for the *grandes écoles* and for the religious institutions, moreover, would raise the 9.6 percent to 11.5 percent or thereabouts. As it happened, 11.2 percent of the age group earned the baccalaureate in 1961.

Altogether, 11–12 percent of the age group probably best characterizes the inclusiveness of the French system at the level of university entry as of 1961. Like baccalaureate awards, university access rates per age group approximately tripled between the 1930s and 1961. Moreover, the rate of change continued to increase during the sixties. One has to imagine what this meant for the social definitions traditionally associated with advanced education, for the expectations of students, and for the whole image and role of the educated man. It is not inappropriate to speak of an educational revolution during the latest phase in the development of the French system.

The course of that development since the mid-nineteenth century is briefly reviewed in Table 3.6, where the main indicators for France are also confronted with their German counterparts. The remarkable thing about the two sets of figures is that they are really very similar. The development of the German system was interrupted by the National Socialists, and the effects remained clearly visible as of 1960. Until the 1930s, however, the main ratios for the two countries were never very far apart. By way of explanation, one can point to the similarities between the baccalaureate and the *Abitur*. The two tests were introduced under comparable circumstances to regulate access to the higher civil service and to the liberal professions, in effect establishing very similar role definitions and patterns of demand for educated men. Both systems apparently experienced a crisis of demand during the 1830s and 40s; both appear to have adjusted to changes in industrial technology after about 1860. The social definitions established with

Table 3.6

The French and German Systems Compared, 1875–1961

(Enrollments and Certificates as Percentages of the Age Group)

	France			Germany		
	Second-ary[a] (% age 11–17)	Bacca-laur. (% age 17)	Univ. Level (% age 19–22)	Second-ary[b] (% age 11–19)	Abitur (% age 19)	Univ. Level[c] (% age 20–23)
1875–76	2.4	0.8	0.5	2.5	0.7	0.6
1885–87	2.4	1.0	0.6	2.6	0.8	0.9
1898–01	2.5	1.2	1.2	2.7	0.9	1.1
1911	2.6	1.1	1.7	3.2	1.2	1.5
1921	3.5	1.4	2.0	6.0	1.3	2.7
1931	6.9	2.3	2.9	8.8	3.3	2.7
1950–51	17.3	5.7	5.4	9.1	4.5	3.8
1960–61	42.3	11.2	9.6	12.4	5.4	5.4

See I, V, IX, and XI for details.

[a] Before 1898, secondary and presecondary enrollments are related to the age group 8 through 17. Girls included beginning in 1921. Includes former higher primary and vocational schools from 1951 on and the former complementary courses in 1961 (without the complementary courses, the percentage for 1961 would be 27.2).

[b] Data are for Prussia until World War One. Girls included beginning in 1921.

[c] Technical institutes included from 1900 on and academies from 1921.

the baccalaureate and the *Abitur* were not radically challenged until around 1930.

Once that much is said, of course, the qualifications begin to announce themselves. (1) The choice of somewhat younger age groups for France than for Germany is based upon impressions of nineteenth-century conditions; fortunately, it cannot give rise to any large errors. (2) More consequential is the use of a ten-year age group as a reference for French secondary enrollments before 1898, and of a seven-year age group thereafter. Given the durations of study actually prevailing, this may slightly understate the inclusiveness of French secondary education until the 1880s, and it may overstate it slightly for the most recent period. (3) For similar reasons, French university access may be somewhat understated until the interwar period. Up to that point and perhaps even beyond it, the average student took longer to complete his university work in Germany than in France. The normal course of study did not in fact reach four years even in Germany until the late nineteenth century. (4) The lower seminaries are not counted among French secondary schools; the error thus intruded is not *relatively* very significant for the period after 1870, but it is not negligible either. (5) If the *grandes écoles* and private higher education were included with the public faculties for France, the enrollment ratios would have to be increased by as much as 10–20 percent, especially for the most recent period. (6) Finally, the two enlargements of the French secondary system since the 1930s could be considered deceptive or partly nominal. The inclusion of the former higher primary and vocational schools from 1950 on should at least be noted. The addition of the former complementary courses in 1960–61 is even more open to challenge. Without this second enlargement, French secondary enrollments in 1960–61 would have been 27.2 percent of the age group.

A closer look at the table leads to the discovery that the two systems were not absolutely alike after all. Until the interwar period, the two secondary enrollment pyramids were shaped quite differently. Despite the notorious rate of failure on the baccalaureate examination, there were generally somewhat more baccalaureates than *Abiturs* per age group. At the same time, total enrollments per age group were always slightly greater in the German than in the French secondary schools. The German pyramid was narrower at the apex, yet wider on the average; it must have been consistently broader than the French pyramid at the base. There was a good deal more early leaving or weeding out in Germany than in France, and we know that most of the early leaving took place in the *Realschulen*. In Germany as in France, the classical secondary stream really did not grow in overall size after the mid-nineteenth century. It merely graduated an increasing portion of its students. In the meantime, the nonclassical programs were added near the base of the enrollments pyramid, as predominantly nondegree forms of secondary schooling. Despite the temporary success of Duruy's special secondary program, however, this widening of the nonclassical base was distinctly less marked in France than in Germany. It is in this area of lower level, modern secondary schooling, more than in any other field, that Germany had a comparative advantage during the nineteenth century.

What of the French higher primary and vocational schools of the 1880s and after—weren't they the French counterparts of the German *Realschulen?* It would be easier to answer that question if more exact information were available on the German "middle schools." As it is, one can only guess that the middle schools matched the French higher primary schools until the interwar period, which would leave the *Realschulen* as a more than nominal German advantage, again until the interwar period.

What happened after the First World War was a little more complex. Though the hopes of serious reformers were disappointed, the common school to age 10 and a few related structural changes were forced through in Germany during the 1920s, while comparable French efforts achieved no successes at all until about 1930. The German middle schools apparently lost some pupils to the secondary schools, which had become a little easier to reach than in the past. In any case, German secondary enrollments per age group moved clearly ahead of French enrollments during the 1920s. However, significantly more *Abiturs* than baccalaureates were awarded for the first and only time in 1931. At that point, secondary education seemed definitely more inclusive in Germany than in France.

But the positions were quickly reversed as Hitler came to power in Germany and a few reforms succeeded in France around 1930 and after 1936. Admittedly, the secondary ratios for the decades since the Second World War may overstate the French advantage that resulted, since new French school categories are counted as secondary. In Germany since the 1950s, the middle schools and the new full time vocational and intermediate technical schools (*Berufsschulen* and *Fachschulen*) which are not counted as secondary education, have developed to a level that may be comparable to parts of the French secondary system. As of 1960, on the other hand, French baccalaureates per age group were more than twice as frequent as German *Abiturs*. In that sense, the enlargement of the French secondary system certainly created a more than nominal difference between it and its German counterpart.

This is confirmed at the university level. Even without Catholic institutions and *grandes écoles*, the French faculties enrolled more students per age group around 1950 and 1960 than all German university-level institutions combined. As a matter of fact, the university enrollment ratios were generally a little larger for France than for Germany from around 1900 on. The only exception to this pattern occurred under the highly unstable conditions of the interwar period, with its economic crisis, veterans at universities, and violent fluctuations in the size of age cohorts. Again, inclusion of the *grandes écoles* would have made the French advantage stand out even more plainly. The only explanation lies in the consistently greater percentage of women among French than among German university students during the twentieth century. That, of course, was as real a difference between the two educational systems—and societies—as can be imagined.

To find clearly higher university enrollments in Germany than in France, one has to turn to the nineteenth century, and specifically to the figures for the 1870s and 80s. The German advantage they indicate was presumably even more marked during earlier decades. Though baccalaureates were slightly more numerous than *Abiturs* in relation to the age group, French faculty enrollments lagged behind. Relatively short French durations of study may be partly responsible, along with the exclusion of the *grandes écoles*. It must also be remembered that theology was practically unrepresented at the French faculties of the nineteenth century. It is this peculiarity, along with the almost total neglect of the arts and sciences, that kept French university-level attendance below the German level during the nineteenth century. The *licence* in law must have been taken as a generalist's degree to some extent, and the baccalaureate must often have served as a terminal degree in letters; otherwise the difference between the French and German secondary and university-level ratios would have been much greater than it actually was.

The comparison with Germany makes the period between 1870 and 1900 look especially important for the French faculties. While secondary enrollments remained practically unchanged, real attendance at the faculties advanced at a steady pace. This ended the role of the baccalaureate as a terminal degree and moved French university enrollments slightly above the German level. The reversal of positions serves as a reminder that the rhythm of change was slightly different in the two systems. In Germany, both university and secondary enrollments reached an early peak around 1830. There followed a sharp decline, a low plateau between 1840 and 1860 or 1870, and renewed growth thereafter. In France, the recovery of secondary enrollments after the revolutionary and Napoleonic era really continued almost uninterrupted from 1809 into the 1870s. At that point, a long-term stagnation set in at the secondary level that extended into the interwar period. At the university level, however, the decades after 1870 witnessed concerted efforts at reform; indeed, university attendance and study really became meaningful only at this stage in the history of the system. The result was the remarkable catching up of the French faculties to French secondary and to German university enrollments during the last three decades of the nineteenth century.

All these differences between the two systems require and deserve some attention. Yet they should not be allowed to erase the really more significant impression of an underlying similarity. It remains true that the major indicators for the two countries were of the same order of magnitude until the 1930s. And in all likelihood, the divergence produced by the National Socialists has been largely cancelled by a renewed convergence since 1960. In their largest outlines, the two systems and their developmental phases resembled each other. No reference to mere levels or rates of industrialization will suffice to account for this circumstance—France gained a comparative advantage in secondary and higher education precisely as Germany outpaced her in the industrial race. This merely reemphasizes the partly autonomous character of educational systems, which has emerged as one of the general conclusions of this study.

4. The French System Compared: Education and Society

Secondary Education during the Early and High Industrial Phases

French government agencies did not begin to publish adequate data on the social origins of French students until the 1930s. To obtain an impression of recruitment patterns in French secondary schools during the early and high industrial periods, one must therefore turn to a handful of specialized works on particular institutions.

Perhaps the most impressive of these specialized studies is Frijhoff and Julia's report on three provincial *collèges* of the seventeenth and eighteenth centuries.[1] Tracing names on the schools' registers to various local records, Frijhoff and Julia were able to determine the tax obligations as well as the occupations of many of the fathers. They could compare the economic situation of specific individuals with their occupational or social standing. This not only clarified the socio-professional categories used in the sources, it also shed light on the relationship between wealth and status as determinants of access to education. Without denying the importance of wealth, Frijhoff and Julia repeatedly noted the partly independent role of status—or of education itself.[2] The son of a lawyer, schoolmaster, or scribe was more likely to reach a *collège* than the son of an equally prosperous merchant, farmer, or artisan.

The consequences are plainly visible in Table 4.1, which roughly summarizes Frijhoff and Julia's results on the social origins of students. The column on Avallon is particularly important, since Avallon was a full-length *collège*, encompassing all grades and therefore comparable

1. Frijhoff and Julia, *Ecole et société*.
2. See pp.24, 31, 83.

Table 4.1

Social Origins of Students
at Three French Collèges of the Old Regime
(Percentages by Column)

Socio-Professional Category	Auch ca. 1600	Avallon ca.1745	Gisors ca. 1770
Nobility	11	10	8
Liberal professions, high officials[a]	7	24	12
Minor professions, officials	10	22	14
Bourgeois[b]	16	7	1
Large merchants }	19	9	–
Small merchants }		15	23
Artisans[c]	16	9	23
Farmers (agriculture)[d]	21	4	17
Workers	–	–	2
Absolute Totals (100%)	1,695	1,113	512

From Frijhoff and Julia, *Ecole et Société,* p.14. Based on catalogue entries for 1598–1607 at Auch, 1711–79 at Avallon, and 1748–90 at Gisors. Absolute totals are those for whom parents' occupations or status could be located, and percentages are taken with respect to these "known" totals. The table ignores Frijhoff and Julia's important distinction between local and out-of-town students, though the latter generally came from families higher on the social scale. Avallon was a complete *collège,* covering all grades, much like a *lycée* of the nineteenth century. Auch and Gisors, by contrast, specialized in the lower grades; they were really not full secondary institutions.

[a] Covers not only lawyers, doctors, and architects, but also a long list of the more lucrative and distinguished "offices" of the old regime; of course the *officiers* were not officials in the modern sense. This applies also to the minor "offices" that are grouped with the less desirable service occupations.

[b] The term *bourgeois* was used in a vague and partly honorific sense by all sorts of middle-class and upper middle-class parents.

[c] Artisans who managed to send their sons to a *collège* were the more well-to-do among their peers.

[d] Some farmers or "agriculturists" (*laboureurs*) were in fact middle-class land-owners.

to a provincial *lycée* of the nineteenth century. Gisors and Auch, by contrast, were really lower secondary schools. At Avallon, over 45 percent of students' fathers were lawyers, doctors, architects, members of minor professions, or *officiers*—holders of one of the many greater and lesser offices that proliferated under the Old Regime. The sum of 45 percent for the nonentrepreneurial middle classes outweighed the 33 percent of fathers who were large or small merchants or well-to-do artisans. Some 7 percent of the fathers were vaguely described as *bourgeois,* which merely hinted at their claim to upper middle-class status. Only 4 percent of the fathers were in agriculture, probably as substantial farmers or nonaristocratic landowners. Another 10 percent were nobility. Altogether, the distribution was far from progressive. The vast mass of the peasantry and the urban lower classes was practically unrepresented. On a unilinear social scale, the significant figure is a sum just under 50 percent for the tiny upper crust of nobles, members of the liberal professions, holders of high offices, *bourgeois* and large merchants. At the same time, with the class/status distinction in mind, one is bound to notice the dominant role of the professions and *officiers* within this middle-class setting.

The figures for Gisors and Auch suggest a somewhat more progressive pattern of recruitment at institutions of an intermediate or lower secondary type. Percentages at Gisors and Auch were significantly lower than at Avallon, not for the nobility or for commerce, but for the major *and* minor professions and offices. In compensation, artisans and farmers were particularly well represented. Many of them were probably unable to obtain full secondary educations for their sons. The children of farmers, artisans, and small shopkeepers typically left school after a few years in the lower grades. As a result, the upper grades were socially more homogeneous—and less progressive—than the lower ones. Aristocratic youths generally advanced into the upper grades, but they tended to skip the terminal classes, which prepared future university students of law, medicine, and theology.

Frijhoff and Julia were able to learn much about the subsequent studies and careers of Avallon graduates by tracing many of them to the records of various university faculties and religious organizations. What they discovered was a sharp class division between law students, who came overwhelmingly from the upper middle classes, and future theologians and schoolmen, who generally came from modest social backgrounds. A variant of this undoubtedly typical division was found in the German data as well. The Catholic church, including the teaching orders, recruited heavily among the less advantaged social strata. In a sense, the church served as a channel of upward mobility for able youths from the humbler classes. Since Catholic priests and monks had no physical heirs, this channel could be used over again in every generation. The effect can be conceived as a continual revitalization of a traditional society's intellectual leadership; but it can also be considered a kind of brain drain upon the lower classes.[3] Certainly by the

3. Frijhoff and Julia on p.87 suggest a "brain drain"; their perspective is informed by Bourdieu and Passeron, *La Réproduction*. The notion of a brain drain depends on the idea that lower-class talent flowing into the church was in some sense lost; this can be maintained partly because Catholic clergy had no heirs and partly because they acquired no significant share of wealth or power.

later eighteenth century, the average member of the French clergy had little share in the society's wealth and power.

It is interesting to speculate how much all this meant for the social dynamics of European societies during the early modern period. Where the Reformation led to clerical marriage, it tended to narrow a traditional path of upward mobility for the sons of peasants and artisans. This may have encouraged alternate, secular, and individualistic modes of social ascent. Clerical marriage also created a whole new category of desirable social positions, which were promptly engrossed by the upper classes, at least in England. In France during the eighteenth century, an unmarried and relatively humble clergy continued to be recruited among the lower classes. Indeed, Frijhoff and Julia discovered practically no other form of upward mobility through education among Avallon graduates, most of whom apparently ended up close to their fathers' social positions.

It is hard to say how far these conclusions can be read back into the seventeenth century or forward into the nineteenth. One cannot dismiss the possibility of small reductions in secondary enrollments per population from the seventeenth century on and again between the 1780s and 1809.[4] During the late eighteenth century, the spreading practice of boarding pupils probably raised the de facto cost of schooling. After examining the tax rolls and other evidence for Auch and Gisors, Frijhoff and Julia suggest that French secondary education may have been marginally less progressive on the eve of the French Revolution than a century or more before that time. After 1789, as we know, there was a reduction in the availability of free places and scholarships. In sum, French higher education may well have been somewhat more closed and regressive during the early nineteenth century than at any time since the seventeenth century.

More direct information on the nineteenth century has been provided by R. Anderson, who worked on an unpublished survey of secondary pupils' social backgrounds that was conducted by the French Ministry of Education in 1864. Table 4.2 summarizes Anderson's findings for the classical stream at the provincial *lycées* of Angers and Dijon, for the highest three grades within the classical stream at the relatively "democratic" *lycée* Charlemagne in Paris, and for the entire student body of the fashionable Parisian *lycée* Condorcet. Anderson was impressed by the strength of the lower middle-class contingent at these schools. It reached about 25 percent at Condorcet, around 30 percent at Charlemagne, and some 20–35 percent at Angers and Dijon, depending on how one interprets some of the categories. The dominant

4. For this and the following, see the discussion in Chapter Three, pp. 131–34.

Table 4.2

Social Origins of Students at Some French Lycées, 1864–1908
(Percentages by Column)

Father's Occupation	Angers and Dijon 1864	Charle- magne 1864	Condor- cet 1864	Condor- cet 1907–1908
1. Doctors, lawyers (bar)	17	9	8	17[a]
2. Other liberal professions	3	2	4	8[b]
3. Magistrates, (high) officials	14[c]	2	4	4[d]
4. Professors, teachers[e]	6	7	4	4
1–4. Learned professions	40	20	21	33
5. Officers	2	3	4	2
6. Agriculture	10	4	–	–
7. Propertied,[f] rentiers	20	20	33	9
8. Entrepreneurs, engineers[g]	21	30	17	39
9. Shopkeepers, artisans	4	14[h]	21	5
10. Employees, clerks	3	7	4	12[i]
11. Lower officials	2	4		–
1–11. Absolute total known (100%)	122	272	1,200	867
12. Absolute number other, unknown	6	33	–	(12)
1–12. Absolute totals	128	305	1,200	(879)

From R. Anderson, "Secondary Education," and Vincent, "Professeurs du second degré," the latter for Condorcet in 1907–1908. The entire classical stream is
counted at Angers and Dijon; the top three grades in that stream alone are covered
at Charlemagne. The 1864 figures for Condorcet encompass the entire student
body, but they appear to be approximate (rounded). There were 1,060 pupils at
Condorcet in 1907–1908; for 879 of them, records for fathers' occupations could
be found, and this number includes 12 fathers in occupations other than those
listed.

[a] Includes a few dentists.

[b] Includes artists, journalists, and notaries.

[c] All officials are included, excepting only army noncoms and police.

[d] Includes some deputies, senators, and police.

[e] Primary teachers mentioned separately (3.3 percent at Angers and Dijon,
1.5 percent at Charlemagne, 1.6 percent at Condorcet in 1907–1908) are nevertheless grouped with other (secondary and university) teachers.

[f] The ubiquitous *propriétaires*, grouped with rentiers and with a few men without profession in the case of Condorcet in 1907–1908.

[g] Covers all kinds of large or wholesale merchants (*négociants*), bankers, industrialists, and other large-scale businessmen (including 3.2 percent executive
employees for Condorcet in 1907–1908), architects and engineers (8.3 percent at
Condorcet in 1907–1908), and contractors.

[h] A few (2.6 percent) workers are lumped with the artisans and shopkeepers
or retail traders (*commerçants*) at Charlemagne.

[i] About evenly divided between middle-level employees (*cadres moyens*) and
clerks (*employés*).

elements within the lower middle class were the small merchants and shopkeepers, substantial artisans, and clerks. The lower officials and primary teachers clearly played less of a role in France than in Germany. Agriculture was rather poorly represented even at the provincial *lycées*, and the lower classes were essentially excluded. To consider this a progressive pattern, as Anderson does, is to imply a comparison with the English "public" schools of the early nineteenth century.

From any other perspective, it is the domination of French secondary education by the upper middle class that really stands out. To begin with, one has to deal with the 20–35 percent contingent of the "propertied" (*propriétaires*) and rentiers. Some individuals in this category may have had relatively modest incomes from bonds, pensions, or bits of real estate. But the group as a whole was strongest by far at expensive and fashionable Condorcet. It probably included a few aristocrats, along with upper middle-class owners of rural estates or of urban and movable capital. Until late in the nineteenth century, wealthy Frenchmen liked to emphasize their ability to live on income rather than having to exercise a profession. This preference was a specifically French outgrowth of the aristocratic ideal, and it made the *propriétaires* a central category in all surveys of students' fathers for that period.[5]

Along with the "property-owners," the active businessmen within the upper middle-class—the large merchants, bankers, and industrialists—were very well represented among fathers of students in French *lycées* during the 1860s. Of course the liberal professions were important as well, and so were the magistrates and high officials, and the secondary teachers and university professors. Yet the percentage for lawyers and doctors was significantly lower at the Parisian schools than at Angers and Dijon. Especially in Paris, at the top of the French secondary pyramid, the propertied and entrepreneurial elite overshadowed the noneconomic elements within the upper middle class. In any case, some two-thirds to three-quarters of pupils at distinguished French *lycées* in 1864 came from some sort of upper middle-class background.

---

5. Harrigan reports 17 percent *propriétaires*/rentiers among fathers of *all* students covered by the 1864 survey. He does this both in "Secondary Education," which has been available for some time, and in "Social Origins," which reached me only at the last minute. In any case, I can do very little with Harrigan's data. In "Secondary Education," some of his percentages (Table 3, p.364) are based on very low absolute numbers (and better information *can* be found); the "high" and "low" professions in Tables 1 and 2 (pp.352, 360) are too diverse to be treated as meaningful groups for statistical analysis; and the information on aspirants and entrants to the *grandes écoles* in Table 1 could be replaced by more direct evidence on the results of entrance examinations. In "Social Origins," too, the categorization is very awkward and ambiguous. The basic data should really be reworked, and the analysis should be focussed upon those responses for particular schools that are couched in relatively specific language.

At Angers and Dijon as well as at Charlemagne and Condorcet, patterns of recruitment were thus considerably more rarefied in 1864 than they had been at Avallon a century earlier. At Avallon about 1745, some 50 percent of students' fathers had been noblemen, members of the liberal professions, high *officiers*, large merchants, and *bourgeois*. The other half had been lesser professionals and officeholders, small merchants, artisans and farmers. By 1864, many nobles, high *officiers*, and *bourgeois* of the Old Regime had presumably become *propriétaires;* much continuity probably lay beneath the changing terms. Yet no matter how one interprets the categories, and even at "democratic" Charlemagne and provincial Angers and Dijon, one cannot assign less than 66 percent of pupils to the upper middle class by 1864. The evidence is not conclusive, of course, but it strongly suggests a regression in French secondary recruitment between the mid-eighteenth and the later nineteenth century. This remarkable change was due less to the probable reduction in enrollments per age group than to the reorientation of religious education. At Avallon, many scholarship boys and other pupils from the poorer classes had prepared to enter clerical careers. By 1864, this whole aspect of secondary schooling had been transferred from the *lycées* and *collèges* to the private schools and especially to the lower seminaries. Thus even if the number of clergy per population remained stable, which is unlikely, the traditionally progressive recruitment into the church no longer affected the social makeup of the public secondary system.

At least at Condorcet, as a matter of fact, the pattern of recruitment by 1907 was even less progressive than in 1864. The distribution percentages for the liberal professions climbed by more than 10 points, and most of this increase took place at the expense of the lower middle class. A sharp decrease in the figure for the property owners was essentially balanced by an enlargement in the share of the entrepreneurial and technical upper middle class, which included executive employees, engineers, and architects. Lower down on the social scale, the almost total disappearance of shopkeepers and artisans among students' fathers was only partly compensated by an increase in the shares of the nonexecutive employees. In sum, the upper middle class accounted for over 80 percent of enrollments at Condorcet by 1907!

Of course none of the columns in Table 4.2 can be considered representative of French secondary education in general. The figures for provincial Angers and Dijon are certainly more typical than those for Condorcet or for the highest grades at Charlemagne; yet even they encompass only the classical stream. Table 4.2 thus entirely neglects not only the popular municipal *collèges,* but also the ancillary vocational and other nonclassical programs that anticipated Duruy's special

secondary curriculum of 1865. This is important, since special secondary schooling undoubtedly became the most progressive segment within
the French secondary system of the later nineteenth century.

In support of this claim, one can cite Gréard's data for the 1880s.
Gréard reported in roughly comparable terms upon the seven Paris
area *lycées* in 1879 and the special secondary stream at public secondary schools in the Academy of Paris between 1865 and 1886.[6] Among
parents of students at the Paris *lycées,* he found 33 percent who were
"without professions," along with 12 percent in the liberal professions,
16 percent in the civil service, 30 percent in "industry and commerce,"
and 7 percent in "private administration." The proportion of parents
"without profession" was particularly low (20–22 percent) at "democratic" Charlemagne and at Vanves, and particularly high at fashionable Saint-Louis and Condorcet (41–43 percent). In compensation,
"industry and commerce" reached only 20–23 percent at Saint-Louis
and Condorcet, as against 40 percent at Charlemagne and 51 percent at
Vanves. Despite the vagueness of the terms, this demonstrates once
again that the liberal and learned professions were not predominant at
the distinguished Parisian *lycées,* and that many of the parents lived—
or pretended to live—on their incomes. Active involvement in business
affairs did not ordinarily bring what the French call *considération.*

All the more striking is the heavy representation of "industry and
commerce" in Duruy's special secondary program after 1865. Gréard
reported with particular care on the special stream in the Academy
of Paris. Like other educational planners, he was apparently anxious
to know whether its pupils were lured away from the practical realm
for which they were trained and from which most of them came.
Gréard's findings are summarized in Table 4.3, which is meant to evoke
the flow of students from their family backgrounds into the schools
and out again into their own occupations.

In fact the figures for 1865–80 not only demonstrate the importance
of industry and commerce for the special secondary track; they also
reveal an extraordinary similarity between the "inflow" and the "out-
flow" of students. The special curriculum, it seems, was totally adjusted
to the needs felt in certain sectors of French society during the 1860s
and 70s. It recruited most of its pupils from the families of well-to-do
artisans, clerks, shopkeepers, and small businessmen, and it gave them
the status of secondary students. It then returned them to their parents'
station in life a little better equipped to take the next step in a slowly
changing business environment. Perhaps they enlarged their fathers'

6. Gréard, *Education et instruction,* vol. 2, p.241.

stores and workshops; perhaps they became middle-level employees in one of the larger firms that were growing up. We do not know the details, but we do have grounds to suspect that few of them really left the social world from which they came.

Apparently, this began to change during the 1880s, as the "special" stream gradually took on the character of the "modern" secondary branch that officially succeeded it in 1891. After 1880, a sharply increased proportion of students in the special curriculum had fathers in "administration" or in "professional" specialties that were neither liberal nor explicitly identified with industry or commerce. Many of these fathers were probably employees, but they claimed the status of professionals. Among the graduates of special secondary education, about a third continued even after 1880 to enter commerce, but there was a marked reduction in those who opted for industry or for agriculture. Almost a fifth sought additional education, and close to another third chose "administration" or one of the "professions."

The shift in the special curriculum after 1880 was thus a movement from vocational to general education. The process can also be regarded as a drift toward the white-collar graduate, away from the skilled artisan or industrial foreman. It is certainly startling that only 5 per-

Table 4.3

Social Origins and Career Choices
of "Special Secondary" Pupils
in the Academy of Paris, 1865–1886
(Percentages by Column)

Father's Occupation	1865–1880		1881–1886	
	IN	OUT	IN	OUT
Liberal professions	2	1	4	2
Other professions	3	7	12	16
Administration	11	8	13	12
Agriculture	23	27	17	16
Without profession	13	–	14	–
Further study	–	11	–	18
Industry	14	14	12	5
Commerce	33	32	28	32
Absolute total known (100%)	4,657	3,542	4,183	3,744
Absolute number unknown	1,168	2,283	58	497
Absolute Totals	5,825	5,825	4,241	4,241

From Gréard, *Education et instruction*, vol. 2, pp.262–65. Social origins are listed under IN, career choices under OUT. Gréard did not precisely define his professional categories.

cent of those leaving special secondary education in the Academy of Paris after 1880 went directly into industry. Against the intentions of its founders, the special stream became a less prestigious form of academic secondary schooling. It catered to the middle and lower middle classes, not to artisans and skilled workers. What set it off from the traditional secondary path was no longer an alternate model of education, but a mere difference in social elevation within the middle-class spectrum. The conflict that raged over the divide between French classical and modern secondary education around the turn of the century was thus essentially a contest between the upper and the lower middle classes.

Gréard's figures for special secondary education during the early 1880s can be compared with the columns on the Prussian *Oberrealschule* in Table 2.1. The Prussian distributions pertain only to graduates of the modern secondary schools, and they cover the whole period from 1875 to 1899. Gréard dealt with all pupils in the special stream and with an earlier and shorter period. Even so, a few tentative comparisons are possible. Some 13 percent of pupils in the French sample had fathers in "administration," and 12 percent in turn chose to enter that field. Among graduates of the *Oberrealschule*, 13 percent came from the families of lower officials, and exactly 13 percent planned to join the civil service at an intermediate level, without further study. So far, the figures are strikingly similar, except that the share of specifically *public* administration may have been somewhat smaller in the French than in the German case.

The only clear difference between the two samples lies in the high 16–17 percent of French pupils who came from farm families or who chose agricultural occupations. Since little can be made of small and inconsistent numbers for the minor "professions," teaching, and the military, the other significant contrasts simply mirror the difference in the strengths of the rural contingents. In the French sample, some 54–55 percent of the fathers were in commerce and industry or "without profession," and the same share of the pupils either entered commerce and industry or chose further study. In the Prussian sample, about two-thirds of the fathers were in commerce and industry or in the technical and artisanal occupations, and the same proportion of the graduates opted for commerce and industry or for the technical specialties. The technical professions in fact attracted 56 percent of graduates from the *Oberrealschule*. Many of these students, as we know, completed their education at the technical institutes. A good number of them eventually entered the technical branches of the civil service, rather than private business.

Thus the *Oberrealschule* appears to stand out for its urban character, for its relatively close ties to the bureaucracy, and for the high

proportion of students who prepared specifically for the technical institutes and/or the technical professions. Yet even these apparently
distinctive characteristics of the *Oberrealschule* would almost certainly
be reduced or eradicated if early school leavers as well as secondary
graduates had been included in the Prussian figures. By the late nineteenth century, there was probably a rough similarity between the
social roles played by the nonclassical secondary stream in France and
the *combination* of *Realschule* and *Oberrealschule* in Germany.

A very different conclusion must be drawn from a comparison between the traditional *lycée* and the *Gymnasium*. In Table 4.4, the
column on the *Gymnasium* represents all Prussian graduates from that
school during the last quarter of the nineteenth century. The French
columns pertain to 1864 and 1907; they deal with all students at Condorcet, with the top three classical grades at Charlemagne, and with
the whole classical stream at Angers and Dijon. All the more striking
is the fact that the *Gymnasium* distribution looks decidedly more progressive than any of the patterns for the *lycées*. No matter how one
groups the occupations, one cannot arrive at an estimate much above
50 percent for the upper middle-class contingent among fathers of
Gymnasium graduates, and the 7 percent for the Protestant clergy
must be included to achieve that estimate. On the other hand, as has
been noted, some 60–80 percent of *lycée* students came from upper
middle-class backgrounds; this was true in the provinces and at Charlemagne, not only at Condorcet. The French and German occupational
censuses of the late nineteenth century cannot be compared in any detail, but they did not differ enough to account for the sharp contrast
between the *lycée* and the *Gymnasium*.[7] Levels of inclusiveness, too,
were roughly comparable in the two countries. Apparently, they simply
were not high enough to prevent a substantial divergence between the
two distributions of educational opportunities. The decisive elements
in the French pattern were the *propriétaires* and *rentiers*, who drove
up the representation of the wealthy upper crust. In general, the economic middle and upper middle classes dominated the classical *lycées*
of the nineteenth century.

At the *Gymnasium*, by contrast, neither the propertied nor the entrepreneurial groups within the upper middle class were particularly
strong. Industrialists made up no more than a twentieth of graduates'
fathers, and all the commercial and artisanal occupations added only
another fifth. One-tenth of the students came from farm families; many

7. The French occupational census of 1872 is described in Table 4.7. It may
be compared with the German census of 1882, which is summarized in the notes
to Table VII.

Table 4.4

Social Origins of French and German
Secondary Pupils, 1864–1908
(Percentages by Column)

Father's Occupation	Angers and Dijon 1864	Charle-magne 1864	Condor-cet 1864	Condor-cet 1907–1908	Gymna-sium 1875–99[a]
1. Liberal professions	20	11	12	25	{ 9
2. Magistrates, high officials	{ 16	2	4	4	
3. Middle and lower officials		4	ca. 2	–	12
4. Professors, secondary teachers	3	5	ca. 3	3	5
5. Lower teachers	3	2	ca. 1	2	7
6. Protestant clergy	–	–	–	–	7
7. Military officers	2	3	4	2	3
1–7. Sum	44	27	26	36	43
8. Propertied, landowners, rentiers	20	20	33	9	ca. 6
9. Farmers	10	4	–	–	11
10. Entrepreneurs, industrialists	{ 21	30	17	39	5
11. Engineers, technical professions					4
12. Merchants	{ 4	14	21	5	} 20
13. Shopkeepers, innkeepers					
14. Artisans					7
15. Employees, clerks	3	7	ca. 2	12	–
10–15. Sum	28	51	40	56	36
16. Others	–	–	–	–	ca. 4

From Tables 2.1 and 4.2.
[a] Graduates (*Abiturienten*) of Prussian *Gymnasien*.

of them were probably preparing to enter the Catholic church. But it was the disproportionate representation of the lower officials and teachers that chiefly distinguished the *Gymnasium* from the *lycée*. Together with the sons of Protestant clergymen, the offspring of the lower officials and teachers lent the *Gymnasium* its distinctive character as a relatively progressive institution and the stronghold of the non-economic middle class.

Because of this difference between the *Gymnasium* and the *lycée*, the classical/modern divide also had slightly different meanings in

France and in Germany. To the east of the Rhine, the segmentation of the secondary system was socially horizontal to an appreciable degree. The contrast between the *Gymnasium* and the *Oberrealschule* was not just a divide between the upper and the lower middle classes. Rather, the *Gymnasium* stood for the noncommercial occupations: the civil service, teaching, the church, and the liberal professions. The modern secondary schools stood for business and technology. Classical learning was linked with the traditional status society in which "cultivation" had acquired its significance, while the nonclassical curriculum evoked the high industrial class society.

The French divergence from this pattern was only a matter of degree, of course. Especially at the provincial *lycées,* the liberal professions were quite well represented, and so were the lower officials. Even in Paris, *considération* was clearly associated with the ability to retreat from active business life into the world of the "property-owner." The *propriétaire* who sent his son to one of the best *lycées* might well have had his eye on an honored position in the public service, rather than on an entrepreneurial career. At the same time wealth itself, whether active or passive, was certainly an inescapable presence at the classical French secondary schools. Especially after 1880, the difference between the classical and the modern stream in France was essentially one of social altitude. Segmentation was predominantly vertical. Classical learning served primarily to enhance and to legitimate social positions that were based on wealth. It did not, or not to the same extent as in nineteenth-century Germany, sustain a rank order at variance with the industrial class structure.

One way to characterize the situation is to describe the French *bourgeois* as a type. He was a member of a very small elite that combined all the social advantages. He was wealthy and economically powerful, but he was also very well educated, in a traditional way, and this made him confident of his right to political and cultural leadership. Adopting the quasi-aristocratic life style of the *propriétaire*, he enjoyed a degree of *considération* above that of the ordinary businessman. As late as the 1960s, only about 8–10 percent of Frenchmen questioned about their class affiliation defined themselves as bourgeois; most of the rest considered themselves "middle class," "working class," or "peasants." Almost 80 percent of the bourgeois, moreover, identified style of life as the criterion they used to determine their class affiliation.[8] Thus *bourgeois* meant something like "upper class." It signaled a confluence of wealth, education, and status. The difference between a *Gymnasium*

8. Rogoff, "Social Stratification," pp.580–82.

and a *lycée* around 1900 was that the *Gymnasium* represented status, while the *lycée* was integrally *bourgeois*.

The *Grandes Ecoles* during the Nineteenth Century

Since nothing has been published on the social origins of students at French faculties before the 1930s, we must be content with a look at the major *grandes écoles*. Table 4.5 deals with the Ecole Polytechnique, the prototypical *grande école* of the nineteenth century and one of the most prestigious institutions in France.

As the table indicates, the Ecole Polytechnique was *bourgeois* to the core, at least until 1880. From 1815 through the 1870s, about one-

Table 4.5
Social Origins of Students
at the Ecole Polytechnique, 1815–1914
(Percentages by Column)

Father's Occupation	1815–1830	1830–1847	1848–1879	1880–1914
Liberal professions	12	15–16	19	11
High officials	17–20	14–17	18	9
Middle officials	15–16	12	6	10
Lower officials	11	4	1	10
Propertied, rentiers	29–31	35–37	32	13
Entrepreneurs	10–11	13	20	25
Shopkeepers (craftsmen)	2–3	4	4	10
Lower class	–	–	1	11
Absolute total known (100%)	883	1,088	2,034	2,717
Absolute number unknown	146	201	257	259
Absolute Totals	1,029	1,289	2,291	2,976

From Daumard, "Les élèves de l'Ecole Polytechnique," and Shinn, *Dawning of a Bourgeois Elite*. Percentages are recalculated with respect to known portions of samples. Daumard surveyed the entering classes (*promotions*) of 1815–30 (N: 1,581, with 1,437 known) and 1831–47 (N: 2,477, with 2,215 known). She divided the "economic professions" into "large merchants and industrialists" and "shopkeepers." Shinn worked with slightly different chronological groupings for the early nineteenth century (1815–29, 1830–47), and he extended his coverage to 1914. He apparently followed Daumard in his socio-professional categories, except that he divided her lower-ranking officials into a middle and a lower group. Daumard's and Shinn's results are remarkably similar; both percentages (rounded) are given where they differ at all. The absolute numbers listed are Shinn's. Sutter et al, "L'Evolution de la taille," seems a bit erratic in its categorization, but it does suggest that white-collar groups were chiefly responsible for the increase in Shinn's 'Entrepreneurs' and 'Lower Class' (*classes populaires*) after 1880.

third of students' fathers were *propriétaires* and another sixth were high officials; these two groups alone accounted for half of the enrollments at the school. The liberal professions and the entrepreneurs each increased their representation from just over 10 percent in the 1820s to around 20 percent during the period 1848–79. The total share of the upper middle class thus advanced from about 70 percent just after 1815 to almost 90 percent before 1880. The corresponding decline took place in the figures for the middle and lower officials, which fell from around 26 percent in the 1820s to a mere 7 percent in 1848–79. Officers and other military men are presumably grouped with the officials in Table 4.5. Before 1848, the rank and file of the civil service, including the military, apparently played as great a role at the Ecole Polytechnique as at the German universities. As the century wore on and the prestige of the school increased, however, its *bourgeois* character became ever more exclusive. The economic lower middle class of smaller merchants and producers, at any rate, was essentially unrepresented at the Ecole Polytechnique before the 1880s.

Both Daumard and Shinn have argued that well-to-do Parisian shopkeepers would have been financially able to send their sons to the Ecole Polytechnique; they abstained because they were not impressed with the generally modest salaries earned by the school's graduates in the military or in public administration.[9] The high status associated with these careers was not particularly attractive, according to this argument, except to families already wealthy enough to indulge a taste for distinction. By way of example, Shinn cites a fascinating letter from a rich businessman to his son at the Ecole. Your learning, the father writes in effect, will raise you above your parents' station; you will move with ease among cultivated men who need not worry about money; your life of state service will bring glory to France and honor to your family. Here is a typical piece of *bourgeois* family strategy: advanced education is used to legitimate wealth; an acquired class position is both consolidated and complemented through an advance in status and power. One can easily imagine that this tactic was most likely to be used above a certain level of capital accumulation. A shopkeeper would have had different immediate objectives.

All the more startling is the abrupt change in the social character of the Ecole Polytechnique after 1880. Comparing the distribution percentages for 1848–79 with those for 1880–1914, one observes an increase

9. Daumard, "Les élèves de l'Ecole Polytechnique," p.229; Shinn, *Dawning of a Bourgeois Elite*. Much of Shinn's manuscript was not finally paginated when I saw it. Since it will be published in any case, I am omitting page citations in much of what follows.

from 7 to 20 percent for middle and lower-ranking officials and a simultaneous advance from 5 to 21 percent for shopkeepers, artisans, petty
employees, and other members of the lower middle and lower classes.
In exchange, the share of the economic upper middle class shrank from
52 to 38 percent and that of the liberal professions and high officials
from 37 to 20 percent. Altogether, the nonbusiness groups lost ground
to the "productive" occupations; but the decisive shift was the decline
of *bourgeois* representation from nearly 90 percent to less than 60
percent of enrollments.

The causes of this minor revolution probably had less to do with the
attractiveness of the Ecole Polytechnique than with its accessibility.
Shinn and Daumard are right to note the preoccupation of parents with
their sons' ultimate career expectations, but they may underestimate
the more immediate influence of costs upon family strategies. According to Shinn, the ordinary student annually paid about 1,600 francs in
tuition and fees to attend the Ecole Polytechnique. To pass the entrance
examination, he also had to graduate from an expensive *lycée* and to
spend a year or more in even more expensive preparatory classes. The
state offered a number of secondary scholarships, especially to the
sons of officials; this may help to account for the strength of the civil
service in the early columns of Table 4.5. At the Ecole Polytechnique
itself, according to Shinn, some 31 percent of matriculants held scholarships between 1830 and 1880, though many of the awards went to
young men from upper middle-class families. For the period 1880–1914,
the percentage of scholarship holders at the school advanced to 57
percent, and lower middle-class students received more of the grants
that were given. This change in financial arrangements, surely, was
one of the causes of "democratization" at the Ecole Polytechnique
toward the end of the nineteenth century.

Another such cause was the development of French secondary
education after 1880. Between 1876 and 1898, baccalaureate awards
increased from 0.8 to 1.2 percent of the age group. Many of the new
graduates came from the modern secondary curriculum, which was
more progressive in its recruitment than the classical stream. Lower
middle-class students at Polytechnique, Shinn notes, often came from
the younger of the two secondary programs. This is easy to understand.
A shopkeeper was presumably readier to invest in modern than in
classical schooling for his son. The modern track was an acceptable
risk, for the boy could fail to excel in it and still return to the family
business with improved skills. The controversy over the accreditation
of modern secondary education after 1880, as already noted, was
clearly a conflict between the upper and the lower middle classes.
Especially from 1890 on, with the modernists in control of the Min-

istry of Education, the Ecole Polytechnique was publicly pressed to abandon its avowedly elitist animus against the modern baccalaureate. Modernist spokesmen explicitly intended a democratization of the nation's politics and elite recruitment. The Ecole Polytechnique did everything in its power to resist this movement, but it could not avoid an occasional compromise.

Among graduates of the Ecole Polytechnique, Shinn found, the proportion entering the military advanced by steps from 56 percent in 1815–29 to 74 percent in 1880–1914. Those accepting assignments in various technical branches of the government service decreased from 27 percent to 13 percent during the same period. The remaining 10–15 percent of graduates took up private occupations; they were eventually joined by a number of others who left their public positions later in life.[10] Graduates of Polytechnique thus ended by filling a whole range of important posts in civil engineering, in public administration, and even in private business. The school was not an exclusively military one, although that was certainly its most important function by the later nineteenth century.

The Ecole Centrale was more specifically designed to prepare managers for French industry. Classifying fathers of 398 students at Centrale between 1900 and 1917, Weiss assigned 11 percent to the liberal professions, 20 percent to executive employees and high officials, 14 percent to officers, professors, and teachers, 27 percent to business owners, 15 percent to middle and lower-level white-collar employees, 8 percent to small merchants and artisans, and 2 percent each to farmers and workers.[11] While the terms are partly ambiguous, they leave no doubt that the Ecole Centrale was almost as thoroughly *bourgeois* as the Ecole Polytechnique. On the one hand, some 60–70 percent of the fathers were in industrial and commercial occupations; active business was significantly better represented at Centrale than at Polytechnique. On the other hand, around 60–70 percent of students at Centrale came from upper middle-class families; this indicative percentage was almost as great at Centrale as at Polytechnique. Certainly the Ecole Centrale catered to a socially more elevated clientele than the German technical institutes, with which it might otherwise be compared.

Here the *écoles d'arts et métiers* provide an important contrast; they clearly served the economic middle and lower middle classes. In Day's sample of 631 fathers of students for the period 1806–90, one-third held

---

10. Shinn, *Dawning of a Bourgeois Elite*, Table 2 and related discussion.
11. Weiss, "Origins of a Technological Elite," table 6 (p.22A). Weiss separately calculated that 11 percent of students' fathers were themselves engineers.

nonbusiness positions: 2 percent were in liberal or related professions, 2 percent in the technical branches of the civil service, and 3 percent in teaching; 13 percent each were lower officials and military. An additional 7 percent were farmers; 21 percent were business owners or executives; 20 percent were artisans; 5 percent were petty merchants, and 9 percent were foremen and workers.[12] In some ways, this pattern reminds one of the German *Oberrealschule*. Here was a channel of upward mobility from the lower to the higher levels of the commercial and industrial hierarchy. Only the number of military men and of lower officials alters this general impression. The lower officials would have been represented at an *Oberrealschule* but not the large military group, which presumably included many noncommissioned officers and ordinary soldiers. Their presence gave the *écoles d'arts et métiers* an integrally lower middle-class character. If the difference between these *écoles* and Centrale or Polytechnique is considered an instance of segmentation, in other words, it was clearly more vertical than horizontal. As in French secondary education, the most visible distinctions were predominantly a matter of social altitude.

The great exception to this rule, of course, was the contrast between the Ecole Polytechnique and the Ecole Normale. About equally distinguished in academic terms, the two great rivals nevertheless differed sharply in their social makeup and not just with respect to altitude. In a way, they represented diametrically opposed models of the relationship between knowledge and society; they were the poles of an antithesis at the heart of French culture.

In analyzing the distributions for the Ecole Normale in Table 4.6, one is struck by the similarity of the data for the two major time periods and curricular divisions. Only two significant changes took place in overall recruitment patterns between the 1880s and the 1930s. The sons of lower-ranking teachers increased their slice of total enrollments from 10 to 16 percent, while the offspring of entrepreneurs, property owners, rentiers, and farmers were reduced in strength from 20 to 11 percent. A slight decrease in the share of shopkeepers and artisans was essentially compensated by an increase in the figure for the lesser employees. Recruitment at Normale thus became slightly more progressive after 1910 and also a little more specialized upon the children of teachers. The rate of change was modest indeed, and this may be the most important point to remember. It is underscored by what information is available on the 1870s and earlier decades. The school's commitment

12. Day, "Transformation of Technical Education," p.15; another 2 percent of the fathers were in other occupations.

Table 4.6
Social Origins of Students
at the Ecole Normale, 1880–1941
(Percentages by Column)

Father's Occupation	Classes of 1880–1909			Classes of 1910–1941		
	Letters	Sciences	All	Letters	Sciences	All
1. Liberal professions[a]	14.9	6.9	11.7	13.1	10.3	12.0
2. High officials, politics[b]	6.6	4.4	5.7	4.7	3.0	4.0
3. Secondary and university teachers[c]	20.2	14.1	17.8	17.6	18.5	18.0
1–3. Sum	41.7	25.4	35.2	35.4	31.8	34.0
4. Officers	3.3	3.0	3.2	4.7	5.6	5.0
5. Middle officials	5.4	4.0	4.8	4.4	4.4	4.4
6. Lower officials	9.0	8.9	9.0	8.7	10.1	9.2
7. Lower teachers[d]	9.9	9.4	9.7	17.1	14.3	16.0
5–7. Sum	24.3	22.2	23.5	30.2	28.8	29.7
8. Farmers, propertied, rentiers[e]	7.6	9.4	8.3	2.5	3.0	2.7
9. Entrepreneurs[f]	10.5	13.1	11.5	9.5	6.0	8.1
10. Shopkeepers, artisans	4.1	9.4	6.2	3.8	3.8	3.8
11. Lower white collar	5.4	8.4	6.6	10.0	11.3	10.5
12. Skilled workers[g]	3.1	9.1	5.5	3.5	7.6	5.1
13. Unskilled	–	–	–	0.5	2.0	1.1
1–13. Absolute total known (100%)	609	405	1,014	771	497	1,268
14. Unknown	114	100	214	216	141	357
1–14. Absolute totals	723	505	1,228	987	638	1,625

Robert J. Smith has kindly allowed me to subsume the results of his archival research under my summary categories. A more highly articulated report on his excellent survey should shortly be available in his forthcoming book on the Ecole Normale. Classes are *promotions*. Smith's sample of 349 *Normaliens* from the *promotions* of 1868–79 did not differ much from what is tabulated above for all students in 1880–1909; the percentage for secondary and university teachers was six points higher, but the difference was almost completely compensated by lower figures for the lower officials and teachers.

[a] Mainly comprises (in order of magnitude) doctors, lawyers, clergymen, musicians and artists, and pharmacists.

[b] Groups some men in national and local politics with larger contingents of technical and other high government officials.

[c] Dominated by teachers and administrators in *lycées* and *collèges,* but also includes substantial numbers of university professors and administrators along with a few education officials above the primary level.

continued next page

to the sons of academics and teachers became more pronounced with time, but there was no notable change in the level of progressiveness.[13]

Before 1910, the scientists at the school came in substantially larger proportions than the humanists from the business classes, especially from the families of tradesmen, clerks, and skilled workers; among the humanists, sons of liberal professionals, academics, and secondary teachers were more numerous. Even after 1910, the scientists were a little more progressively recruited than the humanists, but the difference was no longer significant. Thus, with only minor qualifications in mind, one can take the distribution for all students about 1880–1914 as a roughly adequate representation of both the school's curricular branches from the mid-nineteenth to the mid-twentieth century.

Table 4.7 takes advantage of this circumstance to place the basic pattern for the Ecole Normale into a comparative context, where it can be most adequately interpreted. The obvious contrast between the Ecole Normale and the Ecole Polytechnique during the decades after 1880 was due largely to the numerical strength of academics, teachers, school inspectors, and other educational administrators among the fathers of students at the Ecole Normale. High and middle-level officials, including military men, were somewhat better represented at Polytechnique; but the percentages for the academics and teachers easily outbalanced this difference, so that the noneconomic occupations as a group were considerably more numerous at Normale than at Polytechnique. Among the business groups, both property owners and entrepreneurs were much stronger at the Ecole Polytechnique; the figure for the propertied at Normale is remarkably low in view of the fact that it encompasses ordinary farmers as well. Among the economic middle and lower middle classes, shopkeepers were somewhat better represented at the Ecole Polytechnique. The unusual figure at Normale is the 6 percent for skilled labor, which admittedly included state railroad workers.

---

d Predominantly elementary teachers (*instituteurs*); also includes a number of other nonsecondary teachers along with primary school administrators and inspectors.

e Covers Smith's large category of "farmers, *propriétaires*," along with his very much smaller groupings for rentiers and "small farmers, *propriétaires*."

f Almost entirely wholesalers and "manufacturers, entrepreneurs"; but also includes a few bankers, publishers, and booksellers, and a handful of "business scientists-engineers."

g Includes a few railroad employees and mechanics and a remnant of foremen.

13. A comment on these figures from Smith for 1868–79 is included in the notes to Table 4.6. Seabold, *Normalien Alumni*, pp.299–301, deals with the social origins of 263 selected students in the classes of 1831–69. The special characteristics of Seabold's sample and the occupational categories he uses do not permit comparisons with Smith's data; but Smith's sense of a basic stability over time is not inconsistent with what evidence Seabold presents.

Table 4.7
Social Origins of French and German University-Level Students, ca. 1875
(Percentages by Column)

Father's Occupation	French census 1872[a]	Ecole Polytechnique 1848–1879	Ecole Polytechnique 1880–1914	Ecole Normale 1880–1909	German universities[b] 1874–1876
1. Liberal professions	0.8[c]	19	11	12 ⎫	⎱ 20
2. High officials	0.1[d]	18	9	6 ⎭	
3. Clergy	0.7[e]	–	–	–	14
4. Secondary and university teachers	0.1	–	–	18	3
1–4. Sum	1.7	37	20	35	37
5. Officers	0.2			3	1
6. Other military, police	1.1 ⎫				
7. Middle and low officials	1.2 ⎭	7[f]	20[f]	14	10
8. Lower teachers	0.5	–	–	10	9
5–8. Sum	3.0	7	20	27	20
9. Landowners, farmers	34.7			8 ⎫	14
10. Propertied, rentiers	4.8	32	13 ⎬	⎭	4[g]
11. Entrepreneurs	4.4[h]	20	25	12 ⎫	⎱ 25
12. Shopkeepers, artisans	7.2[i]	4	10	6 ⎭	
13. (Lower) white collar	3.3	1[j]	11[j]	7	–
14. Workers	40.9[k]	–	–	6	1

From Tables 2.4, 4.5, 4.6, and *Statistique de la France, Résultats généraux du dénombrement de 1872.*

[a] Pertains to the male work force ("active population"); about 9.52 million make up the 100 percent; some 378 thousand "active" males were excluded from that 100 percent as army draftees, retired, on welfare, or (in under 10 thousand cases) difficult to classify. As suggested by Karady, "Normaliens et autres enseignants," teachers in the census are distributed between the secondary/university and "lower" categories in a ratio of 1:5, and figures of 20 thousand and 100 thousand are assigned, respectively, to officers and to noncommissioned officers and police. Beyond that, the categories used for the census are slightly different and more detailed than those worked out by Karady.

[b] A composite or average of 1874–76 data on students at the University of Halle, from the state of Württemberg, and at the University of Leipzig.

[c] A few private scholars and writers are included with the secondary and university teachers, not here.

[d] Only magistrates; all remaining civil servants are listed as "Middle and Lower Officials."

[e] Practically all French clergymen, of course, were Catholic.

[f] A number of military men are presumably included with the officials.

[g] Only rentiers are included.

continued next page

The Ecole Normale used to be considered a stronghold of proletarian radicalism, but that myth has now been effectively destroyed.[14] Thus we will do no harm by looking for a moment at the element of truth in the original misconception, which was clearly nourished by the contrast with the Ecole Polytechnique. Among fathers of students at Polytechnique, almost 60 percent were *bourgeois* even after 1880, and the proportion had been nearly 90 percent earlier in the century. At Normale, if academics and teachers are excluded, the comparable figure was only 35–40 percent between 1880 and 1909, and it had not been appreciably higher around 1870. Among officials, the middle and higher ranks seemed to favor Polytechnique, while the lower ranks were about equally well represented at the two institutions. Petty employees and skilled workers were a little stronger at Normale; a few working-class students did indeed manage to reach that school. But what really stood out about the Ecole Normale was the high share of students whose fathers were primary and secondary teachers, professors and scholars, and members of the educational bureaucracy. Normale was almost exclusively a training school for future secondary and university teachers. Joined to this circumstance, its specialized recruitment made it the most purely academic institution in modern Europe. Its "radicalism," such as it was, had more to do with the antithesis between the academic and the *bourgeois* in France than with any significant presence of working-class students.

Dividing the distribution percentages for Polytechnique and Normale by the corresponding percentages in the French occupational census of 1872, one obtains what we have called educational opportunity ratios. These can be taken seriously only as orders of magnitude, since even minor changes in professional categories cause them to fluctuate wildly. It is interesting, nevertheless, that the opportunity ratio for the economic lower middle class of shopkeepers and artisans was somewhere near one; these occupations were roughly as well represented at the two famous *grandes écoles* around 1880–1914 as in the French population. If fertility and death rates had been equal for

---

h Employers/owners (*patrons*) in mining, manufacture, construction, transport, and banking, along with large or wholesale merchants, but excluding executive employees (who *are* listed as entrepreneurs among students' fathers).

i Innkeepers and related occupations are grouped with the shopkeepers and artisans.

j Encompasses the *classes populaires*.

k Various low-skilled assistants (*manoeuvres*) are counted with the workers, as are 14.3 percent of the work force who were agricultural laborers.

14. Much of the credit goes to Smith, "L'Atmosphère politique."

all social groups in France at that time, the son of a shopkeeper or artisan would have had about as good a chance as the average French boy in his generation of gaining access to the Ecole Normale or the Ecole Polytechnique. While very few members of a given age group reached these schools at all, so that absolute access chances were small for everyone, the *comparative* access chance for the shopkeeper's son must have stood somewhere near one.

For the offspring of workers and peasants, of course, the educational opportunity ratios were minute fractions; three quarters of the French population had almost no chance of sending their sons to any of the distinguished *grandes écoles.* The highest opportunity ratios were those for the educated upper middle class: near 200 for the sons of academics and secondary teachers at Normale; 50–100 for the offspring of high officials at Polytechnique; 10–20 at both schools for the liberal professions as well as for the learned occupations as a group. The ratio for property owners and entrepreneurs at Polytechnique stood somewhere near 5, but the figure for the lower-ranking teachers at Normale was four times that high! Indeed, middle and lower officials and teachers appear to have done about as well as the economic upper middle class in educating their children. This is another indication that the rank order of learning was not identical with the economic class hierarchy in nineteenth-century France.

Of course the Ecole Polytechnique and the Ecole Normale were both very small and specialized schools; they cannot be equated with French higher learning generally. It is certainly their uniqueness that stands out when they are compared with German institutions, as in the last column of Table 4.7.

Only the Ecole Normale came at all close to resembling a German university of the later nineteenth century. The sons of Protestant clergymen were almost as large a contingent at the German universities as the sons of secondary and university teachers were at the Ecole Normale, and the lower-ranking teachers were almost equally well represented in the two cases. Allowing for probable differences in the categorization of middle-level officials, the noneconomic occupations were therefore only slightly less numerous at the average German university than at Normale. Farmers' sons were quantitatively more significant among German students; we know that many of them studied Catholic theology, which they could not have done at a public educational institution in France. The figures for the business groups are harder to interpret, but petty employees and skilled workers were apparently a little better represented at Normale than at the German universities.

Altogether, the pattern of recruitment appears to have been roughly as progressive at the German universities as at the Ecole Normale; the percentages for the economic upper middle class in particular were not very high in either case. Obviously, the role of the Protestant and Catholic theological faculties helps to account for this surprising similarity. The sons of pastors and farmers were to the German universities what the sons of secondary teachers, clerks, and skilled workers were to the Ecole Normale.

The essential difference between the Ecole Polytechnique and the German university is now clear—it paralleled the contrast between the Ecole Polytechnique and the Ecole Normale, with the qualification that the middle and upper grades of the bureaucracy, including the military, were naturally somewhat stronger at Polytechnique than at the German universities, and so, more markedly, were the property owners and entrepreneurs. The German universities, it seems, stood very near one of the two poles of an important antithesis in the French system—the antithesis between the Ecole Polytechnique and the Ecole Normale, between the *bourgeois* and the academic. The German universities of the later nineteenth century, in these terms, were still more academic than *bourgeois*. That is the safest and most interesting conclusion to be drawn from the comparison that has been attempted.

The Social Origins of Secondary Students since the 1930s

Systematic information on the social origins of French secondary students finally began to be collected in the 1930s; but until 1958, it was organized under a few very general categories borrowed from the census. The figures brought together in Table 4.8 are therefore not as useful as they might be. They give us no more than a blurred outline of the transition from the high industrial to the late industrial phase in the history of French secondary education.

The three most important columns in the table are those for all pupils in the entering classes (Sixths) of public *lycées* and *collèges*. The distribution for 1936 reflects the increase in access around 1930 but not the major structural change that followed: the integration of the higher primary schools (*écoles primaires supérieures*) into the secondary system as *collèges modernes*. The effect of this 1941 reform can be observed in the column for 1943; it obviously brought about a major advance in the progressiveness of French secondary recruitment. There were sharp reductions in the distribution percentages for the liberal professions, for officials of all ranks, for rentiers and for owners of large and small businesses, who are listed as "entrepreneurs." The

Table 4.8

Social Origins of French Secondary Pupils, 1932–1956
(Percentages by Column)

Father's Occupation	Bacc. cands. 1932[a]	Entering Classes (streams/years)[b]					German Sec. 1931[c]
		All 1936	All 1943	Class. 1943	All 1956	Class. 1956	
Liberal professions	14.3	11	7	10	9	13	7
Officials	25.2	30	24	28	27	30	35
Agriculture	1.3	2	8	6	7	6	4
Rentiers (propertied)	10.6	6	3	3	2	2	2
Entrepreneurs	17.8	25	14	17	12	14	8
Artisans (shopkeepers)	3.9	4	10	9	8	7	24
White collar	24.4	20	19	19	22	21	12
Workers	2.6	3	15	8	12	8	7

See X for details.

   [a] Data on 1932 baccalaureate candidates in the Academy of Paris (N: 6,610) from Commission Carnegie, *Enquêtes:* 'Rentiers, propertied' here includes 8.6 percent "without profession and other"; 'Entrepreneurs' are 6.9 percent industrialists and 10.8 percent merchants; 1.9 percent shopkeepers are grouped with the artisans; 10.8 percent of the employees are described as in executive positions; 0.3 percent domestics are included with the workers.

   [b] Distributions for French entering classes (Sixths) pertain to all streams in traditional public *lycées* and *collèges* in 1936. Thereafter, former higher primary schools (EPS: *collèges modernes*) are included as well. In both 1943 and 1956, about half the students were in the classical stream, so that specific distribution percentages for all pupils generally fell about half-way between those for the classical and those for the modern stream. The occupational categories for these official statistics (taken from the census) are not very helpful or precise: 'Rentiers' here includes those without profession, but not *propriétaires*. 'Entrepreneurs' really means all heads of industrial and commercial enterprises other than "artisans," who have been separated out.

   [c] Distribution for Fifth (entering) grade of German public boys' secondary schools in 1931 from Table 2.2: 'Officials' includes 5 percent high officials, 1 percent military, 29 percent middle and lower officials and teachers; 'Rentiers, propertied' here covers "others, unknown" as well as "without profession"; 'Entrepreneurs' are large-scale owners and directors, along with executive employees.

corresponding increases came in the figures for farmers, artisans, and workers; together, these groups raised their share of secondary enrollments from 9 to 33 percent.

There are indications that this progressive shift was more than nominal. Of course the higher primary schools did not immediately begin to function as full secondary institutions. Yet, as we know, the ratio of baccalaureates to total enrollments for the *enlarged* secondary system eventually recovered its former level; the new schools were thus ultimately integrated into the secondary pyramid. It is significant, in this context, that even the classical stream of 1943 was more progressively recruited than the whole secondary system of 1936. The difference is not great, but the distribution for the classical program in 1943 includes slightly lower percentages for the sons of officials, rentiers, and business owners, and somewhat larger figures for the off-spring of farmers, artisans, and workers. One cannot avoid the impression that a real change did take place, that the incorporation of the higher primary schools did improve educational opportunities for the lower middle and lower classes, at least in the long run.

The difference between the percentages for 1936 and those for 1943 is in fact the only noteworthy contrast in Table 4.8. The distributions for the classical stream in 1943 and 1956 were less progressive than those for all students, but the divergence was not large in either case. There was segmentation, certainly, but it was relatively mild, and it was socially vertical in a thoroughly uncomplicated way. The study of Latin simply attracted a slightly more elevated clientele than the modern curriculum. The distribution for baccalaureate candidates in 1932 was less progressive than that for beginning secondary pupils four years later; but the difference was no greater than one would expect, given the typically higher rates of attrition among lower-class students in the upper grades. The slimness of the gap between the data for 1932 and 1936 suggests, indeed, that the increase in enrollments per age group around 1930 had little immediate effect upon the level of progressiveness in French secondary education. Between 1943 and 1956, while enrollments continued to increase, the pattern of recruitment actually became less progressive, though the change was minute and probably insignificant.

The main point is that only the incorporation of the higher primary schools significantly altered the social makeup of French secondary education between 1930 and 1956. As in Germany, gradual increases in enrollments per age group had little effect on the level of progressiveness; it took the quantum jump associated with a structural change to make a difference at all.

Little is added to this conclusion by the German data in Table 4.8. The appropriate comparison places French secondary entrants in 1936 beside beginning pupils at German secondary schools in 1931. As we know, levels of inclusiveness were similar in French and German secondary education during the early 1930s, after the French expansion around 1930 had been launched and before the German system contracted under the National Socialists. It is no surprise that the degrees of progressiveness were roughly comparable as well. Most of what differences there were between the two pertinent columns can be traced to dissimilarities of classification. The only exceptions are the high German percentages for officials and for workers. The figure for the officials includes a large contingent of lower-ranking civil servants and teachers, who have always been particularly numerous among the fathers of German students. The percentage for the workers suggests that secondary schooling may indeed have been marginally more progressive in Germany than in France around 1931.

If so, the standings had been thoroughly reversed by 1960, as Table 4.9 reveals. The occupational categories that appear in this table were first introduced by French statisticians in 1958. They are much more precise than those in Table 4.8, but unfortunately, it is practically im-

Table 4.9

Social Origins of French Secondary Pupils, 1959–61

(Percentages by Column)

Father's Occupation (and Percent in 1954 Occupational Census)	All Sixth 1959	Class. Sixth 1959	All acad. 1961	All Tech. 1961	All gen. 1961	German sec. 1965
Liberal professions, high white collar[a] (2.9)	15	21	17	6	2	32
Farmers (20.8)	7	6	7	6	10	4
Farm workers (6.0)	1	1	1	2	3	–
Rentiers, without profession (–)	2	2	3	3	2	–
Industrialists (0.4)	2	2	2	2	1	7
Commerce (7.7)	9	9	9	7	7	} 13
Artisans (3.9)	6	5	5	6	6	
Middle-level white collar (5.9)	15	17	16	11	11	} 30
Lower white collar[b] (10.9)	18	17	17	17	17	
Workers[b] (33.8)	19	13	16	33	35	} 12
Domestics (5.1)	1	1	1	2	2	
Others[c] (2.6)	6	6	6	5	5	4

German figures from Table 2.2 pertain to the tenth school year of all (academic) secondary schools. French columns for 1959 pertain to entering classes at public secondary schools of the academic type (classical and modern but not technical), including former higher primary schools, and to the classical stream within those classes, which was generally about half as large as the modern stream. French columns for 1961 pertain to all grades and streams of academic secondary schools, to full-term technical secondary schools (essentially *lycées techniques*, former EPCI), and to the former complementary courses that became "general" (lower) secondary schools (CEG) in 1959. See X for details.

a As inclusive a category in the French as in the German columns, encompassing high officials, professors, and secondary teachers, along with the liberal professions, executive business employees, and nonindependent technicians.

b Public employees and workers are counted with private ones.

c Includes clergy and military.

possible to compare the two schemes. Officials had been a separate group in the older terminology. In the new system, some of them were grouped with the liberal professions and executive employees, others with the middle and lower-ranking white-collar occupations, and the rest with the workers. The new classifications make up an essentially unilinear scale; those who devised them had their eye on the late industrial context, especially on the all-important white-collar hierarchy.

The most important distribution in Table 4.9 is headed *All academic, 1961*. It pertains to all grades in all public secondary schools of the academic type: to both the classical and the modern streams, including the former higher primary schools. No other set of figures could more adequately represent the social makeup of French secondary education during the early 1960s. Just over 20 percent of pupils' fathers were high officials, secondary and university teachers, members of the liberal professions, high white-collar employees or independent technicians, industrialists, and rentiers or men without professions. Middle and lower-ranking white-collar employees, at 33 percent, were considerably more numerous among the parents than independent merchants, shopkeepers, and artisans, at 14 percent. That left 8 percent for agriculture, 17 percent for workers and domestics, and 6 percent for other occupations, including the military and the Protestant clergy. In sum, this was a relatively progressive distribution. The percentages for workers and petty employees were undoubtedly driven up by the inclusion of public officials in these categories. But there can be no doubt that the lower middle and lower classes had finally acquired a share in French secondary education.

Certainly French academic secondary schools of the early 1960s were significantly more progressive in their recruitment than their German counterparts. The contrast between the two pertinent columns in Table 4.9 cannot be traced to minor dissimilarities in terminology or to the difference between the occupational censuses of the two countries. If the figures for industrialists are added to those for the liberal professions and related occupations, the sum comes to nearly 40 percent in the German case, and to only about half that much in the French distribution. The representation of workers and domestics reaches 17 percent in the French column, as against 12 percent in the German one.

The French advantage was due, as has been suggested, to the structural reforms that were begun during the interwar period and completed after the Second World War, chief among them the integration of the higher primary schools into the secondary system. This brought about so thorough a reorientation of social conventions and expecta-

tions that full-length secondary enrollments per age group shot up
from under 7 percent in 1931 to over 27 percent in 1961, while baccalaureates advanced from just over 2 percent to more than 11 percent
of the age group. In Germany, by contrast, average secondary attendance per age group was not significantly higher in 1950 than it had
been in 1931. Both *Abitur* awards and average enrollments did increase
between 1950 and 1960, but the rate of change was nowhere near as
great as in France.

Whether even the French reforms were drastic enough to increase
social mobility through education is impossible to say. My guess would
be that the effect of moderately higher distribution percentages for the
lower middle and lower classes was essentially cancelled by the quantum jump in enrollments per age group, which reduced the value of
secondary certificates in the job market. On the other hand, increased
progressiveness in education can be socially significant, it seems to me,
quite apart from its impact—or lack of impact—upon rates of mobility.

To do justice to the postwar condition of the French secondary
system, one has to look not only at the academic streams but also at
the distributions for technical and for general education in 1961. The
column on the technical schools in Table 4.9 pertains to full-length
technical *lycées*, formerly advanced vocational schools (*écoles pratiques de commerce et d'industrie, écoles nationales professionnelles*),
which have been considered secondary since the Second World War
and which award the technical baccalaureate. "General secondary"
refers to the former complementary courses, which became lower secondary schools (*collèges d'enseignement général*) in 1959. They have
been extremely popular and have helped to move the French system a
few steps toward the interwar ideal of the common school (*école
unique*).

In 1961, as Table 4.9 reveals, recruitment patterns in French technical and general secondary schools were progressive indeed. The two
distributions involved were also nearly identical. The only real difference between the two columns is that the offspring of farmers were
somewhat more numerous in the general program, while the children
of executive employees and liberal professionals were better represented at the full-length technical *lycées*. Beyond that, what stands
out is the large share of the lower middle and lower classes. In both
cases, the most remarkable percentages are those for the artisans (6),
for middle and lower-ranking white-collar employees (28), and for
workers and domestics (35–37).

The precision of the categories used by French statisticians since
1958 makes it possible to put much of this information into a more

significant form. The distributions for 1961 in Table 4.9 can be related to the French occupational census of 1954. Educational opportunity ratios can thus at last be calculated with a respectable degree of accuracy. In technical and general secondary education, none of the ratios were far from one, since most occupational groups were about as well represented in these programs as in the general population. This was true even for workers. The exceptions on the low side were fractions of 0.3–0.5 for domestics and for the agricultural occupations. On the high side, the industrialists reached multiples of 5 and 2.5 at the technical and general schools respectively. The ratio for middle-level employees was roughly 2 at both sets of institutions, and the same proportion held for the high white-collar professions at the technical *lycées.*

The more significant ratios, of course, were those for academic secondary education. Needless to say, they varied more widely than those for the technical and general schools. At the top of the rank order, the liberal professions, executive employees, and high officials were represented at 6 times their share of the census. The industrialists followed with a multiple of 5, the middle-level employees with 3, and the lower white-collar occupations with about 1.5. Clustered around 1 were the smaller merchants and artisans. The figure for the workers was roughly 0.5, a not inconsiderable magnitude. The lowest opportunity ratios were 0.3 for agriculture and 0.2 for domestics. With the possible exception of the results for the farmers, the whole sequence is consistent with an essentially unilinear class analysis of educational inequalities. Whatever may have been true of French secondary education during the nineteenth century, the line between the academic and the nonacademic streams by 1961 was a nearly perfect case of socially vertical segmentation.

Also socially vertical were the further differences of recruitment among the several classes and streams within the academic secondary sector. The central column in Table 4.9, academic secondary schools in 1961, pertains to all grades and curricular options. Of the two columns for 1959 at the left of the table, however, one deals with the Sixth or entering class, and the other is focussed even more exclusively upon the classical Sixth. The differences between the three academic secondary distributions are to be found almost entirely in the figures for the workers on the one hand and for the liberal professions and related occupations on the other. To move upward from the entering class to an average grade (central column) is to encounter a slightly increased proportion of pupils from upper middle-class homes and a correspondingly reduced share of working-class youths. To move within the academic Sixth from all streams to the classical stream is to meet the same kind of "rarefication" in a more pronounced version. Apparently, the social difference between French classical and modern secondary education was somewhat more visible in the mid-1950s than in the early 1960s. It would look more significant, too, if the classical stream were compared with the modern one, rather than with the two combined [X]. Even so, the remaining contrast is but a faint echo of the antithesis that initially arose when Duruy's special secondary program was launched in the 1860s.

Increasingly since the 1950s, the decisive bifurcation in French education has been the socially vertical separation between the primary and the secondary track. In the critical selection at age 11 or 12, as of 1953, about 29 percent of French primary pupils were routed out of the ordinary primary schools [X]. Among these transfers, 40 percent entered complementary courses; 5 percent enrolled in technical *lycées;* and 55 percent went to classical and modern secondary schools, joining those of their age mates who had begun their education in the elementary classes of secondary schools. But the proportion of children who left the ordinary primary schools at this point varied sharply with their parents' occupations: it was 86–87 percent for the liberal professions and high officials, 39–43 percent for lower white-collar employees, and 21 percent for nonagricultural workers. In the further selection among those who transferred at all, the share who reached classical and modern secondary schools ranged from 75–85 percent for the liberal professions and high white-collar occupations to 43 percent for agricultural and 34 percent for nonagricultural workers.

By 1962–63, elementary classes at secondary schools had been abolished; the complementary courses had become "general secondary" schools; and there had been a further increase in the inclusiveness of French secondary education. According to an exemplary study by Sauvy and Girard, some 55 percent of French pupils now reached a secondary Sixth: 28 percent entered general secondary schools, and 27 percent enrolled in classical, modern, or technical *lycées* [X]. Among upper middle-class youngsters, 85–95 percent reached a secondary Sixth; among the children of workers and farmers, the proportion was about half that much. At the *lycées* in particular, access percentages were 75 for the liberal professions and other high white-collar occupations, 55–57 for heads of business enterprises and middle-level employees and officials, 32–33 for the lower white-collar group, and 16 for farmers and nonagricultural workers.

Taking their analysis a step further, Sauvy and Girard grouped pupils not only according to their fathers' occupations but also according to their school grades, which ranged from "excellent" and "good" to "average," "mediocre" and "poor." They were thus able to calculate secondary access percentages for each *occupational category and grade level* [X]. Their results were lowest for farmers and agricultural workers, who obtained secondary school places for only 63–64 percent of their "good" students and 32–40 percent for all their children, regardless of school performance. The next lowest figures were those for the children of nonagricultural workers; the highest were those for the offspring of the high white collar occupations: executive employees and high officials. Below are the secondary access percentages for these two groups and for all occupations (and pupils) combined.

	Excellent	Good	Average	Mediocre	Poor	All grades
High white collar	100	98	92	72	50	94
Nonagricultural workers	91	79	42	10	3	45
All occupational groups combined	93	83	51	15	6	55

It is a disheartening pattern, and probably a typical one. As a result of major structural reforms since the later 1930s, French secondary education by 1962 was considerably more inclusive and somewhat more progressive than its German counterpart. Yet change has been exceedingly slow. Substantial increases in enrollments per age group have failed to accelerate the difficult approach to equality of opportunity in education. In France, at any rate, "meritocracy" is scarcely an immediate prospect.

University Faculties and *Grandes Ecoles* since 1939

The earliest statistics on the social origins of students in French university faculties date from 1939.[15] Unfortunately, they are couched in the rather general categories normally used in French official surveys until 1958, and their value is further reduced by substantial portions of unknowns in the distributions of fathers' occupations. Thus it is only with great caution that a few summary conclusions can be drawn from the data presented in Table 4.10.

15. Data for the early nineteenth century would not be very meaningful in any case, since matriculation in the faculties was often merely nominal at that time. Additional research would be most usefully invested in the period from 1870 to 1940.

Table 4.10

Social Origins of French University Students, 1939–1956
(Percentages by Column)

Father's Occupation	Students in All Faculties			
	1939	1946	1950	1956
Liberal professions	19	17	17	12
Officials	26	27	28	29
Farmers	4	5	5	5
Farm workers	1	1	1	1
Propertied, rentiers, without profession	10	8	6	4
Entrepreneurs[a]	} 16	} 16	} 15	8
Shopkeepers				
Artisans	4	5	5	} 13
Employees	13	13	12	15
Workers	2	2	2	3
Unknown	7	8	8	11

	Students in 1950, by Faculty			
	Law	Med.[b]	Lett.	Sci.
Liberal professions	14	26	12	19
Officials	27	21	40	24
Farmers	5	5	6	5
Farm workers	1	1	1	1
Propertied, rentiers, without profession	6	7	7	4
Entrepreneurs,[a] shopkeepers	16	18	11	17
Artisans	5	4	5	7
Employees	14	11	9	14
Workers	2	1	2	3
Unknown	10	6	8	7

See XII for details.

[a] Heads of industrial and commercial enterprises.

[b] Includes students of pharmacy.

The basic pattern of the late industrial phase in the history of French higher education, the table indicates, was a very gradual increase in progressiveness, at least at the faculties. Between 1939 and 1956, there were slight decreases in the distribution percentages for the liberal professions and related occupations, as well as in those for rentiers, property owners, and others without occupation. Students from the families of petty employees and workers, in the meantime, marginally strengthened their share of enrollments. The figures for fathers of unknown profession also increased, but the increments were too small to raise questions about the overall trend.

The causes of change are not hard to find. French university enrollments per age group advanced from about 4 percent to over 6 percent between 1936 and 1956, and baccalaureate awards simultaneously increased from 4 to 9 percent of the age group. We know that the reclassification of the higher primary schools in 1941 was a particularly important structural reform and led to more progressive recruitment at the secondary level. By the early 1950s, apparently, it began to affect the faculties as well, for much of the shift that can be observed in Table 4.10 was concentrated between 1950 and 1956.

An interesting hypothesis is suggested by the divergent effects of increased inclusiveness at the German universities, in French secondary education, and at the French faculties during the twentieth century. In the German case, as university enrollments per age group slowly rose from 1 to 4 percent between 1900 and 1955, there were no significant gains in the distribution percentages for the lower middle and lower classes. In French secondary education, structural reform led to a quantum jump in inclusiveness, from 7 to 27 percent of the age group between 1931 and 1961. The consequence, while far from "meritocratic," was an unmistakable equalization of educational opportunities at the secondary level. At the French universities between 1936 and 1956, enrollments advanced from 4 to over 6 percent of the age group, and the result appears to have been a modest change in recruitment patterns during the early 1950s. The overall access percentages for the French faculties thus seem to indicate a threshold, near 5 percent of the age group, at which further advances in inclusiveness begin to have a mildly progressive effect.

The distributions for particular faculties in Table 4.10 are not easy to interpret. The occupations grouped with the liberal professions in these figures included not only medical men but also engineers and architects, who probably encouraged their sons to enroll in the faculty of sciences. Teachers were counted among the officials. These peculiarities of categorization help to explain why the liberal professions were well represented in the faculty of sciences as well as in medicine, and why the sons of officials were particularly numerous in the faculty of letters. The faculty of medicine apparently attracted the largest share of students from upper middle-class families, while the children of artisans, employees, and workers showed a mild preference for the faculty of sciences. But none of the social differences among the faculties really looks very significant, at least in the occupational terminology of the early 1950s.

Fortunately, as in the case of secondary education, the quality of official statistics on the French faculties improved considerably after 1958. So great was the change in the categories used that the new classification cannot easily be compared with the old. In the absence of reliable indications to the contrary, one simply assumes that there was little real change between 1956 and 1959. Indeed, that assumption is appropriate and necessary even with respect to the distributions for 1959 and 1963 in Table 4.11. What differences there are between them could be due almost entirely to a few additional alterations of terminology. Thus in the figures for 1963, the lower officials were reclassified as lower white-collar employees or as workers; the lines among the business occupations were slightly redrawn; and artists, clergymen, and the military were counted among the "other" professions. At the same time, the "unknown" category shrank a good deal.

Altogether, it seems best to analyze the data in Table 4.11 in an essentially static fashion. Such an approach can actually profit from variations in nomenclature to clarify the pattern as a whole. The results obtained will give an account of the French faculties at a time when their continuing gradual growth almost certainly produced only minor changes in their social composition.

As of about 1960, to summarize the most important distribution percentages, the nonentrepreneurial upper middle class of liberal professionals, high officials, secondary teachers, and academics accounted for about 23 percent of students at French university faculties. The economic elite of rentiers, industrialists, merchants, and executive employees added another 17 percent, so that the *bourgeois* share as a whole came to 40 percent. The offspring of middle and lower-ranking civil servants and teachers made up some 12–18 percent of enrollments, depending on how one classifies the low officials. The intermediate strata within the business community, made up of middle and lower-level employees, shopkeepers, and artisans, were jointly represented at about 26 percent. That left some 6–8 percent for the agricultural occupations and 1 percent for domestics. It also left 8 percent for the nonagricultural workers, including those employed by public agencies.

As might be expected, educational opportunity ratios varied more sharply at the university faculties than at the secondary level. The highest multiple, 17 for the liberal professions in 1963, probably reflected a particularly narrow definition of that group in the census. Next came a figure of 10 for secondary teachers and university professors; it would have been greater if the Ecole Normale and its sister institution had been counted as well. High officials and industrialists shared an opportunity ratio of 8, while middle-level officials joined

Table 4.11

Social Origins of French University Students, 1959–1963
(Percentages by Column)

Father's Occupation (and Percent in 1954 Occupational Census)	All Faculties		1963: Selected Faculties			
	1959	1963	Law	Med.	Letters	Sci.
1. Liberal professions (0.6)	13	10	11	20	7	7
2. High officials (0.9)	6	7	6	8	6	7
3. Secondary and university teachers (0.4)	5	4	3	4	4	4
1–3. Sum (1.9)	23	20	20	32	16	18
4. Lower teachers (2.0)[a]	5	5	3	3	6	6
5. Middle officials (1.1)	7	7	7	6	7	7
6. Low officials[b] (4.1)	6					
7. Farmers (20.8)	5	7	5	3	7	8
8. Farm workers (6.0)	1	1	—	—	1	1
9. Rentiers, (propertied)[c], no profession (−)	5	8	8	7	10	7
10. Industrialists (0.4) }	6	3	5	4	2	3
11. Merchants (1.0) }		} 9	8	9	10	9
12. Shopkeepers (6.7) }	13					
13. Artisans (3.9) }		4	3	3	5	5
10–13. Sum (12.0)	19	17	16	16	17	17
14. Executive employees (1.0)	5	6	7	6	5	6
15. Middle-level employees (2.8)	6	6	6	4	7	6
16. Low employees[b] (6.8)	6	7	7	7	8	8
17. Workers[b] (33.8)	3	8	4	3	10	10
18. Domestics (5.1)	—	1	1	1	1	1
19. Others (2.6)[d]	—	7	16	3	6	6
20. Unknown (−)	10	2	1	10	—	—

See XIII for details.

[a] Middle-level personnel in the medical and social services are grouped with the lower teachers in the census only.

[b] Lower officials after 1959 are reclassified as ordinary low white-collar and blue-collar workers.

[c] Property owners are explicitly included only in 1959.

[d] Artists, clergy, and military are included in the census and for 1963, but not for 1959.

high white-collar employees at a multiple of 6. There was little trace here of the divergence between public and private employment that played so great a role in nineteenth-century education, especially in Germany. The lower teachers and the middle ranks of white-collar employees reached ratios of 2.5 and 2, respectively, though the teachers' figure would have been higher if their share of the census had not been enlarged by the inclusion of certain medical and social service occupations. Clustered around a ratio of 1 were the low officials, when they were separately mentioned, along with the shopkeepers, artisans, and petty employees; these groups were as well represented at the universities as in the census. Farmers, workers, domestics, and agricultural laborers stood at the bottom of the list. Their ratios were 0.2–0.3 —they had roughly two-tenths to three-tenths as good a chance as the average Frenchman of sending their children to the universities.

Obviously, educational opportunities were still very far from equal in French university education during the early 1960s. The range of opportunity ratios was not as vast as it had been at the two most famous *grandes écoles* during the nineteenth century, but it was large enough. Particularly at the upper end of the scale, the multiples were nearly twice as great at the faculties as in academic secondary education.

The other point to be made about the opportunity ratios has already been mentioned: they suggest that differences in access chances were distributed in a predominantly vertical way, along an essentially unilinear scale of occupational status. Officials and teachers were still able to match wealthier groups in obtaining university educations for their offspring; in that sense the hierarchy of learning still perpetuated itself independently of the class system to some extent. But the incongruities involved were very much milder than they had been during the early and high industrial periods, in France and especially in Germany. *Convergence* is the term normally used to evoke the fading of the old status inconsistencies and tensions in the age of the white-collar employee.

The columns for selected faculties in Table 4.11 are interesting primarily because they confirm, at a more precise and specific level, what has already been observed in the data for the early 1950s. Despite the suspiciously high figures for 'others' and 'unknown' under Law and Medicine, the social differences among the faculties are clear enough. Medicine attracted the largest proportion of upper middle-class students; the distribution percentage for doctors and other members of the liberal professions was 9 points higher in medicine than in law, its closest competitor. The faculties of letters and of sciences, which specialized in the training of secondary teachers, stood at the opposite end of the scale. They were most easily reached by the offspring of the lower-ranking teachers, farmers, artisans, and workers. If one adds the percentages for industrialists and executive employees to those for the liberal professions, high officials, academics and secondary teachers, one obtains a fair index of *bourgeois* predominance in a given distribution. As of 1963, that index came to 42 percent in medicine, 32 percent in law, 27 percent in the sciences, 23 percent in letters, and 29 percent in the French university faculties as a group. Law and the sciences stood close to the overall norm for the universities, medicine ranked well above law, and letters took up the lowest position on the scale.

The probable causes of the social differences among the French faculties include variations in the duration and cost of study and in the other expenses associated with getting started in a profession. Economic considerations come more readily to mind than cultural or attitudinal differences because the distinctions among the faculties, once again, were chiefly of the socially vertical type. They were also rather modest, at least in comparison with similar variations at the German universities. As of 1963, according to Table 2.10, the proportion of German university-level students whose fathers were in the liberal and learned professions was 49 percent in medicine, 38 percent in law, 27 percent in the humanities, 22 percent in the sciences, 22 percent in technology, and 18 percent in economics and business studies. The analogous percentages for German owners, directors, and executive employees in the larger enterprises were 32 in economics and business studies, 28 in technology, 24 in the sciences, 22 in law, 20 in the humanities, and 17 in medicine. The dissimilarity between the two German rank orders faintly recalls the socially horizontal segmentation that characterized the German system during the nineteenth century. The sheer magnitude of the contrasts they represent makes the differences between the French faculties seem relatively mild.

To encounter anything like the German segmentations in French university-level education, one has to turn to the *grandes écoles*. Six of these are described in Table 4.12, and descriptions of several others can be found in the Appendix.[16] Each of the distributions in Table 4.12 includes four indicative sums. A single distribution percentage for the

16. See Table XIV. Girard, *Réussite*, pp.193, 308–9, reports on questionnaires sent in 1958 to members of *promotions* 1947 through 1953 at Normale, Polytechnique, Centrale, and the Institut Agronomique (not to be confused with the less famous higher agricultural schools listed in Table XIV), and on candidates admitted to the Ecole Nationale d'Administration (ENA) from 1952 to 1958. For all but the Institut Agronomique and ENA, Girard's results (based on incomplete returns and on categories less useful than those in XIV) are superseded by the information in Table 4.12 (and XIV). ENA, because of its special admissions policy and function, is most appropriately discussed in a study of the French civil service rather than one of the educational system as such.

liberal and learned professions is obtained, as in previous tables, by adding up the data for the liberal professions, high officials, and secondary and university teachers. In the same way, the percentages for industrialists, merchants and shopkeepers (commerce), and artisans is combined into an indicator of business representation, and the three levels of employees are drawn together into a white collar index. Finally, at the bottom of the table, the percentages for the liberal and learned professions, industrialists, and executive employees are added up to yield a summary figure for the upper middle-class or *bourgeois* share within each distribution. Indeed, the schools in Table 4.12 are listed in order of decreasing percentages for the *bourgeois* contingent.

Nonuniversity institutions of higher education in France, as these indicators suggest, fall into two main groups. On the one hand, there are the oldest and most famous *grandes écoles*, which are clearly dominated by the upper middle class. They include the Ecole Polytechnique, the Ecole Normale, the former Ecole Libre des Sciences Politiques ("Sciences Po") and other Instituts d'Etudes Politiques, and the Ecole Centrale. The *bourgeois* representation at these schools as of 1961 ranged from 50 to 62 percent, which must be contrasted with 29 percent, the comparable figure for the university faculties in 1963. On the other hand, there are the Ecoles Nationales d'Ingénieurs Arts et Métiers (ENAM) and similar institutions, with *bourgeois* percentages near or below those of the faculties. Some of these relatively progressive schools are younger cousins of the ancient *grandes écoles*, chiefly higher technical and professional schools that have grown up since the late nineteenth century. Others, including the ENAM, are not *grandes écoles* in the traditional sense at all. They really represent the apex of the French system of vocational education, though they are nowadays comparable in quality to the newer technical schools. The higher commercial schools, which have also arisen since the late nineteenth century, occupy an intermediate place on the scale of *bourgeois* predominance. Even so, a salient characteristic of the French system as a whole has been the existence of two distinctive clusters of *grandes écoles* and related institutions, one of them far above the faculties in social altitude, the other near or below them.

In 1961 as during the nineteenth century, the Ecole Polytechnique was the most quintessentially *bourgeois* institution in France and probably in the world. As noted earlier, the term *bourgeois* must here be used in the integral sense specific to the French context: it implies political power and social eminence, not only wealth. Graduates of Polytechnique became not only military officers, but also high public administrators, technologists, and business leaders. Among fathers of

Table 4.12

Social Origins of Students in Selected *Grandes Ecoles,* 1961
(Percentages by Column)

Father's Occupation (and Percent in 1954 Occupational Census)	Poly-tech-nique	Nor-male Sup.	Inst. d'Et. Polit.	Cen-trale	Com-merce	Arts et Mé-tiers
1. Liberal professions (0.6)	16	7	15	7	8	3
2. High officials (0.9)	19	7	11	16	8	6
3. Secondary and university teachers (0.4)	8	33	3	4	1	2
1–3. Sum (1.9)	43	47	29	27	17	11
4. Lower teachers (2.0)[a]	9	14	3	5	2	5
5. Middle officials (1.1)	3	5	7	6	6	6
6. Farmers (20.8)	1	1	8	2	4	5
7. Farm workers (6.0)	–	–	–	–	–	1
8. Rentiers, without profession (–)	1	4	3	6	5	5
9. Industrialists (0.4)	5	2	8	3	12	4
10. Commerce (7.7)	6	5	8	7	17	6
11. Artisans (3.9)	2	2	3	2	3	9
9–11. Sum (12.0)	13	9	19	12	32	19
12. Executive employees (1.0)	14	4	15	20	17	8
13. Middle employees (2.8)	3	7	3	7	6	8
14. Low employees[b] (10.9)	8	5	8	9	5	10
12–14. Sum (14.7)	25	16	26	36	28	26
15. Workers[b] (33.8)	2	3	2	2	5	17
16. Domestics (5.1)	–	–	1	–	–	2
17. Others[c] (2.6)	3	1	2	4	1	3
1–3, 3, 12. Sum (3.3)	62	53	52	50	46	23

The institutions involved include the two Ecoles Normales Supérieures at the Rue d'Ulm and at Sèvres, five Instituts d'Etudes Politiques (including the former Ecole Libre des Sciences Politiques), twelve Ecoles Supérieures de Commerce, and six Ecoles Nationales d'Ingénieurs Arts et Métiers. See XIV for details.

[a] Middle-level personnel in the medical and social services are grouped with the lower teachers in the census only.

[b] Low officials are consistently included with other low white-collar and blue-collar workers.

[c] Includes artists, clergy, and the military.

students at the school, 19 percent were high officials and 16 percent were members of the liberal professions; industrialists and executive employees were represented at nearly 20 percent as well. The bourgeois index of 62 percent, the highest in the table, was thus a composite of all major elements within the upper middle class. Some of the highest educational opportunity ratios for institutions in Table 4.12 were those for the Ecole Polytechnique. Multiples of 48 for high officials and 27 for the liberal professions were followed by 14 for executive employees and 13 for industrialists. The overall ratio for the liberal and learned professions was 23; that for the upper middle class in general was 19. The comparable indicators for workers and farmers were well below 0.1. Progressiveness was not among the virtues of the school.

In 1961 as around 1900, the Ecole Polytechnique's most formidable rival was the Ecole Normale. This remarkable institution drew 47 percent of its students, more than the Ecole Polytechnique, from the liberal and learned professions. Its total percentage for the upper middle class was 53, the second highest in the table. Yet one would hardly describe Normale as a *bourgeois* stronghold. To begin with, some 24 percent of its students came from lower middle and working-class families; their fathers were teachers below the secondary level, artisans, petty employees, and workers. At the universities, these groups were represented at about 26 percent; at other famous *grandes écoles,* they reached only 17–21 percent. The secret of the Ecole Normale, of course, was the overwhelming share of its students who came from the families of university professors, secondary, and primary school teachers. Taken together, this academic contingent accounted for almost 50 percent of enrollments at the school. For secondary and university teachers alone, the opportunity ratio at Normale was 37, one of the highest that can be derived from the data in the table. As during the later nineteenth and early twentieth centuries, the Ecole Normale was a kind of antithesis to the Ecole Polytechnique, not because it was unusually progressive but because it was so thoroughly academic in its social makeup.

If one compares the distributions for Polytechnique and Normale in 1961 with their counterparts around the turn of the century, as a matter of fact, one finds no clear indication of an increase in progressiveness at either institution. Gone, to be sure, were the sons of *propriétaires* who had dominated the Ecole Polytechnique before 1880, and who were still represented at about 13 percent between 1880 and 1914. But their place had been taken by additional offspring of high officials and executive employees, not by pupils from humbler backgrounds. By 1961, the upper ranks of the white-collar hierarchy had acquired a commanding place at Polytechnique, as in the late industrial society generally. At the Ecole Normale, the major change since 1900—and even since 1940—had been a further increase in the representation of professors and teachers; the school had become even more specialized in its recruitment. Whether one compares the summed percentages for the liberal and learned professions or those for the upper middle class as a whole, one can detect no increase in progressiveness. If anything, the evidence points in the opposite direction. Much the same is true of what data we have for the Ecole Centrale and even for the ENAM.[17] Although changes in occupational categories were too great in all these cases to permit precise comparisons, the presumption is in favor of long-term stability in the distribution of educational opportunities at the *grandes écoles*.

A moment's reflection will dispose of any surprise that may be felt at this general conclusion. There was very little increase in enrollments at the smallest and most prestigious among French educational institutions. As the population grew, levels of inclusiveness at these schools either declined or remained essentially unchanged. At the German universities, with moderate increases in overall access rates, there were no appreciable improvements in access chances for the lower middle and lower classes. Why should we expect anything different from the *grandes écoles*? To be sure, they probably became more "meritocratic" in their way, as competition for the few available places grew more fierce. But in the white-collar society, there is such a thing as middle-class meritocracy, or even upper middle-class meritocracy, and the Ecole Polytechnique may serve as the perfect example.

The distributions for the other eminent *grandes écoles* in Table 4.12 gain in interest from the strong possibility that they characterize past as well as present patterns of recruitment. Noteworthy among the figures for "Sciences Po" and other Instituts d'Etudes Politiques is the relatively high percentage for farmers. Some of the Instituts are located in the provinces, which may explain their ability to attract the offspring of prosperous notables from the agricultural districts. Presumably, they shared the political ambitions that also drew an unusually large contingent of industrialists' sons to these schools. In any case, the Instituts d'Etudes Politiques were even more *integrally bourgeois* than the Ecole Polytechnique. High officials were numerous among the fathers of students, as one might expect, but so were members of the liberal professions, industrialists, and executive employees. The pertinent opportunity ratios were remarkably similar: 28 for high officials, 25 for the liberal professions, 20 for industrialists, and 15 for executive employees. These numbers do not suggest the exclusive concentration on the upper layers of the government bureaucracy that has sometimes been considered characteristic of these schools.

17. Compare above pp. 173–74.

The Ecole Centrale, on the other hand, surprises us with a very large proportion of students from the families of high officials and with startlingly low percentages for the offspring of industrialists, merchants, and shopkeepers. The opportunity ratio for the high civil service at Centrale was 40; as the second highest for the table, it ranked immediately behind the ratio for the same occupational group at Polytechnique, which was 48. The white-collar employees, especially the highest ranks among them, were more strongly represented at Centrale than at any other *grande école;* the opportunity ratio for executive employees was 20. Even so, the school can scarcely be regarded as a stronghold of the French business community. Its founders explicitly intended that it should provide technical expertise for the leaders of private industry in France, yet by 1961, its recruitment suggested a somewhat altered set of clients and functions. If one can argue from the social origins of a school's students to its output—as within limits one can—then Centrale must have changed course sometime between 1870 and 1960. Following the direction taken by Polytechnique, its older sister, it apparently began to develop ties to the technical civil service and to the public sector generally rather than confining its interests to private industry.

To find large percentages for the business community in French higher education, one must turn to the Ecoles Supérieures de Commerce. Roughly comparable to the German *Handelshochschulen,* these business schools were almost as specialized in their recruitment upon the industrial and commercial middle class as the Ecole Normale was upon academics and teachers. Among fathers of students at the Ecoles de Commerce, the industrialists were particularly numerous, with a distribution percentage of 12 and an opportunity ratio near 30. No less than 60 percent of enrollments at these institutions were the offspring of white-collar employees or of industrialists, merchants, shopkeepers, and artisans. That the higher ranks of the business hierarchy predominated over the middle and lower ones is clear from the *bourgeois* index for the schools, which was 46 percent. At Centrale and at "Sciences Po" as at Polytechnique, the high *bourgeois* representation was the effect of a remarkable alliance among all elements within the upper middle class; at the higher commercial schools it was a narrower and more sectional quantity.

As suggested earlier, however, the Ecoles de Commerce cannot be grouped with the traditionally eminent *grandes écoles* of the nineteenth century. They should be numbered, rather, among the younger professional and technical schools that have grown up since the late nineteenth century and are today considered *grandes écoles* in the extended sense of that term. Typical of the technical schools in this younger group are the Ecoles Nationales Supérieures d'Ingénieurs (ENSI) for such fields as chemistry, electricity, and aeronautics. Among fathers of students at a number of ENSI for chemistry in 1961, some 20 percent were members of the liberal and learned professions, 5 percent were industrialists, and 10 percent were executive employees [XIV]. The total of 35 percent for the upper middle class as a whole was a good deal lower than the *bourgeois* representation at the higher commerical schools, but it still exceeded 29 percent, the comparable percentage at the university faculties.

The most progressive recruitment patterns in French higher education around 1960 were those at the Ecoles Nationales d'Ingénieurs Arts et Métiers and those at the Ecoles Normales Supérieures of Saint-Cloud and Fontenay. In the distribution for Arts et Métiers in Table 4.12, the liberal and learned professions registered only 11 percent, and the total for the upper middle class was confined to 23 percent. Almost 30 percent of students' fathers were artisans, workers, and domestics, and another 15 percent were petty employees and teachers below the secondary level. The lower middle and working classes thus accounted for 44 percent of enrollments in these schools. This was less than 62 percent, their part of the census, but in the context of French higher education it was certainly a remarkable share. To understand the unusual role of the Ecoles d'Arts et Métiers in the French system, one has to think of them as the apex of a pyramid of postprimary vocational schooling that consistently functioned as an alternative to the academic secondary stream.

Even more intimately linked to primary education than Arts et Métiers were the high primary normal schools at Saint-Cloud and Fontenay. In France as in other European countries, one of the oldest educational paths upward out of the primary system led to the primary normal schools or comparable institutions, often by way of higher primary schools or courses. Future primary school teachers almost always came from the primary schools themselves, and many of them were of lower middle-class or lower-class origins. In France, this rather specialized educational ladder terminated in the Ecoles Normales Supérieures of Saint-Cloud and Fontenay, where instructors were trained to teach in the ordinary primary normal schools and sometimes in the higher primary system itself. Thus it is no surprise that the *bourgeois* index at Saint-Cloud and Fontenay was only 18 percent, lower than it was anywhere else in French higher education [XIV]. In fact, 9 of those 18 *bourgeois* percentage points were due to the sons of academics

and secondary teachers; neither the liberal professions nor the industrialists were represented at all. Some 14 percent of students' fathers
were themselves teachers below the secondary level, 10 percent were
lower-level white-collar employees, and 25 percent were artisans,
workers and domestics. In all, the lower middle and lower classes accounted for almost half the enrollments at these remarkable institutions.

One of the virtues of the comparative method is that it points up
national peculiarities as well as international trends in the evolution
of various social arrangements, including those in education. Table
4.13 provides the opportunity to contrast the French and German systems of university-level education, as of about 1960, in a summary
but comprehensive way. Four of the columns in the table represent
the defining constituents of the French system. The Ecole Polytechnique and the Ecole Normale stand for the traditionally most distinguished *grandes écoles*. Arts et Métiers marks the greatest degree of
progressiveness reached by some of the higher vocational/technical
schools, while the university faculties represent the numerically dominant center of the system. The first of the German columns pertains
to the whole spectrum of German university-level institutions, from the
universities to the technical institutes and academies. The distribution
for students of law comes fairly close to the pattern characteristic of
the universities, while the figures under *Technology* reflect conditions
at the technical institutes.

By the early 1960s, as we know, French university education was
roughly twice as inclusive as its German counterpart. At the faculties, it
was also somewhat more progressive. This is clear despite the awkward
differences in the grouping of occupations. The German percentages
for middle and lower officials include a number of men who would
have been reported as petty employees by French statisticians. The
line between German high and intermediate white-collar workers, too,
may have been drawn so as to enlarge the category of "entrepreneurs"
(industrialists and executive employees) at the expense of the "lower
employees." Yet these terminological inconsistencies are probably not
substantial enough to account for all the contrasts between the French
and German distributions, even in the categories that are most directly
affected. Moreover, there appear to be no significant national variations
in the definition of the liberal and learned professions on the one hand
and of the workers and domestics on the other. It therefore seems fair
to conclude that university recruitment was in fact moderately more
progressive in France than in Germany around 1960.

The German distribution for technology came closest to the French
university faculties in progressiveness, while the German law faculties

Table 4.13
Social Origins of French and German
University-Level Students, 1961–1963
(Percentages by Column)

Father's Occupation	France				Germany		
	Poly-technique	Nor-male Sup.	Arts et Mé-tiers	Uni-ver-sity	All Univ. level	Law only	Tech-nology only
Liberal professions	16	7	3	10	14	18	11
High officials	19	7	6	7	9	16	8
Secondary and university teachers	8	33	2	4	6	5	4
Liberal and learned professions	43	47	11	20	29	39	23
Lower teachers	9	14	5	5	5 }		
Middle officials (and military)a	3	5	6	7	13 }	17	17
Agriculture	1	1	6	7	4	3	3
Rentiers	1	4	5	8	–	–	–
Industrialists	5	2	4	3	} 23	22	28
Executive employeesb	14	4	8	6			
Merchants Shopkeepers }	6	5	6	9	} 8	6	9
Artisans	2	2	9	4			
Lower employeesc	11	12	18	13	9	7	10
Workersc (domestics)	2	3	19	9	6	4	6
Others (unknown)	3	1	3	7	5	4	3

From Tables 2.10, 4.11, and 4.12. The German columns report on all university-level institutions and on students of law and of technology within all institutions.

a For Germany, all "middle and lower officials" other than blue-collar workers are included under 'Middle Officials,' and so is military personnel.

b May be somewhat more inclusively defined for Germany than for France.

c For France, lower officials are grouped with lower white-collar employees and blue-collar workers.

were almost as thoroughly upper middle-class in character as the Ecole Polytechnique. The Ecoles d'Arts et Métiers had no real counterparts in the German system, except possibly among the advanced *Fachschulen,* which are fairly recent foundations and little studied as yet.[18] A more general point to be made about the columns in Table 4.13,

18. The reference is to the *Fachschulen* and the (more recently so called?) *Fachhochschulen.* I found little information about them for the period before 1960, perhaps because they are recent foundations, or perhaps because they were too far from my main line of research.

however, is that the German universities took up an intermediate place between the French faculties and the more famous *grandes écoles* in the opportunities they offered to students from the lower middle and lower classes.

The French and German systems differed, too, in their overall structure, not just in levels of progressiveness. In Germany, the secondary schools and universities were deeply segmented and in a partly horizontal way. The divide between the classical and the modern curriculum, between general education and technical training, retained its significance well into the twentieth century, penetrating every level of the educational pyramid. As late as the 1960s, the distributions for all university-level institutions and for students of technology revealed the remnants of a contrast that was once much greater: the percentages for the liberal and learned professions (Table 4.13) were 29 and 23 for all university-level and technology, respectively; those for industrialists and executive employees were almost exactly reversed, 23 and 28 percent respectively. Obviously, what we are dealing with here is only an echo, a memory that is rapidly fading in the late industrial context. Yet the pattern it recalls was once characteristic of the German educational system in its entirety, and therein lies its significance.

In French education, segmentation took a somewhat different form. At the secondary level, the bifurcation introduced with Duruy's special secondary stream in the 1860s was certainly comparable to the opposition of the classical and the modern schools in Germany; the realm of practicality was consciously separated from the world of humane learning. Yet the quick transformation of "special" into "modern" secondary education tended both to weaken the antithesis and to change its meaning. On the one hand, some of the ablest students at the classical *lycées* took courses in theoretical and applied mathematics to prepare for the Ecole Polytechnique and for other eminent *grandes écoles* with a scientific orientation. On the other hand, the modern secondary program and the newer baccalaureate options soon became quite as general and academic as their older competitors, training students for white-collar positions, not for artisanal and other skilled manual work. As a result, the social difference between the two major secondary tracks became predominantly a matter of social altitude. Segmentation in French secondary education, on the whole, was uncomplicated and socially vertical, and so it remained even after the conversion of the higher primary into the modern secondary program in 1941.

What was true of French secondary schools was true of the French university faculties as well. They differed in their social makeup, but the contrasts were comparatively mild and rarely horizontal in any significant sense, at least from 1939 on. It is as if the potential for segmentation had been pushed out of the broad center of French university-level education to the extremes in the *grandes écoles* and related institutions. For those of the higher schools that stood closest to the progressive end of the spectrum, one might be able to find counterparts among the German academies—this applies to the Ecoles de Commerce, to some of the newer engineering schools, to the Ecoles d'Arts et Métiers, and perhaps even to the Ecoles Normales Supérieures at Saint-Cloud and Fontenay.[19]

What of the other end of the scale, the famous *grandes écoles* of the nineteenth century? Surely their separation from the mainstream of French higher education was as extreme an instance of tracking as anything to be found in Germany? The answer is yes—and no. Certainly if one thinks only of socially vertical segmentation, the Ecole Polytechnique, the Instituts d'Etudes Politiques, and the Ecole Centrale are not likely to be outdone in the contemporary world. Yet the socially horizontal differences among these institutions, or between them and the universities, are scarcely significant. On the contrary, we have been struck with the degree to which they resembled each other in their social makeup. All were integrally *bourgeois* in the sense that they brought together the several sectors of the upper middle class, including the entrepreneurial-technical elite. The Ecole Polytechnique and the Ecole Centrale, after all, were technical institutions, and they stood at the very apex of the hierarchy of academic and social prestige in French education. This in itself was an extraordinarily sharp contrast with the German pattern.

The special position of some of the most famous *grandes écoles* was thus perfectly suited to emphasize the social divide between a small *bourgeois* elite and the bulk of the middle and lower middle classes, a divide that ran all through the French educational system from the nineteenth century on. It could help to define and to perpetuate the peculiar plentitude of social advantages that came together in the French *bourgeoisie*. The Ecole Polytechnique has stood for wealth that was enhanced by an accredited grounding in the traditional culture, by technical expertise, by a quasi-aristocratic style of life, and by easy access to the upper ranks of the military and of public administration. Here was a conjunction of status characteristics that could

19. The German Pedagogical Academies may in some ways be comparable to the Ecoles Normales Supérieures at Saint-Cloud and Fontenay, except that the French schools did not function as ordinary primary normal schools.

scarcely fail to enrich—and thus to legitimate—distinctions based on class alone. What the unique character of the eminent *grandes écoles* could not do, however, is equally obvious. It could not sustain the conflict between technological-industrial "civilization" and humanistic "culture" that so profoundly affected German social and cultural life from the nineteenth century to the advent of National Socialism.[20]

The great exception to the generalizations of the last few paragraphs, of course, was the Ecole Normale. As distinguished as any of the *grandes écoles* and at least as unusual in its recruitment, it was the great rival of the Ecole Polytechnique. The two schools differed sharply in their social composition, and the difference could be considered horizontal in part. Here, surely, was an antithesis as great as any in Germany. Indeed, there was a certain similarity of recruitment between the Ecole Normale and the German universities during the nineteenth century. The competition between the ultra-academic Ecole Normale and the most *bourgeois* among the *grandes écoles* might well be interpreted as a variation upon the contrasts typical of German higher education.

Yet the rivalry between Polytechnique and Normale was played out at an exceedingly rarified level; it involved two small schools at the apex of the French educational pyramid. In Germany, the separation between the two main curricular tracks ran through the entire system, from the secondary schools on up to the university level. In France, the antithesis was between the academic and the integral *bourgeois;* in Germany, it opposed humanistic cultivation to the world of practicality, commerce, and technology. Different lines of demarcation in the two countries led to subtle but important disssimilarities in the clustering of social roles and concepts. As the reader was warned at the outset, this study is motivated largely by an interest in social meanings—and by cross-national differences among them. These chapters are meant to establish a framework in which such meanings can be more thoroughly studied and, indeed, understood.

20. Ringer, *Decline of the German Mandarins.*

5. English and American Comparisons

English Institutions

Compared to Germany and France, England (with Wales) has been both slow and unsystematic in developing a national system of education.[1] Until 1870, even primary education was either entirely private or in the hands of religious or philanthropic voluntary associations. While the government gave some support to voluntary schools after 1833, it did not attempt to exercise direct control at the local level until 1870. The Education Act of 1870 called for the institution of school boards, which had the option of supplementing the voluntary system with board schools financed by local taxes and government grants. With the Education Act of 1902, the old boards were replaced by Local Education Authorities (L.E.A.'s), which have remained the basic units of English educational administration until the present day. In each of 146 counties and boroughs, the L.E.A. is charged with the supervision of education. Both voluntary and public schools (successively called board, county, and maintained schools) are financed and inspected by the L.E.A.'s, though voluntary schools have retained a degree of financial and administrative antonomy.

Before the Education Act of 1902, England had no public system of secondary education at all. Instead, a variety of independent presecondary and secondary schools supported themselves primarily from endowments and fees. All of these institutions were of the grammar

1. Basic introductions to English education are Barnard, *A Short History;* Banks, *Parity and Prestige;* Cotgrove, *Technical Education;* Mountford, *British Universities.* Sampson, *Anatomy of Britain,* contains a useful sketch of the postwar system at work. Halsey et al., *Education, Economy and Society,* is an excellent topical reader with a contemporary emphasis.

school type, with a predominantly classical curriculum. Since 1902, grammar and other schools maintained by the L.E.A.'s have made up a rapidly growing sector of English secondary education. Even so, the independent institutions of the nineteenth century have survived and retain much of their special distinction. The English universities too are essentially independent institutions, though most of their income nowadays comes ultimately from the Exchequer.

Central administrative agencies in the whole field of education have grown very slowly in England. A Science and Art Department of the Board of Trade was created in 1853, a separate Education Department in 1856. In 1899, a national Board of Education combined all supervisory authority over primary, secondary, and technical instruction. A University Grants Committee (U.G.C.) was established in 1919. Since 1944, a Ministry (or Department) of Education and Science has consolidated some previously dispersed authority. It now acts as a central overseer for all types of primary and secondary schools: it implements all educational legislation; it distributes funds to the L.E.A.'s and to some individual institutions; and it inspects all schools, including the independent ones. Even so, the U.G.C. has retained a separate role, outside the Department of Education. Though it inspects the universities and distributes vast sums, it really serves as a kind of shield between the universities and the Treasury. Late and incomplete centralization has thus been a notable characteristic of the English system. Its correlate has been a slow and piecemeal approach to reform, which has typically been initiated by specially appointed committees rather than by a permanent bureaucracy.

All the more remarkable is the fact that the institutional divide between primary and secondary education was at least as marked in England as on the Continent during the nineteenth century. Primary education was not made compulsory at the national level until the 1890s. The school leaving age, first set at 11 in 1893, was raised to 12 in 1899. From 1891 on, a special provision insured instruction for children of needy families, but fees were not entirely abolished even at the primary level until 1918. As late as 1900, there was virtually no connection between primary and secondary education. Primary schools, whether voluntary or not, provided the rudiments of literacy and arithmetic between about age 6 and 12. Once a youngster had completed a course of primary schooling, there was little opportunity for further study. Transfers to secondary schools were rare, since primary pupils were academically unprepared for the secondary curriculum.

The private secondary system of the early nineteenth century was made up of "public" schools, endowed grammar schools, and proprietary schools. The public schools were generally church-affiliated establishments with ancient ("public") charters and with a variety of endowed scholarships available under founders' deeds. Most of them were boarding schools for boys aged 13 or 14 to 18 or 19. Many of the endowed grammar schools differed from the public schools only in being more recent foundations, though some were day schools or took in pupils at age 11 or 13. Proprietary schools, as the name implies, were simply private business ventures; they supported themselves exclusively from students' fees. They were free of the statutory limitations that bound many public and endowed grammer schools, both in their curriculum and in their religious affiliation. There is no doubt that the public schools outranked the others in prestige. This was especially true of the Ancient Nine: Eton, Westminster, Winchester, Charterhouse, St. Paul's, Merchant Taylor's, Harrow, Rugby, and Shrewsbury.

The public and endowed grammar schools were in considerable difficulties during the early nineteenth century. Endowments had lost value through inflation and ·neglect, while fees were rising in compensation. Enrollments had apparently been declining during the eighteenth century. There were charges of corruption and lack of effective teaching, of idleness and immorality among students. Dissenters objected to the exclusive Anglicanism of most of the schools, utilitarian reformers to the old classical syllabus, which was taught mechanically if at all. In many cases, founders' deeds prevented the introduction of nonclassical subjects. There were quarrels over the use of endowed scholarships, most of which had originally been intended for poor boys from the vicinity of the school who proposed to enter clerical careers. Neither headmasters nor middle-class reformers were interested in these provisions, which prevented the nation-wide recruitment of pupils on merit principles while burdening impoverished foundations with expensive obligations to the local poor.

One response to the discredit into which the schools had fallen was the kind of pedagogical reform exemplified by the work of Thomas Arnold at Rugby after 1828. Without abandoning the classical curriculum, he encouraged students to approach it in an active and comprehensive spirit. He was also interested in an undogmatic sort of religious instruction and in the formation of moral character. As the public schools gained in reputation, there was some easing of restrictions upon the teaching of nonclassical subjects, though these could generally be provided only in exchange for additional fees.

In 1861, a Royal Commission under Lord Clarendon examined conditions at the Ancient Nine or (thereafter so-called) Clarendon schools. In 1868, a Schools Inquiry Commission under Lord Taunton reported on eight hundred endowed grammar and one hundred twenty-two proprietary schools. The results were embodied in the Public Schools Act of 1868 and the Endowed Schools Act of 1869. In the discussions of the secondary curriculum during the 1860s, continental models played a certain role; they were introduced by Matthew Arnold's reports. Something like the German pattern of *Gymnasium, Realgymnasium,* and *Realschule* appeared in the Taunton Commission's tripartite scheme: three secondary schools with leaving ages of 18–19, 16, and 14 respectively, classical subjects being progressively replaced by practically oriented subjects in the latter two. The shortest and least academic program was considered suitable for the sons of small farmers, tradesmen, and substantial artisans, and the whole tripartite scheme was thought to correspond "roughly, but by no means exactly, to the gradations of society."[2]

The reforms actually initiated in 1868 and 1869, however, dealt less with curriculum than with matters of governance and with endowments. The classical curriculum remained predominant in all the schools, though somewhat less inflexibly at proprietary than at endowed institutions. Fees continued to be charged; they were generally highest at public and lowest at proprietary schools. Scholarship endowments were freed of many statutory and local restrictions. This meant that a small number of "free places" could be awarded on merit principles in nationwide competition. Since "merit" was hard to attain without the proper presecondary schooling, including Latin, however, the "educational ladder" invoked by the Taunton Commission was not likely to carry more than a few pupils up from the world of the ordinary primary schools.

In 1869, many of the public and more distinguished endowed grammar schools drew together in the Headmasters' Conference. Its aim was a certain amount of self-regulation and the prevention of further state intervention. Membership in the Headmasters' Conference came to signify a kind of accreditation. The survival of the Conference to the present day may be taken to symbolize the primacy of the private sector in English secondary schooling, which was not challenged at all until 1902. The English middle classes of the nineteenth century chose not to create educational institutions and programs of their own. The classically oriented public school remained the model for all its less prestigious successors. Mathematics traditionally held a place in its curriculum, and some room was made for paid electives in modern subjects after 1840 and again after 1869. Still, despite the tripartite

2. Barnard, *A Short History*, p.130.

conception of the Taunton Commission, no rival curricular streams or tracks arose at the secondary level. In place of the curricular and social segmentation of Germany and France, the English secondary system knew only gradations of academic and social standing on a continuum that was dominated by the Ancient Nine. The traditional learning of gentlemen and clergymen was transmitted downward along this continuum to a middle class in need of social grace.

What the Ancient Nine were to the English secondary system, Oxford and Cambridge were to university-level education. The only two universities in existence in England and Wales until 1836, they traced their foundations to the Middle Ages. Both were made up of colleges that functioned as autonomous academic and residential units. The colleges had their own statutes and endowments, admissions procedures, headmasters and fellows. At least in theory, the colleges and their teaching fellows, tutors, or dons were responsible for most of what teaching was done.

Like the public and endowed grammar schools, "Oxbridge" suffered a period of decline that extended from the later seventeenth to the early nineteenth century. Traditionally, the two ancient universities had not only given a general education to sons of the aristocracy and gentry; they had also prepared less well-to-do youths for the clerical professions, including that of schoolmaster. As a matter of fact, the colleges—and their fellowships—had been thoroughly integrated into the network of church livings. After the English Reformation and Revolution, the gentry had taken a gradually increasing interest in that network, which helped them provide for their younger sons. In any case, an alliance between the gentry and the Anglican church defined the English universities of the eighteenth and early nineteenth centuries. Catholics and dissenters were excluded. Though limited to bachelors, college fellowships tended to become sinecures that could be held for life and in absentia. Many endowments had declined in value. At the same time, social conventions demanded expensive forms of dissipation from upperclass students who rarely took advantage of what little teaching was offered.

Amid lively public debate and with the aid of several Royal Commissions, a series of reforms were brought about at Oxford and Cambridge between the early 1850s and the late 1870s. Catholics and dissenters were admitted to matriculation and to the B.A. in the mid-1850s and to higher degrees in 1871. Endowments were consolidated and freed of various founders' restrictions. Absenteeism and life tenure among college fellows were ended, their teaching duties were specified, and they were allowed to marry. A new, relatively well-paid and committed type of college don now emerged. At the same time, there was a structural shift from collegiate to university-wide organization. From the 1850s on, students could live outside the colleges, in town. Collegiate resources were used to subsidize a growing number of intercollegiate lectures and university-wide professorships. The new university chairs were meant to encourage specialized and innovative research, rather than the passing on of standard curricula by unspecialized tutors. New programs in the natural sciences were introduced at both universities about midcentury.[3]

Even so, the emphasis at Oxford and Cambridge continued to be on classical and literary studies, plus mathematics at Cambridge. The tutorial system and the generalist don, too, retained a special position at the ancient English universities, despite the advent of the university lecture and of specialized research. Apart from theology, no professional studies ever had or found a place at Oxford or Cambridge. One might read law at Oxford, but one would have to finish one's training at the Inns of Court. Medical education was available in Scotland or else at one of the teaching hospitals of London.

At Oxford and Cambridge, two three-year programs led to the B.A. One terminated in a "Pass," the other in an "Honours" degree. Honours degrees were originally intended for exceptional students, and they remained in the minority until 1914. Today, however, Oxford and Cambridge are almost entirely "Honours" institutions, and other English universities are moving in the same direction. The most important advanced degree of the nineteenth century was the M.A. It was generally earned two years after the B.A., but it was something of a formality for holders of Honours degrees from Oxford or Cambridge. There was in England no such firm connection between university study and professional accreditation via state examinations as on the Continent. Even so, the B.A. became something like a prerequisite for entry into the higher civil service, the clergy, and secondary teaching. Most grammar school teachers held a B.A., while university professors generally had the M.A. in addition. Of course, Honours degrees provided especially easy access to these professions. When the English system of higher civil service examinations was expanded and formal-

3. At Oxford in 1850, new honors schools were created in law and modern history and in natural science; these joined the classically oriented school of *literae humaniores* or "Greats," which had been created about 1800. At Cambridge in 1851, a new natural sciences tripos was added to the triposes that existed in mathematics since 1747 and in classics since 1824.

ized in 1870, the questions were quite obviously patterned after Oxbridge Honours curricula.[4]

Nevertheless, the hegemony of Oxford and Cambridge in English
university-level education did not go entirely unchallenged even during the eighteenth and early nineteenth centuries. Among the Scottish
universities, Edinburgh and Glasgow attracted a number of English
students, especially middle-class dissenters. Diverse and progressive
in their recruitment as well as in their curriculum, the Scottish universities were influential centers of learning during the eighteenth century. Unlike Oxford and Cambridge, they were open to the whole
range of Enlightenment science, philosophy, and social thought. In
eighteenth-century England, privately funded dissenting academies
were similarly associated with religious nonconformism and with the
advanced intellectual currents of the day. Unfortunately, relatively
little is known about the dissenting academies. They were apparently
in decline by the early nineteenth century.

A more immediate challenge to Oxford and Cambridge during the
nineteenth century was the foundation of University College, London,
in 1826. Initially called London University, this was a strictly private
venture; it was supported by a group of prominent liberals as an alternative to the religious and specifically Anglican orthodoxy of Oxbridge.
Fees were kept much lower than at the established universities, so
that opportunities might be provided for students from the middle
and lower middle classes. The curricular emphasis was on modern and
scientific studies, especially on medicine. So threatening was this "godless institution" to good Anglicans and conservatives that they created
King's College to be its rival in 1829. Since neither of the new colleges
was empowered to offer degrees, the University of London was chartered in 1836, strictly as an examining and degree-granting agency for
University College, King's College, and other "approved" institutions.
The only other new university founded before the 1880s was Durham,
chartered in 1837 but a marginal quantity until late in the century.[5]

All the more important was the availability of the University of
London's nonmatriculant or "external" degrees. Beginning in 1858, they
could be awarded to anyone who passed the appropriate examination,
regardless of how he prepared for it. Under the umbrella provided by
this arrangement, a whole cluster of "university colleges" sprang up
during the later nineteenth and early twentieth centuries. Not being

4. Mountford, *British Universities,* p.61.
5. Durham had briefly had a university in the seventeenth century. Its nineteenth century heir was, like King's College, founded partly in reaction against
the "godless institution."

chartered to award degrees themselves, these institutions prepared their students for London examinations. Some of the new university colleges traced their origins to the so-called mechanics institutes, which had flourished from the mid-1820s to the 1850s. These had initially provided vocationally oriented evening classes for artisans; but their curriculum had become gradually more general, and their clients had eventually been drawn more from the lower middle than from the working class. Others among the new university colleges created after 1850 owed their existence to the wealth, the practical outlook, and the civic pride of middle-class entrepreneurs in the new manufacturing cities. The obvious example is Owen's College, Manchester, the first of the university colleges. It opened in 1851, though at first as a very small and predominately part-time institution.

In 1878, women were admitted to the examinations for external degrees at London. This was a significant step forward for the few small women's colleges in existence at that time. In 1881, female students from colleges affiliated with Cambridge were permitted to take the "tripos" examinations there, though they could not earn degrees. It was not until 1920 that women were admitted as ordinary students at Oxford. In England as in France and Germany, the arrival of women in higher education thus took place in stages between 1880 and 1920. The almost exactly simultaneous unrolling of this revolutionary process in three otherwise highly distinctive societies has yet to be fully explained. In England, the University of London clearly played a crucial role.

In 1898, London was given the right to admit students of its own, even while continuing to examine for external degrees. By that time, the University had already become a massive complex of twenty-four loosely affiliated institutions founded at various times and not all located in London. In addition to University College and King's College, there was the Royal College of Science, itself the heir of the Royal College of Mines and the initially very modest Royal College of Chemistry (1845). There were the great teaching hospitals, the London School of Economics (1895), a number of women's colleges, the Central Technical College of the City and Guilds Institute in South Kensington (1884), and others. In 1907, the Royal College of Science, the Central Technical College, and other parts of the South Kensington complex became the Imperial College of Science and Technology, which remained a constituent of the University of London. As some of the dates begin to suggest, growth was particularly vigorous at the University of London from the 1880s to the First World War. The same period, indeed, saw the establishment of a whole series of "provincial," "civic" (now "older civic"), or "red brick" universities, most of them former university colleges. Beginning in 1889, the government channelled financial and moral support to these new foundations via the Committee to University Colleges in Great Britain, the forerunner of the University Grants Committee. Manchester, Birmingham, Liverpool, Leeds, Sheffield, and Bristol were among the institutions chartered between 1880 and 1909. Thereafter, with the exception of Reading (1926), no additional universities were founded until after the Second World War.

In England as in France and Germany, the high industrial phase in the history of education was characterized by an increased emphasis upon scientific, technical, and vocational education, though the dating of this phase cannot be made as precise for England as for the continental counties. The international exhibitions of 1851, 1867, and 1878 are generally credited with having raised a growing English fear of foreign industrial competition, a fear that inspired the usual commissions of inquiry along with increasing government intervention in behalf of "technical instruction."

Just what this technical instruction would consist of was not clear. In connection with the reforms at Oxford and Cambridge during the 1850s, both universities introduced honors programs in the natural sciences. Especially the natural sciences tripos at Cambridge helped to bring about a minor renaissance of research in pure science.[6] But this had little to do with technical instruction. On the other hand, it was generally agreed that industrial or artisanal techniques could not and should not be taught directly in school. It was feared that manufacturing secrets might be lost, and on-the-job training was firmly proclaimed to be best in any case. It thus became established doctrine that technical instruction would convey the scientific principles behind various industrial techniques, without entering into the specifics of their application.[7] What was wanted, in other words, was a rudimentary education in pure science that was applicable but not applied.

The Science and Art Department, created in the wake of the 1851 exposition, began in 1859 to support the teaching of science and arts. Payment was "by results," that is, in specified amounts per pupil. Though the program was intended for "the industrial classes," secondary schools were eligible for grants in support of just about any modern subjects they taught. At a more popular level, evening classes began

6. Ashby, *Technology and the Academics;* MacLeod, "Resources of Science," for this and related subjects.
7. Musgrave, "Definition of Technical Education"; Musgrave, "Constant Factors."

to be offered by a variety of agencies, though little real headway could be made until after the Education Act of 1870.

The fact is that progress in primary education and the active presence of the school boards were necessary conditions for the development of vocational and technical schooling. Thus vigorous expansion in this sector did not take place until the 1870s and 80s. The City and Guilds of London Institute began to offer evening classes in 1877, and the London school board followed suit in 1882. In the same year, Quintin Hogg's Polytechnic opened as the first of a dozen similar institutions founded by 1905. Some of these polytechnics traced their origins to mechanics' institutes. They gave day as well as evening courses, though much of their instruction was necessarily part-time. After the Technical Instruction Act of 1889, the boards were authorized to aid technical education from local taxes, and in 1890, "whiskey money" became available for the same purpose. As of 1905, most of the technical instruction that took place was part-time and essentially prevocational in character, though a more advanced standard was attained in such technical colleges as the Finsbury Technical College (1883) and the Central Technical College in South Kensington (1884). At the university level, the new red brick institutions were undoubtedly more hospitable to modern and technical subjects than Oxford and Cambridge.

Finally, a kind of technical instruction came to be offered in some of the higher primary institutions and classes that were created by the school boards after 1870. These were the forerunners of the present-day secondary "modern" and "technical" schools. Venturesome boards began during the 1870s and 80s to earn grants from the Science and Art Department by offering instruction beyond the age and level of the normal primary schools in so-called higher grade board schools or "higher tops." Cousins to these higher primary institutions were the "organized science schools," later "junior technical schools," that were sometimes affiliated with the new technical colleges. The Technical Instruction Act of 1889 called for secondary schools of the "modern" type, and that is just what the higher grade schools and similar institutions were becoming by the turn of the century.

The real watershed in the history of English secondary schooling, however, was the Education Act of 1902. It created a public system of secondary education, for it empowered the L.E.A.'s to aid and even to establish secondary schools. Particularly in conjunction with the "free place" regulation of 1907, the Act of 1902 thoroughly transformed the English system. To begin with, there was further progress in higher primary education. The school leaving age was gradually raised from

12 in 1889 to 14 in 1918. "Senior elementary classes" were created to provide general terminal education for students over 11 years of age. The so-called selective central schools were among other higher primary institutions that prospered during the decades immediately preceding and following the First World War. The junior technical schools gained in reputation, offering a two to four-year course for students entering at the age of 13 or 14. Young people in increasing numbers attended higher primary, junior technical, and even grammar schools in preparation for middle-level clerical and related occupations, rather than for university study.

The L.E.A.'s did more than establish new grammar schools of their own; they also gave aid from taxes to existing endowed or proprietary grammar schools. In return, these institutions were obliged to reserve at least a quarter of their places for "free students" selected by the L.E.A.'s on the basis of examinations. Schools that agreed to these arrangements were gradually absorbed into the state system. More and more completely controlled by the L.E.A.'s, they eventually became indistinguishable from other maintained schools. After 1900, the government also began to extend aid directly to selected secondary schools. In 1926, government-aided grammar schools were given the option of being administered by the L.E.A.'s, like maintained schools, or of remaining outside L.E.A. control and receiving direct grants from the central government. About one-quarter of the institutions involved took the direct grant option, which still obliged them to reserve one-quarter of their places for scholarship students. Today, "direct grant" grammar schools enjoy many of the privileges of independence. They are members of the Headmasters' Conference, and their curriculum is geared for university entrance.

In England as in France and Germany during the nineteenth century, primary teachers were not educated at the secondary schools. They went straight from the elementary schools to a five-year apprenticeship as student teachers, which might or might not be followed by a couple of years at a training college. This too was changed after 1902. Increasingly, future primary teachers attended secondary schools as scholarship students. They then transferred immediately to a training college, where they completed their professional education.

Public support for secondary education continued to mount during the interwar period, at least until the financial crisis of the early 1930s. Free places at the maintained and direct grant grammar schools rose from 93 thousand in 1920 to 178 thousand in 1931, or from about 30 percent to 43 percent of all places.[8] Unfortunately, the financial diffi-

8. Vaizey, *Costs of Education*, p.31.

culties of the 1930s led to a narrowing of the opportunities thus provided. Many free places were replaced by "special places," in which only a portion of the school costs were remitted. This tended to favor lower middle-class over working-class pupils.[9]

At the university level also, state expenditures rose markedly during the 1920s. In 1925, Oxford and Cambridge became eligible for awards from the University Grants Committee. Government inspection came with government aid. Yet the English universities have maintained their independent status; no standardized or controlled university system has evolved. With the exception of Reading (1926), no new universities were founded between the wars, but the older civic universities continued to grow in importance and size. In 1919, English universities began to offer the doctorate, partly to draw American and other foreign graduate students away from the Continent. Requirements for the English D. phil. include a good Honours B.A. or its equivalent, two or more years of advanced study, and a thesis involving original research. Because they are not prerequisites for university teaching, English doctorates have not been taken as frequently as their continental counterparts, but their number has considerably increased in the last fifty years.

The most important innovations in English education between the wars, undoubtedly, were the new conceptions of secondary education that were advanced. A little like the continental spokesmen of the common school, English Labourites had been urging "secondary education for all" since the turn of the century. As this idea became more widely accepted during the 1920s, it underwent some modification. The Hadow Report of 1926 projected a dual scheme of grammar and modern secondary schools above a foundation of common primary schooling to age 11. Partly because of the success of the junior technical schools, the Spence Committee in 1939 proposed a tripartite scheme instead. This would include a "technical high school," heir to the junior technical school, along with the grammar and modern branches. The Norwood Committee, appointed two years later, supported this project with the convenient discovery that three types of mind were represented among pupils. In addition to those "interested in learning for its own sake," there were potential clients for the technical schools with "interests and abilities" in "applied science or applied art." Finally, for the modern stream, there were youths who "deal more easily with concrete things than with ideas."[10] England had always known only one secondary curriculum, within which social differences were

9. Floud, ed., *Social Class.*
10. Banks, *Parity and Prestige,* p.132.

marked by gradations of expense and prestige. But this changed as "secondary education for all" brought with it a tripartite segmentation of the secondary system.

The plans developed during the interwar period specifically called for an end to "primary" schooling at age 11. At that point all students were to take a series of examinations entitled the eleven-plus, which would determine the type of their secondary education. The brightest pupils would proceed to a grammar school, which traditionally began at age 11. The rest of the students were to attend a "modern school," the successor to the old senior elementary classes and other higher primary institutions. Some, at age 13, would be encouraged to transfer to a technical or vocational school. On September 1, 1939, the legal school leaving age was to be raised to 15.

The war, following upon the depression, kept many of these plans in the blueprint stage. Although by 1939 some 80 percent of senior elementary classes had been reorganized into modern secondary schools, the integration of primary and secondary education was not actually achieved until 1944. The Education Act of 1944 set the leaving age at 15, called for universal free primary and secondary education, and reorganized the whole educational administration in systematic fashion. Above all, the Act provided for machinery and funds to execute these plans. The eleven-plus became compulsory for all students in the public sector. Depending upon their scores on this inevitably traumatic examination, students were channelled to grammar, technical, or modern schools.

The technical schools outranked the modern schools in prestige. In theory, they were academic secondary institutions, equal cousins of the grammar schools. Entrance was set at age 11, which eliminated the previous two-year gap between the primary and junior technical schools. For the first two years of study, a student in a technical school followed the same curriculum as his contemporaries in the grammar school. At age 13, specialized vocational training began. The technical schools were no longer terminal institutions; many of their students went on to university-level technical study. In practice they attracted not only pupils interested in the sciences and technology, but also those unable to gain entrance to a grammar school.

Obviously, the tripartite secondary system had its limitations. Theoretically, students could transfer from one type of secondary school to another at age 13. But this happened infrequently. To combat the rigidities of the tripartite system, so-called bilateral, multistream, and comprehensive schools were created. These provided two or all three types of secondary education, either in separate programs within the same school or in partly or wholly mixed curricular divisions and classes. The tripartite approach to secondary schooling was thus modified to some degree; but it survived in its essentials well beyond the period covered in this study. It was not until the late 1960s and early 70s that the eleven-plus was abolished and the ideal of the common school extended, in steps, to most of English public secondary education.

During the decades after the Second World War, something like a national testing system for secondary students came to be organized in England. The first standardized examinations, the School Certificate and the Higher School Certificate, were created in 1918. These two tests were designed as entrance examinations for universities. In 1950, they were replaced with a greatly expanded set of examinations called the General Certificate of Education (G.C.E.). Offered in some forty-three subjects, the G.C.E. became one of the main prerequisites for university admission. Taken by nearly all students in schools of the grammar type, it was offered at three levels: ordinary, advanced, and advanced with scholarship. To be admitted to a university, a student had to receive five or six certificates, at least two of them at the advanced level. The ordinary-level examinations were usually taken at age 16. Then, after an additional year or two of specialized study at a grammar school, students could attempt the advanced-level tests. Aside from their use for university admission, G.C.E. scores were also considered in applications for various types of white-collar employment. In 1965, the Certificate of Secondary Education (C.S.E.) was specifically established for students not planning university study. Designed to be comparable to the G.C.E.—the highest pass of the C.S.E. is equivalent to the ordinary level pass of the G.C.E.—it was taken chiefly by graduates of secondary technical and modern schools and became a prerequisite for access to certain specialized occupations and nonuniversity forms of further education.

In the two decades after the Second World War, massive changes also took place in English higher education. Five university colleges were raised to university status: Nottingham, Southampton, Hull, Exeter, and Leicester. Seven new universities were established: Sussex, York, East Anglia, Lancaster, Essex, Kent, and Warwick. In addition to these "younger civic universities," a number of so-called Colleges of Advanced Technology (C.A.T.s) were singled out during the mid-1950s from among existing technical colleges and other L.E.A.-maintained institutions of full and part-time technical and further education. The C.A.T.'s were directed to concentrate exclusively upon advanced and specialized technological education and research. They were not intended to supersede the older technical institutions generally, but rather to be the most advanced and prestigious centers in their field. A new degree, the Diploma of Technology, has been created for the C.A.T.s, as well as for some of the regional technical colleges, as an equivalent to the university Honours degree. Since 1963, however, the C.A.T.s have been obtaining university status and the right to grant regular degrees. Their rapid development exemplifies the shift toward science and technology in university study, as well as the generally high rate of change in English education since 1945.

English Enrollments

Little systematic evidence on English secondary enrollments before 1960 is available at all; what there is has been collected in Table 5.1. The estimated percentages of indicative age groups in full-time attendance as of 1870, 1902, 1938, and 1962 are from the Robbins Report. The figure of 40 percent for ten-year-olds in 1870 describes the sorry state of English primary education on the eve of the Education Act of 1870. The estimates of 2 percent for fourteen-year-olds and 1 percent for seventeen-year-olds in 1870 pertain to the upper grades of endowed and proprietary grammar schools. If they are correct, then British secondary education around 1870 was practically as inclusive as its counterparts in France and Germany.

The figures for 1900–1902 are even more surprising, and this time the Robbins Report is backed up by the results of a retrospective survey conducted among British adults in 1949. Both sets of data indicate that the private English secondary system of 1900 exceeded the continental systems in enrollments per age group, at least at the base, among students who reached the grammar schools at all. Of course the French and German secondary pyramids were also wider at the level of entry than at the altitude of "mean" enrollments. Still, beginning pupils in French and German secondary schools around 1900 were never more than 4–6 percent of their age group, which is one-third to one-half the access percentage for English grammar and boarding schools at that time.

There is only one likely explanation for these remarkable results. The ordinary English grammar schools of the decades around 1900 must have taken over some of the functions served by the continental primary and higher primary schools. Given a relatively undeveloped primary system, and despite the appearance of higher board schools and senior elementary classes during the late nineteenth century, many English youngsters must have entered ordinary grammar schools without intending to complete the course or to proceed to a university.

Table 5.1
The Development of Intermediate and Secondary Education
in England and Wales (or Great Britain: GB), 1870–1960
(Indicative Percentages of Specified Age Groups)

About 1870

In full-time attendance at any school (GB): 10-year-olds	40
14-year-olds	2
17-year-olds	1
Compare Germany 1870:	
Mean secondary enrollments per age group	2.3
Abitur certificates per age group	0.8
Compare France 1876:	
Mean secondary enrollments per age group	2.4
Baccalaureates per age group	0.8

About 1900–02

In full-time attendance at any school (GB): 10-year-olds	100
14-year-olds	9
17-year-olds	2
Reached nonboarding grammar schools	9
Reached boarding grammar schools	3
Compare Germany 1900:	
Mean secondary enrollments per age group	2.7
Abitur certificates per age group	0.9
Compare France 1898:	
Mean secondary enrollments per age group	2.5
Baccalaureates per age group	1.2

About 1936–38

In full-time attendance at any school (GB): 14-year-olds	38
17-year-olds	4
Reached nonboarding grammar schools	16
Reached boarding grammar schools	2
Compare Germany 1931:	
Mean secondary enrollments per age group	8.9
Abitur certificates per age group	3.3
Compare France 1936:	
Mean secondary enrollments per age group	7.2
Baccalaureates per age group	3.9

About 1950

Reached maintained and direct grant grammar schools	20
Reached independent grammar schools	3
Percent of age 12–14 in:	
Bilateral, multilateral and comprehensive schools	2.4
Secondary technical schools	2.8

continued next page

Maintained grammar schools 16.4
Direct grant grammar schools 2.3
Independent "efficient" schools 4.2
Pupils aged 15 and over as percent age 15–18 in:
    Secondary modern schools 0.9
    Secondary technical schools 1.0
    Maintained grammar schools 7.2
    Direct grant grammar schools 1.2
    Independent "efficient" schools 2.3
Percent of age year 17 in:
    Maintained and direct grant grammar schools 8
    Independent grammar schools 2.5

Compare Germany 1950:
    Mean secondary enrollments per age group 9.1
    Abitur certificates per age group 4.5
Compare France 1951:
    Mean enrollments traditional secondary per age group 8.9
    Mean enrollments technical and modern secondary 8.4
    Baccalaureates per age group 5.7

About 1960–62

In full-time attendance at any school (GB): 14-year-olds 100
                                     17-year-olds 15
Percent of age 12–14 in:
    Bilateral, multilateral and comprehensive schools 10.0
    Secondary technical schools 2.6
    Maintained grammar schools 16.6
    Direct grant grammar schools 2.2
    Independent "efficient" schools 4.3
Pupils aged 15 and over as percent age 15–18 in:
    Secondary modern schools 2.6
    Secondary technical schools 1.2
    Maintained grammar schools 9.5
    Direct grant grammar schools 1.4
    Independent "efficient" schools 2.6

Compare Germany 1960:
    Mean secondary enrollments per age group 12.4
    Abitur certificates per age group 5.4
Compare France 1961:
    Mean enrollments traditional secondary per age group 22.3
    Mean enrollments technical, modern, and "general" secondary .. 19.9
    Baccalaureates per age group 11.2

From *Robbins Report,* p.11 (estimates for 10-, 14-, 17-year-olds in Great Britain, 1870, 1902, 1938, 1962); Floud, "Educational Experience," p.128 (percent reaching nonboarding and boarding grammar, ca. 1900, ca. 1936); Little and Westergaard, "Trend of Class Differentials," p.304 (percent reaching, and percent of age year 17 in, maintained and direct grant grammar, and independent grammar, ca. 1950); Marsh, *Changing Social Structure,* pp.210–11 (estimates, for various school types, of pupils 12–14 as percent of their age group and of pupils

15 and over as percent of age 15–18: 1951 and 1961). Simplified categories were listed for Marsh's "Bilateral, Multilateral, Comprehensive and Special" and "Other schools recognized as efficient" (i.e., independent schools). Percentages from Little and Westergaard pertain to youths born in the late 1930s. Percentages from Floud were recalculated for both sexes from her separate data for males and females. Her information stems from a 1949 sample of adults that was divided into birth cohorts which reached nonboarding and boarding grammar schools as follows:

Born	Reached sec. age about	% Reaching nonboarding	% Reaching boarding	Total % grammar
Before 1890	1890s	8.4	3.5	11.9
1890–99	1900s	10.0	2.5	12.5
1900–09	1910s	9.0	2.1	11.1
1910–19	1920s	14.7	1.6	16.3
1920–29	1930s	16.4	1.7	18.1

Entered into Table 5.1 were rounded averages for the 1890s and 1900s under *About 1900–02* and rounded percentages for the 1930s under *About 1936–38*. It should be noted that there was a steady reduction in the proportion of youths reaching boarding schools from the 1890s to the 1930s, and that nonboarding (generally maintained) grammar school enrollments per age group also stagnated from the 1890s to the 1920s, so that increases in the figures for the 1930s stem entirely from the interwar period and from the L.E.A. schools.

Among boys leaving grammar schools around 1908–1909 and around 1936–37, in any case, only a handful went to the universities, while most of the rest took middle-level clerical jobs in commerce and industry.[11] Only about 2 percent of British seventeen-year-olds were still in school around 1900. Even the 2 percent, to be sure, was roughly twice the rate at which *Abitur* and baccalaureate certificates were awarded on the Continent at that time.

By the 1930s, the difference between the English and the continental systems had been reduced but not eliminated. Some 38 percent of British fourteen-year-olds were in full-time education, many of them presumably in higher primary schools. The rate of entry to English

11. Banks, *Parity and Prestige*, esp. pp.169–171: Among boys leaving grammar schools after age 12 in 1908–09, 3 percent went to universities and 10 percent to other institutions of further education; 8 percent became student teachers; 5 percent transferred to other secondary schools; 42 percent took professional or clerical positions; 17 percent went into industrial, manual, or agricultural work; and 15 percent remained at home or left school for other or unknown reasons. Among boys leaving grammar schools after age 14 in 1936–37 other than to transfer to other secondary schools, 5 percent went to universities and 6 percent to other educational institutions; 2 percent became student teachers, and 67 percent entered professional, commercial, industrial, and other business occupations. (Four percent went into the armed forces or police; 3 percent took up agricultural or rural occupations, and 14 percent remained at home or left for other, miscellaneous or unknown reasons.)

grammar and boarding schools was around twice as high as the mean
secondary percentages for France and Germany. Thus large numbers
of ordinary English grammar schools must have continued to serve
essentially as lower secondary or higher primary schools, since the percentage of British youngsters still in school at age seventeen was now
almost identical with the rate of French baccalaureate awards. Near
the apex, the French and English secondary systems were probably
very similar by the late 1930s, while the German system had begun to
suffer the destructive effects of National Socialist policies.

After the Second World War, further enrollment increases at the
English grammar schools were accompanied by the emergence of
technical, modern, and mixed types of secondary education. The non-
grammar streams clearly lost many of their pupils before graduation,
but by 1960 they had begun to assert their secondary character. The
rounded access percentages below may be taken to summarize the state
of the English secondary system about 1960.

	Age 12–14	Age 15–18
Independent and direct grant	6.5	4.0
Maintained grammar	16.5	9.5
Total grammar	23.0	13.5
Other secondary: without modern	12.5	1.0
with modern	77.0	4.0

It is this pattern that should be compared with the French and German data for 1960. As might be expected, the German indicators lag
rather far behind, while the English and French distributions look
roughly similar. One could argue that the English system was the most
inclusive of the three, but the point is debatable since the enrollment
pyramids are not measured at clearly comparable altitudes.

The slice of English secondary enrollments taken up by the independent and direct grant grammar schools, it will be noticed, was never
very large. The percentage of the age group in secondary boarding
schools actually decreased between 1890 and 1920. On the other hand,
the independent and direct grant institutions lost few of their students
before they reached the upper grades. In this respect the independent
schools were the English counterparts of the German *Gymnasien*
and the French *lycées*. Until the 1930s, they took significant portions
of the entering classes from private elementary institutions.[12] Their

12. Floud, "Educational Experience," p.130. Among adults surveyed in 1949
who had reached secondary grammar or boarding schools during the 1890s, nearly

graduates filled a vastly disproportionate share of places at the universities, especially at Oxford and Cambridge. Thus among students from the United Kingdom who entered Oxford and Cambridge or other British universities, the percentages below (by row) came from independent, direct grant, and maintained grammar schools.[13]

	Independent	*Direct grant*	*Maintained*
Oxford and Cambridge	54	16	30
Other British universities	15	13	72

Although in the early 1960s the independent schools accounted for less than one-fifth of twelve to fourteen-year-olds in English grammar schools and for less than one-fifth of fifteen to eighteen-year-olds in all types of English secondary schools, they still had a comfortable majority at Oxford and Cambridge. Here is conclusive evidence for the persisting weight of the English public school tradition or for the special position of Oxbridge among English universities.

Until 1836, of course, Oxford and Cambridge were the only universities in existence in England and Wales. This circumstance has made it relatively easy to reconstruct the history of English university-level enrollments up to the middle of the nineteenth century. The decisive contribution has been Lawrence Stone's calculation of decennial average rates of entry to the two universities from the sixteenth to the end of the nineteenth century.[14] In Table 5.2, Stone's most important findings are brought together and related to rough estimates of the relevant age group. The resulting percentages adequately describe the inclusiveness of the English system at the level of university entry, at least until the 1840s or 50s.

The pattern of enrollments is certainly a startling one. In relation to the population or age group, there were over three times as many university students in England during the seventeenth as during the nineteenth century. Even in absolute terms, enrollments at Oxford and Cambridge reached a peak near one thousand in the 1630s. Attendance decreased during and immediately after the Civil War, and the recovery of the 1660s remained incomplete. More important, it was followed by a decline that led to an absolute low at about three

---

two-thirds had begun their schooling in private elementary schools, and the corresponding figure was still 30–40 percent about 1900–1920 and around 20 percent during the 1920s and 30s.

13. *Robbins Report*, p.80.

14. My reservations, here and later in this chapter, about Stone's interpretation of his own data in "Size and Composition" (the best we have on the subject) are discussed in Ringer, "Problems in the History of Higher Education."

Table 5.2

Annual Admissions to Oxford and Cambridge, 1630–1900
(In Decennial Averages and Percentages of the Age Group)

Decade	Oxford admissions	Oxford and Cambridge admissions	Age group (thousands)	Admissions (percent of age group)
1630s	530	996	97	1.0
1660s	458	857	97	0.9
1700s	316	565	110	0.5
1750s	182	331	116	0.3
1800s	236	416	181	0.2
1810s	328	619	208	0.3
1820s	410	850	243	0.3
1830s	384	811	278	0.3
1840s	410	863	316	0.3
1850s	389	825	356	0.2
1860s	488	991	400	0.2
1870s	684	1,360	454	0.3
1880s	766	1,693	515	0.3
1890s	821	1,762	576	0.3

From Stone, "Size and Composition," pp.91–92, 103, for decennial average freshman admissions at Oxford and Cambridge (figures for Oxford 1630s and 1660s and for Cambridge 1700s and 1750s are interpolated by Stone), for total population estimates (England and Wales) 1630s through 1750s, and for the age group ratio (see below). Stone calculates the median age of entry at Oxford as 17 in the 1630s, 17.5 in the 1660s and 1700s, 18 in the 1750s, and 18.5 during the nineteenth century. To get from the total population to the size of university entrants' age groups, he applies a demographer's estimate that 0.95% of the total population were males in the relevant age year, and this from the 1630s to 1900. Without verifying this estimate, I doubled it to obtain 1.9% as the male *and* *female* age group ratio, which I applied to decennially averaged population totals (England and Wales) from Mitchell, *Abstract.*

hundred and thirty annual entrants in the 1750s and a relative low at 0.2 percent of the age group in the 1800s.

What confronts us here is a major social and cultural disaster, one that is very far from being understood. We know that university enrollments declined in Germany during the eighteenth century. In French secondary education, too, there may have been a slight loss of enrollments per population after 1789 and perhaps earlier as well. Richard Kagan has shown that attendance at the universities of Castile dropped from a high during the early seventeenth century to a low around 1770, with a mild recovery thereafter.[15] Thus the evidence

15. Kagan, "Universities in Castile."

mounts for a European-wide collapse of secondary and university-level education that coincided, roughly, with the Enlightenment. How does one explain so revolutionary a set of changes?

Part of the answer undoubtedly has to do with the availability of positions considered appropriate for educated men. Contemporary accounts suggest a scarcity of places in the church during the early seventeenth century. The enrollment boom that culminated in the 1630s had apparently overshot the point of equilibrium between the supply and the demand for university graduates. As Lenore O'Boyle has shown, a similar glut recurred about two centuries later. After a period of rising admissions to Oxford and Cambridge from the 1800s to the 1830s, there was *thought* to be an excess of educated men.[16] In fact, as we know, parallel enrollment fluctuations gave rise to job shortages even more clearly in France and especially in Germany during the 1830s and 40s. Yet if there really was an excess of graduates in England about 1840, it occurred when enrollments per age group were less than one-third what they had been in the 1630s. Obviously then, the enrollment decline of the late seventeenth and eighteenth centuries was due, not to a short-term disequilibrium, but to a long-term change in the relationship between supply and demand in higher education. How did seventeenth-century societies support—and then employ—contingents of students per population and age group that were not matched again until the twentieth century? And how was this demand for education reduced during the later seventeenth and eighteenth centuries—why did England lose its earlier capacity to place graduates in appropriate positions? These are some of the further questions that have to be asked.

Unfortunately, the answers run out at this point, and one is left with conjectures. There may well have been a contraction in the size of the English church, at least in relation to the population. Perhaps pluralism played a role as well. Various "clerical" positions outside the church could also have been more numerous in the early seventeenth century than in the society that was created by the Industrial Revolution.

Whatever its ultimate origins, the shortage of places was accompanied by a socially regressive trend at the ancient universities and in the English church, a trend that may have been a cause or an effect of the job crisis, or even both at once. Tuition and other expenses rose steeply at Oxford and Cambridge, while an unprecedented emphasis upon status differences added to the psychic cost of university attend-

16. O'Boyle, "Excess of Educated Men," pp.478–84.

ance for lower-class students. At the same time, the younger sons of the
gentry began to compete with poor scholars for the available livings.
The fact that Anglican clergymen could marry may have helped to attract the offspring of the social elite into the church. The sons of clergymen, in turn, took up places that might once have gone to poor out-
siders. In any case, there certainly was a long-term transformation in
the social makeup and character of the English church. The Anglican
Establishment of the decades around 1800 not only rested on an ex-
clusionary alliance of gentry and clergy, it was also a system of patronage, a major asset for the social groups that controlled it. The reduction
in university access after 1670 was probably linked, somehow, with
an upper-class conquest of a resource that only gradually revealed its
potential.

Of course hunches of this sort are hard to sustain in the present state
of research. Even so, they accord better with what we do know than
any attempt to link higher education before 1860 with industrialization or the industrial bourgeoisie. Indeed, the downward movement of
English university enrollments during the eighteenth century should
really suffice to do away with the all-too-tenacious assumption that
early industrialization increased opportunities for the highly educated.
Until the late nineteenth century, absolutely all the available evidence
points in the opposite direction. The English figures for the eighteenth
century suggest, indeed, that education was one of the forms of preindustrial social wealth that were *used up* or *transferred* to the industrial sector during the proverbial take-off into sustained growth.

Following the movement of English university-level enrollments into
the nineteenth century, one encounters a serious gap in the available
information. For the years 1840–1900, there are attendance statistics
only for Oxford and Cambridge. There is no comparable evidence for
the University of London (founded in 1836), for the university colleges that offered work for London degrees (Owen's College, 1851),
or for the older civic or red brick universities that were chartered
between 1880 and 1909. In all probability, these institutions were numerically insignificant before 1860, and they certainly grew most
rapidly toward the end of the century.[17]

The situation from 1900 on is briefly outlined in Table 5.3, which is
based on estimates contained in the Robbins Report. By the turn of

17. Sanderson, *Universities and British Industry*, p.96, estimates the total
number of day students (not necessarily full-time and excluding medical students)
at the civic universities, in thousands, as 0.8 in 1880, 1.8 in 1888, 3.0 in 1893,
3.3 in 1900, and 4.3 in 1913. He also estimates average annual graduations with
degrees as 93 in 1889–93, 222 in 1895–97, and 566 in 1910–19.

Table 5.3

University-Level Education in Great Britain, 1900–1961
(Enrollments in Thousands, Entering Students
as Percentages of Age Group)

Year	Total enrollments: thousands			Entering: % of age group[a]		
	Universities	Teacher training[b]	Further education[c]	Universities	Teacher training[b]	Further education[c]
1900–01	20	5	–	0.8	0.4	–
1924–25	42	16	3	1.5	1.0	0.2
1938–39	50	13	6	1.7	0.7	0.3
1955–56	85.2	28.7	13.6	3.4	2.0	0.7
1960–61	107.7	40.5	30.8	4.1	2.7	1.5

From the *Robbins Report*, pp.15–16, App. One, p.163; see also App. One, p.342, App. Two (A), pp.18, 24, 28 for all tabulated figures, including percentages of the age group. University entrants in 1900 were estimated to be one-third of total enrollments, which implies a three-year duration of study. (Calculated durations were 3.3 years by 1938 and 3.7 years by 1960.) Entrants to further education were assumed to be one-half of total enrollments. Women were 23.3% of British university students in 1938 and 25.5% in 1960. The shares of enrollments falling to various universities were as follows.

Year	Oxford and Cambridge	London	Civic, Wales	Scotland
1938–39	22	26	32	20
1961–62	16	20	47	17

(Scotland's population was about 11 percent of Great Britain's in 1938.) In 1961–62, 28 percent of British university enrollments were in the humanities, 4 percent in education, 11 percent in social studies, 25 percent in science, 15 percent in technology, 2 percent in agriculture, and 15 percent in medical subjects.

[a] The Report defines the percentage of the age group as the sum of percentages calculated separately for each age year represented among entering students.

[b] Covers training colleges in England and Wales and colleges of education in Scotland.

[c] (Approximate figures through 1939). Refers to full-time advanced (beyond G.C.E. advanced level) courses in C.A.T.'s, regional technical colleges, colleges of commerce, schools of art, and central institutions in Scotland.

the century, roughly 0.8 percent of the age group reached all universities *in Great Britain.* This must be compared with admissions to Oxford and Cambridge (Table 5.2), which came to 0.3 percent of the age group *in England and Wales* during the 1890s, and indeed over the whole period between 1870 and 1900. Part of the difference between the two percentages is due to the fact that university enrollments per age group were considerably higher in Scotland than in England and Wales. In 1938, Scottish institutions accounted for 20 percent of British university enrollments, even though Scotland's population was only

11 percent of Great Britain's. If these percentages are applied to the British enrollment total and age group ratio for 1938, one obtains separate enrollment estimates of about 3.1 percent of the age group for Scotland and 1.5 percent for England and Wales. Projecting this difference backward in time to 1900, one obtains 0.5–0.7 percent as a rough estimate of English enrollments per age group at that time, or somewhere around twice the rate of entry at the two ancient universities. Developments outside Oxford and Cambridge, in other words, roughly doubled English university enrollments per age group sometime during the later nineteenth century.

Obviously, this rough sketch leaves many questions unanswered. Still, there is a presumption in favor of rapid and accelerating growth at the English universities from 1860 to the end of the century. This expansion may be associated with a high industrial phase in the history of the English system. In Germany at this time, the technical institutes grew along with the universities. In France, enrollments increased in a group of younger *grandes écoles* as well as in the faculties. In England, London and the red brick universities rose to numerical equality with Oxford and Cambridge. It is worth noting that the expansion of English higher education was not interrupted in any way by the great recession that affected England, along with the rest of Europe, from the late 1870s on. Once again, the movement of university attendance figures appears to have been *inversely* related to the state of the economy.

Both in France and in Germany, university-level enrollments stood at about 0.5 percent of the age group in the 1870s, before advancing to near 1 percent by the turn of the century. Thus, England undoubtedly lagged well behind the two continental countries in university attendance during the nineteenth century. Indeed, this difference persisted into the twentieth century. In the 1920s and 30s, as enrollments at British universities and institutions of further education advanced to near 2 percent of the age group, the comparable measures of inclusiveness approached 3 percent in Germany and 4 percent in France. The setback suffered by German higher education under National Socialism accounts for the fact that in 1960, British university-level enrollments per age group, at about 5.5 percent, slightly surpassed the comparable figure for Germany. On the other hand, the rate of access to the French university faculties alone by that time came close to 10 percent.

The British disadvantage in these comparisons was real; it cannot be traced to obvious faults in the methods or indicators used. True, British teacher training was not counted as university-level education, but neither were its French or German counterparts. In Britain as on the Continent, future elementary teachers did not normally attend universities. It has sometimes been suggested that English university students have more often completed their courses than their colleagues on the Continent, but this hypothesis requires further exploration. The average duration of university study in Britain was probably around 3 years in 1900; it then increased to 3.3 years by 1938 and 3.7 years by 1960. But this change was taken into account when total enrollment figures were converted into access percentages. In France and Germany the average duration of study was about 4–4.5 years by 1960, and again the enrollment estimates have been adjusted accordingly.

There certainly were some genuine differences in the distribution of university-level education in England, France and Germany. The proportion of women among university students, for example, was highest in France, reaching 27 percent in 1936 and 40 percent in 1961. The comparable percentages for Britain were 23 in 1938 and 25 in 1960. In Germany, only 16 and 22 percent of university students were women in 1931 and 1960, respectively. In short, England consistently fell almost as far behind France as did Germany in providing university-level education for women.

The distribution of British students over the various subject areas as of 1960 indicates a special emphasis upon the humanities, the natural sciences, and technology, as against the professional programs. The difference between England and the continental countries in this respect may be partly nominal; it certainly does not suffice to account for the lower overall enrollments per age group in Great Britain. Still, some portion of the British disadvantage in university access rates may well be due to the generalist tradition that originated at Oxford and Cambridge. There is every indication that this tradition was transmitted to the younger English universities and that it has survived as a distinctive trait of the British system until the present day.

Education and Society in England

During the early industrial phase in the history of the English system, the public schools were notoriously the most aristocratic institutions of secondary education that could be found in Europe and probably in the world. At eight of the most famous of these schools between 1801 and 1850, according to Bamford, the gentry and aristocracy accounted for about half of total enrollments.[18] Another 12 percent of

18. Bamford, "Public Schools," p.229.

the pupils' fathers were clergymen, around 4 percent were officers, and 5 percent were professional men. A category of "others" included many "gentlemen and ladies living on incomes"; it made up an additional quarter of the parents. That left only about 3 percent for the "middle class" of traders and farmers, and less than 1 percent for the "lower classes." Breakdowns for individual decades between 1801 and 1850 actually suggest a *decline* in the representation of the middle and lower classes and of "gentlemen on incomes" as well. Together, these groups lost about 10 percent of overall enrollments to the aristocracy, gentry, and officers. The figures for the middle and lower classes declined from 7 percent to 2 percent, while the shares of the clergy and professions remained fairly stable. The term *gentry* probably had a broad meaning at the time, and it may have been further enlarged between the beginning and the middle of the century. Still, there is no doubt that the "productive" middle class was very poorly represented at the English public schools of the early industrial period.

Unfortunately, little is known about developments at the public schools between 1850 and 1900 or about the whole spectrum of endowed and proprietary grammar schools during the nineteenth century. It is quite clear, nevertheless, that enrollments expanded very rapidly between 1870 and 1930, especially at the ordinary grammar schools.

We have already remarked upon an interesting peculiarity of the English educational system, which was the generalization of the grammar school model beyond the limits of academic secondary education on the Continent. The traditionally classical secondary schools in France and Germany were always predominantly university-preparatory institutions. Even the modern streams that began as lower secondary schools eventually guided a large portion of their pupils toward the secondary leaving certificate and subsequent university study. As a result, curricular tracking took place within secondary systems that nevertheless remained predominantly academic in orientation and that served a relatively small fraction of the school-age population. In England, by contrast, the classical curriculum that was initially developed at the public schools was transmitted more or less unchanged to all the rest of the grammar schools, including those maintained by the L.E.A.'s after 1902.

Thus the English secondary system was not really segmented in the sense required by our definitions. There were differences of academic and social status in English secondary education—no one could mistake the distance that separated one of the Ancient Nine from an ordinary

L.E.A. grammar school—yet these differences were not as thoroughly institutionalized in England as in France and Germany. Until after the Second World War, no curricular distinctions arose to emphasize and perpetuate any particular discontinuities on the scale of prestige. Indirectly, until 1944, the unwavering English commitment to the old generalist curriculum tended to obscure the boundary between academic and nonacademic secondary education as the public school model was extended downward to the less clearly university-preparatory grammar schools of the early twentieth century. After 1944, to be sure, "secondary education for all" was initially achieved at the cost of a tripartite segmentation of the English secondary system. Even the common secondary schools of more recent times may house distinctive tracks of the type to be found in American high schools. Yet the contemporary English educational system still appears less obviously segmented than its French and German counterparts.

The best data on levels of progressiveness in English grammar school education since the late nineteenth century are to be found in an admirable book by Floud, Halsey, and Martin.[19] Floud and her colleagues concentrated on South West Hertfordshire and Middlesbrough, the former a residential and light industrial area near London, the latter a heavy industrial district in Yorkshire. The three authors were chiefly interested in the share of grammar school places going to students from the "working class," which they defined in the inclusive sense current among contemporary English sociologists.[20] Combining their figures for skilled and unskilled manual workers among the fathers, one obtains the distribution percentages below for working-class boys among male students entering grammar schools in the two districts between 1884 and 1953.[21]

19. For the following, see Floud, ed., *Social Class,* esp. pp.3–8, 29–30, 42.

20. Among children taking the secondary selection examination in 1952–53, according to the authors, 67 percent were from the working class in S.W. Hertfordshire and 77 percent in Middlesbrough. Since practically all children took this examination, the percentages reflect the social structure (and the strength of the "working class") in the two districts. The authors also cite census statistics to show that S.W. Hertfordshire closely resembled England and Wales in its social structure, whereas Middlesbrough had an unusually high percentage of unskilled manual workers in its population. In making this argument, the authors work with census categories that identify two-thirds or more of the English population as "working class." The analytical problems raised by so inclusive a definition of the working class will be discussed in connection with Table 5.6 below.

21. Excluded are Catholic schools in Middlesbrough and students from well-to-do families who may have attended independent schools outside their home districts. Dates listed are only approximately representative of years in which sampling was possible. Skilled workers accounted for the bulk of the working-class

	1884–1900	1904–1918	1922–1930	1934–1938	1950–1953
S.W. Hertfordshire	11	15	19	16	42
Middlesbrough		23	38	46	45

The rise in the working-class percentage in both districts between 1900 and 1930 resulted from the free place regulation of 1907. The decline in the figure for South West Hertfordshire during the 1930s was due to economic stringency and fiscal retrenchment during the 1930s and particularly to the conversion of free into special places at that time. Under the special place arrangement, the portion of school fees remitted varied with the parents' means. This did not significantly affect the working class in Middlesbrough, where both the number of special places made available and the working-class share of the population were high. In South West Hertfordshire, however, working-class boys lost ground in an aggravated competition for special places with pupils from lower middle-class families. In its ultimate effect, the special place system was thus clearly regressive.

The Education Act of 1944 and the abolition of fees in all maintained and grant-aided schools in 1945 produced a renewed improvement in educational opportunities for English working-class students. In this respect, the figures for South West Hertfordshire reflect national trends more adequately than those for Middlesbrough. By 1953, according to careful calculations by Floud and her colleagues, about 22 percent of males in the age group reached grammar schools in South West Hertfordshire, and 17 percent did so in Middlesbrough. Among boys from the families of skilled manual workers, some 18 and 14 percent went to grammar schools in South West Hertfordshire and Middlesbrough, respectively. The corresponding proportion among the sons of unskilled workers was 9 percent in both districts. If these *access percentages* (or chances) for the two working-class groups are related to the access percentages for the whole age group, one obtains educational opportunity ratios (or *relative* access chances) of about 0.8 for the sons of skilled manual workers, and 0.4–0.5 for the sons of unskilled workers, both as of 1953.[22]

---

representations in both districts. The highest distribution percentages for the sons of unskilled workers were 8% in Middlesbrough in 1950–53 and 16% in S.W. Hertfordshire in 1935–38.

22. The other way of arriving at opportunity ratios yields comparable results. One divides the 1953 working-class distribution percentages in the two districts by the working-class (distribution) percentages among all boys taking the 1952–53

After analyzing their data, Floud and her associates were disturbed by a pattern of diminishing returns in the evolution of working-class access. As free places gradually increased in number after 1930, they found, there was a decline in the proportion of additional places obtained by working-class pupils. What happened, even apart from the economy measures of the 1930s, was that middle-class youngsters increasingly entered the scholastic contest for the available places; from 1945 on, they were in effect forced to compete for opportunities they might previously have paid for. The result was a worsening of the terms upon which working-class boys competed for the increasing number of scholarships. Pursuing the problem raised by this trend, Floud's group devised a hypothetically ideal distribution of grammar school places in accordance with the pupils' tested intelligence. They thus in effect defined the meritocratic level of progressiveness at grammar school entry. When they compared this standard with the actual distribution of places, they found surprisingly little difference between the two. The pattern of diminishing returns in the development of working-class access was thus apparently created by a gradual approach to meritocracy, by the increasing adjustment of educational opportunities to measured academic ability. While this is not the place to take up the whole issue of meritocracy, we might just note that it was first raised in England,[23] perhaps because the English educational system of the postwar era moved rather quickly and visibly toward the meritocratic level of progressiveness.

Turning from the English secondary schools to the English universities, we begin with some data on Cambridge. Table 5.4, like several earlier tables, is organized to evoke the flow of students into the university from social origins identified by their fathers' occupations and out again into their own professions. While the categories used are not precise, they leave no doubt that Cambridge was utterly dominated by an alliance between the gentry and the clergy from the mid-eighteenth to the mid-nineteenth century. There was almost no change in the distributions between 1752 and 1849. On the output side, no less than 60 percent of the graduates entered the Anglican church; 15 percent took up the pursuits typical of the landowning class; somewhere near 10 percent went into the professions or public administration; and another

---

secondary selection examination in these districts (67 in S.W. Hertfordshire, 77 in Middlesbrough, according to note 23 above). For the skilled and unskilled categories combined, the ratios thus obtained come close to 0.6 in both districts.

23. Floud, ed., *Social Class*, was published in 1957. Young, *Rise of the Meritocracy*, first appeared in 1958.

10 percent decided on teaching of one sort or another. No one left Cambridge to go into business. Among the fathers of students, about a third each were clergymen and "landowners or of that class." Another 15–20 percent might be loosely described as professional people: they were lawyers, doctors, teachers, or public administrators. Only some 5–10 percent of the parents were bankers or businessmen.

The net flow of students through Cambridge before 1850 was chiefly from the gentry to the church. The professional categories were about as well—or as poorly—represented among the sons as among the fathers, but about half the offspring of gentry who entered Cambridge joined

Table 5.4
Social Origins and Subsequent Careers
of Students at Cambridge University, 1752–1938
(Percentages by Column)

Occupational category[a]	1752–99 IN	1752–99 OUT	1800–49 IN	1800–49 OUT	1850–99 IN	1850–99 OUT	1937–38 IN	1937–38 OUT
1. Landowners or of that class	38	14	31	14	19	7	2	0
2. Church	31	60	32	62	31	38	7	6
3. Public administration[b]	2	3	2	1	3	6	8	10
4. Law	4	6	8	9	9	14	7	11
5. Medicine	4	1	8	2	10	7	8	12
6. Teaching	3	9	3	9	4	12	7	16
3–6. Professions	13	19	21	21	26	39	30	49
7. Business, banking[c]	9	0	6	0	15	7	46	31
8. Miscellaneous	9	7	10	3	9	9	15	14
1–8. Absolute numbers sampled (100%)	318	421	319	412	352	420	2,006	2,295

From Jenkins and Jones, "Social Class," which is a carefully constructed sample from Venn, *Alumni Cantabrigienses* (Part II), subdivided into three chronological groupings of matriculants and supplemented by a 1938 survey by the Cambridge University Appointments Board. Until Sheldon Rothblatt completes his statistical study of Cambridge, the piece by Jenkins and Jones is still the best available work in this field. It is largely supported by Anderson and Schnaper, *School and Society,* which is unfortunately not subdivided chronologically, and it does not actually clash with the very differently categorized results for the eighteenth century in Hans, *New Trends.*

[a] Fathers' occupations are listed under IN, the graduates' own professions under OUT.

[b] Includes the civil, colonial, and diplomatic services.

[c] Groups accounting, finance, and stockbroking with banking, and interprets business broadly to "include occupations, not otherwise listed, directed to profit-making."

the large clerical contingent upon graduation. The few sons of businessmen who reached the university at all, of course, invariably abandoned their fathers' careers. Thus higher education at Cambridge during this period had absolutely nothing to do with the Industrial Revolution or with the industrial class structure that was coming into existence. It is hard to imagine a more actively incongruent role for higher education.

It is equally difficult to conceive a less progressive pattern of recruitment. In nineteenth-century Germany, significant numbers of university students came from the families of lower officials and teachers as well as from the rest of the burgher stratum. At Cambridge during the early industrial period, these groups were practically unrepresented. One obvious reason for the contrast was the presence of a civil service in Germany that was selected at least partly on the basis of academic merit. Further opportunities in France and Germany were provided by the standardized state examinations for the liberal professions, which were based on university work. Finally, religion played a very different social role in France and Germany than it did in England. Particularly the Catholic priesthood as a destination for the sons of farmers and petty tradesmen had no clear counterpart across the Channel.[24] Here again, the peculiar coalition of clergy and gentry was the decisive element in the English pattern.

Just when and how change came to Cambridge after 1850 is not clear, but one should probably picture a gradual evolution that began about 1860 and accelerated toward the end of the century. Rothblatt has warned against the assumption that the aristocratic-clerical mold was quickly broken during the 1860s, or that it was the entrepreneurial elite that chiefly led the attack on the status quo.[25] His work on currents of opinion at Cambridge suggests, rather, that the professional man was the first heir of the traditional gentleman and that business became acceptable only gradually, toward the end of the century, when it was appropriately redefined as a form of public service. This interpretation is not only consistent with the sequence of events in Germany and France, it also accords rather well with the data in the later portions of Table 5.4.

To begin with, change was apparently less rapid during the later nineteenth than during the early twentieth century. While landowner-

24. C. A. Anderson and Schnaper, *School and Society*, pp.7–8, regard the English clergy as a principal avenue of upward social mobility, but this seems to me a questionable conclusion. True, a humble clergyman was more likely to have his son reach the university than many a wealthy noble; but when the son left Cambridge, he generally became a clergyman himself.

25. Rothblatt, *Revolution of the Dons*, esp. pp.86–93.

ship declined as an occupation of graduates even before 1900, it disappeared entirely between 1900 and 1937. Similarly, the share of graduates entering the Church fell from a still substantial 38 percent during the later nineteenth century to 6 percent in the 1930s. On the input side, the proportion of students' fathers in the landowning class was reduced from 31 percent in 1800–1849 to 19 percent by 1850–99; but it then dropped to an insignificant 2 percent by 1937–38. The sons of clergymen remained as numerous at Cambridge during the later nineteenth century as they had been before 1850. They held their place at just over 30 percent of total enrollments until the twentieth century, but they were then reduced to a mere 7 percent by 1937–38. Thus the rapid and thorough transformation of Cambridge between 1900 and 1937 began as a very gradual process during the closing decades of the nineteenth century.

Moreover, it was the professional elite, rather than the entrepreneurial upper middle class, that initially occupied the ground being vacated by the gentry and clergy. The proportion of students entering law, medicine, teaching, and public administration advanced from 21 percent in 1800–1849 to 39 percent in 1850–99. Among the fathers of students, too, the business representation remained modest at 15 percent during the later nineteenth century, though it then advanced quickly to over 45 percent by 1937–38. Even in the 1930s, the net flow of students through Cambridge was away from business toward law, medicine, and teaching.

New evidence recently collected by Stone and summarized in Table 5.5 permits us to extend some of these observations to Oxford. At the top of the table, we are dealing with the very general status categories traditionally entered into the registers of the university. The terms in the lower portion of the table first appeared in a supplementary record begun in 1870; in 1891, they were taken over into the main register itself.

Hampered by the imprecision of the traditional status categories until 1870, we can say only that "plebeians" were largely replaced by "gentlemen" at Oxford during the eighteenth and early nineteenth centuries. "Plebeians," some of them presumably artisans and tradesmen, accounted for as much as 50 percent of Oxford matriculants during the decades around 1600. The steady decline in their representation thereafter must be considered a major instance of social regression in university recruitment. On the other hand, as Stone warns, the growth in the contingent of "gentlemen" during the nineteenth century was due in part to an increasingly informal assumption of that appellation by the middle class. Thus, although the lower middle and lower classes

Table 5.5
Social Origins of Oxford Students, 1760–1910
(Percentages by Column)

Father's status or occupation	1760/61	1785/86	1810	1835	1860	1885
Peer, baronet, knight	5	5	7	4	3	2
Armiger (Esquire)	29	30	40	51	34	33
Gentleman	28	32	23	21	32	39
Higher clergy, clergy, Dr.	21	23	29	24	31	26
Plebeian	17	10	1	–	–	–
Absolute total known (100%)	203	238	324	370	394	742
Absolute number unknown	1	–	–	–	–	7

Father's status or occupation	1870	1891	1910
1. Knights, baronets, peers	2	1	1
2. Esquires, gentlemen	36	16	8
3. J.P.'s, M.P.'s	2	1	–
4. Landowners, farmers	–	3	6
1–4. Sum	40	21	15
5. Clergy	28	24	17
6. Civil servants	1	3	5
7. Armed forces, police	5	4	4
8. Teachers	1	2	6
9. Lawyers	7	12	9
10. Doctors	5	4	6
11. Artists, publishers	2	2	1
6–11. Sum	21	27	31
12. Industrialists, businessmen	7	19	21
13. Tradesmen, shopkeepers, agents	2	6	7
14. Secretaries, clerks	–	2	2
12–14. Sum	9	27	30
15. Working class	–	–	1
16. Unknown	2	1	5
1–16. Absolute totals (100%)	418	669	1,030

From Stone, "Size and Composition." The limitations of categorization are those of the university records themselves.

were certainly excluded from Oxford during the eighteenth and early nineteenth centuries, it is difficult to say just when and how the professional and entrepreneurial wings of the upper middle class arrived to challenge the early industrial alliance of gentry and clergy.

In interpreting the more detailed distributions for 1870, 1891, and 1910, Stone finds it hard to believe that the proportion of nobles, esquires, and gentlemen among the fathers actually decreased from 40 percent in 1870 to 18 percent in 1891. He is equally reluctant to accept the simultaneous increase from 7 to 19 percent in the share of the industrialists and businessmen. He therefore supposes that "at least 10 percent were still describing themselves under landed status categories in 1870 who in fact belonged to the commercial and industrial bourgeoisie."[26]

The difficulty with this supposition lies in the assumption that everyone falsely listed under "esquires, gentlemen" in 1870 was a member of the "commercial and industrial bourgeoisie." If this was true of "at least 10 percent," then industrialists and businessmen were practically as numerous among fathers of Oxford students in 1870 as in 1891. But that in turn is hard to believe, and there is nothing in the evidence that would demand it. Some of the "gentlemen" of 1870 may have been farmers; others could have been solicitors, physicians, or other members of the liberal and learned professions. The only force behind Stone's speculative emphasis upon the commercial and industrial elites is the old temptation to link the development of higher education to industrialization and the rise of the entrepreneurial bourgeoisie.

A more plausible interpretation would call attention to the role of the professions and to the continuing importance of the noneconomic elites more generally. As late as 1891, after all, the educated upper middle class, including the clergy, accounted for over 50 percent of enrollments at Oxford. This was at a time when the share of the nobility, gentry, landowners, and farmers stood just above 20 percent, that of the industrialists and businessmen just below 20 percent, and that of the economic lower middle class somewhat below 10 percent.

Of course the business classes did eventually arrive at Oxford and Cambridge in considerable strength. It was important for the whole direction and speed of English developments that there was no meritocratic civil service in England before 1870 and that the English universities were never tied to a state examination system of the French and German type. As a result, the liberal and learned professions, including the officials, reached the universities later and in smaller numbers in England than in France and Germany. The English universities of the early industrial period were left in the hands of the gentry and clergy. The professional elite did spearhead the middle-class conquest of the English universities during the high industrial

26. Stone, "Size and Composition," p.67.

period, but its leadership was of short duration. For a few crucial decades, it served as a kind of mediator between the old gentry culture and the needs of the new economic middle class. But once the commercial and industrial bourgeoisie began to reach the English universities at all, it quickly captured a remarkably large share of enrollments. At Cambridge by 1937/38, for example, some 46 percent of students' fathers were in business and banking as against 30 percent in public administration, law, medicine, and teaching.

As closer ties were formed between the English universities and the business community, a growing number of English university graduates took jobs in commerce and industry. At Oxford and Cambridge from the 1890s on, appointments committees helped them to find positions. It took an effort to breach the traditional barrier between business and higher education. But by the eve of the First World War, according to Sanderson, some 15–20 percent of Oxford students went into industry and commerce. By the interwar period, the percentage of businessmen among graduates had risen to some 20–30 at Oxford and 33–50 at Cambridge.[27] The Cambridge percentage is particularly remarkable; it actually exceeded the comparable figure for the red brick universities, even though the red bricks apparently drew most of their students from the intermediate and lower levels of the business hierarchy.[28]

Here again, as in the development of the grammar schools, the unspecialized character of the English system strikes the eye. Certainly the older civic universities ranked far below Oxford and Cambridge in academic and social prestige. In all likelihood, they were also readier than the two ancient universities to make room for applied scientific, technological, and other practical studies. Yet they did not come to function as a distinctive curricular track; instead, they adapted and extended the generalist model created at Oxford and Cambridge. Until recently, the German technical institutes, business schools, and other academies have had no clear counterparts in England. Neither the older nor the younger civic universities ever approached the professional specialization of the younger *grandes écoles*. Oxford and Cambridge graduates of the early 1960s took up the same *sorts* of occupa-

27. Sanderson, *Universities and British Industry*, pp.52–53, 278–79, for yearly percentages at Oxford and Cambridge 1906–14 (somewhat erratic fluctuations with high of 20 percent in 1913), Oxford 1922–39, and Cambridge 1919–39. Absolute totals are not large.

28. Sanderson, *Universities and British Industry*, pp.278–79 (for interwar period, as above), and pp.98–99 for fathers of Birmingham students in 1893: 37 percent professional; 17 percent manufacturers, merchants; 21 percent trades and special skills; 13 percent "semi-professional" white-collar occupations; 13 percent "probable artisans"; absolute total: 270.

tions as their colleagues from the other universities.[29] Gradations of prestige, though certainly present, were not reinforced or perpetuated by parallel curricular divides.

The unsegmented character of the English educational system probably made it easier to extend the traditional culture to new social groups; there were few institutional obstacles to retard the process of adaptation and redefinition. The rate of change in English education since 1870, in any case, has been remarkable. During most of the nineteenth century, the English system obviously ranked well below the French and German systems on the scale of progressiveness. By around 1960, however, this difference had disappeared; the English system now easily equaled the French and surpassed the German level on that scale. The similarity between the pertinent indicators for France and England as of 1960 is particularly striking; it suggests that late industrial systems of education may be converging toward a common point. What chiefly interests us at present, though, is the rapidity and visibility of change in the English system after 1870.

This is demonstrated in Table 5.6, which summarily describes the evolution of English secondary and higher education from about 1890 to 1960. The table is based primarily upon a survey of English adults in 1949. Those questioned were classified according to their years of birth and their fathers' occupational status. The figures tabulated are percentages of those in given age and status groups who reached ordinary grammar schools, independent or boarding grammar schools, and universities. Thus the table deals with access at the lowest, entering level of secondary and university education. The professions of fathers are grouped according to the empirically derived Hall-Jones scale of seven occupational status categories. These range from the "professional and higher administrative" and the "managerial and executive" positions, which are sometimes combined, via the upper and lower "inspectional and supervisory" grades, to the skilled manual and routine non-manual occupations, and the semi- and unskilled jobs, which are also frequently subsumed under a single rubric of the "unskilled."

The figures for ordinary grammar schools in the table are not as precise as those in the study of South West Hertfordshire and Middlesbrough by Floud and others. But they outline the main trends at the

29. *Robbins Report*, app. two (B), p.166, occupations of 1962 university graduates six months after graduating; percentages for graduates from all universities are followed by percentages, in parentheses, for Oxford and Cambridge graduates: school teaching 28 (17), industry 23 (20), commerce and law 7 (12), public service 7 (6), other employment 18 (27), post graduate study 18 (18). Note the similarities in the figures for industry, public service, and postgraduate study.

Table 5.6
Percentages of English Age and Status Groups
Who Reached Secondary Schools and Universities, ca. 1890–1960

*a) Percent who reached grammar schools
among those born (and aged 11) ca.*

From father's status category	Before 1890 (1890s)	1890s (1900s)	1900s (1910s)	1910s (1920s)	1920s (1930s)	Late 1930s (1950)
Professional, managerial Upper inspectional and supervisory	23	31	26	40	42	41
Lower inspectional and supervisory	10	12	11	19	24	31
Skilled manual and routine nonmanual	3	4	6	11	12	17
Unskilled	2	1	1	4	7	10
Whole age group	8	10	9	15	16	20

*b) Percent of same age groups
who reached boarding independent schools*

	Before 1890 (1890s)	1890s (1900s)	1900s (1910s)	1910s (1920s)	1920s (1930s)	Late 1930s (1950)
Professional, managerial Upper inspectional and supervisory	12	10	9	8	10	21
Lower inspectional and supervisory	2	2	2	1	—	4
Skilled manual and routine nonmanual	1	—	1	—	1	—
Unskilled	—	—	—	—	—	—
Whole age group	3	3	2	2	2	3

*c) Percent who reached universities
among those born (and aged 20) ca.*

	Before 1910 (1900–29)	1910–29 (1930–49)	1940–41 (1960–61)
Professional and higher administrative Managerial and executive	8.7	15.2	33
			11
Upper inspectional and supervisory Lower inspectional and supervisory	1.4	3.5	6
Skilled manual and routine nonmanual	0.6	0.9	2
Semi- and unskilled manual	0.2	0.5	1
Whole age group	1.3	2.3	4

From Floud, "Educational Experience"; Little & Westergaard, "Trends of Class Differentials"; *Robbins Report*, p.50. Floud sampled the educational back-

continued next page

national level, and they permit us to calculate some additional opportunity ratios. Major increases in grammar school access, they indicate, came sometime between 1900 and 1930, and again after 1945. While working-class youths were by no means the only ones to profit from greater levels of inclusiveness, the access percentages for the working class did rise somewhat more rapidly than those for the whole age group. Thus the opportunity ratio for the skilled manual and routine nonmanual occupations advanced from 0.4 during the decades around 1900 to 0.7–0.8 during the interwar period and 0.8–0.9 around 1950. The ratio for the children of semi- and unskilled workers increased from 0.1 before the First World War to 0.3–0.4 during the interwar years and 0.5 in 1950. In South West Hertfordshire and Middlesbrough in 1953, as we noted earlier, the ratios were 0.8 for skilled manual and 0.4–0.5 for unskilled manual workers.

At the boarding and independent schools, to be sure, recruitment patterns were much less progressive. While only 2–3 percent of the age group reached these institutions at all, children from upper middle-class families did so in much greater numbers than that. There was no visible change, in this respect, between 1900 and 1950. As late as 1950, the access percentage for the professional and managerial category at the independent schools was 21 percent, which made for an opportunity ratio near 7, while the corresponding figures for the working class were still too small to be statistically significant.

If one adds the access percentages for the boarding or independent schools to those for the ordinary grammar schools, of course, one obtains access rates for English academic secondary education in general. As of about 1950, the summed percentages were 23 for the whole age group, 62 for the professional and managerial elite, 35 for the inspectional and supervisory occupations, 17 for skilled and 10 for un-

grounds of various age groups among adults in England and Wales as of July 1949; her results for the two sexes are combined in the table. Little & Westergaard supplemented Floud's work on secondary education by gathering official data on children born in the late 1930s. The Robbins Report included a survey of twenty-one-year-olds *in Great Britain,* i.e., of boys and girls born in 1940–41. Only universities and academic secondary schools are considered. Floud distinguished between boarding grammar and ordinary grammar schools; Little & Westergaard, between independent and other grammar schools. Though somewhat varied by Little & Westergaard (who used the Registrars General scheme) and by the Robbins Report, the basic social categories (applied by Floud) are those of the Hall-Jones status scale. According to Marsh, *Changing Social Structure,* p.200, the Hall-Jones distribution of the English and Welsh population during the early 1950s was roughly as follows: Professional and higher administrative, 3 percent; Managerial and executive, 4.5 percent; Upper inspectional, supervisory, and other nonmanual, 10 percent; Lower inspectional, supervisory, and other nonmanual, 12.5 percent; Skilled manual and routine nonmanual, 41 percent; Semi-skilled manual, 16.5 percent; Unskilled manual, 12.5 percent.

skilled labor. The corresponding opportunity ratios were just under 3 for the professional and managerial elite, about half that much for the inspectional and supervisory occupations, 0.7–0.8 for skilled and 0.4–0.5 for unskilled labor. The principal role of the independent schools, as these figures make clear, was sharply to augment the educational opportunities of children from well-to-do families. Without significantly affecting the opportunity ratios for the working class itself, the independent schools widened the gap between the highest and the lowest access chances in English secondary education.

The special role of the independent schools may be partly responsible for the fact that the level of progressiveness rose much more slowly at the English universities than at the secondary schools between about 1910 and 1960. The university access percentages for the working class, as shown in Table 5.6, increased rapidly enough from 0.6 for skilled and 0.2 for unskilled labor during the decades before 1930 to 2 for skilled and 1 for unskilled labor about 1960. But the access percentage for the whole age group climbed almost as quickly, so that the net effect on the social distribution of opportunities was modest. As of 1960, the opportunity ratio for skilled workers was about 0.5 and that for unskilled workers was about 0.25. Even so, the level of progressiveness in university as in secondary education was at least as high in England as in France around 1960.

Before this can be demonstrated, some problems of method will have to be raised. Opportunity ratios inevitably tend to look lowest where the most disadvantaged social groups are observed in isolation, where unskilled workers are separated from skilled workers, for example. Similarly, the advantages of the professional and managerial elites are bound to be clearest when they are not diluted by an enlargement of their socio-occupational category to include other middle-class groups as well. At the top as at the bottom of the social scale, in other words, the narrower the occupational classifications, the more concentrated the evidence of inequality. This is why it is important that the typical English definition of skilled and unskilled labor is a good deal more comprehensive than the French term for workers (*ouvriers*) in industry and commerce. If the two were simply equated in a comparison of opportunity ratios, the disadvantages of the French *ouvriers* would inevitably look more serious than those of skilled and unskilled labor in England.

To deal with this difficulty at all, I have calculated opportunity ratios as follows. For English students reaching grammar and independent schools about 1950, as well as for those reaching universities about 1960, I have focussed on the "professional and higher administrative" status category (3 percent of the English working population), the "skilled manual and routine nonmanual" group (41 percent of the population), and the "semi- and unskilled manual" classification (29 percent of the population). For French beginning secondary pupils and university students in 1959,[30] I have grouped the liberal professions, high officials, secondary and university professors, and executive employees as "professional and executive" (2.9 percent of the French occupational census of 1954), farmers and low white-collar employees, including petty officials, as "farmers and clerks" (31.7 percent of the census), and industrial and agricultural workers and domestics as "workers and domestics" (44.9 percent of the census). Given below are the opportunity ratios for these roughly comparable social groups in English and French education during the 1950s.

English social groups	Those reaching grammar and independent schools	Those reaching universities
Professional and higher administrative (3%)	?	8
Skilled manual and routine nonmanual (41%)	0.7	0.5
Semi- and unskilled manual (29%)	0.4	0.25

French social groups	Beginning secondary pupils	University students
Professional and executive (2.9%)	5	10
Farmers and clerks (31.7%)	0.8	0.5
Workers and domestics (44.9%)	0.5	0.1

The two sets of ratios, of course, are remarkably similar; they certainly confirm the hypothesis that the English system was at least as progressive as the French system by 1960. It should be noted that the French figures pertain only to the universities, not to the *grandes écoles*. They thus exclude the academically and social most prestigious sector of French higher education, which was also most dominated by the upper middle class. Without this omission, obviously, the working-class opportunity ratio for the French university-level system as a whole would be even lower.[31]

Particularly interesting about the English pattern is that a fair degree of progressiveness was achieved at a low level of inclusiveness—English

---

30. See Tables 4.9 and 4.11 and Tables X and XIII, along with Table 5.6.

31. The English ratios are derived from access percentages, the French ones from distribution percentages; the English figures are for anyone who reached the universities at all, the French ones for all university students, but neither of these differences is likely to be very significant.

university enrollments per age group scarcely exceeded 5 percent around 1960. In France at that time, roughly 10 percent of the age group reached university-level education. The German figure was slightly lower than the English one, but university recruitment was clearly less progressive in Germany than in France as of 1960. England thus combined low enrollments per age group with a comparatively "democratic" distribution of access chances.

This configuration is especially likely to engender social mobility through education. It is also very hard to achieve, for it requires that many pupils from upper middle-class homes be excluded from higher education. Despite the special role of the independent schools, this has apparently been done to some extent in England, perhaps by way of the eleven-plus and other examinations. Among offspring of the English "professional and higher administrative elite," as Table 5.6 indicates, only 33 percent actually reached the universities about 1960. It is hard to imagine an equally rigorous selection taking place in the United States. In France and Germany, the baccalaureate and *Abitur* examinations have officially been considered meritocratic devices, but they may in fact have been used as much to limit the total number of secondary graduates as to discriminate among them. Since both examinations can be taken more than once, they have also favored those who could afford an extended period of cramming, perhaps with the aid of private tutors.

Altogether, the rapid evolution of the English system during the twentieth century constitutes something of a challenge for the historian of education. How could the most blatantly aristocratic of the three major European systems of the nineteenth century change so fast? How was a comparatively progressive pattern of recruitment reached without large enrollment increases and despite the survival of the independent schools? Halsey has pointed to the "remarkable absorptive capacity, the judicious and un-Marxist Fabianism of the upper classes,"[32] to which one could add the determined and un-Marxist reformism of the Labour Party. At a more specific level, I have been inclined to stress the eleven-plus and the absence of clear curricular segmentations. It is obvious that much additional work will have to be done before some of these issues are resolved.

American Contrasts

The American college of the eighteenth and early nineteenth centuries was in many respects a marginal institution. A private venture,

32. Halsey, "British Universities and Intellectual Life," esp. p.506.

it was typically affiliated with a religious denomination or philanthropic association. It generally catered to a local rather than a national clientele. In its academic standards, it resembled a European secondary school rather than a university. The large majority of college presidents were clergymen. With the aid of a few tutors, often aspiring clergymen themselves, these college presidents tried to instruct their charges in Latin and in piety. Among the students, some may have been destined to join the local social and political elites, but most were preparing to become schoolmasters or ministers. In the 1830s, roughly one-third of American college graduates entered clerical careers, and the percentage was even higher during the late eighteenth century.[33]

There was no connection between higher education and government service. This important element in the history of the French and German systems was simply absent in the United States. At the same time, the standardized state examinations for the major professions that played so large a role on the European continent were essentially unknown in America. Professional education in the United States long retained the character of practical apprenticeship. Even college teachers normally held no more than a B.A. degree, which required no specialized scholarship. In fact, as has been suggested, teaching was closely allied to the clerical careers.

Clearly, the American system followed English precedents in important ways, but it failed to achieve the standards and prestige of Oxford and Cambridge. Two major differences between English society and its colonial offspring may account for this failure. First, there was no American aristocracy or gentry that could have been identified with the institutions of higher education and lent them the capacity to confer status. Second, the place of the Anglican Establishment was taken in the United States by a welter of competing religious denominations, none of which could acquire the cultural authority of the English church. As a result, higher education never really became an important or autonomous force in nineteenth-century America.

Not that colleges were progressive or critical elements in the culture. Jencks and Riesman have described the pre-Jacksonian college as a "pillar [of the] locally established church, political order, and social conventions," but as "by no means a very important pillar": "only a minority of those who controlled the established institutions of pre-Jacksonian America sent their children to college, and an even smaller minority had itself been to a college."[34] Nor should one assume that competing educational institutions consciously contributed to the

33. Metzger, *Academic Freedom*, pp. 21–22.
34. Jencks and Riesman, *Academic Revolution*, p.1.

heterogeneity of a rapidly changing society. Jencks and Riesman suspect that many colleges were founded in "a vain struggle to maintain the old standards and the old ways."[35]

Here as always, however, results were more important than intentions. Especially during the second and third quarters of the nineteenth century, all kinds of sectional interests and social groups sought to protect their subcultures by founding colleges of their own. The factual diversity that was thus institutionalized helped to reduce the coherence and authority of higher education and of traditional culture generally. In the context of opportunities provided by the frontier and later by industrialization, education was totally overshadowed by other avenues to wealth and power. Upward social mobility took place more often around than through the existing educational institutions. In that sense, America became a "materialist" society: its essentially irrelevant educational system could not sustain a value and status alternative to the emerging industrial class structure.

In the evolution of American educational institutions, a divide is commonly located sometime between 1860 and 1880. European parallels suggest that this was an era of transition from the system's early industrial to its high industrial phase. The most important institutional changes taking place were the rise of the university with its graduate and professional schools and the emergence of academically demanding colleges that sent a portion of their graduates on to obtain higher degrees. German models helped to shape a new ideal of original scholarship and specialized research. No American Ph.D.s at all were conferred before 1861, but one hundred sixty-four of them were awarded in 1890 and more than twice that many by 1900. The number of postgraduate students rose from less than two hundred in 1871 to nearly three thousand in 1890.[36] Academic standards continued to be uneven; they are much less uniform in America than in Europe even today. Among some five hundred institutions of higher education in the United States in 1903, according to Veysey, only about a dozen were universities of the first rank.[37] Nevertheless, the closing decades of the nineteenth century did inaugurate a new era in American higher education, an era that was to be increasingly dominated by the graduate university and by specialization in scholarship and professional training.

From the 1880s to the 1960s, the American educational system grew in a largely continuous fashion; there were no outstanding institutional changes to break up the process. Throughout the high industrial and

---

35. Jencks and Riesman, *Academic Revolution*, p.7.
36. Metzger, *Academic Freedom*, p.104.
37. Veysey, *Emergence of the American University*, p.359.

late industrial periods, the demand for education rose steadily, without major interruptions. While no state of the economy can be supposed to dictate specific levels of inclusiveness, the rapid expansion of American secondary and higher education was certainly accompanied by the emergence and growing importance of certain kinds of white-collar employment. At least in a general way, one may safely conclude, the rise in enrollments was stimulated by the increasing complexity of twentieth-century technology and of contemporary social organization.

Some of the main characteristics of the American educational system offer interesting contrasts with European patterns. Neither curricular segmentations nor differences of academic and social status have been as prominent in the United States as they have been in Europe, particularly on the Continent. Of course there have been distinctions between academic and vocational courses in high schools and between "pure" and "applied" college programs, but they have not been visible at the institutional level. Similarly, secondary schools, colleges, and universities have differed in prestige; but no *particular interval* in the rank order has been as important as some of the discontinuities within the European systems. One thinks of the line between English grammar and independent schools or between the ordinary universities and Oxbridge. Although not aggravated by curricular tracks of the French and German type, these barriers in English education have been much more significant than anything comparable in the United States. The American system, in short, has been relatively free of segmentation and is, in that sense, amorphous or fluid.

It has also been particularly flexible, capable of responding quickly to new demands for education. Private colleges and universities, whether endowed or not, have done most to maintain this flexibility, at the cost of a certain market orientation among institutions seeking patrons and "customers." Also worth noting is the fact that while individual American colleges and universities have exercised the right to reject some of their applicants and have thus severally had the means to select their students on "merit" principles, they have seldom *as a group* rejected a mediocre candidate who could pay for his education. Particularly in conjunction with the availability of the great state universities, this has enhanced the general fluidity of the system's internal rank structure, as well as the elasticity of its reaction to the many different demands it has faced.

Between 1880 and 1960, the American system did in fact respond easily and quickly to a rising demand for intermediate and advanced instruction. It lacked the authority conferred on nineteenth-century European educational institutions by their traditional connection with an aristocracy, an established church, and/or the civil service of a powerful and centralized state. Its internal organization put few obstacles in the path of expansion and change. And so it adjusted, with a minimum of resistance, to the evolving "needs" of the high and late industrial society, which were defined by the market for education—or for certificates. From a position of social marginality or even irrelevance before 1880, the American system thus moved quickly toward a condition of functional adjustment. It bypassed the phase in the history of the continental European systems when conflicts between modern and traditional curricula were most visible as socio-cultural incongruities. Since it never played an actively incongruent role, it encouraged the simple view of education as an essentially dependent, passive element in the social process.

There is little statistical evidence on American secondary and higher education, especially for the period before 1880, but what there is falls into a familiar pattern. According to Metzger, the ratio of college students to the total population in New England decreased from 0.66 per thousand in 1826 to 0.59 in 1855 and 0.52 in 1869.[38] Even during the 1870s, as Laurence Veysey notes, enrollments at twenty leading colleges increased much more slowly than the total population.[39] There is reason to believe, in short, that access to American higher education stagnated or actually fell during the second and third quarters of the nineteenth century. One is reminded of similar traits in the German and English curves of enrollments per age group between 1830 and 1870. In the case of the United States, even the new graduate programs of the 1860s and 70s apparently led to no increases in college attendance until the 1880s.

The expansion of enrollments from about 1880 to 1960 is the subject of Table 5.7. More specifically, the table deals with estimated percentages of relevant age groups who finished high school and who completed four years of college (with or without a degree) as of the years listed. The lower figures are derived from degree awards reported to the Office of Education; the higher ones are based on the census. The true percentages presumably lay somewhere between the two sets of estimates, but that still leaves a large margin of uncertainty.

Nevertheless, a couple of conclusions can be safely drawn from the material in Table 5.7. There is no doubt, for example, that secondary and university enrollments rose without interruption from 1880 to

38. Metzger, *Academic Freedom,* p.38.
39. Veysey, *Emergence of the American University,* p.4. Veysey also refers to other data suggesting stable or declining enrollments per population for most of the nineteenth century.

1960, and at a roughly similar rate. Those completing four years of college were generally about one-fifth to one-fourth as numerous as high school graduates. They were also generally some two to three times as numerous, in relation to the age group, as German and French secondary graduates. The figures for 1960 are an exception: while German *Abitur* awards lagged behind, French and English secondary graduations were now slightly more than half as frequent as American college completions. English and German university entrants, however, were still only about 4–6 percent of their age group, while French university entrants were about 10 percent and American college graduates were approaching 20 percent of their generation. Thus levels of

Table 5.7

Percentages of American Age Groups Who Completed High School and Four Years of College, 1880–1960

Year	Completed high school	College: four years	German Abitur	French Bacca- laureate
1880	2.5–11.5	1.0–2.0	0.6	0.8
1890	3.5–14.0	1.5–2.5	0.9	1.0
1900	6.5–17.0	1.5–3.5	0.9	1.2
1910	9.0–20.5	2.0–4.0	1.2	1.1
1920	17.0–28.5	2.5–5.0	1.3	1.4
1930	29.0–40.5	6.0–7.5	3.3	2.3
1940	51.0–54.5	ca. 8		
1950	59.0–60.5	ca. 11	4.5	5.7
1960	ca. 65	ca. 18	5.4	11.2

From Jencks & Riesman, *Academic Revolution*, p.77, based on Census and U.S. Office of Education (USOE) estimates. *The higher American figures* stem from the Census (1940 and 1960); they are percentages of those born during stipulated five-year intervals (1855–59, 1860–64, etc.) who finished high school and who finished four years of college, not necessarily with a degree. Jencks and Riesman estimate those not obtaining degrees as probably more than 20 percent of those completing four years of college (according to the Census) before 1910, 20–21 percent around 1910–20, 15 percent around 1930, and 10–11 percent around 1940–50. *The lower American figures* stem from USOE; they are based on institutional reports of all awarded degrees (not Bachelor only). Jencks and Riesman followed USOE in assuming that the median age at high school graduation was 17; they chose 22 as the median age at college graduation on the basis of a 1961 survey. They used these estimates to relate the USOE returns for various graduating classes to the appropriate five-year birth cohorts in the Census (1855–59, 1860–64, etc.). This procedure is simply reversed in the above table. Figures listed for 1880, for example, are percentages of those born 1860–64 who finished high school (aged 17) about 1877–81 and of those born 1855–59 who finished college (aged 22) at about the same time.

inclusiveness have been almost incomparably higher in the United States than in Europe.

The situation has not been as clear with respect to progressiveness. One does have the impression of an unusually broad middle-class influx into the American colleges during the decades after 1880. Members of the liberal professions were joined by many well-to-do farmers and ordinary businessmen among the fathers of students.[40] Partly because the educational system was so rich in gradations of academic standing and social prestige, it appears, there was no sharply visible divide between a highly educated minority and the rest of the substantial middle class.

This impression is confirmed by Reynolds' 1925 sample of American college students, which is described in Table 5.8. About 18 percent of the students' fathers were members of the professions, broadly speaking, and only a handful more were in public service. Another 8 percent, not a large number, were artisans and workers, including artisan-proprietors. That left some 23–24 percent each for agriculture, business owners, and the various service occupations. The comparatively large share of agriculture is particularly remarkable, but the whole industrial and commercial middle class was well represented also. The opportunity ratios ranged from 5 for the professions to 0.07 for "common" labor. The business proprietors, with a ratio of 3, ranked little below the professions. The managerial and commercial service occupations attained a ratio just over 1.5. They were followed by agriculture at just under 1, transportation and clerical service at 0.7, public service at only 0.4, the skilled trades at 0.2, and personal service and "common" labor at around 0.1.

As these figures suggest, the American colleges of the 1920s were "middle-class" in an unusually inclusive sense of that term, but they were not especially progressive. Opportunity ratios dropped off rather sharply toward the lower end of the social scale. Even if one takes artisans and workers as a group, one obtains a ratio of only 0.2 for a 39 percent share of the occupational census. That figure is no higher than the opportunity ratio for the children of semi- and unskilled workers in English universities during the 1930s. Yet the English universities at that time *took in* about 2 percent of the age group,

40. Veysey, *Emergence of the American University*, pp.291–92. Among fathers of students at Michigan in 1902, about 30 percent were businessmen, 22 percent were farmers, and 17 percent were members of nonacademic lay professions (law, medicine, engineering, pharmacy, etc.); only 5.2 percent were mechanics, craftsmen, or skilled workers. (Percentages cited by Veysey do not add up to 100.)

Table 5.8

Social Origins of Students in Fifty-five
American Colleges and Universities, ca. 1925
(Percentages by Column)

Occupational Category	Students' fathers	1920 census
1. Professional	18.3	3.8
2. Public service	0.6	1.6
3. Agriculture	23.3	28.5
4. Business proprietors	24.2	8.0
5. Managerial service	10.1	7.2
6. Commercial service	7.0	3.9
7. Transportation service	3.8	5.0
8. Clerical service	2.0	3.0
4–8. Business	47.1	27.1
9. Artisan-proprietors	1.4	–
10. Skilled trades[a]	5.9	28.1
11. "Common" labor	0.5	7.2
12. Personal service	0.4	3.7
9–12. Artisans and workers	8.2	39.0
13. Unknown	2.5	–

From Reynolds, *Social and Economic Status;* based on a sample of 6,104 students (16 percent of those who had been sent questionnaires) at 55 colleges and universities of mixed locations and types. Reynolds' results fall 0.8 percent short of 100 percent; this 0.8 percent is here added to his unknowns.

[a] The building (3.0 percent), machine (1.5 percent), printing and other trades (1.1 percent), which are grouped with 0.3 percent miners and lumber-workers.

whereas the American colleges *graduated* around 5 percent.[41] Thus the comparison scarcely sustains the widespread belief that educational opportunities were distributed more equally in the United States than elsewhere.

Among more recent surveys of American students, some of the best unfortunately deal only with high school graduates. Thus a study by Folger, Astin, and Bayer in effect asks what percentages of 1960 high school graduates reached college from specified socio-economic back-

41. See Table 5.6; the English opportunity ratio for the semi-skilled and unskilled was just under 0.2 as of 1900–1929 and just over 0.2 as of 1930–49. Note that the English category of the semi- and unskilled accounted for 29 percent of the English census at that time; enlarged to include some skilled workers (as in the American survey) it would give rise to an even higher English opportunity ratio. Those completing four years of college in America were 2.5–5.0 percent of their age group in 1920 and 6.0–7.5 percent in 1930, and about 80–85 percent of those who finished college in those years did so with a degree.

grounds and levels of aptitude.[42] Having divided the graduates into quintiles according to their parents' status and, separately, according to their test scores, Folger and his associates determined college access percentages for every combination of status and aptitude. Their results revealed somewhat larger access differences between aptitude quintiles, with social origins held constant, than between status quintiles, with aptitude factored out. But the margin in favor of test scores as the more important determinant was not at all large. Since Folger's percentages were calculated with respect to high school graduates, not the whole age group, they cannot be compared with the more general indicators for the French and German universities. Even so, they constitute a further challenge to the conventional image of American education as particularly open. They show the American system of 1960 a goodly distance away from the meritocratic level of progressiveness, which suggests that educational opportunities were no more evenly distributed in the United States than in England at that time.

Somewhat more direct evidence on this subject can be found in the form of a comparison between the distribution according to income of "families and unrelated individuals with principal earner between forty-five and fifty-four in 1965" and "families with children entering college, fall 1966."[43] Those earning less than $4,000 were 15.5 percent of all families, but only 6.6 percent of all college families (10 percent of families with children entering public four-year colleges and 3.3 percent of families with children entering private universites). Thus the opportunity ratios for this income group were 0.4 at colleges in general, 0.6 at public four-year colleges, and 0.2 at private universities. For the 2.7 percent of families with principal incomes of $25,000 or more, the distribution percentages were 7.1 percent at all colleges, 2.5 percent at public four-year colleges, and 17.9 percent at private universities. The opportunity ratios for this group were 2.6 at all colleges, 0.9 at public four-year colleges, and 6.6 at private universities. These figures begin to suggest some of the social differences between the more prestigious of the private institutions and the less distinguished of the public ones. The data also indicate considerable differences of educational opportunity between the rich and the poor in America. Undoubtedly, both sets of differences would look even greater if they were described in narrower and more refined categories.

42. Folger et al., *Human Resources and Higher Education*, p.310; the table is reproduced in Jencks and Riesman, *Academic Revolution*, p.103.

43. Jencks and Riesman, *Academic Revolution*, p.118, based on calculations by the Bureau of the Census.

Why do people *believe* that there has been more equality of educational opportunity in the United States than in Europe? (I myself used to think that.) One possible answer has to do with the relationship between inclusiveness and progressiveness. There must be a point, one is tempted to think, when additional increases in inclusiveness cannot help but raise the level of progressiveness as well. While this is clear in the abstract, however, there is no way of telling when an educational system will reach that point. Much depends, of course, on the degree of selectivity that is maintained as inclusiveness increases, and therein lies the difficulty. Though constitutionally quicker than the European systems to respond to new demands for education, the American system *as a whole* has never been selective. It has not often denied college degrees to students who could pay for them; its obvious market orientation has almost certainly favored the wealthier classes. Of course it has been much more inclusive than the European systems; but there is no clear evidence that it has been more progressive as well. What, then, accounts for its vaguely "democratic" appearance?

To deal with this situation, I must refer briefly to the current debate over American social mobility.[44] Lipset and Bendix began that debate by showing that rates of intergenerational upward mobility from blue-collar to white-collar occupations have been roughly similar in all advanced industrial societies; there has been no more mobility in the United States than in other highly developed countries, including the European ones. Despite certain criticisms and qualifications, this general thesis has not been radically challenged. Indeed, there has been additional evidence and argument to the effect that social mobility in America today is about what it was some decades ago or even around 1900, perhaps even during the nineteenth century. The issue is by no means settled—Thernstrom has suggested that there may have been somewhat greater mobility in the United States than in Europe during the nineteenth century, and Kaelble has argued that some types of upward mobility were rarer in Germany than in America between 1900 and 1960. Neither of these arguments can be fully reconciled with the notion of similar rates of mobility at comparable states of industrialization. Still, Lipset and Bendix have made most of their case. No one today would claim that social mobility in the United States has ever

44. For the following, see Lipset and Bendix, *Social Mobility;* Miller, "Comparative Social Mobility"; Blau and Duncan, "Occupational Structure"; Jencks and Riesman, *Academic Revolution*, pp.73–74; Thernstrom, *The Other Bostonians*, pp.257–59; Kaelble, "Sozialer Aufstieg." I am aware that the possibility of increasing rigidity in the American social structure was an issue well before Lipset and Bendix launched their cross-national comparisons.

been high enough to justify the traditional image of America as the open society, the land of opportunity, and the antithesis of class-bound Europe.

Precisely at this point, however, there is a gap in the argument put forward by Lipset and Bendix. They acknowledge that Americans have believed their society to be particularly open. There has been a Horatio Alger myth, a conviction that in America the hard-working individual could rise to a position of wealth and power. Lipset and Bendix treat this belief as largely gratuitous; they fail to explain what has kept it alive. They do point out that America never knew an aristocratic regime of the European type, that there have been some highly visible opportunities near the bottom and the top of the American business hierarchy, and that immigrants and blacks have been available to fill the lowest positions in the American social system. They also refer to the absolutely high level of wealth in the United States, which may have obscured social differences in living standards by putting many consumer goods at the disposal of low income groups. Yet none of these suggestions is fully convincing, and Lipset and Bendix themselves seem unable to decide which of them to take seriously.

My hunch is that the American educational system has fostered a climate of equality that has needed no confirmation from the facts of mobility. Lipset and Bendix themselves call attention to the "materialism" at the foot of American egalitarianism. Americans are determined, they write, to "think of the differences of status and power, not as being what they really are, but as differences in the distribution of material goods."[45] Having reduced social differences to income inequalities, Americans tend to regard them as more or less accidental and superficial—and therefore transitory. But if this "materialistic" outlook is indeed fundamental to the American belief in mobility, one ought to try to explain it. One certainly cannot trace it to the high standard of living, the availability of consumer goods, the chance to start a small business, or anything else of that sort. Even educational opportunities as such will not meet the case.[46]

The American educational system has been "democratic," I would argue, to the extent that it has encouraged the "materialist" reduction of social stratification as a widespread—if unconscious—popular attitude, whereas the European educational systems have discouraged it. Perhaps differences of education have always been experienced as more

45. Lipset and Bendix, *Social Mobility*, p.80.
46. Lipset and Bendix include increased educational opportunities in their list of supports for the American faith in mobility, but they do not elaborate upon this suggestion.

essential, personal, and legitimate than other inequalities. This has been the case, at any rate, in Europe, where education has been a significant and partly autonomous element in the social process and where highly visible barriers have separated the several segments of the educational systems. In Europe, education has conferred status upon highly select groups of students, whose elite position was legitimized by the personal grace derived from the traditional learning. In Europe, education has thus helped to make social differences seem profound and indelible. In America, by contrast, the educational system has had no such effect; if anything, it has fostered the notion that social stratification is "merely" a matter of money, of good luck in the market.

Most of the pertinent peculiarities of the American system have already been mentioned. Marginal institutions during much of the nineteenth century, American colleges and universities have since moved to a position of functional adjustment. Differences of academic and social standing in secondary and higher education have not been reinforced by curricular distinctions. There have been no prominent breaks on a continuous scale of prestige. Indeed, an amorphous structure has helped to *disguise* the realities of stratification within the educational system itself.

The other vital element in the American situation has been the impact of sheer numbers. Without an artistocracy, a powerful civil service, or an established church in its past, American education has never had the status significance of the European tradition. Yet it might have created a purely meritocratic elite, if enrollments per age group had remained at European levels for any considerable period of time. But this is where the advent of "mass" higher education has made a difference. The unusual inclusiveness of the American system has tended to devalue the individual college degree, and not only in the job market. The significance of education as an independent source of status was never high to begin with, but it has been further reduced by an educational inflation that is only just beginning to affect Europe as well.

It is important to recognize that rapid enrollment increases can have democratic implications even when they have little or no impact upon levels of progressiveness in education or upon rates of mobility in the society at large. Numbers alone can reduce the status significance of education; they can eliminate the support given by educational differences to the maintenance of a social hierarchy. The effect will be to reduce the experienced social distances among people. Social differences, indeed, will be demystified or trivialized, depending on one's viewpoint. The place of the traditional European sense of social stratification will be taken by the untutored "materialism" observed by Lipset and Bendix. The American educational system has had a vaguely democratic effect, in short, because it has lent credence to this optimistic and fundamentally egalitarian outlook even when the European systems did the opposite. Time will probably reduce the difference.

Conclusion:

Contemporary Perspectives

While it has not been possible to extend this study beyond 1960, a few concluding remarks on contemporary issues do suggest themselves. The educational systems of the major Western countries have been in a state of nearly perpetual crisis since 1960. Perhaps the historical context will help to clarify current prospects for education as a social force.

In Germany, France, and England, as in the United States, there were particularly sharp increases in secondary and university attendance between 1945 and 1960, even before the large birth cohorts of the immediate postwar years reached the university level. The stage was thus set for the enrollment boom of the 1960s, which has been slowed but not reversed during the 1970s. It must be remembered that enrollment increases tend to be self-accelerating to some extent. There is a multiplier effect, because high enrollments create a demand for teachers, which in turn encourages enrollments. In any case, the boom of the 1960s apparently created an excess of educated men in the United States and elsewhere. The deceleration of the 1970s has been accompanied by the kind of anxieties that were raised by earlier, more or less temporary disequilibria between supply and demand in education.

This is not to say that the enrollment increases since 1945 have been strictly short-term phenomena. They are also part of the long-term rise in the demand for postprimary education that has characterized the late industrial era as a whole. In all the educational systems that have been studied, student numbers began to move upward at an increased rate during the interwar period. In Europe, this accelerated enrollment growth was accompanied by a lowering of the traditional barrier between higher primary and secondary education, as well as by other approaches to the ideal of the common school. Thus the Second

260

World War and the subsequent fluctuations in birth rates merely interrupted and complicated a trend that dates back at least to the 1920s and 30s. The need for highly skilled white-collar personnel in a technologically advanced and highly complex society has undoubtedly helped to launch this trend, but it cannot fully account for it. Germany and the United States, for example, have similar economies but dissimilar university systems and enrollment levels. Even today, social conventions have at least as much to do with the demand for education as any supposedly objective requirements of the economy.

More particularly, one cannot ignore the role of social and political conflict in the history of education. The demand for increased opportunities, for "democratization," has been an important factor in the enlargement of European secondary systems since 1918 and in the growth of enrollments more generally. A reform consensus emerged during the interwar period that has only recently been challenged. The political importance of this consensus stemmed from the rather wide support it had from the center and left of the political spectrum, from moderate socialists as well as democratic liberals. In theoretical terms, the consensus was built upon a few basic propositions that no one thought to question. Segmentation in education was rejected as tending to preserve privilege. Neither institutional barriers nor economic inequalities were any longer to prevent an enlarged and more equal access to advanced education. Greater inclusiveness was recommended both as an aid to the economy and as a democratic measure; it was expected to break down class barriers, to increase educational opportunities for lower-class students, and thus to encourage social mobility. Particularly if merit rather than wealth or family background determined access to education, the theory ran, inclusiveness was bound to mean progressiveness as well.

This expectation, of course, has been largely disappointed. Taking our stand at 1960, we can see that wider access has led to no really satisfying improvements in the social distribution of educational opportunities. Some increments of progressiveness have apparently been achieved in England and to a lesser degree in France, but the overall effect has not been encouraging. Access percentages have increased, but opportunity ratios have proved rather sluggish, and of course the two are not the same. The difference between overall access rates and relative access chances in education should be quite as clear as that between per capita national income and its proportional distribution among various social groups. Greater educational wealth has simply failed to engender the redistribution that had been anticipated.

If this is true, as I think it is, there is no need for complex models of the relationship between educational opportunity and social mobility.[1] Obviously, the effect of an increase in progressiveness will be diluted by any accompanying increase in inclusiveness, since the social advantages or claims that come to be more equally distributed are simultaneously "devalued" by their more general availability. But the case I have tried to make does not depend upon such inflationary dissipation of a potential for social mobility. The evidence suggests that there was little such potential to be dissipated, since levels of progressiveness did not rise substantially enough to create it in the first place. This fact is at the bottom of the widespread disillusionment with education as a means of "democratization."

To make matters worse, contemporary societies are apparently paying for benefits they have been denied. For increased inclusiveness has led to a "devalution" of education even without the expected equalization of opportunities. An American college degree or a French baccalaureate "means" less today than it once did, whether in the job market or as a mark of social distinction.

It is worth noting that this type of inflation can make itself felt with equal intensity at different levels of inclusiveness. An educational certificate is "devalued" whenever it is awarded more frequently than it used to be. The experience of inflation is a disappointed expectation, the sense of a social convention that has been violated. It arises from a *change* in the level of inclusiveness, not from the level itself. In France, the rate of baccalaureate awards rose from 2.3 percent of the age group in 1931 to 11.2 percent in 1961. This was a more serious disturbance of established conventions than the approximately simultaneous increase in the rate of American college graduations from around 7 to about 18 percent of the age group. Thus the apparently universal inflation of academic credentials since the Second World

---

1. Boudon, *Education, Opportunity, and Social Inequality,* is based largely upon an Organization for Economic Cooperation and Development survey of 1970, i.e., on evidence beyond the limits of this study. I do feel that the authors of the OECD survey use an awkward method of assessing inequalities of access; they divide the access percentage for the most favored by that for the least favored social group. For reasons I outline in Chapter Five, this aggravates the potential effect of national differences in socio-occupational codes. Boudon's *theoretical* model, moreover, seems needlessly complicated and uncomfortably tautological. Infinitely small differences of preference can be made to yield infinitely large differences in the social distribution of advanced education, as long as the occasions of choice for the individual student can be made—or imagined—infinitely numerous. Doesn't the American high school student, for example, "choose" almost continually whether to be academic or vocational in his electives—and in his approach to homework?

War has been most traumatic in France and Germany, where very small systems were significantly enlarged. It has been less severe in the United States, where the colleges were never really elite institutions, and in England, where an unusually rigorous selection at the level of university entry has kept the numbers down.

What seems to me most significant about the academic inflation is the crisis of expectations it brings about. I am not impressed by vague complaints about "mass education," which tend to imply, falsely, that university access has become socially more progressive after all or that the maintenance of academic standards is actually impossible at the new levels of inclusiveness. Nor am I afraid that too much education for too many people might be socially wasteful, or that students might be overeducated in some way, or that we might be raising another academic proletariat. I do not believe we know what amounts and types of schooling would be most useful to contemporary societies, and I do not accept the narrowly functional view of education that is implied in the notion of overeducation. On the other hand, I cannot help but sympathize with individual students who experience the "devaluation" of education as a threat to their future and to their self-esteem.

During the nineteenth century, especially in Europe, as I have tried to show, university study opened the way not only to well-paid and interesting jobs but to a measure of status and power as well. The positions it gave access to, moveover, were normally coupled with a degree of personal autonomy that must have been satisfying quite apart from any question of power. The traditional liberal professions, it seems to me, were liberal in a way that most twentieth-century white-collar occupations are not. The typical university graduate of the nineteenth century enjoyed the status, the life-style, and the *independence* of a notable, of the lawyer or doctor in a provincial town. The individualism of cultivation, if not that of the market, was reasonably well attuned to his situation. He could identify with the language of intellectual autonomy and with the model of the liberally educated man, whereas the contemporary white-collar employee might well experience them, more or less consciously, as utopian, irrelevant, or contradictory.

I am suggesting that much of the dissatisfaction of today's student is neither accidental nor transitory. It is linked, rather, to a transformation in the social character and situation of the middle classes that has been under way since the turn of the century. The contemporary student is a future member of the white-collar army. That is one of the things he learns after reaching the university. He senses the contrast between his prospects and the norms and orientations that have survived—so far—in his education. His disillusionment is not only resentment at lost status, but also fear of being humanly impoverished and used by the technological apparatus or by the "system."

Next to the crisis of expectations, the most serious issue in contemporary education is the problem of "meritocracy." It has caused concern especially in England, where fairly rigorous techniques of selection have been tried, and in the United States, where racial minorities have suspected that "merit" principles are designed to exclude them from the educational system.

Extending some of the concepts in Young's *Rise of the Meritocracy,* one may characterize meritocracy in terms of three related problems. The first is psychological. Since jobs are increasingly tied to educational qualifications, no one can afford to do badly on standardized examinations or in school. Grades and test scores are threatening to become the only measures of personal worth, and the psychic cost of academic failure is rising to intolerable levels. It does not seem to matter that success in school cannot guarantee a good position or that the relationship between schooling and professional performance is unclear. What matters is that *poor* school records and test scores can have a *negative* effect on someone's career chances. Without "credentials," a working-class student cannot expect to get a good post, and his upper middle-class colleague at least runs the risk of falling below his father's place in society. Meritocratic selection is particularly dangerous for students from favored backgrounds, who have little to gain and much to lose; but it can be oppressive for everyone. On the other hand, it may be the only secure path to increased progressiveness without academic "inflation." Really to change the social distribution of educational opportunities, one has to reject some middle-class students.

A second problem of meritocracy is best illustrated by the development of working-class access to the English grammar schools since the 1930s. It was found that the provision of additional free places did not improve the access chances of working-class students as decidedly as had been anticipated. Instead, a pattern of diminishing returns set in, and this at a time when the distribution of places came fairly close to the meritocratic level of progressiveness. Does the effort to democratize the educational system reach something like a natural limit?

Merely to ask the question, of course, is to provoke a whole series of objections. Measurable academic ability may be unevenly distributed over the various ranks in society, but much of the variance is culturally conditioned. Educational institutions, like tests, probably do as much to reward and confirm the cultural advantages of privileged students as to aid those from less favored backgrounds.[2] In any case, the distribution of test scores must not be turned into a biological justification for social inequality; for that would lead to the frightening caste system of Young's fable.

In the United States, some of the radical opponents of meritocracy did not confine themselves to theoretical criticisms; they sought practical alternatives to test scores as means of academic selection. For disadvantaged minorities, at least, they demanded a greater share of college places than "merit" alone would justify. Though their efforts were not very successful, they threatened an important part of the old reformist consensus. Their attack has provoked a defensive reaction, in which meritocratic principles have been identified with civilization itself.

The third problem of meritocracy was of particular concern to Young himself. His book can be read as an extended critique of the tripartite scheme of grammar, technical, and modern schools that has dominated British secondary education since the Second World War. Young was a disappointed advocate of the common school. He did not see the tripartite approach as a modern extension of certain traditional segmentations; he saw it as an attempt to adjust the educational system to the late industrial economy. The raising of the grammar and technical schools above the modern ones struck him as an anticipation of the social divide between white-collar experts on the one hand and workers on the other. The merit that was emphasized, it seemed to him, was much too narrowly defined and its nurture too much motivated by considerations of efficiency. For Young, the tripartite model was an example of functional adjustment, and meritocracy was a close ally of technocracy.

Young's objection to meritocracy, in short, was based upon a modern humanism. The working-class spokesmen who initially sought secondary education for all, he suggested, were interested in social equality as a precondition for human diversity. A classless society, they thought, would respect and foster the whole range of man's qualities. Education in such a society would pursue "sweetness and light" for their own sake; it would not treat students as mere "functionaries of society": "The schools should not be tied to the occupational structure

2. Bourdieu and Passeron, *Les Héritiers*, contains some interesting material on the unconscious preference shown even by professional educators for the student (from a privileged background) who is so "gifted" and so at home with the traditional culture that he need not be slavish in its acquisition. In fact he doesn't need the teacher very much.

. . . but should be devoted to encouraging all human talents. . . . The arts and manual skills should be given as much prominence as science and technology . . . and common schools at last established."[3] One of the dangers of the meritocratic mentality, in other words, is that it will impoverish our vision of education.

Altogether, the world of contemporary education is rich in theoretical and practical dilemmas. Hopes for an equalization of educational opportunities have been largely frustrated. We are faced with the discomforts of academic inflation on the one hand and with the disturbing aspects of meritocracy on the other. The developments of the last few decades have challenged practically every assumption that used to guide reformers. Distinguished scholars on both sides of the Atlantic have warned of the futility of trying to use education to reduce social inequalities.[4] There is a spreading sense of helplessness and resignation.

Yet the old left liberal consensus on reform in education is by no means as indefensible, even in today's situation, as some of its critics seem to believe. In its practical purposes, if not its theoretical foundations, it remains viable despite all disappointments. No alternate program has been formulated with any degree of coherence, which is why opposition to it so often seems merely discouraging. We might well review some of the main elements in the consensus to appreciate their strengths.

To begin with the matter of inclusiveness, the notion that "more is better" remains perfectly sound even today. Higher access rates may not do much to increase progressiveness or to encourage social mobility; they may instead aggravate the dissatisfactions and pains of academic inflation. But these eventualities are largely irrelevant. After all, advanced education is valuable in itself; it is a benefit, an advantage, and it should be made available to as many people as possible. If we tried to return to the overall enrollment percentages of the nineteenth century, we would soon find ourselves overwhelmed by the moral and practical difficulties of the selection that would have to be made.[5] A

3. Young, *Rise of the Meritocracy*, p.170.
4. Examples are Jencks et al., *Inequality*, and Boudon, *Education, Opportunity, and Social Inequality*. Both authors recommend that we change the distribution of income instead, but they say less about that than about the futility of traditional reform in education. A certain passivity is suggested, in Boudon's case, by the treatment of inequality as a kind of market phenomenon, the effect of everyone's being allowed to make his own "choices."
5. Lasch, "Inequality and Education," seriously suggests that advanced education be restricted to a small, socially mixed but highly selected group of students, who would prepare to be either critical (because poorly paid) intellectuals or

ruthless application of meritocratic techniques might identify a small elite of able students, many of them from socially and culturally advantaged backgrounds. But only coercion would sustain the exclusion of others from the educational system. The consequences of being excluded, it must be remembered, would be far more serious today than they were during the nineteenth century. Even if our methods of selection were absolutely unbiased and infallible, which is unlikely, a restrictive policy would not be easy to justify.

The further expansion of the educational system, conversely, is to be recommended on grounds of prudence alone. The great complexity of contemporary social life demands a kind of counterweight in education. To be something more than a pawn in contemporary politics, for example, one must know a good deal more than one can learn in the existing primary or secondary schools. To leave advanced education to a small minority, in present-day circumstances, would be to permit a dangerous concentration of power. Some of what goes on in contemporary universities and colleges may be indoctrination, not teaching, but ignorance will scarcely solve that problem.

Similar arguments can be urged in behalf of reducing the segmentation of educational systems. As noted earlier, the limiting case of segmentation is the line between those who are highly educated and those who are not. During much of the nineteenth century, this limiting form of segmentation was socially horizontal to some degree, but nowadays it appears to be almost exclusively vertical in character. It thus legitimates and perpetuates the existing class structure, rather than confronting it with a partly incongruent hierarchy of status. This helps strengthen and justify the egalitarian demand for universal secondary education. Efforts to move in that direction, as in England, may initially result in the reappearance of the primary/secondary divide *within* the secondary system. Even so, the overall effect of increased inclusiveness will be to obscure, and actually to lower, curricular and social barriers that may be further reduced by the introduction of common schooling at ever more advanced levels. For all forms of educational segmentation sustain experienced social distances. Certainly

---

members of the liberal professions (as in the nineteenth century). Lasch regrets that mass culture has impoverished both high culture and "popular culture," and that education does not "mean" much nowadays. All the ordinary citizen needs, he says, is the training in his own language that will enable him to resist tyrants and demagogues. I would ask how Lasch defines "popular culture," in what sense education should "mean" more, how one should educate scientists, journalists, and other such contemporary professionals, and how the citizen should deal with arguments in economics or biology. My objections to the suggestion that intellectuals be poorly paid, however, are largely personal.

this is true of the limiting divide between the educated and the uneducated.

What I am suggesting, partly, is that higher education today must not be rare. On the contrary, it *should* be "devalued" through general availability. Of course I do not mean to urge a disrespect for intellectual standards, or to defend the easy indifference that sometimes passes for liberality. I am talking about power and status, not about intellectual orientations. For it is only as a claim to power and status that education would be devalued by increased enrollments. Numbers alone may threaten academic norms in exceptional circumstances, but they are probably less dangerous to the fabric of intellectual life, as a rule, than scholars who convey no sense that their work is serious and demanding. The chief effects of increased inclusiveness and decreased segmentation, in sum, would be social, not intellectual. The value of educational qualifications in the job market would be further reduced, and an even larger range of social positions would be considered appropriate for educated men and women.

Additional encouragement would thus be given to a view of society that has been described as "materialistic." I refer to the notion that social differences are "merely" a matter of money. Construed in an optimistic way, this view has apparently been an important support of the egalitarian ideology in the United States. I have argued that the absence of education as an autonomous status source in America has enhanced the plausibility of this view in the past. If I am right, a further devaluation of education should have the same effect in the future. The wider distribution of advanced education should further diminish experienced social distances, even when it does not increase social mobility. To devalue education is to reduce its capacity to legitimate—and thus to deepen—existing inequalities.

Another objective of the old left liberal program, of course, was the removal of all economic and institutional obstacles in the path of an enlarged and more easily accessible higher education. The experience of the last few decades has taught us to be cautious about the efficacy of such reforms. Both educational costs and curricular segmentations can be reduced, it seems, without really major improvements in the level of progressiveness. But here again, there can be no question of abandoning the effort that has been begun. Even minor changes in the social character of educational institutions can be very important in the long run, since they will eventually affect the choices made by parents and students. Some of the roots of inequality in education may lie deeper than we thought, but that is no reason to stop cutting those we can reach. Our ignorance about causes is so great, in fact, that we had better be systematic about the cutting.

The promotion of "merit," too, remains a vital objective. Failure to pursue it, despite the difficulties that have been encountered, would almost certainly have a regressive effect. In 1953, when an English L.E.A. abandoned the use of intelligence tests in the selection of grammar school students, for example, there was an immediate decline in the opportunity ratio for the sons of manual workers.[6] Thus meritocratic techniques do in fact play the progressive role assigned to them in the reformist consensus. We cannot do without them.

We have not moved nearly as close to the meritocratic level of progressiveness, moreover, as some commentators appear to believe. In the United States, individual colleges and universities have certainly tried to make room for able students from less favored backgrounds, but the educational system as a whole has never been very selective. Wealthy parents have always been able to find a place for their children. Even in England, private educational institutions have continued to protect privileged social groups from the full impact of meritocracy. If this were clearly and generally recognized, the debate over meritocracy would gain in coherence. As it is, meritocratic principles themselves are sometimes blamed for the consequences of their not being extensively realized in practice. This sort of confusion is intellectually unsound and tactically dangerous.

Even on a purely theoretical level, it is hard to see how meritocratic standards could ever be entirely abandoned in the selection of students. Of course one could distribute access to higher education in a compensatory fashion, giving preference to students from disadvantaged backgrounds—such an approach could be justified as a counterweight to the apparently ineradicable influence of social inequality upon measured academic ability. Or a more general theory of compensation could be developed. Yet the compensatory principle would have to be applied *in conjunction* with meritocratic machinery, as a supplementary correction. To use education in an entirely compensatory way would require an intolerable degree of coercion. In the merit question, as in other respects, the old reformist consensus retains much of its force.

There is only one area of concern, it seems to me, in which we confront the current crisis in education without any conceptual help from reform programs of the past. I refer to the potential impoverishment of

6. Floud and Halsey, "Social Class, Intelligence Tests, and Selection for Secondary Schools," pp.209–14.

our culture by an education that is merely an extension of the occupational structure. The threat in this quarter is greater today than ever before, for we no longer have the firm fabric of tradition that partly insulated European educational systems of the nineteenth century from the early industrial economy. Education is in danger of losing its partial autonomy within the social system, even as some of the inherited educational ideals are losing their coherence. The old classical humanism had its faults. As routinized in the secondary curriculum, it was socially as well as intellectually narrow. Yet it had the virtue of endurance; it survived as an incongruent element in a rapidly changing environment. Few of us would be willing to revive it, even if we could. But what shall we put in its place?

Appendix

Table I

Prussia and Germany: Secondary Enrollments and Population, 1860–1960
(Enrollments in Thousands, Population in Millions)

Year	Mittel-schule	Girls' post-elementary	Ober-real-schule	Real-gym-na-sium	Gym-na-sium	Gym. as % of sec.	All secondary	Total population	Sec. per 1000 pop.	Pop. aged 11–19	Sec. per 1000 aged 11–19	Abitur certifs.	Certifs. per 1000 aged 19	% of certifs. from Gym.
Prussia														
1860			6	12	39	69	57	18.5[a]	3.1			1.9		94
1865			2	21	48	68	71	24.0[a]	3.0			2.2		90
1870			4	31	63	64	98	24.6[a]	4.0	4.3	23	3.6	8	88
1875			5	40	70	61	115	25.7	4.5	4.7	25	3.0	7	83
1880		72[b]	7	40	79	63	125	27.3	4.6	4.9	26	3.1[c]	6	80
1885		204[b]	15	33	83	63	131	28.3	4.6	5.1	26	4.2	8	85
1890		212[b]	21	34	82	59	138	30.0	4.6	5.5	25	4.2	9	87
1895		226[b]	30	31	82	57	143	31.9	4.5			5.2		82
1900		287[b]	45	23	95	58	163	34.5	4.7	6.1	27	5.7	9	82
1905[d]		328	62	33	105	52	200	37.3	5.4	6.7	30	7.1	10	77
1911[d]	243	?	73	52	108	46	233	40.2	5.8	7.3	32	9.1	12	66
Germany: Weimar Republic and National Socialist Regime														
1921[e]	329	248[f]	184	116	152	32[g]	723[h]	62.5	11.6	12.0	60	16.8	13	
1926[e]	259	271[f]	224	134	161	29[g]	823[h]	63.6	12.9	11.6	71	21.0[l]	17	
1931[e]	230	283[j]		495[k]		25[g]	778	65.4	11.9	8.8	88	40.6[m]	33	
1937[e]	272	238[j]		433[k]			671	67.8	9.9	9.7	69			

(For 1931 and 1937 the figures 495[k] and 433[k] are bracketed as a combined total of the Oberrealschule, Realgymnasium, and Gymnasium columns.)

272

Year	Mittel- schule	Girls' post- elemen- tary	Ober- real- schule	Real- gym- na- sium	Gym- na- sium	Gym. as % of sec.	All second- ary	Total popu- lation	Sec. per 1000 pop.	Pop. aged 11–19	Sec. per 1000 aged 11–19	Abi- tur cer- tifs.	Certifs. per 1000 aged 19	% of certifs. from Gym.
								Germany: Federal Republic without West Berlin						
1950	214[n]	255[j]		374[k]			629[n]	47.9	13.1	6.9	91	29.8[m]	45	
1955	349[n]	330[j]		481[k]			811[n]	50.2	16.2	7.5	108	34.9[m]	41	
1960	351						824	53.2	15.5	6.6	124	52.1[m]	54	

NOTE: All calculations are made from raw data (or thousands, in the case of population), not from rounded figures listed.

TERMS: 'Mittelschule' does not include advanced classes at primary schools. 'Oberrealschule,' 'Realgymnasium,' and 'Gymnasium' include enrollments at Realschulen, Realprogymnasien, and Progymnasien, respectively. 'Population Aged 11–19' covers nine full age-years, i.e., to just under 20, with slight variations described below.

[a] 1861, 1867, 1871.

[b] Only public schools 1878 (not 1880), then public and private 1886, 1891, 1896, 1901, 1906, 1911, with figures through 1906 including girls' postelementary education.

[c] One-half the two-year total for 1880–81.

[d] Certificates for school years 1905–1906 and 1910–11, and secondary enrollments for winter semesters 1905–1906, 1910–11, excluding girls' schools recognized as secondary in 1910 from figures for 1911.

[e] Enrollments from surveys done early in the academic years 1921–22, 1926–27, 1931–32, and 1937–38, and certificates conferred during preceding school years.

[f] Enrollments at girls' secondary schools, including a few boys but excluding girls at boys' secondary schools, who are counted with the boys' schools.

[g] Gymnasium shares of all boys' secondary schools, not just of the traditional threesome.

[h] Totals include enrollments in the *Deutsche Oberschule* and *Aufbauschule.*

[i] For the first time includes 1.9 thousand certificates separately listed as conferred at girls' schools.

[j] Girls in all (including boys') secondary schools, excluding only a few in so-called *Frauenschulen* in 1931.

[k] Boys in all types of secondary schools.

[m] Certificates awarded to girls (included in totals), in thousands, were 9.5 in 1931, 9.7 in 1950, about 11.5 (see [n]) in 1955, and 18.5 in 1960.

[n] Pupils at new comprehensive schools in Bremen, 1951, and Hamburg and Bremen, 1955, are divided between *Mittelschulen* and secondary schools according to a key provided by *Statistik der Bundesrepublik*, with secondary share added also to boys' and girls' secondary subtotals and *Abitur* figures (see [m]) on 50/50 basis.

SOURCES: *Preussische Statistik*, vols. 101, 120,

Sources: 151, 176, 209, 231, for *Mittelschulen* and girls' postelementary through 1911. Lexis, *Unterrichtswesen*, vol. 2 for all secondary through 1900. *Statistische Mitteilungen*, vols. 3 (1886), 18 (1902), 23 (1906), and 28 (1911) for *Vorschulen* 1885/86, 1900/01 and for secondary 1905/06, 1910/11. *Statistisches Jahrbuch*, vols. 48 (1929), 52 (1933), 57 (1938), vols. for 1952, 1957, 1962, for *Mittelschulen* and secondary 1921–1960 and for vocational 1921, 1931, and 1960. *Jahrbuch für das höhere Schulwesen*, vol. 1 (1933) for some secondary breakdowns 1931. *Statistik der Bundesrepublik*, vol. 199 for 1951 and 1955 Hamburg and Bremen comprehensive schools. For Prussian and German age distributions: *Statistisches Handbuch für den Preussischen Staat*, vol. 2 (1893); *Statistisches Jahrbuch für den Preussischen Staat*, vols. 1 (1903), 5 (1907), 11 (1913); *Statistisches Jahrbuch*, vols. 42 (1921/22), 48 (1929), 54 (1935), 57 (1938), vols. for 1952, 1957, 1962.

Age Distributions: For Prussia 1870–1905, the figures are for survivors of relevant birth years as of December 1, 1871, 1875, etc., i.e., those aged 10 years, 11 months to those just under 19 years, 11 months on those dates; one-half of those aged about 18 and 19 are used to estimate those aged 19 in the cases of 1900 and 1905. For Prussia in 1911, the reference is to relevant years of birth (and age) as of January 1, 1911. For Germany in 1921, the table reports birth years 1900 through 1908 living as of October 8, 1919. For 1931, because of violent fluctuations in birth rates 1914–20, recourse is had to survivors of birth years 1912 through 1920 as of June 16, 1933. Age years 11 through 19 are directly stated in the sources for 1925, early 1938, September 9, 1950, end 1955, and average 1960; but one-half those aged 19 and 20 are taken to estimate those aged 19 in the case of 1950.

Comparability of Prussian and German Data: Lexis, *Unterrichtswesen*, vol. 2, p. 220, cites the figures in Table I.1 for Prussia and for the German Empire as of the beginning of the winter semester of 1902. Altogether, the

Table I.1

Students per 10,000 inhabitants	Prussia	Germany
Gymnasien and *Progymnasien*	28.3	27.3
Realgymnasien and *Realprogymnasien*	7.4	7.5
Oberrealschulen	5.0	5.6
Realschulen	9.9	13.1
All secondary schools	50.6	53.5

comparison supports the general impression that Prussia was not only large and influential in policy matters, but also fairly typical of Germany as a whole.

Among the German states with particularly high secondary enrollments per population, some of the larger and more prominent were (in order of descending enrollments per population) Bremen, Lübeck, Hessen, Baden, and Württemberg. The northern cities of Lübeck, Bremen, and Hamburg also stood out for particularly high enrollments per population in *Realschulen*. Baden and Württemberg had particularly strong *Oberrealschulen*, as did Bremen.

New Schools of the Weimar Period: If one subtracts enrollments in the three traditional secondary schools from overall totals for enrollments in boys' secondary schools in 1921 and 1926, one is left with about 23 thousand students in 1921 and about 33 thousand in 1926. These figures should come very close to describing the progress of the two main new school types of the Weimar period—the *Deutsche Oberschule* and the *Aufbauschule*.

Vocational Schools: Little is known about such full-time vocational/technical schools of the earlier nineteenth century as the *Provinzial-Gewerbeschulen* in Prussia (from 1817 on). Apparently, they took their pupils from advanced primary and even intermediate secondary classes, preparing a few of them for higher vocational/technical instruction at the Prussian *Gewerbe-Institut*, at "polytechnical schools," or at other forerunners of the technical institutes. Lundgren, *Bildung und Wirtschaftswachstum* and "Industrialization," estimates enrollments in Prussian *Provinzial-Gewerbeschulen* at one thousand during the period 1830 to 1870, but he provides no details on the basis for this estimate. In 1878, the Prussian *Provinzial-Gewerbeschulen* were transferred from the Ministry of Commerce to the Ministry of Culture, simultaneously being transformed into *Oberrealschulen*, full nine-year nonclassical secondary schools. Part-time vocational schools (*Fortbildungsschulen*) seem to have existed throughout most of the nineteenth century, but there is practically no information about them before 1914. Some part-time vocational education after graduation from primary schools was first made compulsory during the Weimar period, and the program has been extended since the Second World War. In 1921, over two million pupils were, at least nominally, enrolled in part-time vocational schools: the *Fortbildungsschulen* and *Berufsschulen*, and the *Fachschulen* at a somewhat more advanced level. In 1931, about 339,000 part-time students attended the *Fortbildungsschulen*, another 1,146,000 were registered as "obligatory pupils" in the *Berufsschulen*, and some 170,000 were enrolled in public *Fachschulen*. As of 1960, about 1,602,000 students went to *Berufsschulen*, which have taken over the whole field of part-time vocational training, while 131,000 were enrolled in full-time vocational schools (*Berufsfachschulen*) for two or three years beyond completion of primary schools, and 154,000 attended the more advanced *Fachschulen*.

Middle and Girls' Postelementary Schools: Quite apart from a few advanced classes at elementary schools (not considered middle schools and not counted in the table), higher primary schools certainly existed in Prussia even before 1816. Often called burgher schools (*Bürgerschulen*) before 1870, these later "middle schools" (*Mittelschulen*) were not at first sharply distinguished from nonclassical secondary schools or even from primary education. Only in 1878, just as the *Provinzial-Gewerbeschulen* were being turned into full secondary schools, did Prussian statisticians begin to report separately upon the *Mittelschulen*, a group of institutions that were commonly entered at age nine or ten and that usually took pupils a year or two beyond the eight-year run of the primary schools. But even after 1878, official statistics on the *Mittelschulen* continued to include enrollments at "higher girls' schools" (*höhere Mädchenschulen*), postelementary institutions for girls that were considered more similar to the middle schools than to the accredited (boys') secondary schools. Indeed, girls dominated "middle school" enrollments until after 1945, but most markedly so before 1914. Thus 1886 enrollments in public *Mittelschulen* and *höhere Mädchenschulen* were about 135 thousand, of which 82 thousand were girls. In addition, some 13 thousand boys and 56 thousand girls attended private versions of these schools. For the first time, in 1896, official Prussian statistics distinguished between girls' *Mittelschulen* and *höhere Mädchenschulen*. By 1906, there were about 171 thousand pupils in boys', girls', and coeducational *Mittelschulen*, plus 157 thousand girls in *höhere Mädchenschulen*. The last decade before 1914 saw an important change in the standing of girls' postelementary education in Germany. In a gradual process most clearly marked by a Prussian regulation of 1910, higher girls' schools that met certain standards were raised to the level of full secondary schools, while the rest were all the more surely grouped with the middle schools. For 1911, the source used indicates 181 thousand pupils in public *Mit-*

telschulen, just under half of them girls, plus 18 thousand boys and 44 thousand girls in private *Mittelschulen*. No data was found for Prussian girls' secondary education between 1910 and the war; but the numbers could not have been very large. What we do have is a figure of 248 thousand for all girls' secondary schools in Germany in 1921, and we also know that in 1926, for the first time, a separate tabulation was given for *Abitur* certificates at girls' schools (about 1.9 thousand of 21 thousand). Altogether, it seemed reasonable to begin including girls' secondary schools in the totals for all secondary enrollments only in 1921.

Realgymnasium, Oberrealschule, Six-Year and Seven-Year Schools: Six- and seven-year variants of the three main types of boys' secondary school existed for much of the period covered. Often located in provincial towns, these schools could send their graduates on to complete their education in the upper grades of a corresponding nine-year institution, which is why only the joint sums for the three main branches were tabulated. Thus the *Progymnasien* taught the lower grades of the *Gymnasium*. The earliest separate figure for them in Lexis (2,480 pupils) dates from 1865 and is included in the *Gymnasium* total for that year. Secondary schools not formally accredited as *Gymnasien* (with the right to confer the *Abitur*) in 1812 were variously called Latin schools, higher burgher schools, or "modern" schools (*Realschulen*, with a predominantly nonclassical curriculum) until 1859. Some of them were given their own leaving certificates in 1832, but these were of little academic value. A reclassification of 1859, slightly modified in 1882, resulted in the following pattern: *Realgymnasien* (initially called *Realschulen* of the First Order) were nine-year schools with some modern emphasis but Latin throughout. Higher burgher schools that had come to function as lower *Realgymnasien* were renamed *Realprogymnasien* in 1882. The remaining higher burgher schools and *Realschulen*, six-year institutions that taught little or no Latin, did not acquire a big sister until 1878 and then in the form of the strictly nonclassical but nine-year *Oberrealschule*, the heir of the old Prussian vocational/technical *Provinzial-Gewerbeschulen*. The earliest tabulation for *Realgymnasien* (first-order *Realschulen*) and *Realprogymnasien* (higher burgher schools with Latin) dates, appropriately, from one year after the standardization of 1859. But what is listed under the *Oberrealschule* before 1880 are really enrollments at six-year *Realschulen* only. Even in 1880, only about 1.7 thousand of the rounded 7 thousand recorded actually pertain to the *Oberrealschule* itself.

Earliest Data on Prussian Middle and Secondary Schools: Not included in the table are scattered figures for the decades before 1860, both from sources already listed (Lexis) and from Conrad, *Universitätsstudium*. For 1816, we have an estimate of 115 thousand students in Prussian middle (burgher) schools, higher burgher schools, and *Realschulen*. Enrollments at Prussian boys' middle schools (public and private, in thousands) were 48 in 1822, 60 in 1828, 38 in 1846, 51 in 1851, and 44 in 1864. At boys' and girls' middle (postelementary) schools, public and private, there were an estimated 90 thousand students in 1864, and 110 thousand in 1882, as against the 72 thousand tabulated for public schools alone in 1878. Conrad estimates decennial average enrollments at Prussian higher burgher schools and *Realschulen* as 0.9 per thousand population in the 1830s, 1.0 in the 1840s, and 1.3 in the 1850s. The comparable figure in the table for 1860 (from Lexis) comes to about 1.0 per thousand population. Enrollments at Prussian *Gymnasien* and *Progymnasien* per thousand population may be estimated and calculated from closely converging figures by Conrad and Lexis as 1.8 in 1831, 1.5 in 1837/38, 1.6 in 1846/47, 2.0

276

secondary certificates; but only some 60–90 of them are included (in each case) in the totals for 1835–60 given above.

in 1853, and 2.2 in 1860 (where table comes to 2.1 for *Gymnasien* alone), as well as at decennial averages (from Conrad) of 1.6 for the 1830s, 1.6 for the 1840s, and 1.9 for the 1850s. Combining these figures with Conrad's (high) estimates for the modern secondary schools, one obtains 2.5 Prussian secondary students per thousand population in the 1830s, 2.6 in the 1840s, and 3.2 in the 1850s, as compared to the (more conservative) 3.1 for 1860 in the table.

Earliest Data and Comments on the Prussian Abitur: The Prussian *Abitur* examination was first introduced in 1788 and further defined in 1812. Lexis lists the following numbers of *Abiturs* conferred, in thousands: 1.1 in 1821, 1.6 in 1825, 1.8 in 1830, 1.0 in 1835, 1.1 in 1840, 1.2 in 1845, 1.4 in 1850, 1.7 in 1855, and 1.8 in 1860. The table lists 1.9 for 1860, because for the first time in that year, i.e., just after the elevation of the future *Real-gymnasium* in the regulation of 1859, Lexis reports just over a hundred certificates conferred at that institution. The figures again suggest a first peak reached around 1830, followed by a setback in the 1830s and early 40s, and recovery thereafter until 1860. It should be noted, however, that the totals for 1821, 1825, and 1830 include (in each case) between 400 and 500 maturity or entrance

examinations passed at universities. These, according to Conrad, were made very easy and could be taken after years of university attendance (without full matriculation), even by students who had failed the test for the *Gymnasium Abitur*. Along with the *Immaturi* (students not yet certified or matriculated at all), the so-called *Extraner* (or *Extranei*, students certified and matriculated without successful and formal study at accredited secondary schools) were therefore quite numerous at German universities through 1830. (A rough estimate, based on Conrad's scattered data, might be that about a third of students were *Extranei*, and somewhere around another tenth were *Immaturi* during the 1820s.) Complaints about their poor qualifications led in 1831 to certain restrictions upon the time *Immaturi* could spend at universities. Then a more decisive regulation of 1834 in effect terminated university entrance tests, locating all secondary graduate examinations at the *Gymnasium* and, later, at other secondary schools. Some *Extraner* continued to enter the universities as fully qualified students, but they now took on the role of external students of secondary schools at which they had been tested and given the *Abitur*, and their numbers were very much reduced. The table consistently reports *Abiturs* earned by *Extraner* along with other

Distribution of Students over the Nine Grades: German secondary classes or grades have traditionally been named in ascending order, *Sexta* (Sixth Form, first year of secondary education, fourth or fifth year of schooling), *Quinta* (Fifth), *Quarta* (Fourth), *Untertertia* and *Obertertia* (Lower and Upper Third), *Untersekunda* and *Obersekunda* (Lower and Upper Second), *Unterprima* and *Oberprima* (Lower and Upper First). Only the *Realschulen* were described in an ascending six-year sequence I-VI until their status improved during the later nineteenth century. The pyramid of rising grades in German secondary schools tapered rather sharply toward the top, especially during the nineteenth century. A great deal of weeding out apparently occurred well before the *Abitur* examination was given. Many students left voluntarily as well, having attained intermediate leaving certificates and/or partial exemptions as "one-year volunteers" from ordinary conscription. This was true especially at the modern schools, where graduate certificates were long of relatively little value as academic qualifications. Available breakdowns show that about 57 percent of students at Prussian *Gymnasien* in 1832 were enrolled in the lowest three grades, the percentage falling to 53 for 1865. (Conrad's arguments for a contrary trend during the earliest years do not withstand close scrutiny). For the years 1885, 1900, and 1911, one finds the lowest third of the *Gymnasium's* nine grades slowly falling in its share of total enrollments (always counting the *Progymnasium* with the *Gymnasium* figures) from 46 to 43 percent, the top third rising from 18 to 21 percent, and the middle third stable at about 36 percent. For the same three years, the comparable proportions for the *Realgymnasium* hovered around 51 percent in the lowest, 35 percent in the middle, and 14 percent in the highest thirds. (This is discounting an inevitably somewhat slower start in the highest grades before 1885 and somewhat erratic figures for 1900, when a ten-year campaign against the school was about to end.) The *Oberrealschule* had only 1 percent of its students in its highest three grades in 1885, and the proportion rose only slowly to 4 percent in 1900 and 8 percent in 1911. The *Realschule-Oberrealschule* combination is best characterized by the fact that about two-thirds of its students were enrolled in its lowest three grades in 1865 and 1885, though the percentage fell to 61 in 1900 and 52 in 1911.

According to a 1931–32 survey of public boys' secondary schools (few were private), only about 9 of 10 students admitted actually enrolled in the first secondary grade (the Sixth), and 8 completed that year. Some 10 percent of all pupils in all grades were not permitted to advance to the next grade at the end of the year; about 3.5 percent chose to repeat a grade, while 6.5 percent left. Nonacademic factors also contributed to a high rate of attrition. Compounding the percentages of students lost between grades (as observed separately for each pair of grades over the course of the year studied), government statisticians projected that for every 100 students in the Sixth, there were 89 in the Fifth, 82 in the Fourth, 75 in the Lower Third, 62 in the Upper Third, 58 in the Lower Second, 37 in the Upper Second, 30 in the Lower First, and 28 in the Upper First. The actual distribution of pupils over the nine grades differed from this projection because of sharp fluctuations in the size of age groups and entering classes during this period. Thus the percentage distribution of actual enrollments between the lowest, the middle, and the highest three grades as of 1931 was 44:30:26 for institutions of the *Gymnasium* type, 47:30:23 for the *Realgymnasium* and its relatives, 49:31:20 for the *Realschule-Oberrealschule* combination,

and 46:31:23 for all boys' secondary schools including the new *Deutsche Oberschule* and *Aufbauschule*. Of those students who reached the Upper First, about 91 percent received the *Abitur*, while just under 4 percent left and just under 6 percent chose to repeat the class. A total of some 40.6 thousand young people received the *Abitur* in 1930–31. Of these, about 27.1 thousand intended to go on to university-level study, 2.6 thousand were undecided, and 11.0 thousand meant to enter occupations not requiring advanced academic credentials.

Role of the Preparatory Schools: In Prussia and in several other German states, preparatory schools (*Vorschulen*) attached to the secondary schools functioned as presecondary institutions for many would-be secondary pupils from the nineteenth century to the 1920s (when they were phased out). Acting in place of the public primary schools, they took pupils from about age six onward, sending them on to the secondary schools at about age nine. It is difficult to assess the quantitative significance of these institutions, because they encompassed only three grades (or less for late entrants), as against nine years of secondary schooling, and because students were very unevenly distributed over the nine secondary grades. It is probably best to compare *Vorschule* enrollments with enrollments in the lowest three regular grades for each of the three main branches of the secondary system. There is reason to suspect that the highest of the three preparatory classes was generally the most popular, but so was the lowest of the three secondary grades that are being compared. For the years 1885, 1900, and 1911, one generally finds preparatory enrollments at all three major school types (surprisingly) not very far above or below one-third of enrollments in the lowest three regular grades, again with the exception of an erratic figure for the *Realgymnasium* in 1900. The safest conclusion appears to be that roughly a third of all German secondary students normally came from preparatory schools until the 1920s. This is not to say, however, that the rest came from the public primary schools. There were many private and special elementary schools in Germany, quite apart from the preparatory schools. Enrollments in these institutions were high enough to convince Conrad (*Universi-*

tätsstudium, p. 178) that as of the 1880s, few Prussian *Gymnasium* and university students came from the public schools.

Ratios of Enrollments and Certificates to the Age Groups: The unequal distribution of students over the nine grades raises a question about the meaning of the enrollment-to-age-group ratios in the table. What they really report is the relationship of an average-sized class, one located near the middle of the secondary pyramid, to members of an average age-year in the range 11 through 19. One may take ages 11 *through* 19 to be appropriate (if not as perfect as 10.5 *to* 19.5) in this connection. While children *could* begin school at age 6 plus and thus enter secondary institutions at age 9 plus (from the preparatory schools), rather than 10 plus (from private or public primary schools), most seem to have completed their nine years of secondary education (if at all) with the *Abitur* at age 19. (More of those earning the *Abitur* in Prussia ca. 1820-80 were 19

than 18 or 20, i.e., they were ca. 18.5-19.5 during their last year of schooling, according to Conrad, *Universitätsstudium*, p. 29, and confirmation in Table V notes.) Table I shows that the ratio of secondary graduates to those aged 19 was considerably smaller than the ratio of all secondary students to those aged 11 through 19. The top of the pyramid was much narrower than the middle, and the bottom must have been proportionately wider. In fact, the ratio of first-year secondary (Sixth-Form) pupils to those aged 11, which is also the proportion of children who received any secondary education at all, was 32 per thousand in 1870/71, ranged between 32 and 38 through 1900, then climbed to the lower 40s before 1914, to 114 by 1931, and reached 144, 170, and 164 per thousand in 1950, 1955, and 1960, respectively. Thus this interesting fraction was generally about a third to a half again as large as the ratio of all secondary students to those aged 11 through 19.

Table II

Prussia: Career Plans and Social Origins of Secondary School Graduates, 1832–1911

(Graduates in Thousands, Occupations as Percent of Graduates)

Careers Intended by Graduates

Year: Institution	Graduates	Learned professions						Nonacademic occupations					
		Law, gov.	Theology	Med.	Hum.	Nat. sci.	Total[a]	Military	Civ. serv.	Tech. prof.	Agricult.	Commerce	Industry
1832 *Gymnasium*	0.7[b]	40	41	5			98	11[e]					
1860 *Gymnasium*	1.8	14	39	16	9	4	82	9	27	19		43	
Realgymnasium	0.1	–	–	–	–	–	–	11[e]	2	1		3	
All Secondary	1.9	13	37	15	8	4	76						
1880 *Gymnasium*	2.5[d]	28	17	23	15	5	88	4	5	1		1	
Realgymnasium	0.6[d]	22	14	18	12	4	46	7	24	11		12	
All Secondary	3.1[d]		14	13	9	4	80	5	9	3		4	
1900 *Gymnasium*	4.6	29	17			6	73	6	2	11		6	
Realgymnasium	0.7						31	6	6	33		19	
Oberrealschule	0.3						5	3	9	48		23	
All Secondary	5.6	23	14	11	7	5	64	6	3	16		9	
1911 *Gymnasium*	6.0	20	14	15	16	12[e]	80	7	3	–		8	
Realgymnasium	1.8	11	1	15	17	23[e]	72	6	3	–		15	
Oberrealschule	1.3	9	–	9	16	31[e]	72	2	6	–		17	
All Secondary	9.1	16	10	14	16	17[e]	77	6	3	–		11	

Year: Institution	Gradu-ates	Learned professions						Nonacademic occupations					
		Law, gov.	The-ology	Med.	Hum.	Nat. sci.	Total[a]	Mili-tary	Civ. serv.	Tech. prof.	Agri-cult.	Com-merce	In-dustry
1875–99 *Gymnasium*	71.2	23	22	20	10		75	7	5	7	2	4	—
Realgymnasium	12.6	2	2	4	18		26	7	19	30	4	10	—
Oberrealschule	1.2	—	–	1	11		12	3	13	56	2	11	—
All Secondary	85.0	20	19	18	12		68	7	7	11	3	4	—

Occupations of Graduates' Fathers

Year: Institution	Gradu-ates	Learned professions						Nonacademic occupations					
1875–99 *Gymnasium*	71.2	5	7	4	5		21	3	19[f]	4	13[g]	20	12[h]
Realgymnasium	12.6	1	1	2	3		7	2	19[f]	7	9[g]	26	22[h]
Oberrealschule	1.2	–	1	1	3		5	2	15[f]	9	5[g]	27	30[h]
All Secondary	85.0	5	6	4	4		19	3	19[f]	5	12[g]	21	14[h]

NOTE: The table should be read from left to right; all figures but those in the first column are percentages (by row, not column) of absolute totals in the first column.

TERMS: 'Graduates' are those having passed the Abitur at secondary schools (including Externer) and having decided whether or not to attend universities. A few who had not decided are left out in 1860 and 1900. 'Learned Professions' in the section on 'Careers Intended' are graduates who planned to attend universities or who (in the summary for 1875–99 only) listed career plans almost certainly requiring university study. Students planning university study whose choice of subject was not indicated in the sources (as for the Realgymnasium and Oberrealschule in 1880 and 1900), or who had not decided on a subject, or who had chosen unspecified subjects other than those listed are counted only in the total for the learned professions, i.e., for university study. 'Nonacademic occupations' in the section on intended careers, are those not planning to attend universities or (in the 1875–99 summary) not headed for occupations requiring university study. Those among them who had not chosen occupations or who had selected unspecified occupations other than those listed are not itemized in the table. This is chiefly why rows of percentages do not add up to 100 in this section; but note that the imaginary category 'Undecided, Unknown, Other' exceeds 4 percent of totals only for the *Gymnasium* and all secondary in 1860 (where the source itself was incomplete) and for the nonclassical schools in 1900 (where absolute numbers were low). Professional categories used in the section on 'Occupations of Fathers' are described in detail below. Some 7–8 percent of fathers were in occupations other than those itemized, which is why the four rows of percentages in question add up to 92 or 93 only. The percentages listed midway between 'Humanities' and 'Natural sciences' in these rows report university professors, secondary teachers, and school principals (*Rektoren*).

a Independently derived from raw data, not from percentages listed for subjects, which are rounded.

b Excludes students passing entrance examinations at universities, for whom no information on plans was available.

c Includes an indeterminate number of students from nonclassical schools.

d One-half the two-year total for 1880–81, with a mere 29 graduates of the *Oberrealschule* included in all secondary only.

e Includes 6 percent of graduates opting for technical subjects in the case of the *Gymnasium*, 12 percent in that of the *Realgymnasium*, 13 percent in that of the *Oberrealschule*, and 9 percent for all three schools.

f Includes 7 percent, 4 percent, 2 percent, and 6 percent of fathers who were "lower teachers" for the three schools and all secondary in descending order.

g Includes 2 percent of students' fathers who were landowners in the case of the *Gymnasium* and of all secondary education, and 1 percent in the case of the *Realgymnasium*.

h Includes 7 percent, 13 percent, 17 percent, and 8 percent of fathers who were artisans for the three schools and all secondary in descending order.

SOURCES: Lexis, *Unterrichtswesen*, vol. 2 for career choices 1832, 1860, 1880, and 1900. *Statistische Mitteilungen*, vol. 28 (1911) for career plans 1911. Ruppel, *Berufswahl der Abiturienten*, for career intentions 1875–99 and fathers' occupations in same sample 1875–99 (my categories and recalculations).

Choice of University Subject: The sources for individual years, 1832–1911, subdivide those planning university study according to a few conventional subject categories: "law," "government" (*Staatswissenschaft*, a few students included with law), "theology" (around half Protestant, half Catholic, and very few Jewish), "medicine" (unclear whether pharmacy is included, but probably not dentistry), "philology, history, philosophy" ('Humanities,' including German language studies), "mathematics and natural sciences" ('Natural sciences,' covering only pure sciences, not technical subjects), and "other subjects" (very few students, included only in the total for university study).

Nonacademic Occupations: Through 1900, sources for individual years broke down graduates not planning to attend universities into six groups: "military service" (sometimes specified "with chances of advancement," i.e., commissioned officers, often after training at military academies), "construction engineering," "mining" (the latter two combined in 'Technical professions'), "forestry, tax and other state service" ('Civil service,' presumably the middle ranks not requiring university study in law), "agriculture, commerce and industry" (a lumped figure, details being apparently uninteresting to those who gathered the material), and "other occupations" (sometimes also "undecided" or "unknown," a relatively small grouping not reproduced in the table).

Technical Professions and Subjects: After 1900, the 'Technical professions' disappear from the nonacademic occupations itemized in the sources. In their place, a series of new subjects is listed for those planning to attend universities. In order of magnitude, these new subjects are "machine engineering," "construction engineering," "architecture," "mining," and "ship-building." Together, they attracted slightly more graduates than the pure sciences in 1911. They are included under 'Natural sciences,' but are also listed separately as "technical subjects" in note e. Note that both 'Technical professions' through 1900 and "technical subjects" thereafter were especially attractive to graduates of the *Realgymnasium* and *Oberrealschule*. Consider that there was a smaller percentage of graduates in "technical subjects" in 1911 than had been in 'Technical professions' in 1900. Add that the technical institutes were officially recognized as university-level institutions (with the right to confer doctorates) at the turn of the century. The obvious inference is that a portion of secondary graduates, especially from the nonclassical schools, really prepared for various qualifications in technical fields throughout the later nineteenth century. Some of them did this without any postsecondary education; but many passed through the technical institutes. Their ultimate goal was probably as often government service (in a technical branch) as private business, which is one reason statisticians distinguished them from the common run of aspirants for "agriculture, commerce, and industry." A substantial portion of these graduates simply became prospective "university students" after the accreditation of the technical institutes.

Career Choices of Graduates 1875–99: The figures tabulated for 1875–99 are my calculations based on a complete but unsystem-atic long-term summary by Ruppel. Under "choice of occupation," Ruppel sometimes reported subject choices, sometimes professions. Indeed, the distinction between the two tended to blur, since Ruppel, or those he reported, liked composite nouns involving the concepts of service (*Dienst*) and speciality or subject (*Fach*), as in *Eisenbahnfach, Reichsbankfach, Intendanturdienst,* and *Bureaudienst* (not to be confused with *Verwaltungsfach*). However, the most popular and traditional subject choices are disentangled and reproduced under 'Law, government' (though there is no separate mention of *Staatswissenschaft* in Ruppel), 'Theology,' and 'Medicine' (including pharmacy, veterinary medicine, and dental medicine). A single figure for future professors and secondary school teachers includes those listing purely academic subjects in the humanities (plus economics and unspecified specialties), as well as those headed for "teaching" (*Lehrfach*). Note that primary teachers did not ordinarily attend secondary schools (or universities) before the 1920s, and that graduates of nonclassical schools before 1900 were essentially restricted to teaching nonclassical subjects in nonclassical secondary schools or *Mittelschulen*. Adding future professors and higher teachers to those planning on law, theology, and medicine, one obtains a total for the learned professions that happens to approximate the proportion of graduates actually planning to attend universities (separately reported by Ruppel as 77 percent for the *Gymnasium*, 30 percent for the *Realgymnasium*, 20 percent for the *Oberrealschule*, and 69 percent for all secondary schools). Following the practice of Prussian statisticians through 1900, one can list as 'Technical professions' such subject choices as (in order of magnitude) construction, machine engineering, chemistry, mining, general and electrical engineering, shipbuilding, surveying, railway transport, and metallurgy. (The list includes chemistry, the only pure science detailed by Ruppel, which was heavily represented among nonclassical graduates and could be pursued at technical institutes as well as universities.) Ruppel's terms strongly suggest that many of these technical professionals really meant to enter government service. 'Military' includes quartermasters, military doctors, and engineers; 'Civil service,' those planning, without study of law or technical subjects, to become public officials, to enter the tax or postal service or the *Reichsbank*, or to go into administration (*Verwaltungsfach, Bureaudienst*); 'Agriculture,' those listing forestry and agriculture (more often the former). That leaves only four groups for 'Commerce' (in order of magnitude): merchants, banking, bookselling, and "subjects of trade and commerce."

Occupations of Fathers: 'Law, government', covers only "jurists" (*Juristen*), men with university training in law, many of them certainly high officials. 'Medicine' includes pharmacists, dentists, and veterinarians. University professors, secondary teachers, and school principals are listed under the bracketed academic subjects 'Humanities' and 'Natural sciences'. Summing at this point, one obtains figures for the learned professions that again coincide almost exactly with percentages of fathers who had university educations: 22 for the *Gymnasium*, 7 for the *Realgymnasium*, and 4 for the *Oberrealschule*, according to Ruppel's separate tabulation. Among the nonacademic occupations, military doctors and officials are included with commissioned officers under 'Military'. In order of magnitude, 'Civil service' covers: a single grouping of state, municipal, and "private" officials (*Privatbeamte*) without higher education, "lower teachers" as detailed in note *f*, postal and tax officials, forestry officials, and noncommissioned officers. 'Technical professions' comprises railroad officials, building officials, engineers, higher and lower mining officials, surveyors, and chemists. Again, among the technical profes-

sionals, one notices the predominance of "officials." Admittedly, those who reported "private officials" (banking, insurance, etc.?) might also be inclusive in their concept of "building officials" (*Baubeamte*). Percentages of landowners included with farmers under 'Commerce' are spelled out in note *g*. 'Commerce' covers merchants, most of them "independent," and innkeepers. 'Industry' includes "industrialists" (*Industrielle*, most of them "independent") and a goodly portion of artisans (*niedere Gewerbetreibende*), as detailed in note *h*, but it excludes a handful of "workers" and servants. Finally, a remnant of 7–8 percent of fathers (not reproduced in the table) were in professions other than those listed, and about half of this remnant were "rentiers." Reporting on fathers of Bavarian *Gymnasium* and Latin school pupils in 1869–71, Conrad (*Universitätsstudium*, p. 50) lists 40 percent for public officials of all ranks, along with 7.5 percent for lower teachers. More valuable is the following report on fathers of 1,591 pupils in selected but roughly representative Prussian secondary schools around 1800 (range 1784–1808) in Jeismann, *Das Preussische Gymnasium*, p.165: officials and other educated professions, including university professors, judges, doctors, apothecaries, officers—40.1 percent; secondary teachers and clergy—32.5 percent;

landowners—1.7 percent; merchants and manufacturers—6.3 percent; noncommissioned officers and soldiers, lower teachers, artisans, workers—14 percent; farmers (*Bauern*) and day laborers—5.4 percent; nobility included in the above—4 percent.

Some Percentages by Column: For convenience, Table II.1 shows the absolute numbers of graduates entering the various nonacademic occupations, and the percentages of these who came from the *Gymnasium*.

Table II.1

Year	Military	Civ. Serv.	Tech. Prof.
1880	144	269	103
	72%	47%	36%
1900	316	180	885
	84%	59%	56%
1911	582	284	789
	76%	54%	50%
1875–99	5,682	5,936	9,458
	83%	56%	53%

Year	Agricult.	Comm. ind.	All grads.
1880	107		3,100
	33%		81%
1900	505		5,600
	59%		82%
1911	986		9,100
	51%		66%
1875–99	2,204	3,224	85,000
	75%	55%	84%

284

Table III

Germany: Social Origins of Secondary Students, 1931–1965
(Percentages of Fathers in Stated Occupations)

Academic secondary, 1931

Father's Occupation	All	Gymnasium	Boys' public	5th grade	13th grade
1. High officials	7.3	13.1	6.8	5.3	10.0
2. Liberal professions with univ. educ.	5.0	7.3	4.3	4.0	5.9
1–2. Sum	12.3	20.4	11.1	9.3	15.9
3. Liberal professions without univ ed.	3.5	2.8	3.1	3.4	3.2
4. Officers	1.1	1.6	1.0	0.8	1.3
5. Other military	0.2	0.2	0.2	0.2	0.2
6. Middle officials	22.6	23.6	22.5	20.5	25.1
7. Lower officials	6.9	6.7	7.8	8.6	5.8
4–7. Sum	30.8	32.1	31.5	30.1	32.4
8. Landowners	0.9	1.3	0.8	0.7	1.0
9. Farmers	4.4	7.8	5.1	3.6	5.3

Academic secondary, 1965

Father's Occupation	10th grade	13th grade
1. High officials	5.3	7.1
2. Professors	3.2	4.4
3. Clergy	1.0	1.4
4. Medical professions	4.5	6.9
5. Lawyers, notaries	1.2	1.9
6. Indep. engin., architects	0.8	1.0
7. Other lib. professions with univ. education	0.8	1.0
1–7. Sum	16.8	23.7
8. Other lib. professions without univ. educ.	2.3	2.4
9. Military	1.2	2.0
10. Middle officials	6.5	6.2
11. Lower officials	5.3	4.1
12. Lower teachers	2.8	2.8
9–12. Sum	15.8	15.1
13. Indep. farmers	3.7	3.1

Table III continued

Academic secondary, 1931

Father's Occupation	All	Gym- nasium	Boys' public	5th grade	13th grade
10. Co. owners, directors	4.5	4.0	4.0	3.7	4.4
11. Executive employees	4.4	3.2	4.2	4.1	4.6
10–11. Sum	8.9	7.2	8.2	7.8	9.0
12. Artisans, tradesmen	15.3	12.5	15.5	17.4	13.8
13. Other independents	6.0	4.6	5.3	6.4	5.2
14. Nonexec. employees	9.9	5.6	10.1	12.4	7.0
15. Industrial workers	2.5	1.7	3.2	3.0	2.4
16. Other workers	3.0	2.4	3.6	3.7	2.8
17. Other occupations	1.4	0.8	1.4	1.4	1.0
18. Without occupation	1.1	0.8	1.1	0.8	1.0
1–18. Total	100[a]	100	100[b]	100	100

Academic secondary, 1965

Father's Occupation	10th grade	13th grade
14. Manufacturers, wholesale merchants	4.2	4.1
15. Executive employees	13.9	14.0
16. Employed engin., archit.	2.5	3.2
14–16. Sum	20.6	21.3
17. Retailers, innkeepers	3.3	3.0
18. Indep. artisans	5.0	4.0
19. Other independents	4.3	3.9
20. Nonexec. employees	14.6	12.4
21. Foremen	1.8	1.3
22. Workers	10.0	6.4
23. No occupation, unknown	1.9	3.4
1–23. Total	100[c]	100[d]

TERMS: The column headed 'All' for 1931 pertains to all boys' and girls' public and private secondary schools, classical and modern, including the *Deutsche Oberschule* and the *Aufbauschule*; the columns headed '5th Grade' and '13th Grade' for 1931 deal with the Sixth and the Upper First, respectively, of boys' public secondary schools. For 1965, the table reports upon all boys' and girls' academic secondary schools (*Gymnasien*, used in the newly inclusive sense), and specifically upon students in Lower Second and Upper First, i.e., after about 6 and 10 years of secondary education. *Occupational categories for 1931* are generally literal translations from the source. 'High Officials' are *höhere Beamte*; 'Officers' includes high military officials; 'Landowners' are *Grossland-wirte*; 'Farmers' are *mittlere und Kleinland-wirte*; 'Company owners and directors' are owners of factories, directors of factories, banks, and corporations (A.-G., G.m.b.H., etc.); 'Artisans, tradesmen' are independent artisanal masters and tradesmen (*Kleinge-*

"professional" specialties (law, medicine). A very few academics are included among 'Retailers, innkeepers' and 'Independent artisans'. 'Foremen' are Werkmeister.

[a] N: 776,988.
[b] N: 511,774.
[c] N: 100,488.
[d] N: 52,826.

SOURCES: *Jahrbuch für das höhere Schulwesen*, vol. 1 (1933). *Wirtschaft und Statistik*, 1967.

Social Makeup of the Tenth Grade: It is worth noting that, as of 1931, the tenth grade (sixth secondary class, or Lower Second) of German boys' public secondary schools roughly resembled the schools as a whole (all grades) in its social makeup (distribution of fathers' occupations).

werbetreibende); 'Other independents' are simply businessmen (*Handel- und Gewerbetreibende*) not specifically identified as company owners and directors or as artisans and tradesmen; 'Other workers' are workers and subordinate assistants (*Gehilfen*) not specifically identified as industrial workers (*Industriearbeiter*). *Occupational categories for 1965* are based on the source's primary distinction between "academics" (i.e., men with university education) and "nonacademics" (without university education), and its secondary distinction between officials, employees (*Angestellte*), members of the liberal professions, and "independents" (*Selbständige*). As summed up in the table, 'High officials' are judges, state attorneys, and other academic officials in medical, technical, and other specialties, as well as nonacademic officials in the "higher grades" (*höherer Dienst*: 1.1 percent in 10th, 1.3 percent in 13th); 'Professors' are university professors and other academic teachers, including a few employees and liberal professionals as well as officials; 'Medical professions' covers doctors, dentists, veterinarians, and pharmacists, including a few employees; 'Lawyers, notaries' also covers a few employees trained in law; 'Middle officials' are nonacademic officials in the "intermediate grades" (*gehobener Dienst*); 'Lower officials' are a single group of nonacademic officials in the *mittlerer und einfacher Dienst*; 'Lower teachers' are nonacademic teachers, including a few employees, as well as officials; 'Manufacturers, wholesale merchants' includes a few men with university education, among them a number (0.3 percent in both 10th and 13th) of "other independents" in commerce and industry; 'Executive employees' are predominantly nonacademic employees in "leading positions," but there are also some employed accountants and other academic employees not specifically identified with any of the

287

Table IV

Prussia and Germany: Secondary Preparation of University Students, by Field of Study, 1887–1931
(Students in thousands)

Year: Secondary Preparation	All fields	Major fields (faculties)					Within Arts & Sciences (philosophy)						
		Prot. theol.	Cath. theol.	Law, gov.	Med.	Arts & sci.	Hum.	Nat. sci.	Econ., bus.	Agri-cult.	Pharm., dent.	Educ.	Other
1887													
Gymnasium	11.0[a]	2.7	0.6	2.0	3.6	2.0	1.4	0.5	0.1	—	—	—	—
Realgymnasium	1.1	—	—	—	—	1.1	0.4	0.6	0.1	—	—	—	—
None	0.9	—	—	—	—	0.9	0.1	0.2	0.2	—	0.4	—	—
Totals 1887	13.0	2.7	0.6	2.0	3.6	4.0	1.9	1.3	0.3	—	0.5	—	0.1
1911													
Gymnasium	16.7	1.2	1.0	4.3	3.0	7.3	4.8	1.6	0.3	—	0.1	0.4	0.4
Realgymnasium	3.9	—	—	0.8	0.7	2.4	1.3	0.9	0.2	—	—	0.1	0.1
Oberrealschule	2.4	—	—	0.3	0.3	1.9	0.8	0.9	0.1	—	—	—	—
None	2.4	—	—	—	—	2.4	0.6	0.2	0.6	—	0.7	0.3	0.3
Totals 1911	25.5	1.3	1.0	5.4	4.0	14.0	7.4	3.6	1.2	—	0.8	0.9	0.9
1931													
Gymnasium	33.3	3.0	1.9	8.8	7.8	11.8	5.2	2.6	1.1	0.3	2.2	0.2	0.2
Realgymnasium	28.5	1.7	0.2	6.6	6.4	13.6	5.4	3.4	1.4	0.2	2.4	0.5	0.3
Oberrealschule	23.8	1.1	0.1	3.9	4.5	14.3	4.1	4.8	1.5	0.2	2.3	1.1	0.3
Reform	3.8	0.2	—	0.4	0.5	2.6	0.9	0.5	0.1	—	0.3	0.7	0.1
Girls'	5.8	0.1	—	0.3	1.0	4.3	2.4	1.0	0.3	—	0.4	0.1	0.1
Other	0.7	—	—	0.1	0.2	0.4	0.1	0.1	0.1	—	0.1	—	—
Special	3.5	0.1	—	0.1	0.2	3.1	1.1	0.3	1.2	0.1	0.1	0.2	0.1
Totals 1931	99.4	6.2	2.2	20.3	20.5	50.2	19.2	12.7	5.9	0.8	7.7	2.8	1.1

NOTE: All tabulated figures are independently rounded from raw data, which is why additions within the table do not always work out exactly.

TERMS: *For 1887 and 1911:* Data are from summer semesters 1887 and 1911 for all German students (male and female) at Prussian universities. Major fields (faculties) for these years are simply the traditional faculties of theology, law, medicine and philosophy (arts and sciences). Breakdowns by subject clusters within arts and sciences in the sources are as follows: "philosophy (mentioned 1887 only), philology, history"–'Humanities'; "mathematics, natural sciences, chemistry (mentioned 1911 only)"–'Natural sciences'; "cameralia, agriculture, economics (mentioned 1887 only)"–'Economics, business' and 'Agriculture'; "pharmacy" and "dentistry"–combined under 'Pharmacy, dentistry'; "other objects within the faculty of philosophy"–'Other.'
For 1931: Data are from summer semester 1931 for German (male and female) students at German universities. Among types of secondary preparation, 'Reform' covers the new *Deutsche Oberschule* and *Aufbauschule* of the Weimar period; 'Girls' means *Oberlyzeum*, the main secondary school for girls, perhaps most similar in curriculum to the *Realgymnasium*; 'Other' includes institutions in Danzig or German-speaking Austria, as well as "institution unknown"; 'Special' covers a variety of newly instituted graduate certificates given on the basis of special examinations, as well as leaving certificates of teachers' preparatory institutions (*Seminare*), foreign qualifications judged sufficient, and a few students without any certificates. The source for 1931 uses a fairly detailed breakdown by subject groupings or fields, and these coincide perfectly with the traditional faculties only in the case of theology. A grouping of "law and government" (*Rechts- und Staatswissenschaft*, the latter possibly including some economics) comes close to the old law faculty and "general medicine" to the old medical faculty. Beyond that, 'Humanities' includes philosophy and psychology, religion, ancient and modern languages, German studies, journalism, art with art history and archaeology, music, history, and geography. 'Natural sciences' covers mathematics and actuarial mathematics, physics, chemistry, mineralogy and geology, and biology. 'Economics, business' includes general economics (*Volkswirtschaftslehre*) and business management (*Betriebswirtschaftslehre*); 'Agriculture', agriculture and forestry; 'Pharmacy, dentistry', dentistry, veterinary medicine, and pharmacy; 'Education', pedagogy for primary and vocational teachers only. Figures for 'Arts, sciences' are simply sums of those subject groupings (as already tabulated in rounded form) that used to be associated with the "philosophical" faculty, i.e., headings from 'Humanities' to 'Other'.

SOURCES: *Preussische Statistik*, vols. 102 (for 1887), 236 (for 1911). *Deutsche Hochschulstatistik*, vol. 7 (for 1931), for the technical institutes (see below).

The Situation at the Technical Institutes: There appear to be no data on the secondary preparation of students at the technical institutes (*technische Hochschulen*) before the Weimar period. From information in Table II, however, one can arrive at some rough estimates. Among Prussian secondary school *graduates* who planned to enter one of the technical professions (presumably often, though not always, via the technical institutes), 36 percent came from the *Gymnasium* in 1880, 56 percent in 1900, 50 percent in 1911, and 53 percent over the whole period from 1875 to 1899. In 1931, among the 20.3 thousand German (male and female) students at German technical institutes, 4.5 came from the *Gymnasium*, 6.0 from the *Realgymnasium*, 7.9 from the *Oberrealschule*, 0.7 from the *Deutsche Oberschule* and *Aufbauschule* ('Reform'), 0.2 from the *Oberly-*

zeum ('Girls'), 0.3 from other or unknown secondary institutions ('Other'), and 0.7 with special graduate examinations or certificates ('Special').

The Early Nineteenth Century: While no exact figures on the secondary preparation of university students are available for the periods before 1887 and after 1931, it may be worth emphasizing that the dominant position of the *Gymnasium* was probably more characteristic of the second and last third of the nineteenth century then of the first. This has to do with the institutionalization of the *Abitur* and the restrictions on university entrance that were introduced in the early 1830s. (See notes to Table I, and Conrad, *Universitätsstudium.*) Through 1830, some 30 to 50 percent of German university students may well have been *Extranei*, admitted without complete or successful secondary schooling on the basis of easy university entrance examinations, and *Immaturi*, who had not (or not yet) passed even these entrance tests. As a rule, the *Immaturi* were concentrated almost exclusively in the faculty of philosophy, where they were sometimes permitted to matriculate as special students. *Immaturi* were also particularly common among students of pharmacy, practical surgery, dentistry, veterinary medicine, and agriculture. Until well past the middle of the century, some universities counted students in these fields as fully matriculated, while others did not; most but not all listed them in the faculty of philosophy. Conrad and other German statisticians of the later nineteenth century standardized counting procedures according to the practices of their own day. They regarded as full (matriculated) students within the faculty of arts and sciences all those who would have been so considered in the later nineteenth century, including all students of pharmacy, dentistry, veterinary science, and agriculture, but not students of practical surgery or *Immaturi* in other fields. This procedure still left a fair number of *Extranei* and *Immaturi* among "full students" at German universities, especially until the regulations of the early 1830s introduced the monopolistic position of the *Gymnasium* that we observe, already being challenged, as of 1887.

Table V

Germany: University-Level Enrollments and Population, 1831–1960
(Enrollments in Thousands, Population in Millions)

Year	University Faculties					Total for univ.	Tech. inst.	Acad-emies	All univ. level	Popu-lation	Students per 1000 pop.	Pop. aged 20–23	Students per 1000 aged 20–23
	Prot. theol.	Cath. theol.	Law	Med.	Arts & sci.								
	German States and Empire (Territory of Empire)												
1831	4.2	1.8	4.4	2.4	2.7	15.5			15.5	29.8	0.52		
1835	2.7	1.1	3.2	2.4	2.6	11.9			11.9	30.9	0.39		
1840	2.3	0.9	3.2	2.1	3.0	11.6			11.6	32.8	0.35		
1845	2.1	1.0	3.6	1.7	3.4	11.8			11.8	34.4	0.34		
1850	1.7	1.4	4.4	1.9	2.9	12.2			12.2	35.4	0.35		
1855	1.8	1.2	3.9	2.2	2.8	12.0			12.0	36.1	0.33		
1860	2.5	1.3	2.4	2.1	3.6	11.9			11.9	37.7	0.32		
1865	2.4	1.1	3.1	2.5	4.4	13.5			13.5	39.7	0.34		
1870	2.1	0.9	3.2	3.1	4.9	14.2	2.9[a]	1.0[a]	14.2	40.8	0.35	2.8[b]	5.0
1875	1.6	0.8	4.4	3.3	6.2	16.4	5.4	1.1	16.4	42.5	0.38	2.8	5.8
1880	2.3	0.7	5.2	4.0	8.8	21.0	3.4	1.4	21.0	45.1	0.47	3.1	6.8
1885	4.5	1.1	4.9	7.6	9.0	27.1	2.5	1.9	27.1	46.7	0.58	3.2	8.5
1890	4.5	1.3	6.7	8.7	7.7	28.9	4.2[c]	2.4[c]	28.9	49.2	0.59	3.4	8.4
1895	3.0	1.5	7.7	7.9	8.5	28.5	6.9	2.9	28.5	52.0	0.55		
1900	2.4	1.7	9.7	7.4	12.7	33.8	10.4[d]	3.3[d]	44.2	56.0	0.79	4.1	10.8
1905	2.2	1.8	11.8	5.8	19.2	40.8	12.2	3.9	53.0	60.3	0.88		
1911	2.7	1.8	10.7	11.6	28.8	55.6[e]	11.2[f]	2.4[f]	66.8	65.4	1.02	4.5[g]	14.7

Table V continued

Year	University Faculties					Total for univ.	Tech. inst.	Academies	All univ. level	Population	Students per 1000 pop.	Pop. aged 20–23	Students per 1000 aged 20–23
	Prot. theol.	Cath. theol.	Law	Med.	Arts & sci.								
Weimar Republic and National Socialist Regime													
1921	3.3	2.1	19.7	16.7	45.8	87.8	24.2[h]	8.8[i]	120.7	62.5	1.93	4.4[j]	27.4
1926	2.1	1.7	19.0	8.5	33.4	64.6	21.1	8.6	94.3	63.6	1.48	5.0[k]	19.0
1931	6.5	2.3	20.8	21.5	52.8	103.9	22.3	8.6	134.8	65.4	2.06	5.0[m]	27.1
1938[n]						43.0	9.6	5.7	58.3	68.6	0.85	3.8	15.4
Federal Republic without West Berlin													
1951[o]	2.9	2.0	11.2	11.9	45.4	73.4	22.8	13.0[p]	109.3	48.4	2.26	2.9[q]	38.2
1955[o]	2.3	1.8	14.5	10.0	59.8	88.3	26.8	11.5	126.7	50.2	2.52	3.0	42.7
1960[o]	2.7	1.7	18.2	16.2	109.7	148.6	38.0	14.5	201.1	53.2	3.78	3.8	53.5

TERMS: In general, enrollments are all matriculated German and foreign students, male or female (though women were not admitted as regular students in Prussia until 1908/09) as of summer semesters of years listed. (Summer enrollments were often, but not always, marginally lower than winter enrollments.) Exceptions, other than those noted below, are made in the case of technical institutes and academies through 1905, where year-end enrollments are reported and where auditors and special students are included. The medical academy at Düsseldorf (after its foundation in 1919) and the ancient philosophical-theological academies of Münster (before it became a full university) and Braunsberg (*Lyzeum Hosianum*) are counted, and traditionally ranked, with the universities, except that Braunsberg, with about one hundred students in 1937/38, was regrouped with the newer philosophical-theological academies at that time. The breakdown by faculties is the traditional one through 1911, after which the focus shifts to fields of study. Theology, law (with government, i.e., *Rechts- und Staatswissenschaften*), and "general medicine" are now subject groupings, though essentially continuous with the old professional faculties, while 'Arts & sciences' encompasses all remaining university enrollments. 'Academies' are those of forestry, mining, veterinary medicine, and agriculture through 1911, plus philosophical-theological academies and business schools (*Handelshochschulen*) from 1921 on, plus art and music academies and a small sports academy from 1951 on. 'All university-level institutions' are the universities alone through 1895, plus technical institutes from 1900 on, plus academies from 1921 on. The age-group 20–23 covers four years, from beginning age 20 to just under 24, with slight variations described below. All calculations are from raw absolute numbers (or thousands, in the case of population), not from rounded figures listed.

[a] Year-end 1869.
[b] December 1871.
[c] Year-end 1891.
[d] Year-end 1899.
[e] About 2.5 thousand women students included, for the first time.
[f] The sources for 1911 and after (except in the case of technical institutes in 1921) use a slightly narrower definition than the source through 1905 in arriving at a count of students in these columns.
[g] December 1910.

[h] See note f; the wider definition current through 1905 is reverted to for this figure only.

[i] Philosophical-theological institutes and higher business schools also included in this column from here on.

[j] October 1919.

[k] 1925.

[m] Inferred from data for 1933.

[n] Enrollments are for winter semester 1937/38.

[o] Enrollment totals for universities, technical institutes, and academies in these lines include students on leave; subtotals for university professional faculties (which are for previous winter semester in 1960) exclude these students along with foreign students; theology subtotals for 1951 and 1960 are estimated on the assumption that distribution of theology students at all university-level institutions between universities and theological academies was the same in these years as in 1955; subtotals for arts and sciences contain all university students not assigned to professional faculties by way of these steps.

[p] Art and music academies and a small sports academy included in this column from here on.

[q] September 1950.

SOURCES: *Preussische Statistik*, vol. 204 for tabulated enrollments and some comments through 1905; vol. 236 for universities in 1911; vols. 125, 236 for doctorates 1880–1911; vols. 102, 204, 236 for age and length of study 1887–1911. *Deutsche Hochschulstatistik*, vol. 7 for technical institutes, academies, and some comments 1911 through 1926, university totals 1921 and 1926, and all enrollments, breakdowns and comments 1931. *Statistisches Jahrbuch*, vols. 42 (1921– 22), 46 (1927) for university fields of study (breakdown only) and art schools 1921 and 1926; vol. 57 (1938), vols. for 1952, 1956, 1961 for enrollments, breakdowns, and some comments since 1937/38; vol. for 1962 for doctorates 1959/60; vol. 2 (1881), vol. for 1962 for population totals; and vols. 9 (1888), 15 (1894), 24 (1903), 34 (1913), 42 (1921–1922), 48 (1929), 54 (1935), 57 (1938), vols. for 1952, 1957, 1962 for age groups 20–23. Eulenberg, *Frequenz*, for enrollments to 1830 and for age and length of study before 1880. Conrad, *Universitätsstudium*, for enrollments to 1830, for age and length of study to 1880, technical institutes, academies, and arts and sciences breakdowns to 1870 and doctorates to 1880. Lexis, *Unterrichtswesen*, vol. 4 for technical institutes before 1870. Kath, *Das soziale Bild* 1963, for age and length of study since 1950. See also Table I with notes on *Abitur* and university entrants to 1830.

Auditors and Special Students (Hörer, Hospitanten): These are excluded from all *university* figures throughout, except that students in such fields as pharmacy, dentistry, and veterinary medicine who were not fully matriculated (and were often *Immaturi*, having passed neither secondary graduate nor, before 1834, university entrance examinations) at some universities during the early nineteenth century were included by the sources, on the grounds that they were elsewhere and/or later (from 1873 for pharmacists in Prussia) fully matriculated students. However, in the case of the academies through 1905, and of the technical institutes through 1905 and in 1921, the sources did not or could not exclude auditors and special students; the source through 1905 argues that an inclusive approach was more appropriate for these institutions than for the universities at that time. It may help to know that, as of 1913, auditors and special students (excluded from the tabulated figures for that year) amounted to about 2.0 thousand at the technical institutes and 0.2 thousand at those institutions included under 'Academies' through 1911. Note also that the source for universities from 1921 through 1931 (and for other institutions from 1911 through 1931) lists just under nine hundred students more than the source through 1911 for the same group of universities as of 1911 (the point of overlap between the two sources), and also differs slightly from the Statistisches Jahrbuch in 1921 and 1926. The 1911 difference seems to involve no shift in categorization, is relatively insignificant (about 1 percent of total), and occurs for a year that is less carefully documented in the

later source than the period during which the table is actually based on it. In short, the sources used for any period appear to be the most authoritative and carefully annotated ones available for that time.

Foreign Students: No special attention has been given to foreigners among all students reported in Table V. The share of foreigners among all students averaged near 7.5 percent at Prussian universities during the academic years 1900/01 through 1902/03. At all German universities, it stood just over 4 percent in 1931 and near 7.5 percent again in 1960. Variations in the share of foreign students among all students could not have accounted for major fluctuations in overall enrollments at the German universities.

Students on Leave, and the Data for 1951–60: In 1925, perhaps because of the crisis produced by postinflationary currency stabilization, some students began to be reported as "on leave," excused from registering even nominally for the traditionally obligatory lectures, often while privately preparing for examinations. They numbered, in thousands, 2.0 at the universities and 0.7 at the technical institutes in 1926; 8.2 at the universities, 1.5 at the technical institutes, and 0.7 at the academies in 1931; 1.7 at the univer-

sities, 0.9 at the technical institutes, and 0.2 at the academies in 1937/38. Had they been included in the table, they would have raised the ratio of students per thousand population by about 0.04 in 1926, 0.16 in 1931, and 0.04 in 1937/38; the numbers of students per thousand aged 20–23 by about 0.5 in 1926, 2.1 in 1931, and 0.7 in 1937/38. They were not included, because the Deutsche Hochschulstatistik of 1931 does not treat them as "matriculated students" and because nothing is known about their fields of study. The source for 1951, 1955, and 1960, however, not only considers these students "matriculated," but also makes it very difficult to separate them from other students. It reports (1) enrollment totals for the several categories of university-level institutions that include students on leave and (as all previous sources do) foreign students, (2) separate subtotals for foreign students, (3) for 1955 only, a list of German students, excluding foreigners and students on leave, at the three main types of institutions, according to their fields of study, and (4) for 1951 and 1959/60 (winter semester, not summer 1960), lists of German students, excluding foreigners and students on leave, according to their fields of study, that do not distinguish among categories of university-level institutions. Thus one can calculate that students on leave, in thousands, were 4.5 at all university-level institutions in 1951, and 3.3 at universities, 0.6 at technical institutes, and 0.6 at academies in 1955. But one cannot determine how many there were in the summer semester of 1960 or how they were distributed among the three main classes of university-level institutions in 1951. Since their numbers were *relatively* small in any case, and since they are clearly becoming a regular category of "matriculated" students, it seemed best to include them in the totals for universities, technical institutes, and academies. The problem of the subtotals for the university faculties or fields of study is discussed in note (o) above.

Estimates of the Age Group 20 through 23: The procedures and sources here resemble those described in the notes to Table I. Figures actually used are 80 percent of the five most relevant birth years (i.e., those most closely resembling age years 20 through 24) surviving as of December 1, 1871, 1875, 1880, and 1885, 80 percent of age years 20 through 24 as of December 1, 1900 and September 1950, the *four* most relevant birth years as of December 1, 1890, 1910, and 1919, birth years 1908 through 1911 (not 1909 through 1912) surviving as of June 1933, and age years 20 through 23 for 1925,

beginning of 1938, year-end 1955, and year-average 1960.

Women Students: While there were just over 200 female students at non-Prussian universities as of 1906 and just over 300 by 1907/08, Prussia decided to let women enter the universities only in 1908. At all German universities, the number of women students then grew quite rapidly—for summer semesters, in thousands, from 1.4 in 1909 to 2.5 in 1911 and 8.3 in 1921. At all university-level institutions, the figure rose from 8.6 in 1926 to 21.2 in 1931, so that the 1920s must be regarded as a decisive period in this respect. Women's share of all university-level enrollments, after falling from 16 per-

cent in 1931 to 11 percent in 1937/38, reached 16 percent again in 1951, 18 percent in 1955, and 22 percent in 1960.

Distribution of Students Over the Fields of Study: Table V.1 shows the percentages (by row) of students at all German universities who were in specified fields of study. The figures for the combined faculties of theology, for law, for medicine, and for arts and sciences as a whole are calculated directly from the main table through 1931. The breakdown within the arts and sciences (percentages of all students, not just of those in arts and sciences) is calculated from substantial samples obtained by Conrad for 1841, 1851, and 1861, and from full reports by the

Table V.1

	Theol. (both)	Law, gov.	Med.	Arts & sci.	Hum.	Nat. sci.	Econ., bus.	Agri-cult.	Pharm., dent.	Other
1831	39	28	15	18	15	3	4		3	1
1840	28	28	18	26	14	4	2		3	1
1850	25	36	15	24	18	4	3		4	1
1860	32	20	18	30	18	4	3		4	1
1870	21	22	22	34	21	6	3		4	—
1880	14	25	19	42	22	13	3		3	—
1890	20	23	30	27	10	8	4		5	—
1900	12	29	22	37	14	14	5		4	—
1911	8	19	21	52	23	14	6		4	5
1921	6	22	19	53	14	12	13	4	7	3
1931	8	20	21	51	18	14	6	1	8	4
1955	5	18	12	65	22	15	20	1	6	—

sources for 1870 (1871) through 1931. For 1955 (for reasons explained above) the distribution pertains to German students, excluding foreigners and students on leave, not to figures listed in the main table.

'Other' covers students in technical fields through 1860; about 18 percent of those under 'Other' in 1931 were preparing to be lower teachers; but the category is particularly vague in 1911 and 1921, where it certainly includes some humanists and scientists. 'Pharmacy, dentistry' seems to cover pharmacy alone through 1860; then essentially pharmacy and dentistry through 1921, with the addition of veterinary medicine for 1931 and 1955. Listed jointly under 'Economics, business' and 'Agriculture' through 1911 is a single grouping of "cameralia, agriculture" (through 1860) or "agriculture, cameralia, economics," plus a few foresters (separately mentioned through 1860). 'Economics, business' is broadly but vaguely defined (*Volkswirtschaft*) in 1921, explicitly includes business management (*Betriebswirtschaftslehre*, about 40 percent of the grouping) in 1931, and is expanded to cover all the social sciences in 1955, except to the extent that politics (*Staatswissenschaft*) is grouped and taught with law. The line between the humanities and natural sciences is drawn so as to include geography with the sciences, a

convention violated for 1931 in Table IV, but not here. (Otherwise, see Table IV for detailed subject breakdowns.) All categorizations are clearly somewhat imprecise in the sources, partly because conceptions of various disciplines have changed. The figures from 1921 on simply exaggerate the standard practice of German statisticians before that time, which was to assign all students not specifically in the professional faculties to arts and sciences. On the other hand, as Conrad observed, future secondary teachers and other humanists often enrolled (at least nominally) in the theological faculties during the early nineteenth century, and scientists in the medical faculty. Still, the somewhat erratic figures for 1890 derive from the same source and method of classification as those for 1880. The temporary shifts that took place around that time deserve further study (along with the whole evolution of enrollments by discipline); the present survey is concerned only with the obvious long-term trends.

The Technical Institutes: While four of these institutions date back to the 1820s and 30s, they evolved only gradually from "higher trade schools" to "polytechnical schools" and eventually "technical institutes." This process, which naturally differed from institution to institution, was apparently more or less com-

plete by the late 186os, though the technical institutes did not achieve full university rank, with the right to confer doctorates, until 1899 (in Prussia). Thus German statisticians inevitably differed in counting students at "technical institutes" before 1870. The following enrollment estimates, in thousands, by Lexis and by Conrad (in parentheses) must be regarded as covering polytechnical schools as well as technical institutes: 0.2 (0.8) ca. 1831, 0.6 (0.9) ca. 1835, 0.7 (1.2) ca. 1840, 0.9 (1.2) ca. 1845, 1.2 (1.6) ca. 1850, 1.3 (1.7) ca. 1855, 2.2 (2.6) ca. 1860, 2.0 (2.7) ca. 1865. Enrollments at the technical institutes expanded especially fast from 1870 to about 1876, declined sharply for about ten years, climbed steadily again from the mid-1880s to the early 1890s, only to remain essentially stagnant until 1914. During the interwar years, enrollments fluctuated less violently at the technical institutes than at the universities; the overcrowding at the universities around 1931 had no full equivalent at the technical institutes. Among students at the technical institutes in the summer semester of 1931, about 26.5 percent were taking architecture and construction, 21.5 percent machine engineering, 15 percent electrical engineering, 9 percent other types of engineering (aviation, naval, automotive, surveying, mining, metallurgy, textiles, paper, brewing), 7 percent chemistry, 7 percent mathematics, physics, and "technical physics," 8.5 percent lower-level teaching (including vocational, secondary music, drawing, sports, and a handful in "general studies"), 4 percent economics, business, and business-school teaching, and 1.5 percent pharmacy, agriculture, and forestry. For a diagram of the situation in 1955, see below.

The Academies: Enrollments summarized under this heading in the main table can be broken down at roughly ten-year intervals, in thousands in Table V.2.

a school of social science are also included under this heading for 1960. The philosophical-theological academies, generally run by religious organizations, stood at 1.4 in 1907 and 1.3 in 1911, but were not included under academies until 1921. Art and music schools (including some 300–500 students at a higher sports academy since 1951) stood at 5.8 in 1926, but were not counted until 1951. Never included among academies are the new higher academies or schools of pedagogy for future primary and vocational teachers, some of which (as in Hamburg) are affiliated with universities. A creation of the 1920s, they stood at 0.2 in 1926, 3.2 in 1931, 13.2 in 1954/55 (winter semester), and 25.0 in 1959/60 (winter semester). It should be noted that the academies are not included among university-level institutions (and calculated ratios) until 1921.

The Category of University-Level Institutions: There are good grounds to include the universities alone under this heading until just before 1900, when the technical institutes were formally recognized as their equals. On somewhat more impressionistic evidence, one can justify waiting until the Weimar period to include the academies (with business schools and philosophical-theological academies), and until 1951 to

bring in art and music schools *as* academies. The limits of available information leave little other choice in any case. On the other hand, the pedagogical academies might have been included from 1931, even though they alone were still reported separately from the now very inclusive list of university-level institutions (*Hochschulen*) in German official statistics for 1960.

Students at All Institutions by Subject in 1955: During the summer semester of 1955, matriculated German students (excluding those on leave) at all German university-level institutions were enrolled (in thousands) at the classes of institutions and in the fields of study given in Table V.3.

Academies are defined as in the main table under 1955. Apart from demonstrating the contribution of the various institutions, this breakdown can also help to clarify the counting procedure in the main table for 1955.

Doctorates Conferred at Prussian and German Universities: Table V.4 shows ordinary (*rite*, excluding honorary) doctoral degrees and theological licentiates conferred at Prussian universities through 1911, and doctorates at all German university-level institutions in 1959/60. The figures for 1863 and 1869

Table V.2

	Mining Acads.	Agric. Forest.	Veteri-nary	Busi-ness	Phil.- theol.	Art, Music
1869	0.1	0.6	0.3			
1880	0.3	0.7	0.4			
1891	0.4	1.0	1.0			
1899	0.8	1.2	1.3			
1911	0.4	1.3	0.7			
1921	0.9	2.8	0.7	2.8	1.5	
1931	0.4	1.2	1.0	4.0	2.0	
1955	1.1	0.3	0.5	2.2	2.4	5.1

Auditors and special students are excluded from 1911 on. Business schools (*Handelshochschulen*) stood at about 0.8 in 1907 and 1.0 in 1911, but were not counted among academies until 1921; some 200 students at

Table V.3

	Universities	Tech. institutes	Academies	All institutions
Protestant theology	2.3	–	0.4	2.7
Catholic theology	1.8	–	1.6	3.4
Law, government	14.5	–	–	14.5
General medicine	10.0	–	–	10.0
Pharmacy, dentistry, vet. medicine	4.9	0.5	0.5	5.8
Agriculture, forestry	0.9	0.6	0.3	1.8
Humanities	18.1	0.3	0.1	18.4
Economics, business, social sciences	16.4	0.6	2.0	19.0
Natural sciences	12.1	4.2	0.2	16.6
Architecture, engineering	0.1	17.1	–	17.2
Mining	–	1.4	0.8	2.2
Music, art, sports, other	0.2	–	4.6	4.7
All Fields	81.2	24.6	10.5	116.3

Table V.4

	Prot. theol.	Cath. theol.	Law	Medicine	Phil.	Total
Prussia ca. 1863	2	3	23	246	132	406
ca. 1869	5	4	39	286	175	509
1879/80	3	–	76	224	263	566
1889/90	4	2	51	499	389	945
1899/1900	8	10	115	316	332	781
1910/11	10	13	336	468	837	1,664
Germany 1959/60	91 }		641	1,567	3,207	5,506

(and increasingly as he moved toward 1830) with enrollment figures for selected universities, Eulenburg estimated that close to 8 thousand students attended German universities around 1620 and again around 1655, and the total actually hovered just below 9 thousand during the first half of the eighteenth century. Enrollments then declined gradually after 1750, reached a low of about 5.7 thousand around 1801–05, climbed to about 7.7 thousand after the Napoleonic Wars in 1817, and then rose sharply to 15.3 thousand ca. 1826–30. Conrad's samples, and Prussian figures for 1820–41 in Hoffman, Sammlung, confirm the impression of a very sharp rise during the 1820s, and a decline that can be dated rather precisely from a peak at 1830. The tabulated figure for the summer semester of 1831 probably comes very close to marking that peak, at about 0.52 students per thousand population, though enrollments at Prussian universities were slightly higher in the summer of 1830 than a year later. The figure for 1817 can be related to a population total for 1816, to yield a ratio of about 0.31 students per thousand population, which is very close to the subsequent low of 0.32 for 1860.

Other Critical Periods in the Curve of Enrollments: Absolute total enrollments (not re-

are Conrad's averages for 1861/62–1865/66 and 1866/67–1870/71. Thereafter, 1879/80 means winter semester 1879/80 plus summer semester 1880, etc. Degrees listed under 'Philosophy' for 1959/60 are in all subjects other than theology, law, and general medi-cine. As of 1911, students at Prussian universities were about 49.5 percent of students at all German universities.

University Enrollments Before 1831: Working partly with matricular records, partly

lated to the population) at German universities after 1831 declined steadily to a low in the later 1830s, from which, despite a brief rally ca. 1849–52, they did not really begin to rise until 1859. Steady growth thereafter, briefly interrupted ca. 1866–68 and 1871, was particularly rapid between 1877 and 1885. A dip in the curve after 1889 was not fully made good again until 1896, but it was succeeded by a continuous and steady rise until the First World War. High enrollments immediately after the war were not significantly eroded before the winter semester of 1923/24, but the currency stabilization (not the inflation itself) then produced a sharp dip that reached its bottom in 1926 and was not fully cancelled until 1928/29. Enrollments rose and remained high during the depression of the early 1930s, though they apparently began to decline even before the National Socialist regime's restrictive measures of 1933–34.

Age of Students: As noted in connection with Table I, Prussian students ca. 1820–80 were more often 19 than 18 or 20 when they earned the Abitur. New entrants or first-semester students, too, were most often 19 at Prussian universities in 1886–87 and 1911/12 and at all German universities, technical institutes, and university-level institu-

tions in 1926–31. The mean age of entry appears to have risen a little between 1820 and 1880. It has surpassed 20 since the Second World War. A student may earn the Abitur at 19, enter the university shortly thereafter, and still be 20 during most of his first year of studies. Even without interim military service (an important factor since the Second World War), this may help to explain why, among students at Prussian universities in 1886/87 and 1911/12, each of the four age years 20 through 23 was more heavily represented than any older or younger one. Samples for all German university-level institutions in 1947/48, 1956, and 1963 are somewhat inconsistent and incomplete in their breakdowns, but they do show the two-year age group 22–23 as generally central, and those 24 and over more numerous (and increasingly so) than those under 22. Still, those aged 20 through 23 constitute the best single four-year group to which students may be compared for most of our period. A much more important and difficult question is whether four years, rather than three or five, was in fact the time the average student spent at the university.

Duration of Study and the Choice of a Four-Year Age Group: Eulenburg's and Conrad's calculations suggest that the average German

student stayed 1.7 to 2 years at a single university from the early modern period through the nineteenth century. Since he also tended to change universities freely, however, this tells us nothing about the average duration of university attendance. After 1886, Prussian statisticians began to obtain breakdowns of students according to their semesters of study. On this basis, they calculated average durations of study over 3 periods of about 10 semesters from 1886/87 to 1911/12, arriving at roughly 4 years for theology, 3.3 years for law, 6.3 years for medicine, and 5.8 years for the humanities and natural sciences. Certainly too high, these results neglect students who left in the early semesters, even before completing the mandatory time for state examinations in these fields, along with those in minor subjects within arts and sciences. For the period 1925–31, a more general approach reveals that roughly half the students at all German university-level institutions were in their first nine semesters, the rest in the tenth and higher ones, so that 4.5 years was a kind of median length of attendance. Undoubtedly the most direct and summary approach to the whole question is to calculate the ratio of all enrollments to first-year students or its inverse, the percentage of all students who are in their first year. This is essentially what Conrad did for

Prussia ca. 1820–80, except that he used secondary graduates (including *Extranei*) in the place of first-year enrollments, relating them to all university students who held secondary certificates (including *Extranei*). He thus obtained averages of about 3.4 years for the 1830s and ca. 1856–65, and 4.1 years for the 1870s. The first-year method does produce a special kind of measure. When the duration it yields is used to define the denominator in the ratio of enrollments to a number of age years, the result must come very close to describing first-year enrollments in relation to their one-year age group. The method also understates durations during periods of absolutely increasing university entry. Large first-year percentages may be caused by enrollment growth, and thus falsely suggest too short durations of study. This problem cannot be entirely overcome by averaging; it is particularly serious immediately after recoveries from lows or plateaus in the enrollment curve and least damaging during periods of relatively level enrollments. Average ratios of first-year to all students and corresponding durations of study (in parentheses) were 25.6 percent (3.9 years) for Prussian universities during two semesters in 1886/87, 21.5 percent (4.7 years) for Prussian universities during two semesters in 1911/12, 26.1 percent (3.8 years) for all German university-level institutions (plus pedagogical academies, unfortunately) during five summer semesters from 1927 to 1931, 22.6 percent (4.4 years) and 21.5 percent (4.7 years), respectively, at German universities and German technical institutes in 1931, and 24.4 percent (4.1 years) for four selected semesters 1951/52–1959/60. This suggests that the "true" duration of study at German universities rose from 3.5 years during the earlier nineteenth century to 4 years by the 1870s, and roughly 4.5 years (with or without the technical institutes) from the eve of the First World War through the Weimar period. At all university-level institutions it probably stood slightly above 4 years during the 1920s, but reached 4.5 years after the Second World War. The tabulated ratios of enrollments to the four-year age group 20 through 23 therefore tend to understate the access to university-level study by up to 15 percent before 1870, and to overstate it up to the same limit from around 1880 on.

Table VI

Germany: Social Origins of University Students, 1770–1885

(Percentages of Fathers in Stated Occupations)

Father's occupation	At the University of Halle, ca:						At Halle ca. 1852 by faculties:			
	1770	1821	1834	1852	1874	1879	Theol.	Law	Med.	Arts & sci.
1. High officials	18.6	13.1	12.4	12.3	10.6	6.1	3.2	28.0	11.9	7.6
2. Professors	3.4	3.0	1.8	3.9	2.4	5.2	4.3	3.2	3.6	4.8
3. Clergy	27.8	26.0	19.4	28.0	18.8	16.0	40.6	14.0	19.0	15.2
4. Medicine	4.8	3.7	4.7	4.7	5.2	5.2	1.8	5.2	15.5	5.7
5. Officers	1.0	2.3	1.4	2.4	0.7	0.8	0.9	5.4	1.2	1.9
1–5. Sum	55.6	48.1	39.7	51.3	37.7	33.3	50.8	55.8	51.2	35.2
6. Lower officials	13.9	16.5	21.2	19.0	22.1	22.9	24.1	11.0	12.5	28.6
7. Landowners	4.2	3.7	3.9	4.9	7.4	5.8	1.8	10.3	6.0	1.9
8. Farmers	3.9	6.6	7.9	5.9	6.3	6.9	6.6	5.2	6.5	3.8
9. Industrialists	–	1.6	1.5	1.6	3.4	3.4	0.9	2.4	3.0	1.0
10. Merchants	8.3	8.3	11.2	7.4	10.0	11.2	5.5	6.9	13.7	12.4
11. Artisans	12.3	13.7	11.7	7.6	8.2	11.4	8.1	5.4	6.0	17.1
12. Workers	0.8	0.9	1.7	1.0	1.1	0.8	1.6	0.6	–	–
9–12. Sum	21.4	24.5	26.1	17.6	22.7	26.8	16.1	15.3	22.7	30.5
13. Rentiers	1.1	0.5	1.3	1.1	3.9	4.3	0.5	2.4	1.2	–
Absolute totals (100%)	830	1,102	1,516	1,479	2,127	2,594	742	464	168	105

301

Table VI continued

Father's occupation	From Württemberg ca:			At Leipzig ca:			At Leipzig ca. 1876 by faculties:				
	1837	1875	1885	1866	1876	1886	Theol.	Law	Med.	Hum.	Sci.
1. Higher officials	16.6	11.5	9.8	17.0	14.3	11.9	2.6	24.1	11.0	7.6	8.2
2. Professors	3.9	4.7	4.4	5.8	3.6	3.9	3.9	2.9	3.8	5.2	2.8
3. Clergy	14.3	14.0	11.6	15.9	10.3	8.7	39.9	5.0	5.5	10.8	5.6
4. Medicine	7.8	7.4	5.2	7.3	5.8	5.9	1.9	4.6	16.4	3.7	7.9
5. Professions	0.1	0.7	0.5	1.8	2.5	3.8	1.2	2.4	2.9	2.9	2.7
6. Officers	2.2	0.6	0.8	1.0	1.1	1.8	0.2	1.8	0.8	0.8	0.7
1–6. Sum	44.9	38.9	32.3	48.8	37.6	36.0	49.7	40.8	40.4	31.0	27.9
7. Lower officials[a]	21.1	20.9	23.0	15.1	13.1	12.6	18.9	8.6	10.4	20.2	12.7
8. Landowners	0.9	0.6	1.4	2.1	3.8	2.9	0.8	5.8	1.3	1.8	4.6
9. Farmers	6.6	13.7	10.4	6.7	9.9	8.7	8.6	8.4	8.8	10.2	14.9
10. Entrepreneurs	2.7	6.0	11.2	3.3	4.6	5.9	2.4	5.2	5.1	3.9	5.3
11. Tradesmen	23.2	17.6	18.5	12.7	18.9	20.7	8.6	21.6	23.7	16.0	19.7
12. Artisans[b]	0.4	0.3	0.7	8.9	6.8	6.8	9.4	3.4	4.0	12.0	9.0
10–12. Sum	26.3	23.9	30.4	24.9	30.3	33.4	20.4	30.2	32.8	31.9	34.0
13. Rentiers	0.1	1.8	2.5	2.6	5.4	6.5	1.5	6.4	6.4	4.9	5.9
Absolute totals (100%)	818	1,724	2,439	2,861	9,086	9,428	1,019	3,767	910	1,905	1,485

TERMS: For Halle, years listed in the table are approximate median dates of samples covering 1768–71, 1820–22, 1832–36, 1850–54, 1872–76, and 1877–81. Note that the theological faculty was unusually large and dominant at Halle, especially before 1850, and that foreigners and students of pharmacy and agriculture were excluded by the source for Halle. Under Württemberg, samples are of students with secondary certificates who came from Württemberg and were enrolled at any German university during the years 1835–40, 1871–81, and 1881–91. For Leipzig, samples cover 1864–68, 1874–78, and 1884–88. Faculties are the traditional ones, except that the source for Leipzig splits the total for arts and sciences into natural sciences and "historical disciplines," broadly defined. 'High(er) officials' comprises judges, lawyers, national state and local officials, all with university education, except that some separately mentioned high forestry officials (Oberförster) are also included for Württemberg and a few higher-level officials without university education for Leipzig. 'Professors' are teachers with university education or university and Gymnasium teachers, except that a few separately mentioned scholars are also included for Württemberg. 'Medicine' almost certainly includes dentists, veterinarians, and pharmacists in all cases. 'Professions' covers artists for Württemberg; and artists, writers, architects, and engineers for Leipzig. 'Officers' also includes a few high nobility for Württemberg. 'Lower officials' comprises all officials and teachers without university education, except that some higher-level officials without university education are moved from this category to that of 'Higher officials' in the case of Leipzig. The distinction between 'Landowners' and 'Farmers' is inevitably imprecise. Landowners are defined as large agrarian proprietors (Grossgrundbesitzer or Gutsbesitzer) or stewards (Pächter, in the case of Württemberg only), but "agriculturists of equivalent standing", are

also included for Halle, which makes for a particularly inclusive definition in that case. Farmers are defined essentially as peasant-farmers (Bauern) for Halle and Leipzig, but much more inclusively as agriculturists (Landwirte) for Württemberg. As of about 1875, the sums of percentages for landowners and farmers were actually very similar in the three samples. On the other hand, the difference between the concept Landwirt and the combination Gutsherr-Bauer reflects real differences between agrarian structures in Württemberg and in the northeast. As for the categorization of the industrial, commercial, and artisanal occupations, it is quite various in the three cases. For Halle, 'Industrialists' is a literal translation of Industrielle, meaning industrial producers quite generally; 'Merchants' covers merchants and innkeepers; 'Artisans' literally translates Handwerker; 'Workers' are workers (Arbeiter) and servants (niedere Bedienstete). For Württemberg, 'Entrepreneurs' covers large-scale businessmen (Grossgewerbetreibende) in industry and commerce, along with "private officials in executive positions"; 'Tradesmen' covers small-scale businessmen (Kleingewerbetreibende) in industry and commerce, along with "private officials in subordinate positions"; 'Artisans' is in this case a narrowly defined low-status category of

workers, unskilled assistants (Gehilfen) and occasional workers (Taglöhner), a group more restricted than 'Workers' for Halle. For Leipzig, 'Entrepreneurs' covers industrialists (Industrielle, as for Halle), plus large or wholesale merchants (Grosskaufleute); 'Tradesmen' comprises merchants and innkeepers (as 'Merchants' does for Halle); 'Artisans' includes workers as well as artisans. See further details below.

ª Somewhat more inclusively defined for Württemberg than for Leipzig, as explained below.

ᵇ Much more inclusively defined for Leipzig (artisans and all workers) than for Württemberg (unskilled workers and servants), as explained above.

SOURCES: Conrad, Universitätsstudium, for Halle and for addenda below (a few mistakes in Conrad's absolute numbers corrected on internal evidence, and all percentages recalculated, since Conrad's contained scores of errors). Rienhardt, Universitätsstudium, for Württemberg (percentages are recalculations from verified absolute numbers). Eulenburg, Entwicklung der Universität Leipzig, (again internal corrections of a few absolute numbers, especially of totals, and percentage recalculations). Lenz, *Geschichte der König-lichen Friedrich-Wilhelms Universität*, for addendum below.

Industrial, Commercial, and Artisanal Occu-pations ca. 1874/75: To grasp differences of categorization for these occupational groups, it is useful to compare data for 1874 and 1875 in the three samples. In the case of Württemberg only, the source supplies two further breakdowns not reproduced in the table. 'Entrepreneurs' for Württemberg ca. 1875 (6.0 percent of sample) consists of 1.8 percent large-scale businessmen in industry, 3.6 percent large-scale businessmen in com-merce, and 0.6 percent private officials in ex-ecutive positions; 'Tradesmen' (17.6 percent) consists of 12.4 percent small-scale business-men in industry, 4.4 percent small-scale busi-nessmen in commerce, and 0.8 percent private officials in subordinate positions. The "pri-vate officials" in this breakdown are so few that the executive ones can be included with large-scale industry, and the subordinate ones with small-scale commerce. This gives us the rough scheme, shown in Table VI.1, of over-lapping categorizations in the three samples for 1874/75.

The scheme is an inference based on terms that are vague in the sources, especially in

Table VI.1

	Halle	Württem-berg	Leipzig
Large industrial producers	3.4	2.4	4.6
Large-scale merchants	10.0	3.6	
Small(er) merchants		5.2	18.9
Small-scale producers	8.2		
Artisans		12.4	
Skilled workers	1.1		
Unskilled, servants		0.3	6.8
Total: all the above	22.7	23.9	30.3

the case of Leipzig. It should be particularly noted that the German word for merchant (*Kaufmann*) can be used almost as broadly as *business*. It is no surprise, on the other hand, that Leipzig, partly because of its location, should have attracted a larger rep-resentation of the older and newer business middle classes than Halle, with its traditional emphasis on theology.

Lower Teachers Among Lower Officials: 'Lower officials' includes lower-level teachers, defined as "primary school teachers" by the source for Leipzig, and as "teachers without university education" by the sources for Halle and Württemberg. At Halle, they were 5.4 percent of fathers about 1770, 7.5 percent ca. 1821, 7.9 percent ca. 1834, 7.9 percent ca. 1852, 11.8 percent ca. 1874, and 10.8 per-

cent ca. 1879. Among fathers of students from Württemberg, they accounted for 7.0 percent ca. 1837, 9.7 percent ca. 1875, and 10.7 percent ca. 1885. At Leipzig, 6.6 percent of fathers were in this category ca. 1866, 5.8 percent ca. 1876, and 5.3 percent ca. 1886. In other words, they generally made up from about one-third to one-half the percentages listed for lower officials in general.

Additional Data for Tübingen and Berlin: Conrad reports briefly on fathers of Württem-berg *Gymnasium* graduates at the University of Tübingen. The percentage of fathers who could be assumed to have university educa-tions, he says, was 52 in 1821–30, 57 in 1840–49, and 53 in 1873–77. Lenz breaks

Table VI.2

	Educated	Propertied	Burgher
1810	47	25	28
1815	50	26	24
1820	45	30	24
1830	45	32	23
1840	48	32	20
1850	48	31	21
1860	45	32	23
1870	38	33	29
1880	31	42	28
1890	33	41	26
1900	34	41	26
1909, male	32	39	30
1909, female	42	45	13

down fathers of students at the University of Berlin into three large groupings. The first, which may be called the educated class, consists of higher officials, clergy, judges and lawyers, university and *Gymnasium* teachers, the medical professions, officers, architects, engineers, writers, and artists. The second (propertied class) comprises large landowners, large and small "industrialists" and merchants, along with rentiers. The third and last of Lenz's groupings (burgher class) is made up essentially of middle and lower officials and teachers, artisans, and farmers. Table VI.2 gives Lenz's listing of the percentages of Berlin students traceable to the three types of family backgrounds during selected years.

Table VII

Germany: Social Origins of University Students, 1885–1925
(Percentages of Fathers in Stated Occupations)

Father's Occupation	Prussia ca.		Prussia, 1900, by faculties					By fields within "Philosophy"			
	1889	1900	Prot.	Cath.	Law	Med.	Phil.	Hum.	Sci.	Cam.	Pharm.
1. High officials	7.0	6.3	2.3	1.5	12.2	4.4	4.1	3.7	4.5	4.8	3.6
2. Professors	3.3	4.8	4.1	1.2	5.6	3.9	5.3	7.0	5.6	2.6	2.9
3. Clergy	7.0	6.3	30.2	0.1	4.2	5.3	3.7	5.2	3.0	2.4	2.8
4. Medicine	5.1	5.4	1.4	1.1	5.0	10.5	4.4	2.5	4.8	2.2	10.6
5. Professions	0.6	0.6	0.2	0.4	0.5	0.5	1.0	1.4	0.9	0.4	0.4
6. Officers	1.4	1.8	0.5	–	3.0	1.4	1.6	1.8	1.4	2.2	0.8
1–6. Sum	24.5	25.1	38.5	4.4	30.4	26.0	20.1	21.6	20.2	14.7	21.1
7. Lower officials	19.7	21.3	33.1	21.6	17.1	19.8	22.7	28.3	21.5	15.8	18.2
8. Landowners	1.9	1.6	0.4	–	3.1	0.6	1.5	0.4	0.9	6.5	0.8
9. Farmers	11.9	10.6	7.9	26.1	8.8	9.6	10.9	8.1	8.1	27.4	8.3
10. Entrepreneurs	15.6	15.1	7.8	22.2	14.1	13.6	17.6	16.6	21.2	13.3	15.8
11. Tradesmen	18.8	21.7	8.9	15.2	23.9	26.3	21.5	18.7	22.3	17.4	30.7
12. Employees	2.6	2.6	2.4	3.5	1.8	2.2	3.6	3.4	4.0	3.6	2.8
13. Workers	0.8	0.8	0.5	4.4	0.2	0.5	0.9	1.5	0.6	0.4	0.3
10–13. Sum	37.8	40.2	19.5	45.2	40.0	42.6	43.5	40.3	48.2	34.7	49.6
14. Others	4.1	1.2	0.5	2.7	0.8	1.4	1.4	1.4	1.2	1.0	2.1
Absolute totals (100%)	12,565	14,798	1,310	889	4,418	3,099	5,082	1,895	1,738	723	726

	Württemberg ca.		Leipzig ca.		Bavaria ca.		Prussia	Prussia, 1925		
	1895	1905	1895	1905	1914	1925	ca. 1911	Univ.	Tech.	Acads.
1. High officials	9.4	8.8	8.9	8.0	8.0	13.0	5.9	13.9	13.2	11.6
2. Professors	6.2	5.2	5.0	6.1	3.9	4.7	4.0			
3. Clergy	12.1	10.2	8.0	7.4	2.8	2.6	4.6			
4. Medicine	5.7	4.8	5.9	5.4	7.1	7.2	4.3	8.6	8.4	5.5
5. Professions	0.3	0.3	4.3	4.3	1.0	0.9	0.7			
6. Officers	0.6	0.8	1.5	1.5	0.9	1.0	1.5	1.4	2.1	1.9
1–6. Sum	34.3	30.1	33.6	32.5	23.7	29.4	21.1	24.0	23.7	19.0
7. Lower officials	24.0	24.8	14.6	16.1	18.5	18.8	26.8	26.5	24.8	27.2
8. Landowners	1.0	0.8	2.8	2.1	–	–	4.5	2.9	1.5	5.3
9. Farmers	9.0	10.3	7.6	7.5	9.6	6.3	6.1	5.0	3.9	6.8
10. Entrepreneurs	11.8	11.0	6.3	7.7	7.7	8.9	11.7	8.9	14.9	12.4
11. Tradesmen	14.6	17.2	22.9	23.0	23.9	20.1	23.4	21.9	21.0	17.3
12. Employees	1.8	2.6	–	–	2.3	4.5	3.2	6.0	6.4	6.0
13. Workers	1.0	1.0	5.3	4.9	3.0	2.6	1.6	1.3	0.7	1.8
10–13. Sum	29.3	31.7	34.5	35.8	36.9	36.1	39.9	38.1	43.1	37.4
14. Others	2.4	2.4	6.9	6.1	11.3	9.4	1.8	3.6	3.1	4.2
Absolute totals (100%)	2,381	3,050	9,095	11,640	18,574	19,486	24,218	30,001	8,603	4,880

307

TERMS: Under 'Prussia 1889', 'Prussia 1900', and 'Prussia 1911', the table reports on German students at Prussian universities during an average semester between 1887 and 1891, during the academic years 1899/1900 and 1911/12 (average of the two semesters in each case), on the traditional faculty breakdown for 1899/1900, and on the source's further subdivision of arts and sciences ("philosophy") into "philosophy, philology, and history," "mathematics and natural sciences," "agriculture, cameralia, and economics," and "pharmacy and dentistry." 'Württemberg' covers secondary graduates *from* Württemberg at German universities (as in Table VI), the two samples being for 1891–1901 and 1901–1911. The columns on the University of Leipzig report on 1894–98 and 1904–1908; see Table VI for earlier data on Leipzig. Columns under 'Bavaria' contain figures for German students at Bavarian universities during two periods of two semesters in 1913/14 and 1924/25. The last three columns at the lower right of the table are for Prussian institutions in the winter semester of 1924/25, i.e., for universities, for technical institutes, and for academies of forestry, agriculture, veterinary medicine, mining, and commerce. Reports are for all students in each case, though women were not explicitly mentioned (or numerically significant) be-

fore 1924. *Occupational categories of fathers* are basically those of the *Preussische Statistik* before the First World War (inspired by Conrad), though with variations as follows. 'High officials' are officials, judges, and lawyers with university education (with a few high foresters separately mentioned for Württemberg), plus high officials (*höhere Beamte*) regardless of education for Leipzig and Bavaria; they form part of a single grouping of *höhere Beamte*, professors, secondary teachers, and clergymen for Prussia in 1925. 'Professors' are teachers with university education or *Gymnasium* teachers and university professors, except that university professors specifically designated as in theology, law, or medicine were moved to these classifications by the Prussian source for 1911, and *Gymnasium* teachers generally (regardless of education) are included for Leipzig. 'Medicine' includes a few Prussian military doctors, as well as veterinarians, apothecaries, and (almost certainly) dentists, though dentists were explicitly listed only for Württemberg and Bavaria. 'Professions' are writers, artists, and private scholars, with the addition of architects and engineers for Leipzig (3.2 percent of fathers ca. 1905) and of a minute group in university-educated professions not itemized under other headings for Bavaria; the category is most inclu-

sive for Prussia ca. 1925, where it covers all "liberal" and "academic" professions (i.e., lawyers, doctors, apothecaries, writers, private scholars, etc., with university education), as well as a small number (1.4 percent of university students' fathers) in "liberal professions without university education." 'Officers' includes a handful of military officials for Prussia and high nobility for Württemberg. 'Lower officials' comprises teachers and officials not classified as high officials or professors, with the addition of a few noncommissioned officers for Prussia. 'Landowners' are narrowly defined as owners of noble estates (*Rittergutsbesitzer*) for Prussia through 1900, more broadly as large landed proprietors for the remaining samples, with the explicit addition of lessees and stewards for Prussia in 1911 and 1925. 'Farmers' are all remaining independents in agriculture, with the explicit inclusion of a few men in forestry, commercial gardening (or vegetable farming), and fishing for Prussia through 1911 and of small leaseholders for Prussia in 1925. 'Entrepreneurs' are independents in industry and insurance for Prussia through 1900; owners, managers, and executive employees of large-scale concerns in industry, commerce, insurance and transportation for Prussia from 1911 and for Württemberg; "industrialists" and wholesale mer-

308

chants for Leipzig; and industrial owners and highly educated technical personnel (4.1 percent of fathers ca. 1925) for Bavaria. 'Tradesmen' are all independents in commerce, transport, and innkeeping for Prussia through 1900; small-scale and artisanal independents (all those not "entrepreneurs") in industry, commerce, insurance, transport, and innkeeping for Württemberg and for Prussia from 1911; smaller merchants and innkeepers for Leipzig; and all merchants, artisans, and innkeepers for Bavaria. 'Employees' are nonexecutive "private officials" or supervisory and clerical personnel in all sectors. 'Workers' are nonindependent and nonclerical "assistants" in all sectors, servants, and/or "workers" (occasional or without description of sector), with the addition of "artisanal workers" (*Handwerker*) for Leipzig and of "others members of the lower classes" for Bavaria. 'Others' includes those without, or with unknown, occupations for Prussia; rentiers or pensioners (*Rentner*) for Württemberg and Leipzig; and *Rentner* (including former officials and those on social security), unknowns, and a handful of minor health professionals for Bavaria.

SOURCES: *Preussische Statistik*, vol. 125 for 1887–91, vol. 193 for 1899/1900, vol. 236

for fathers with university education 1886–1911 and for tabulation 1911, vol. 279 for Württemberg. Rienhardt, *Universitätsstudium*, for Württemberg. Eulenburg, *Entwicklung der Universität Leipzig*. Bavaria, *Sozialer Auf- und Abstieg*, for Bavaria. *Statistisches Jahrbuch*, vol. 8 (1887) for occupational census 1882.

Lower Teachers Among Lower Officials: 'Lower officials' consistently includes lower-level teachers, defined as teachers without university education in all samples for Prussia and Württemberg and as primary school

teachers for Leipzig and Bavaria. Among fathers of all university students, they made up 8.2 percent in Prussia both ca. 1889 and 1900, 11 percent in Prussia ca. 1911, 11.5 percent for Württemberg both ca. 1895 and ca. 1905, 6.8 percent at Leipzig ca. 1895 and 7.1 percent ca. 1905, 8.1 percent in Bavaria ca. 1914 and 6.7 percent ca. 1925. They were not distinguished from lower officials in the Prussian sources for 1925.

Industrial, Commercial, and Artisanal Occupations ca. 1905–1914: Table VII.1 represents an inferential scheme of the sources'

Table VII.1

	Prussia	Württemberg	Leipzig	Bavaria
Larger industrial owners and managers	8.2	4.8		5.1
Executive or educated employees (with range to commerce)		1.3	7.7	2.6
Owners and directors in commerce, transport, insurance	3.5	4.9		
Smaller independents in commerce, etc.	15.9	6.2	23.0	16.1
Innkeepers	1.6			
Nonexecutive employees	3.2	2.6		1.8
Small producers to artisans	5.9	11.0		2.3
Skilled workers			4.9	6.0
Unskilled, servants	1.6	1.0		3.0

categorizations in this field. Breakdowns for Prussia ca. 1911 (with the most accurate and detailed definitions) are compared with all (irreducible) groupings listed in the sources for Württemberg ca. 1901–11, Leipzig ca. 1901–11, and Bavaria ca. 1914.

Fathers with University Education in Prussia, 1886–1911: Among fathers of German students at Prussian universities, some 25.7 percent were themselves academically educated during the period between 1886/87 and 1891, 27.5 percent ca. 1891/92–1895/96, 27.0 percent in 1899/1900, 25.7 percent in 1902/03, 24.2 percent in 1905/06, 23.0 percent in 1908/09, and 22.1 percent in 1911/12. As of 1899/1900, the percentage of university students' fathers with university education was 38.6 percent in Protestant Theology, 4.6 percent in Catholic Theology, 33.0 percent in Law, 26.8 percent in Medicine, 22.8 percent in Arts and Sciences generally, 21.5 percent in the humanities, and 24.1 percent in the natural sciences.

German Occupational Census of 1882: Rounded percentages of the German labor force in major sectors and social positions as of 1882 were as follows:

Independents, officials, and employees in government, the liberal professions, nonprofit organizations, and services:	5%
Independents in agriculture, forestry, fishing, and gardening:	12%
Helping family members and workers in agriculture, etc.:	31%
Independents in industry, commerce, transport, and insurance:	14%
Officials and employees in industry, commerce, agriculture:	2%
Family helpers and workers in industry, commerce, etc.:	29%
Domestic service personnel:	7%

“Industry” is used in the extended sense of all production, including crafts. “Independents” include not only owners or co-owners, leaseholders, and directors, but also administrators and employees in executive positions. However, about 340 thousand “independents” who were working in their own home for the account of others are counted as workers. “Officials” in the German census does not include “private officials”; officials in transportation, for example, include state railroad officials. To contrast the proportions of students' fathers who were officials or members of the liberal professions with the 5 percent of the work force in that sector is to ignore officials in industry, commerce, etc. But the distortion is balanced by the inclusion of many minor and private service professions in the 5 percent that is used as a point of reference.

310

Table VIII

Germany: Social Origins of University-Level Students, 1931 and 1963
(Percentages of Fathers in Stated Occupations)

At universities, by fields of study, and at technical institutes: 1931

Father's Occupation	Total[a]	Prot.	Cath.	Law	Med.	Hum.	Sci.	Econ.	Pharm.	Other	Tech.
1. High officials, professors, clergy	15.0	22.0	2.9	18.5	17.2	14.6	12.4	9.1	10.8	8.6	12.9
2. Academic professions	6.9	1.8	1.1	7.5	14.1	4.1	4.0	4.2	8.6	2.0	4.3
3. Officers	1.4	1.0	0.2	2.2	1.5	1.4	1.1	1.4	0.9	0.9	1.7
1–3. Sum	23.3	24.8	4.2	28.2	32.8	20.2	17.5	14.7	20.3	11.5	18.9
4. Other professions	1.8	1.8	0.9	1.7	1.7	1.4	1.3	2.1	4.1	1.0	3.3
5. Lower officials	31.5	37.0	30.3	26.6	25.2	36.9	37.8	25.7	34.1	37.6	28.3
6. Landowners	1.2	0.7	0.4	1.6	1.3	0.7	0.7	1.1	1.3	2.9	0.9
7. Farmers	4.2	5.0	19.3	3.2	3.2	3.8	4.6	3.6	4.5	6.5	2.7
8. Entrepreneurs	10.6	5.7	4.9	13.1	11.0	9.1	10.5	16.7	9.1	7.6	17.7
9. Tradesmen	17.9	12.3	21.3	18.7	19.0	16.6	15.9	24.6	19.3	15.4	16.8
10. Employees	6.0	7.7	6.5	4.5	4.0	6.8	7.7	7.4	5.4	8.7	7.5
11. Workers	2.9	4.1	11.3	1.8	1.2	3.5	3.5	3.5	1.0	8.0	2.8
8–11. Sum	37.3	29.8	43.9	38.1	35.2	36.1	37.5	52.2	34.8	39.8	44.8
12. Others	0.7	0.9	1.0	0.6	0.7	0.8	0.6	0.6	0.9	0.7	1.1
Absolute totals (100%)	99,432	6,249	2,197	20,328	20,494	19,249	12,744	5,850	7,689	4,632	20,280

Table VIII continued

At all university-level institutions, by fields of study: 1963

Father's Occupation	Total^b	Prot.	Cath.	Law	Med.	Hum.	Sci.	Econ.	Educ.	Other	Tech.
1. High officials	8.6	6.7	3.5	15.8	10.3	8.5	7.5	5.8	5.5	8.8	8.0
2. Professors	6.0	5.7	3.1	5.0	6.1	8.4	6.9	3.4	6.5	7.2	4.2
3. Clergy	1.8	19.1	0.1	1.3	1.9	2.1	1.0	0.7	1.8	1.7	1.0
4. Medicine	7.2	2.9	2.8	4.8	26.2	4.2	3.3	2.9	3.3	6.3	3.1
5. Academic professions	5.1	2.8	1.8	11.1	4.8	4.0	3.5	5.0	3.2	5.0	6.1
1–5. Sum	28.8	37.3	11.3	38.0	49.3	27.1	22.2	17.8	20.4	29.0	22.3
6. Other professions	1.6	1.1	0.8	1.8	1.3	1.5	1.2	2.1	0.9	1.8	1.8
7. Lower officials	17.6	16.9	16.6	16.9	13.5	21.4	19.8	15.6	24.6	17.6	16.9
8. Agriculture	3.7	4.1	15.7	2.9	2.9	3.7	3.3	3.6	4.6	4.2	3.2
9. Entrepreneurs	22.8	17.2	11.4	21.5	17.0	20.1	24.1	31.6	16.7	21.6	28.0
10. Tradesmen	7.7	5.6	11.1	5.7	5.1	7.3	8.2	11.3	8.2	7.0	9.0
11. Employees	9.0	8.8	10.2	6.6	5.0	9.9	11.6	9.7	11.9	8.4	10.4
12. Workers	5.9	6.4	20.6	3.5	2.9	6.6	7.4	5.7	10.1	5.8	6.2
9–12. Sum	45.4	38.1	53.3	37.4	29.9	43.8	51.3	58.3	46.9	42.7	53.5
13. Others	3.0	2.6	2.3	2.9	3.1	2.5	2.3	2.7	2.6	4.7	2.3
Absolute totals (100%)	192,342	3,922	3,181	14,962	27,367	30,852	22,213	25,116	5,195	32,962	26,572

a Distribution for all university students, i.e., in all *university* fields of study.
b Distribution for all students, all fields of study, at *all university-level institutions*.

TERMS: University fields of study for 1931 (summer semester) are the traditional faculties, except that arts and sciences is broken down into humanities; natural sciences; economics and business; pharmacy, dentistry, and veterinary medicine; and all remaining subjects, including education for primary and vocational teachers, agriculture, and forestry. Education for lower teachers at universities was not yet common in 1931 (2,761 students). The line between the humanities and the natural sciences is drawn exactly as in Table IV, which may be consulted for further

312

details. 'Technical' for 1931 covers all students (all fields) at technical institutes during that summer semester. Figures for 1963 are based on a survey of all students at all university-level institutions, broken down by fields of study: 'Medicine' here includes dental and veterinary medicine; 'Humanities' comprises history, German studies, ancient and modern languages; 'Sciences' covers mathematics, physics, and chemistry; 'Economics' includes business management; 'Education' means preparation for primary and vocational school teachers; 'Other' is a very inclusive category, covering pharmacy, sociology, political science, philosophy, psychology and pedagogy, archeology, anthropology, comparative literature, art, journalism, sports, surveying, mining, and other subjects—it is therefore not to be compared to the "minor" subjects within arts and sciences normally listed under 'Other'; 'Technical' subjects are construction, mechanical engineering (including aviation and naval construction), and electrical engineering, i.e., the main subjects (other than chemistry) commonly taught at the technical institutes. Occupational categories for 1931 are still those originated by Conrad and the Preussische Statistik, though with slight simplifications and alterations. 'High officials, professors, clergy' has become a single grouping including all höhere

Beamte, chiefly but not exclusively with university education, as well as all teachers with university education. 'Academic professions' are members of the liberal professions (lawyers, doctors, apothecaries, writers, private scholars, etc.) with university education. 'Officers' include "higher military officials." 'Other professions' are members of liberal professions without university education. 'Lower officials' are predominantly "middle-level" civil servants, a few among them with university education, but also teachers without university education (not separated out), a small group of "lower-level officials," and a few military personnel other than officers. 'Landowners' are all owners and leaseholders of domain or other large landed properties. 'Farmers' are middle and small farmers and peasants. 'Entrepreneurs' are owners and directors of factories and corporations in all sectors, as well as executive employees. 'Tradesmen' are small independents in all sectors, down to the level of the independent artisan. 'Employees' are all those not included with entrepreneurs. 'Workers' are predominantly but not exclusively in industry, including occasional workers. 'Others' covers those not already classified, unknowns, and a few "without profession." Occupational categories for 1963 are discussed below.

SOURCES: Deutsche Hochschulstatistik, vol. 7. Kath, Das soziale Bild 1963. Statistisches Jahrbuch, vol. 53 (1934), vol. for 1963 for census 1933 and 1961.

Details on Fathers of All University-Level Students in 1963: Occupational categories in the source for 1963 are very similar to those in the source for fathers of German secondary students as of 1965 in Table III, but the summary presented in Table VIII is a little more condensed than Table III. Table VIII.1 is a breakdown that duplicates the scheme of Table III where possible (see III for detailed annotation) and that incidentally provides a contrast between the social origins of women students and those of all students. (Arabic numerals indicate categories used in Table VIII.)

German Occupational Census, 1933 and 1961: Table VIII.2 gives the percentages of the labor force in major sectors and social positions as of 1933 and 1961 (microcensus). 'Officials' does not include "private officials"; officials in transport, for example, include state railroad officials. 'Independents in professions, services' for 1933 includes some high officials. About 1.3 million apprentices are excluded from the working population for 1961.

Career Plans of German Students in 1931: Table VIII.3 shows the percentages of German students at German universities and at German technical institutes who planned to enter the occupations listed. "Independent" here apparently means self-employed, not (as in German census usage) self-employed or of equivalent status.

Table VIII.1

	All students	Female students
1. High officials	8.6	10.7
(including without university education)	(3.3)	(3.7)
2. Professors	6.0	7.9
3. Clergy	1.8	2.1
4. Medical professions	7.2	9.9
4. Lawyers, notaries	1.9	2.7
5. Independent engineers, architects	1.4	1.7
5. Other liberal professions with university education	1.8	2.0
6. Other liberal professions without university education	1.6	1.8
7. Military	2.5	2.8
7. Middle officials	6.5	5.5
7. Lower officials	3.5	2.3
7. Lower teachers	5.1	4.9
8. Independent farmers	3.7	3.1
9. Manufacturers, wholesale merchants	4.4	4.8
(including "others" in business with university education)	(0.2)	(0.2)
9. Executive employees	14.8	13.7
9. Employed engineers, architects	3.5	4.1
10. Retailers, innkeepers	2.6	2.2
10. Independent artisans	3.0	2.3
10. Other independents (business)	2.1	2.0
11. Nonexecutive employees	7.8	5.9
11. Foremen	1.2	0.7
12. Skilled workers, dependent artisans	5.4	2.7
(not a category in source for Table III)		
12. Unskilled and agricultural workers	0.5	0.3
(not a category in source for Table III)		
13. No occupation, unknown, others	3.0	3.8
Absolute totals (100%)	192,342	44,159

Table VIII.2

	1933	1961
Independents in professions, services	1	2
Officials in the government, nonprofit and services sector	3	4
Employees in the government, nonprofit and services sector	3	6
Independents in agriculture, forestry, fishing, and gardening	7	5
Independents in industry, commerce, transport, banking, insurance	9	6
Officials in agriculture, industry, commerce	2	2
Employees in agriculture, industry, commerce	10	15
Family helping in agriculture	14	8
Workers in agriculture	8	2
Family helping in other than agriculture	2	3
Workers in other than agriculture	38	46
Domestic service personnel	4	–
Absolute Totals (100%, in millions)	32.3	24.6

Table VIII.3

	Universities	Technical institutes
Government service	11.9	18.0
Professor, librarian, archivist	1.2	0.1
Secondary teacher	24.2	6.2
Other teacher	5.9	9.2
Clergy	8.7	–
Medicine	27.6	–
Lawyer, patent lawyer	6.8	0.5
Other free professions	2.9	9.1
Industry, commerce, agriculture:		
as owners or "independents"	1.2	4.4
as (executive) employees, etc.	6.7	47.6
Other, unknown	2.8	5.0
Absolute totals (100%)	99,432	20,280

Table IX

France: Secondary Enrollments and Population, 1809–1961
(Enrollments in Thousands, Population in Millions)

Year	Complementary	Vocational	Higher primary	Girls' secondary[a]	Public secondary[a]	Private secondary[b]	All secondary[a]	Total population[c]	Sec. per 1000 pop.	Age group[d]	Sec. per 1000 age group	Baccalaureates	Baccs. per 1000 aged 17
1809					27.6	22.6	50.1	28.6	1.8				
1820					33.8	16.8	50.6	30.3	1.7			3.1	
1831					39.8	20.6	60.4	32.6	1.9			3.2	
1842					45.3	25.3	70.5	34.5	2.0	6.1	12	2.8	5
1854					46.4	64.4	110.8	35.9	3.1	6.4	17	4.3	7
1865					65.7	74.6	140.3	37.9	3.7	6.5	22	5.9	9
1876					79.2	75.4	154.7	36.9	4.2	6.4	24	5.4	8
1887	10.2[e]		21.0[e]	10.4	89.9	68.3	158.2	38.2	4.1	6.6	24	6.6	10
1898	30.2[e]	6.1[f]	33.2[e]	9.0	63.9	48.8	112.7	38.7	2.9	4.6	25	7.8	12
1911	48.6	14.5	54.4	22.0	67.0	52.7	119.7	39.6	3.0	4.6	26	7.2	11
1921	90.2	20.2	65.6	28.6	75.3	63.2	167.1	39.2	4.3	4.8	35	9.8	14
1931	149.2	41.4	78.0	37.3	86.2	105.0	228.5	41.8	5.5	3.3	69	15.6	23
1936		60.9	100.3	53.5	116.7	147.1	317.3	41.9	7.6	4.4	72	15.4	39
1946	217.5	137.5	159.7	164.5			657.4	40.5	16.2	4.5	146	28.3	44
1951	278.6	173.1	171.0	178.2			708.9	42.0	16.9	4.1	173	34.5	57
1956	387.5	208.4	249.0	252.5			935.8	43.6	21.5	3.8	246	51.2	90
1961	769.1	245.4		823.4		317.3	2,155.2	45.9	47.0	5.1	423	66.2	112

TERMS: Except as noted, enrollments are counts made late in years listed, or pertain to academic years beginning in calendar years listed. Baccalaureates are for entire calendar years listed through 1898, for academic years listed in calendar years listed thereafter. Because data cannot be regarded as precise, many calculations are made from rounded figures listed. 'All secondary' covers public and private secondary through 1911, with the addition of girls' secondary from 1921, of higher primary and vocational from 1946, and of 'Complementary' in 1961. 'Complementary course', except as noted for 1887, refers to the public and private *cours complémentaires* (CC), postprimary classes generally attached to primary schools, and to their reclassified heirs after 1959, the *collèges d'enseignement général* (CEG, including vocational classes at these *collèges* in 1961). 'Vocational' includes neither part-time nor agricultural vocational education, nor the *centres d'apprentissage* that sprang up after 1940 and were reorganized as *collèges d'enseignement technique* (CET) in 1960/61. It does cover (1) the *écoles pratiques de commerce et d'industrie* (EPCI, higher primary schools of a vocational-technical character) and similar institutions (1936 only) through 1936, (2) the *écoles nationales professionnelles* (ENP, somewhat less numerous and more advanced than the EPCI) through 1956, (3) the *collèges techniques* (former EPCI) and *sections techniques* at public and private secondary schools in the 1940s and 50s (together with a few vocational classes among the *cours complémentaires* during the same period), and finally (4) the whole vocational-technical (*enseignement technique*) sector of public and private secondary education in 1961, i.e., the consolidation of all the above (except vocational classes among the CC, now counted with the CEG). 'Higher primary' are the public *écoles primaires supérieures* (EPS) and their reclassified heirs after 1943, the *collèges modernes* (carried under *enseignement moderne* in general statistics on secondary education). 'Girls' secondary' comprises the *cours secondaires de jeunes filles*, not-quite-secondary schools created in 1867, and the public girls' *lycées* and *collèges* that originated in 1881, quickly outstripped the *cours secondaires*, and were reorganized as full equals of the boys' schools by the mid-1920s. 'Public secondary' draws together the traditional public boys' (later boys' and girls') state *lycées* (*collèges royaux* between 1815 and 1848) and municipal *collèges*, excluding (1) classes below the 6e from 1898 on, (2) attached higher primary or vocational-technical sections (numerically significant only since the late 1930s and counted with 'Vocational' from 1946), and (3) "modern" sections since the Second World War (listed under 'Higher primary'). 'Private secondary' excludes the *petits séminaires*, but encompasses all other (lay and religious) private secondary institutions, including the "modern" (but not the vocational-technical) sections thereof since the 1940s. It should be noted, however, that "external" day students at public institutions through 1898 described as in residence (internal students) at private institutions were counted only once, *with the public schools*, their total being subtracted from enrollments reported for the private schools.

[a] Through 1887, enrollments are for all grades, including 7e, 8e, and *classes primaires*; from 1898 on, however, enrollments in classes below the 6e are excluded.

[b] Same as note a, except that figures for 1911 through 1946 are estimated as described below.

[c] Some of the figures are estimated as described below.

[d] Age 8 through 17 (10 years) before 1898; then age 11 through 17 (7 years); some of the figures are estimated as described below.

[e] Academic years 1886–97 and 1897–98;

and baccalaureates per population and age group for metropolitan France. After the opening of a first lycée in 1848 and of four collèges in 1859–60, there were about 1.2 thousand students in public and private secondary institutions in Algeria by 1865. This amounted to less than 1 percent of 'All Secondary' enrollments for that year. The proportion then climbed to around 2 percent between 1876 and 1898. In 1950–51, however, the comparable ratio for public and private boys' and girls' secondary education (including modern but not primary and vocational-technical sections) stood near 5 percent. No attempt has been made to correct for this error in the text.

The Lower Seminaries: Enrollments at the *petits séminaires* were generally ignored by French statisticians and are not included in the table. Though officially preparatory schools for the higher Catholic seminaries (*grands séminaires*), they clearly managed to enlarge their function during much of the nineteenth century. From Villemain, the statistics for 1865, the Ribot report, and comments by Prost (*L'Enseignement*, pp.27, 32) and Anderson, one can obtain a rough account of these institutions. Suppressed during the Revolutionary and Napoleonic period, they recovered so rapidly during the Resto-

figure for 'Complementary' in 1886–87 includes public courses only.
f Figure is for 1900.

SOURCES: Villemain, *Rapport*, for public and private secondary through 1842; Fortoul, "Rapport," for 1854 private only; *Statistique de l'enseignement secondaire en 1865* for rest through 1865; *Statistique . . . secondaire en 1876* through 1876; *Statistique . . . secondaire en 1887* (including girls' secondary) through 1887; Ribot, *Enquête*, through 1898; Piobetta, *Le Baccalauréat*, for baccalaureates through 1898. *Annuaire statistique*, vol. 72 (1966) for total population through 1946 and all enrollments and baccalaureate data not taken from sources already cited; BUS, *Recueil 1936–42* and *1949–51*, for some detailed breakdowns ca. 1936–1950; *Informations statistiques*, nos. 36–45, 82–83, for some distributions 1960–65; R. Anderson, "Conflict in Education," pp. 57–63, for comments on private secondary education ca. 1842–1899. INSEE, *Population*, for age groups and for total population 1951–61.

Estimating Total Population and Age Groups: The total population of metropolitan France (boundaries of relevant years, excluding Algeria) is available for census years 1801, 1821, and 1831 and at five-year intervals

thereafter, except that the 1871 census was delayed until 1872 and that yearly estimates (as of January 1) are available since 1946. Population figures for other years are estimated from bracketing years, on the assumption that population change was steady over the period involved. Distributions by age year of the total population are available for census years since 1851 and yearly since 1946; but for 1921, age years 11 through 17 had to be defined as 7/10 of age years 10 through 19 and age year 17 as 1/5 of age years 15 through 19. To obtain age groupings for years not covered in the sources, the *ratios* of age group to total population for bracketing census years were converted into a time-weighted ratio to be applied to the estimated total population for the year in question. The known age group/population ratio for 1851 was also applied backward to a calculated total population figure for 1842. It should be noted that these procedures were used only for periods of relative demographic stability.

The Problem of Algerian Enrollments: Tabulated enrollments and degrees from 1865 on cover all French "academies," including that of Algiers. It has not been possible consistently to eliminate Algerian enrollments. The result is a slight overstatement of students

ration that a law of 1828 was designed to limit their enrollments to a maximum of 20 thousand, and to confine them to their narrow function. After the Falloux Law of 1850 removed these restrictions, they enjoyed another period of prosperity. Apparently their enrollments, in thousands, grew from negligible proportions in 1812 to somewhere near 20 by the time of the 1828 law, then fell quickly to just below 15 by 1830, recovered to 18 by 1839 and to 20 by 1842, stayed at or just below that level (18 as of 1850, according to Anderson) for a decade, climbed to 23 by 1865, reached a peak near 26 in 1878, and still exceeded 22 in 1891 and 1898. Presumably, they then declined during the course of the twentieth century; what enrollments they retained may well be included in other data on private secondary education since 1911. In any case, the relative error they intrude into the figures on 'All secondary' per population and age group after 1898 cannot be large, since absolute enrollments then were high. Moreover, roughly one-third of pupils in the lower seminaries (judging from the situation in other private schools) were probably in grades below the 6e, where they could not affect the 'All secondary' totals after 1898.

Public Secondary Education: Lycées and collèges through 1936: During the early nineteenth century, the municipal *collèges* (with partial state support) were more popular than the state *lycées* (*collèges royaux* under the monarchy). Total enrollments in the *collèges* were about twice as great as those in the *lycées* until the 1830s. Thereafter, however, the *lycées* expanded more rapidly than the *collèges*, equaling them in enrollments from the late 1850s into the 60s, and outstripping them by some 50–80 percent from the 1890s to the Second World War. On the other hand, it was always possible to transfer from the *collèges* (many of which did not teach the higher grades at all) to comparable programs and grades in the *lycées*. In the classical curricular stream, some 400–500 such transfers took place annually during the early 1860s, some 600–900 annually from 1866 to 1882, and some 900 to 2000 annually during the later 1880s. Even in the nonclassical stream (*enseignement spécial*), between 100 and 500 students annually moved from *collèges* to *lycées* during the decade after 1877, and there must have been many children entering the secondary grades of *lycées* from presecondary classes in hometown *collèges*. All this makes the invariably well-documented distinction between *lycée* and *collège* enrollments practically irrelevant until the Second World War.

Public Secondary Education: Bifurcation and Curricular Structure through 1936: Grades in French secondary schools have traditionally been numbered, in *ascending* order, 8e, 7e, 6e, etc., up to the 2e. This has typically been followed by at least two *classes terminales*, named according to the subjects emphasized. In the classical stream, the place of the 1re has until recently been taken by a *classe de rhétorique*, commonly followed by a *classe de philosophie*. At the same time, students have typically been able to enter two classes in mathematics (*élémentaires* and *spéciales*) after the 2e or even the 3e, sometimes while simultaneously enrolled in the *rhétorique* or *philosophie*. The mathematics classes could be repeated, and the elementary one was generally two years in length. In addition, *classes préparatoires* to train students for entry into the scientific *grandes écoles* (*écoles spéciales, écoles du gouvernement*) were available, though often coupled with the higher mathematics classes. Altogether, it is probably best, at least for the period through 1936, to think of the 3e as being followed by *three* additional years of schooling, with two main curricular options, making for a de facto bifurcation at the apex of the system. At the bottom of the pyramid, things generally began with a *classe élémentaire* or *primaire* (more recently a preschool *classe enfantine*

Table IX.1

	1842	1865	1876	1887	1898
Elementary (below 6e)	10.3	17.9	23.7	24.5	(22.0)
Classical 6e-4e	16.2	14.8	14.3	18.7	13.6
Classical 3e-philos.	12.5	12.2	12.4	14.7	16.5
Spécial first three yrs. (later: modern 6e-4e)	–	13.4	19.5	19.3	18.3
Spécial higher yrs. (later: modern 3e-1re)	–	3.5	3.2	3.6	9.7
Mathematics	6.3	3.9	6.1	9.0	5.8
Total	45.3	65.7	79.2	89.9	63.9

followed by several classes primaires) below the level of the 8e. Moreover, a few lycées and many collèges have periodically had small attached higher primary and vocational-technical branches (most recently called sections techniques). But these arrangements remained exceptions until Victor Duruy created the practical and technical-experimental enseignement spécial between 1863 and 1865. This was a fully separate curricular stream beginning as early as the 6e (though grades were at first called preparatory year, 1st year, 2nd year, etc.), available to students for up to four, later five and six years. As the popular spécial expanded and lengthened, however, a series of steps after 1881 tended to reduce its practical emphasis, while simultaneously developing it into a full-length "modern" branch of secondary education with its own baccalaureate by 1891. A new settlement of 1902 nominally merged the classical and modern baccalaureates and streams, while introducing several curricular branches and baccalaureate options at the higher levels. The pattern thus set remained basic to the system until the Second World War.

Public Secondary Education: The Pyramid of Grades through 1898: The distribution of French secondary students among the various grades and curricular streams from 1842 to 1898 is summarized in Table IX.1, in thousands.

As of 1842, the grades reported as élémentaires apparently encompassed the equivalents of the 8e and 7e only. Not counted as secondary were 3.8 thousand pupils in "elementary primary" and another 3.8 thousand in "higher primary" classes attached chiefly to collèges. Villemain's statistical report of 1842 actually listed lump sums of elementary and higher primary pupils affiliated with the collèges from 1809 on (1809: 0.2 thousand, 1820: 0.6 thousand, 1831: 1.5 thousand), without including any of these numbers in the secondary totals. The statistical report of 1865, however, listed and counted as secondary some 3.2 thousand students in a classe primaire ou 9e at the lycées and some 5.2 thousand in écoles primaires attached to collèges. By 1887, several classes primaires led to the 8e at the lycées; by 1898, a single rubric of 7e, 8e, 9e et classes primaires (plus enfantines at lycées) enrolled some 22 thousand students, who were excluded for the first time from the secondary total tabulated for that year. Even while the French public secondary system apparently extended downward after the Ferry reforms of the 1880s, the 6e and age 11 emerged by the later nineteenth century as the critical point of entry into secondary education proper. Latin was postponed from the 8e to the 6e in 1880, though a living language continued to be taught below the 6e until the First World War. It became standard practice to report lycée and collège enrollments below the 6e in a lump sum as classes primaires.

The enseignement spécial had its forerunners among some 1.2 thousand pupils reported as attending special vocational courses in 1842, most of them simultaneously enrolled in the regular secondary program. It is significant that neither vocational nor higher primary enrollments at secondary schools were reported from 1865 through 1887 while Duruy's *spécial* remained in force more or less unchanged. After the 1880s, the transformation of *spécial* into *moderne* coincided not only with the vigorous growth of regular higher primary schools outside the secondary system but also with the reappearance of some 0.4 thousand students in vocational courses attached to *collèges* (not counted as secondary) by 1898.

As of 1842, some 9.7 thousand students were enrolled in classes of mathematics and physics and 0.9 thousand in preparatory courses for the *grandes écoles*. But many of these, as in the case of the 1.2 thousand in vocational programs, simultaneously attended the regular classical courses. The 6.3 thousand pupils listed as mathematics students for 1842 above are pupils included in the enrollment total for that year but *not* registered in the elementary or ordinary classical grades. From 1865 through 1898, a precise distinction was made between mathematics and other classes; but pupils preparing for the *grandes écoles*, though separately listed (see below), were still in simultaneous attendance in other grades, presumably those in mathematics for the most part. In 1898, candidates for the *grandes écoles* were explicitly grouped with the elementary mathematics class, and a distinction was made between 3.4 thousand mathematics students who had come from the classical stream and 2.4 thousand who had come from the modern curriculum.

The ratio of secondary enrollments below the 6e to all secondary pupils at public schools was 23 percent in 1842, 27 percent in 1865, 30 percent in 1876, 27 percent in 1887, and 26 percent in 1898. But the secondary system apparently extended downward after 1842 and especially after 1880. One can assume, given the curricular pattern discussed above, that the 8e and 7e were always more heavily attended than the 9e and lower grades. The proportion of public pupils entering *all curricular streams* of the public 6e from a public 7e was probably not far below 100 percent until the 1880s, whereupon it gradually fell to a level nearer 75 percent or even 50 percent by the end of the century. On the other hand, both this ratio and the relatively mild narrowing of the public pyramid of classical grades was modified by a continuous replenishment of public from private secondary education.

Public Secondary Education: From 1911 through 1936: The distinction between classical and modern secondary enrollments was apparently dropped after the settlement of 1902. The *Annuaire statistique* breaks down totals for *lycées* and *collèges* into two subgroups only. One of these, "secondary schooling" (i.e., academic 6e and up), is reproduced in the main table. In the other category of "primary classes," the *Annuaire* reports 30.5, 38.1, 55.3, and 55.9 thousand pupils for 1911, 1921, 1931, and 1936, respectively. BUS, *Recueil*, provides a somewhat more detailed breakdown for 1936 (in thousands), shown in Table IX.2.

Table IX.2

Elementary, preparatory, and infant classes	(40.2)
Vocational-technical sections, and higher primary	(15.4)
Secondary classes (6e-1re)	103.1
Philosophy	4.4
Mathematics	4.3
Preparatory classes for *grandes écoles*	4.8

Enrollments in the preparatory classes for the *grandes écoles* are no longer intermingled with the mathematics classes. Despite a minor divergence between the two sources, it is clear that the *Annuaire's* rubric of "primary classes" covers attached vocational-technical sections and higher primary classes as well as classes below the 6e. BUS, *Recueil*, does show, however, that enrollments below the 6^e remained relatively as significant (26 percent of all enrollments other than vocational and higher primary ones) in 1936 as in 1898.

Public Secondary Education: Girls' Schools through 1936: A beginning was made in this field with the essentially higher primary *cours secondaires* during the late 1860s. More important were the girls' *lycées* and *collèges* created during the early 1880s. Following the pattern established by *spécial*, secondary grades were initially numbered 1–5, then 1–6, though most pupils entered these grades from affiliated primary classes. Enrollment beyond the third year was at first very light, as shown in Table IX.3, the distribution for 1887 (in thousands).

Table IX.3

Lycées and collèges	
Primary and infant classes	2.5
First through third year	2.6
Fourth and later years	0.9
Cours secondaires	
Primary classes	1.3
Secondary classes	3.1
Total girls' secondary	10.4

For 1898 through 1936, the *Annuaire* provides only the distinction between primary

and secondary classes at girls' *lycées* and *collèges*, along with overall totals for the *cours secondaires*. For 1936, BUS, *Recueil*, supplies the breakdown (in thousands) given in Table IX.4. The numbers in parentheses correspond to the *Annuaire's* "primary classes"; the rest, to what is tabulated as secondary from 1898 on. Classes below the 6^e accounted for 29 percent of all enrollments other than vocational and higher primary ones. What portion of the low and stagnating total enrollments in the *cours secondaires* to include under 'Girls' secondary' from 1898 through 1931 could only be estimated on the basis of (rather similar) bracketing distribu-

Table IX.4

Lycées and collèges	
Elementary, preparatory, and infant classes	(21.5)
Attached vocational and higher primary	(4.2)
Secondary classes (6e-1re)	46.9
Philosophy	2.2
Mathematics	0.4
Preparatory for *grandes écoles*	0.5
Cours secondaires	
Elementary, preparatory, and infant classes	(1.6)
Attached vocational and higher primary	(0.2)
Secondary classes (6e-1re)	3.4
Philosophy	0.1
Total girls' secondary	53.5

tions available for 1887 and 1936. It should be noted that French girls' secondary education expanded vigorously at the beginning of the present century, was assimilated to boys' schools in curriculum (elective Latin and Greek) and grade structure during the early and mid-1920s, and is thus included in the tabulated total for 'All secondary' from 1921 on.

Private Secondary Education through 1936: Apart from the *petits séminaires*, French private secondary schools fell into two broad groups: those run by laymen and those sponsored by religious orders or authorities. Nothing is known directly about the distribution of students in these institutions over the various grades before 1898, though something may be inferred from the fact that they supplied only 7 percent of successful candidates for the baccalaureate during the three-year period ending in 1842. We do not even know, before the 1850s, which of the so-called *institutions* and *pensions* were lay and which religious. The sources provide only overall totals, including a certain number of double counts, which had to be subtracted before the rest were tabulated. "Double counts" are pupils who took at least some courses at public institutions as "external students," while simultaneously residing as "internal" students" in supervised private establishments. *Reported* cases of this sort, in thousands, were 1.0, 2.7, and 4.0 at *lycées* alone in 1809, 1820, and 1831, respectively; 5.1 and 1.0 at *lycées and collèges* in 1842; 4.3 at all public secondary schools in 1854; 2.8 and 0.5 at *lycées and collèges* in 1865; 2.2 and 0.4 at *lycées and collèges* in 1876; 1.7 and 0.2 at *lycées and collèges* in 1887; and 1.6 at *lycées* alone in 1898. No double counts are reported in the sources for 1911 and after.

As Anderson has signaled, Fortoul's official report of 1854 understated enrollments in religious secondary schools by failing to carry some 5,000 pupils forward from the subtotals by academy to the national totals. Though the report contains about a dozen arithmetical or typographical errors, the "loss" of these 5,000 students does not appear to have been accidental. The true totals were 42,462 pupils in lay private schools and 26,202 in religious private schools. Since Fortoul (credibly) reports 4,305 "double counts" (which Anderson overlooked), one obtains 64,359 pupils who received their entire schooling at private schools.

Among all students in private institutions, some 38 percent were attending religious (almost exclusively Catholic) schools in 1854, 45 percent in 1865, 60 percent in 1876, 71

percent in 1887, and over 87 percent in 1898.

In 1898, for the first time, information was made available on the distribution of students in private institutions over the various grades (in thousands). See Table IX.5. As in the

Table IX.5

8ᵉ, 7ᵉ, and primary classes	(23.4)
Attached higher primary schools	(1.7)
Attached vocational courses	(1.9)
Classical stream: 6ᵉ-philosophy	32.6
Modern stream: 6ᵉ-1ʳᵉ	13.8
Preparatory for higher commercial and industrial schools	1.0
Preparatory for baccalaureate and *grandes écoles*	3.0
Minus double counts	<1.6>
Total Private Secondary	**48.8**

case of public secondary from 1898, the figures in parentheses have not been taken over into the main table. In addition, the double counts are subtracted from enrollments in the 6ᵉ and higher grades. If the resulting distribution is compared with the pattern in the public schools for 1898, it becomes clear that the private schools were disproportionately strong in the grades below the 6ᵉ (32 percent as against 26 percent of all enrollments other than the vocational and higher primary ones) and in the classical stream, rather than the modern curriculum.

In any case, the 1898 breakdown indi-

cates that some 65 percent of all students in private secondary schools (including double counts here) were enrolled in regular secondary classes. The next similar distribution available in BUS, *Recueil*, is for 1943–44 and shows the same ratio of "secondary" to all pupils in private schools. This ratio was therefore applied to totals supplied by the *Annuaire*, to arrive at the tabulated figures under 'Private secondary' for 1921 through 1936. For 1911, however, the only basis for estimating private secondary enrollments was the set of bracketing numbers for 1898 and 1921. It was simply assumed that the total growth in private secondary education between the bracketing years was distributed over the two subintervals 1898–1911 and 1911–21 in the same proportion as the increase in public secondary education during the same period. This assumption is open to challenge, of course, and so is the postulate that 65 percent was the ratio of secondary to all students in private secondary establishments between 1898 and 1943. As J. M. Chapoulie has been kind enough to warn, private presecondary students might well have been more than 35 percent of the total during periods of expansion in the private secondary sector and less than 35 percent at times when that sector was relatively threatened or unpopular. In all likelihood, 1921 and 1936 were boom years for private secondary (really primary) education; but so, presumably, was 1943, given Vichy sympathies. Conversely, 1911 was probably *not a* year of expansion, but neither (probably) was 1898. It is all the more remarkable that the 65 percent ratio obtained in *both 1943 and 1898*. Particularly since no substitute is available, it seems reasonable to use 65 percent as a guide, as long as the resulting estimates are recognized as rough orders of magnitude.

Higher Primary, Vocational, and Complementary Education through 1936: While a few of the higher primary schools projected in Guizot's law of 1833 were actually created and survived as models into another era (e.g., *Ecole Turgot* in Paris), what higher primary education there was before the late 1870s took place predominantly in special courses attached to *collèges*. Some 3.8 thousand higher primary and 1.2 thousand vocational students were thus affiliated with *collèges* in 1842. Duruy's *spécial* apparently took the place of these courses for a time after 1865, though 0.4 thousand vocational students reappeared at the *collèges* in 1898, after the transformation of *spécial* into *moderne*. As of that year also, some 1.7 and 1.9 thousand students, respectively, attended higher primary and vocational classes attached to private secondary schools. By 1936, as noted above, affiliated higher primary and vocational enrollments added up to 15.4 thousand at public boys' and 4.2 thousand at public girls' secondary schools. *It is unclear whether these affiliated pupils were included in the totals reported in the sources on higher primary and vocational education through 1936.*

In any case, the main initiative in the whole higher primary and vocational field was taken at the public level beginning in the later 1870s under Octave Gréard in Paris. As formally instituted by Ferry's law of 1881, the new *écoles primaires supérieures* (EPS) were consciously designed to prepare for middle-level skilled positions in industry and commerce and *not* to compete with the secondary system, as Duruy's *spécial* had ended by doing. A few of the students the EPS took in from ordinary primary schools, initially at age 13–14, managed to go on, after up to four years of additional schooling, to the primary normal schools, to specialized *collèges* (Chaptal in Paris), or to certain higher technical and professional schools (chiefly *arts et métiers*). As this pattern implies, some of the EPS were from the beginning less general than vocational in their curriculum. After a tug of war between the ministries of education and commerce, a few of the more professional EPS were renamed *écoles pratiques de commerce et d'industrie* (EPCI) by 1892. They were joined in the full-time vocational sector by the somewhat more advanced and much smaller *écoles nationales professionnelles* (ENP), some of which also evolved from the model EPS of the 1880s. The column on 'Vocational education' through 1936 sums up enrollments in the EPCI and ENP.

The figures on private and public boys' and girls' *cours complémentaires* (CC) cover a postprimary program attached to primary schools in 1886. Initially limited to one year, it managed gradually to expand its length and function, eventually sending some of its own graduates to the primary normal schools.

Expanded Public Secondary Education, 1936 through 1956: The reform projects of the Popular Front (particularly of Jean Zay beginning in 1936), consolidated under Vichy, brought the EPS and EPCI into the public secondary system as six-year *collèges modernes* and *collèges techniques*, respectively, while leaving the CC as terminal postprimary schools or preparatory institutions for the primary normal schools. For 1946 through 1956, the *Annuaire* thus reports on an enlarged secondary system in which (1) girls

Table IX.6

	1946	*1951*	*1956*
Primary classes at *lycées* and *collèges*	(67.9)	(73.8)	(97.8)
Modern branch (*6e-1re*)	159.7	171.0	249.0
New classes	9.2	18.1	12.1
Classical branch (*6e-1re*)	120.5	117.4	179.3
Terminal classes	25.5	29.8	46.0
Preparatory classes for *grandes écoles*	9.4	12.8	15.1
Sections techniques reported with secondary education	26.1	33.3	41.7
Collèges techniques and *sections techniques* at *collèges modernes* and *lycées* reported with vocational education	101.2	94.9	111.0
Vocational courses at CC	10.2	23.3	27.0
Écoles nationales professionnelles	10.2	12.8	15.1

were about as well represented as boys, (2) the former EPS were included with remnants of the older nonclassical secondary stream under the rubric of a six-year "modern" branch, (3) a group of "new" (later "pilot") classes encompassing the *6e* through *3e* played a minor role as common or multistream lower secondary ("first-cycle") schools, and (4) attached vocational-technical sections (*sections techniques*) were reported in connection with secondary education as well as under the vocational rubric, where they were grouped with the *collèges techniques* (former EPCI) and joined by the ENP and by vocational classes at CC. Table IX.6 describes the resulting distributions of enrollments.

Private Secondary Education, 1936 through 1956: Private secondary education was similarly organized, though the breakdowns provided by the *Annuaire* are incomplete, especially for 1946. What share of 1946 total enrollments to assign to the *6e* and higher grades (62 percent) was estimated from the bracketing proportions (65 percent for 1943,

59 percent for 1949) provided by BUS, *Recueil*. The results are shown in Table IX.7. The tabulated 'Vocational' figures for 1946 through 1956 cover all "technical" *collèges* and sections, public and private, no matter how affiliated or reported.

Further Changes between 1956 and 1961: The pattern of 1956 was further modified in 1959. A leaving age (14 since 1936) of 16 was projected for 1967, and the CC were transformed into four-year *collèges d'enseignement général* (CEG). They did some vocational as well as general postprimary teaching. In the vocational sector, they were joined by the *centres d'apprentissage*, founded in 1949 and renamed *collèges d'enseignement technique* (CET) in 1960. The new *collèges d'enseignement secondaire* (CES) of the early 1960s were conceived as a step in the direction of a common trunk in the lower grades ("first cycle") of the secondary sys-

Table IX.7

	1946	*1951*	*1956*
Primary classes	(119.9)	(145.3)	(184.0)
Secondary classes (*6e-1re*), classical, modern, and new classes	195.7	174.2	211.3
Terminal classes		10.8	12.5
Preparatory classes for *grandes écoles*		1.6	2.2
Sections techniques	?	8.8	13.5

tem. Together, the CEG, CET, and CES ultimately made up a whole new ancillary sector of the secondary pyramid. Their proliferation caused most of the older types of secondary schools to rename themselves *lycées*, whether classical, "modern" (former EPS, mostly), or "technical" (former EPCI, ENP, and vocational-technical sections). While the CET were most commonly entered at age 14, either directly from primary or from first-cycle secondary schools, the four-year CEG and CES admitted their students at age 11, whether to give them their terminal schooling or to send them eventually to the CET or into the upper grades of modern or technical *lycées*. The numerically significant CEG in particular were thus at least marginally a part of the French secondary system as of 1960, though they really functioned as intermediate schools.

Characteristics of the New Pattern: The ratio of enrollments below the 6e to all students other than higher primary and vocational ones had been 26 percent at public boys' schools in 1898 and 1936, 29 percent at public girls' schools in 1936, and near 33 percent at private secondary institutions in 1898 and 1936. For the full-term classical and modern branches of the consolidated postwar system (excluding CEG and technical schools and sections), the ratio dropped from 17 percent at public institutions in 1946 and 1951 to 16 percent in 1956 and 6 percent in 1961. At private schools, however, it actually rose from 38 percent in 1946 to 44–45 percent in 1951–56, before falling to a still substantial 35 percent in 1961. For public and private schools together, it held its place at some 27–29 percent from 1946 through 1956 and then declined to 16 percent in 1961. BUS, *Recueil*, reports that among pupils entering the 6e at *public* secondary schools in 1936, some 48 percent came from a public 7e, 7 percent from a private 7e, and 45 percent from public primary schools. For the expanded system of 1950, the comparable percentages were 25, 6, and 68, respectively. Among pupils in the 6e through 1re of full-term public secondary schools by 1961, 19 percent were in the technical branch, 16 percent in the 6e shared

vate equivalents of the CEG (often still called CC, 135.9 of their pupils in general and 5.5 in vocational programs). The rest tabulated for 1961 is clearly distinguished in the sources as full-term ("long") *general and vocational* education (classical, modern, and technical *lycées*), and is broken down in Table IX.8 (in thousands). Apart from rounding problems, this configuration is reproduced exactly in the main table, if in simplified form, the public and private "technical" 6e through terminal classes being summed under 'Vocational'.

Table IX.8

	Public	Private
Preschool and elementary classes	(52.1)	(170.3)
Classical and modern 6e consolidated	145.5	61.3
Classical 5e–3e	172.2	161.9
Modern 5e–3e	210.2	
Classical 2e–1re	63.3	74.4
Modern 2e–1re	135.4	
Classical and modern terminal classes	66.7	17.2
Technical 6e–3e	100.5	
Technical 2e–1re	75.0	59.8
Technical terminal classes	10.0	
Preparatory for *grandes écoles*		
Higher technical sections (2 years)	19.3	
	8.9	
Other preparatory courses	1.7	2.5

Left out of account in the tabulated figures for 1961 are some 218.4 thousand full-time pupils in the public CET (former *centres d'apprentissage*), along with 30.7 thousand students in private institutions of a similar character. The CES were not yet in existence. Included in the 'All secondary' total under the 'Complementary' heading, however, are 627.8 thousand pupils in public CEG (573.3 in general and 54.5 in vocational programs) and 141.3 thousand in priby the modern and classical sections, 38 percent in the upper grades of the modern, and 26 percent in the upper grades of the classical stream.

Among youngsters who had stayed in public primary schools until the legal leaving age (still 14 at that point) as of 1959–60, according to *Informations statistiques*, some 40 percent rejoined their families or went directly to work (and part-time vocational courses), 12 percent continued in primary school, 10 percent transferred to CEG, 18 percent to CET, 13 percent to other vocational or agricultural schools, and only 1.5 percent managed to enter the modern and 0.3 percent the classical branch of full-term public secondary schools. Age 11 thus remained the critical divide in fact, although CEG, CET, and (later) CES have apparently come to provide a very narrow bridge from primary to secondary modern and technical education at age 14.

All Secondary Enrollments in Relation to Population and Age Group: If students in the lower seminaries are included with those in ordinary secondary schools, public and private, one arrives at the following ratios of secondary enrollments *per thousand population* through 1887: 1.8 in 1809, 2.3 in 1831, 2.6 in 1842, 3.6 in 1854, 4.3 in 1865, 4.9 in 1876, and 4.7 in 1887. Enrollments *per age group* changed very little between 1876 and 1911, and this would be true even if no change had been made in the definition of 'All Secondary' (and of the corresponding age group) as of 1898. The proportion of secondary pupils per thousand aged 11 through 17 did change from 26 to 35 between 1911 and 1921; but the figure for 1921 would be no more than 29 if only *public* girls' schools were excluded.

Enrollments in boys' and girls' public *lycées* and *collèges* (secondary classes only and without *cours secondaires*) increased moderately, in thousands, from 100.4 in 1921 to 115.7 in 1925, with girls contributing more substantially than boys to the overall expan- sion. At private secondary schools (all grades), enrollments, in thousands, advanced from 97.2 in 1921–22 to 111.6 in 1925–26. But then the small birth cohorts of 1914–19 reached the 6e about 1925–30, followed by especially large cohorts in 1931–32, and this raises some problems of interpretation. With the aid of unpublished figures from the Ministry of Education, Jaubert, *La Gratuité*, was able to establish the numbers of pupils entering the public 6e (in thousands) and to relate them to the sizes of the relevant birth years (literally: thousands of births in years listed, not 11 year-olds surviving at age 11). See Table IX.9.

Enrollments in all secondary grades of *lycées* and *collèges* and in all grades of private

Table IX.9

Academic Year	Public 6e	Birth year: no. births	Pupils as % births	Total public	Total private
1924–25	19.8	1913:746.0	2.7	115.7	109.2
1925–26	19.6	1914:593.8	3.3	111.9	111.6
1926–27	15.3	1915:387.0	4.0	107.4	113.5
1927–28	12.0	1916:313.0	3.8	103.0	118.9
1928–29	13.9	1917:342.5	4.0	101.1	120.9
1929–30	16.0	1918:399.5	4.0	107.1	128.9
1930–31	22.0	1919:403.5	5.5	119.8	147.5
1931–32	30.0°	1920:833.5	3.6	135.2	161.5
1932–33	34.5	1921:811.8	4.2	143.3	181.3
1933–34	31.9	1922:759.7	4.2	143.7	194.0
1934–35	29.6	1923:761.3	3.9	156.8	211.4
1935–36	29.0	1924:753.5	3.8	166.7	224.5
1936–37	29.5	1925:770.1	3.8		226.3

secondary schools are provided (not from Jaubert) in the last two columns. Jaubert argued that no real increase in access took place around 1930, since the ratio of beginning secondary pupils to births in their generation was as high during the later 1920s as during the mid-1920s. But this argument takes the very useful ratio in question a little too seriously. After all, it was already unusually high during the late 1920s, having advanced at an abnormally rapid rate from 1924 to 1926. Clearly, small birth cohorts tend, other things being equal, to make for small entering classes but increased access percentages, while large cohorts tend to produce enlarged entering classes at reduced access percentages. The growth in enrollments per age group after 1924 was probably artificial in part; yet it was not cancelled by the large cohorts of the early 1930s. Thus there surely was a real and permanent increase in secondary access *sometime* during the decade after 1925, and the years 1930–31 appear to mark the most important advances. Unfortunately, when enrollments in all grades of public and private schools are related to the seven-year age group 11–17, a clear view of these short-term changes is sacrificed for the increased scope of the overall measure. The most serious problem is that the small birth cohorts of 1914–19 continued to pro-

duce small seven-year age groups 11–17 even after the large postwar birth cohorts reached the 6e in 1931. The summary enrollments to age group ratio for 1931 in the main table thus partly disguises the upturn in secondary access about 1930.

Some of the distributions detailed above suggest that the increase in secondary enrollments since the Second World War has been due in part to a lengthening of the normal secondary curriculum in the upper grades. As of 1964–65, according to *Informations statistiques*, some 22–26 percent of each of the age years 12 through 17 attended full-term secondary institutions, along with just under 17 percent of age years 11 and 18. This implies 7.5 years as the normal duration of secondary schooling. Among twelve year-olds, 22 percent in full-term secondary institutions were joined by about 25 percent in CEG and their private equivalents and 3 percent in CES, as against just over 50 percent remaining in primary schools. Among fifteen-year-olds, 24 percent in full-term secondary schools were joined by about 15 percent each in the CEG and CET, while 1.5 percent each remained in the CES and in primary schools and 42 percent had left school altogether. This means that the tabulated composite ratio of 'All Secondary' enrollments per age 11 through 17 since 1946

in fact describes a situation in which enrollments in full-term secondary schools per age group climbed gradually toward about 25 percent by the early 1960s, while a slight lengthening of the course of full-term study combined with the additional enrollments in the CEG to drive the calculated ratio over 40 percent.

The Baccalaureate: Not included in the table are supplementary scientific baccalaureates required of bachelors in letters who wished to study for medical doctorates between 1821 and 1896, as well as extremely small numbers (range 1–126 per year) of ordinary science baccalaureates earned before 1853 when the baccalaureate in letters was a prerequisite for them. Apart from these special cases, only baccalaureates in letters were conferred from 1809 (when the degree was established) until 1852. From 1853 until 1891, separate and parallel baccalaureates in letters and sciences could be earned. Yearly awards (thousands) in letters and sciences, respectively, were 2.0 and 2.2 in 1854, 4.1 and 1.8 in 1865, 3.3 and 2.1 in 1876, 3.9 and 2.7 in 1887. From 1892 to 1905, separate baccalaureates were given in the classical and modern branches of the secondary system, and there were several options available in each branch. For 1898, the figures, in thou-

failure on the baccalaureate examination. In the three years ending in 1842, according to Villemain, *Rapport*, an annual average of 5,038 candidates presented themselves for the "bac," and 2,938 passed. Of those who

Table IX.10

	1946–47	1951–52	1956–57	1961–62
Philosophy	15.6	17.6	21.5	29.4
Experimental sciences	5.8	7.8	15.6	16.7
Mathematics	6.6	8.1	11.9	16.7
Mathematics-technology	0.3	1.1	2.1	3.0
Technology-economics	–	–	0.1	0.3

passed, 1,377 came from *lycées* (*collèges royaux*), 758 from *collèges* (*municipaux*), 166 from private schools, and 637 from "domestic studies." In 1932, according to Commission Carnegie, *Enquêtes*, about 37 percent of all candidates passed the first part of the examination, 49 percent passed the second part, and the overall ratio of passes to candidates was just over 42 percent.

sands, were 4.7 in classical-stream "letters and philosophy," 1.3 in classical-stream "letters and mathematics," 0.5 in modern-stream "philosophy," 0.9 in modern-stream "mathematics," and 0.3 in modern-stream "sciences." A few awards continued to be made under these rubrics until 1910.

By 1905, however, a new system had grown out of the curricular settlement of 1902 that was to remain in force, with minor modifications, until the Second World War. A newly introduced first part of the examination, taken before entry into the terminal classes, could be passed in Latin and Greek, Latin and Modern Languages, Latin and Sciences, or Sciences and Modern Languages. Those who also succeeded on the second part of the test earned degrees labeled "philosophy" or "mathematics," like the terminal classes. In 1911–12, some 4.5 thousand final awards were made in philosophy and 2.7 thousand in mathematics. In 1921–22, the first part of the baccalaureate was passed by 1.8 thousand candidates in Latin-Greek, 3.2 in Latin-Modern Languages, 3.4 in Latin-

Sciences, and 3.2 in Sciences-Modern Languages, while 6.2 and 3.6 thousand students passed the second part and earned degrees in philosophy and mathematics, respectively. The Latin-Modern Languages option was gradually phased out after the mid-1920s, while the role of the natural sciences was increased in all three remaining first-part options, now labeled A, A', and B, the last without Latin. In 1931 and 1936, the distribution of final awards between "philosophy" and "mathematics" was essentially identical with the divide between A-A' and B (Latin/no Latin) on the first part of the examination. Some 10.7 and 4.8 thousand degrees were given, respectively, in philosophy and mathematics in 1931–32, and 10.8 and 4.6 thousand in 1936.

Since 1946, a whole new series of options has been created for the second as well as for the first part of the test. Table IX.10 shows the distribution of final awards (in thousands). No statistical account of French secondary education is complete without at least a few figures on the staggering rate of

Table X

France: Social Origins of Public Secondary Students, 1936–1961
(Percentages of Fathers in Stated Occupations, Absolute Totals in Thousands)

Father's Occupation	1936	1943 Class.	1943 Mod.	1943 Both	1946 Class.	1946 Mod.	1946 Both	1951	1956 Class.	1956 Mod.	1956 Both
1. Lib. professions	10.6	10.3	3.0	7.0	11.2	3.9	7.2	8.1	12.6	4.1	8.8
2. Officials	29.9	28.4	19.7	24.4	31.2	21.6	25.9	26.6	30.0	23.1	26.9
3. Agriculture	1.7	6.0	10.9	8.2	6.0	11.3	8.9	7.2	5.6	8.4	6.8
4. Entrepreneurs	24.6	16.5	11.0	14.1	19.1	14.6	16.6	14.1	14.0	10.6	12.4
5. Artisans	4.3	8.7	11.0	9.8	8.1	11.3	9.9	8.7	6.8	9.7	8.2
6. White collar	20.3	18.9	19.7	19.3	15.4	17.6	16.6	18.8	20.7	22.9	21.6
7. Workers	2.7	8.0	22.4	14.5	6.1	17.5	12.4	12.7	7.6	17.7	12.3
4–7. Sum	51.9	52.1	64.1	57.7	48.7	61.0	55.5	54.3	49.1	60.9	54.5
8. Rentiers, etc.	5.8	3.2	2.3	2.8	2.8	2.3	2.5	1.6	1.9	2.1	2.0
9. Deceased	—	—	—	—	—	—	—	2.2	0.8	1.4	1.0
Absolute totals (100%)	28.8	27.0	22.2	49.1	25.4	31.7	57.1	65.5	51.9	46.9	101.8[a]

Father's Occupation	1959 Class.	1959 Mod.	1959 Both	1959 CEG	1959 Tech.	1959 Voc.	1961 Lycées	1961 CEG	1961 Tech.	1961 Voc.	1954 Census
1. Professions, executive employees	21.3	7.9	14.8	2.3	4.1	1.3	17.1	2.4	5.7	1.4	2.9
2. Farmers	5.9	7.1	6.5	10.2	5.8	5.6	6.5	10.0	6.0	6.0	20.8
3. Agricult. Workers	1.1	1.6	1.3	2.6	2.0	4.1	1.2	2.7	1.7	3.9	6.0

Father's Occupation	1959						1961				1954 Census
	Class.	Mod.	Both	CEG	Tech.	Voc.	Lycées	CEG	Tech.	Voc.	Census
4. Industrialists	2.3	1.5	1.9	0.8	1.5	0.5	2.1	0.8	1.7	0.5	0.4
5. Merchants	9.2	8.7	9.0	8.0	6.9	3.9	9.2	7.4	7.4	3.8	7.7
6. Artisans	5.4	6.7	6.0	6.6	7.0	4.7	5.3	6.3	6.1	4.6	3.9
7. Middle white collar	16.9	12.8	14.9	10.3	10.4	5.7	15.9	10.6	11.1	5.6	5.9
8. Low white collar	16.6	19.3	17.9	16.2	16.1	11.8	17.0	16.7	17.4	11.9	10.9
9. Workers	12.5	24.7	18.6	35.5	34.9	49.0	15.9	35.0	32.5	49.9	33.8
10. Domestics, etc.	0.9	1.6	1.2	1.7	2.7	3.8	1.2	1.8	2.0	3.1	5.1
11. Rentiers, etc.	1.6	2.0	1.7	1.3	3.3	4.0	2.5	1.8	3.4	3.9	–
12. Others	6.3	6.1	6.2	4.5	5.3	5.6	6.1	4.5	5.0	5.4	2.6
Absolute totals (100%)	74.8	70.3	145.0	141.1	165.9	76.5					

NOTE: The data for 1961 pertain to all pupils, the rest only to entering classes (6e) of public institutions involved. Years are academic years 1936–37, etc.

TERMS: Most of the students listed under 'Modern' after 1936 were enrolled in the formerly higher primary schools (EPS) that were brought into the secondary system as *collèges* (later *lycées*) *modernes* in 1941. The source for 1961 entirely drops the classical/modern distinction. '*Lycées*' for 1961 are all "academic" (classical and modern) *lycées*, including former EPS but excluding technical secondary schools and students in preparatory classes for the *grandes écoles*. The CEG (*collèges d'enseignement général*, former *cours complémentaires*) were integrated into the secondary system as four-year lower-level or transitional institutions in 1959. 'Vocational' for 1959 and 1961 refers to the full-time *centres d'apprentissage*, renamed *collèges d'enseignement technique* (CET) in the early 1960s, but not considered secondary before then. 'Technical' for 1961 refers to the *lycées techniques* or similar institutions, formerly vocational-technical institutions which have been considered secondary since the Second World War. 'Technical'

for 1959, however, covers all "technical" schools and classes, including the *centres d'apprentissage*, entering classes of which are more fully described under 'Vocational' for that year. *Occupational categories* used in French official statistics were changed in 1958. *In the upper half of the table*, 1936–56, terms used literally translate the sources; but 'Agriculture' (*cultivateurs*) clearly includes farm workers as well as all types of working farmers; 'Entrepreneurs' are "heads of enterprises in commerce and industry"; 'White collar' covers all "employees in commerce and industry"; 'Workers' clearly excludes those in agriculture or public em-

331

ployment; and 'Rentiers' also comprises men "without profession." In the lower half of the table, 1959 and 1961, occupational categories are those used in recent census reports on the male and female working population, except that a rubric is added for "rentiers, without profession." "Professions, executive employees" includes the highest ranks of white-collar workers (cadres supérieurs) in the public and private sectors, i.e., secondary and university teachers with literary and scientific occupations (0.4 percent in 1954 census), engineers in the private sector, managerial-administrative posts in the private sector, and high officials (0.9 percent in 1954 census). 'Farmers' covers all of agriculture other than agricultural workers (salariés agricoles). 'Industrialists' (industriels) appears under a general heading for all owners or directors (patrons) in industry and commerce that also covers artisans and the 'Merchant' group (1954 census: patrons pêcheurs 0.1 percent, gros commerçants 0.9 percent, pet:ts commerçants 6.7 percent). 'Middle white collar' (cadres moyens) covers primary teachers and the lesser medical and social service professions in the private and public (1954: 1.4 percent) sectors, technicians and middle-level administrative personnel in the private sector, and middle-level officials (1954: 1.1 percent). 'Lower white collar' (employés) comprises commercial and office clerks, the latter about evenly divided between the private and public (1954: 4.1 percent) sectors. 'Workers' includes foremen and skilled workers in the private (13.8 percent) and public (1.9 percent) sectors and semi-skilled workers (spécialisés: 8.2 percent private, 1.5 percent public). 'Domestics' (personnel de service) covers butlers, maids, and similar occupations. 'Others' in the 1954 census and presumably also in the figures on students comprises artists (0.2 percent), clergy (0.8 percent), and the military and police (1.6 percent).

a Includes 2.9 thousand students in common "pilot" classes.

SOURCES: Peyre, "L'Origine sociale," for 1936 absolute numbers (some of Peyre's percentages are miscalculated) and for comments on higher grades. BUS, Recueil 1949–51, for 1943 and 1946; Girard and Pressat, "Deux études, I: L'origine sociale," for 1956 and 1959; Informations statistiques, no. 60–61 (1964) for 1961; INSEE, Recensement général 1954, Population active, I: Structure professionelle, for 1954 census. Also Girard, "Enquête nationale," and Sauvy and Girard, "Les diverses classes," for addenda below.

Changing Distributions in the Higher Grades: In 1955–56, according to Peyre, the liberal professions accounted for 12.7 percent of the classical and 4.2 percent of the modern 6e in French public lycées; workers, for 7.5 percent and 17.9 percent, respectively. In the 1re (a year or two before graduation) of the same institutions during the same year, however, the proportions were 16 percent and 6.3 percent for the liberal professions in the classical and modern stream, respectively, as against 3.7 percent and 10 percent for the workers. The sons of entrepreneurs also gained ground in this way, while the offspring of artisans and farmers became less numerous. In other words, as might be guessed from the tabulated figures for 1959 and 1961, the social clientele of the higher secondary grades was markedly more elevated than that of the entering classes.

Academic Selection, Social Origins, and School Performance: In a 1954 survey of students leaving public and private primary schools (excluding primary classes at secondary schools), Girard distinguished between those who left at age 11 or 12, generally to transfer to a secondary school, and those who left at or after the legal leaving age of 14 (not raised to 16 until 1967). Having drawn his sample from schools in different communities and of varying size, Girard reported his results in weighted form, so as to represent all of France outside of Paris (Department of the Seine, which had been separately surveyed earlier). Only 2 percent of those (all of France in this case) who stayed in primary school until 14 subsequently reached any form of secondary education; some 6 percent transferred to vocational schools and 7 percent to "commercial courses," while almost all the rest went home or to work, or became apprentices in various firms. In the critical selection around age 11, only about 29 percent of all pupils were routed out of the primary system. But the percentage of those who left before 14 varied sharply with the parents' occupation. It was 87 for the liberal professions, 86 for high officials, 81 for the higher white-collar occupations, 68 for industrialists, 47 for lower officials, 39 for merchants (*commerçants*) and artisans, 43 for the lesser employees (*employés*) and foremen, 21 for workers (*ouvriers, manoeuvres*), 16 for farmers (*cultivateurs*), and 13 for agricultural workers. The result, of course (shown in Table X.1), was a difference in the social makeup of the group who left before 14 and those who remained until the leaving age.

Among those who left around age 11, about 55 percent entered classical or modern secondary streams, 5 percent went to technical *lycées*, and 40 percent enrolled in complementary courses. But again the percentage of those who reached classical or modern secondary schools varied from 80–85 for the liberal professions and higher white-collar groups, 75 for the high officials, and 61–68 for farmers, industrialists, lesser officials, and merchants, to 47–55 for the lesser employees, foremen, skilled workers, and artisans, and 43 and 34, respectively, for agricultural and nonagricultural workers. Girard noted that among students who left before 14, the share of those who marked "excellent" or "good" by teachers on a five point scale did not differ greatly from social group to social group. He concluded that school performance was certainly an important and at least partly independent factor in academic selection at age 11. But he did not provide the breakdowns or totals necessary to pursue this issue

Table X.1

	Those leaving before 14 (%)	Those remaining until 14 (%)
Liberal professions, industrialists	4	} 1
High officials, higher white collar	6	
Lower officials	11	5
Merchants, artisans	19	9
Lesser employees, artisans	20	12
Workers	17	27
Farmers	15	29
Agricultural workers	2	8
Retired, unknown	6	9
Total	100	100

Table X.2

Father's Occupation	School grades					All grades
	Excellent	Good	Average	Mediocre	Poor	
Liberal professions, business executives	97	97	90	59	10	90
High white collar	100	98	92	72	50	94
Middle white collar	96	94	76	30	21	84
Low white collar	98	91	64	22	5	67
Artisans, shopkeepers	97	91	67	25	11	66
Workers	91	79	42	10	3	45
Farmers	76	64	32	9	5	40
Agricultural workers	92	63	27	3	0	32
All groups	93	83	51	15	6	55

very far. Fortunately, much more careful and subtle work was done in connection with a survey of over 20,000 pupils in 1962–63, undertaken partly to check the effects of the 1959 reforms. This work is summarized in an excellent 1965 article by Sauvy and Girard. By 1962–63, elementary classes at secondary schools had been abolished, and the complementary courses had become "general secondary" schools (CEG). Some 55 percent of the age group were entering some type of secondary 6^e, and social differences of access had been somewhat further reduced since 1954. Nonetheless, Sauvy and Girard ob-

tained the percentages given in Table X.2 of each social group *and* grade level who reached the enlarged secondary system. While 55 percent of pupils reached a secondary 6e, only 27 percent entered the *lycées* (rather than the CEG, which drew the other 28 percent). But again the access percentages for the *lycées* were 75 percent for the liberal professions and high white-collar occupations, 55–57 percent for heads of business enterprises and middle-level employees, 32–33 percent for petty employees, artisans, and shopkeepers, 16 percent for farmers and nonagricultural workers, and 11 percent for

agricultural workers. Further losses in the share of the lower social groups then occurred between the 6^e and the 1re, and between secondary graduation and university entry. Following a generation of nonagricultural workers' children through the school system between 1957 and 1964–65, Sauvy and Girard thus estimated that they were 35 percent of all pupils to begin with, 27 percent of those academically qualified to enter a 6^e, 20 percent of those who did so, 14 percent of those reaching the 3^e, 12 percent of those in the 1re, and 8 percent of those entering the universities.

Table XI

France: Public Faculty Degrees, Enrollments and Population, 1851–1961
(Degrees and Enrollments in Thousands, Population in Millions)

Year	Degrees (in parentheses) and students in:					All faculties	Total population	Students per 1000 pop.	Pop. aged 19–22	Students per 1000 aged 19–22
	Law	Medicine	Pharmacy	Letters (& Theol.)	Sciences					
1851[a]	(1.0)	(0.4)	(0.2)	(0.1)	(0.1)		35.8			
1856[a]	(0.8)	(0.4)	(0.2)	(0.1)	(0.1)		36.0			
1861	(0.8)	(0.4)	(0.2)	(0.1)	(0.1)		37.4			
1866	(1.1)	(0.5)	(0.3)	(0.1)	(0.1)		38.1			
1876	(1.0) 5.2	(0.6) 4.0	(0.4) 1.4	(0.1) 0.3	(0.1) 0.3	11.2	36.9	0.3	2.4	4.7
1881	(1.3) 5.2	(0.7) 4.1	(0.4) 1.1	(0.2) 0.9	(0.2) 0.7	12.0	37.7	0.3	2.6	4.6
1886	(1.4) 5.7	(0.5) 5.7	(0.4) 1.6	(0.3) 2.1	(0.4) 1.2	16.3	38.2	0.4	2.7	6.0
1891	(1.2) 7.7	(0.6) 6.2	(0.6) 2.5	(0.3) 2.7	(0.3) 1.6	20.7	38.3	0.5	2.6	8.0
1896	(1.2) 8.8	(1.1) 8.5	(0.8) 3.1	(0.4) 3.5	(0.3) 3.1	26.9	38.5	0.7	2.7	10.0
1901	(1.5) 10.2	(1.2) 8.6	(0.6) 3.3	(0.5) 3.9	(0.3) 3.9	29.9	39.0	0.8	2.5	12.0
1906	(1.7) 14.3	(1.1) 8.1	(0.6) 2.7	(0.5) 5.0	(0.5) 5.6	35.7	39.3	0.9	2.5[b]	14.3
1911	(2.0) 17.3	(1.0) 9.9	(0.3) 1.6	(0.5) 6.2	(0.5) 6.1	41.2	39.6	1.0	2.5	16.5
1921	(2.3) 17.4	(1.4) 11.3	(0.4) 2.2	(0.8) 8.1	(0.8) 10.9	49.9	39.2	1.3	2.5[b]	20.0
1926	(1.5) 17.4	(1.5) 12.3	(0.4) 3.7	(0.6) 12.5	(0.7) 12.6	58.5	40.7	1.4	2.7[b]	21.7
1931	(2.1) 20.7	(1.1) 18.1	(0.8) 5.5	(1.2) 18.7	(0.8) 15.5	78.7	41.8	1.9	2.7	29.1
1936	(2.9) 21.6	(1.4) 17.7	(0.8) 5.7	(1.6) 17.5	(0.8) 11.3	73.8	41.9	1.8	2.0	36.9
1946	(6.3) 42.3	(1.5) 20.5	(1.1) 8.5	(2.0) 29.0	(1.8) 22.9	123.3	40.5	3.0	2.5	49.3
1951	(3.0) 38.7	(2.3) 30.2	(1.1) 7.1	(1.8) 36.6[c]	(1.2) 27.0	139.6	42.0	3.3	2.6	53.7
1956	(3.1) 37.0	(2.2) 30.0	(0.8) 7.9	(2.4) 43.2	(1.8) 39.3	157.5	43.6	3.6	2.4	65.6
1961	(1.9) 34.3	(2.3) 31.7	(0.9) 9.2	(4.0) 64.4	(6.3) 70.2	210.9[d]	45.9	4.6	2.2	95.9

TERMS: Years listed are academic years 1875–76, etc., except that calendar years are used in the case of degrees from 1861 through 1881, and from 1901 through 1961. All matriculated students are counted, including foreigners and those attending Algerian faculties (see below). Because of other imprecisions in the data, calculations are made from rounded figures (as tabulated), except that the total for 'All faculties' is taken directly from the sources, not from rounded subtotals for the several faculties. In general, the term *faculty* is used loosely, since various nineteenth-century "higher schools" (*écoles supérieures*), especially in the professional fields, played roles similar to those of independent faculties in the absence of an integrated university system. Students listed under 'Medicine' include those studying medicine at "mixed" faculties of medicine and pharmacy and at *écoles de plein exercise* and *écoles préparatoires de médecine et de pharmacie* during the nineteenth century. Similarly, 'Pharmacy' includes pharmacy students at these institutions. Theology students included under Letters were never numerically significant. Degrees reported are those most commonly taken in each of the several faculties or schools, i.e., the doctorate in medicine, the state pharmacist's diploma, and the *licence* in law, theology (insignificant numbers), letters, and sciences. See below for details. The 'Population aged 19–22' comprises four full age years, i.e., to just under 23.

[a] Figures on degrees in these lines are five-year averages for 1851–55 and 1856–60.

[b] Age years 19 through 22 defined as one-fifth of age years 15 through 19, plus three-fifths of age years 20 through 24.

[c] Arithmetic mean of data for 1950 and 1952.

[d] The total exceeds the sum of figures for the several faculties by about 1.1 thousand in the source, and only the total could be independently verified.

SOURCES: *Statistique de l'enseignement supérieur 1878–1888* and same title *1889–1899* for enrollments 1876 through 1896. *Annuaire statistique*, vol. 42 (1926) for degrees through 1886 and vol. 72 (1966) for total population through 1946, degrees from 1891, and enrollments from 1901. INSEE, *Population*, for age group 19–22 and for total population from 1951. Also BUS *Recueil 1942–1945* and *1949–1951*; *Informations statistiques*, no. 82–83 (1966); UNESCO, *World Survey of Education*, vol. 3; Sutter et al, "L'Evolution de la taille"; Halls, *Society*; *Schools and Progress*, pp.140–46 for additional comments.

The Problem of Algeria: It has been impossible to eliminate enrollments in Algerian faculties with any consistency. While only a small *école de plein exercise* existed in Algeria as of 1876, the tabulated enrollment figures for 1896 include a total of just under 0.5 thousand students in Algerian faculties and schools of law, medicine, pharmacy, letters, and sciences. Subsequently, enrollments in Algerian institutions rose to just over 5 thousand by 1951 and 1956, and about 7.5 thousand in 1961. Since the population figures pertain to metropolitan France alone, this problem intrudes an error into the ratios of enrollments per population and age group that amounts to about 2 percent for 1896, and around 3.5 percent for 1951–61.

Pattern of Degrees: A general difficulty in the interpretation of data on French degrees (especially in the nineteenth century) is that students could earn several certificates in succession or even work on them simultaneously, and not necessarily in the same faculty. The best way to minimize this problem, if not to eliminate it, is to concentrate on the degrees most commonly sought, as was done in the table. The full pattern, of course, was

336

more complex than the figures suggest. Degrees awarded by public faculties in theology, including a baccalaureate, the *licence*, and a doctorate have never been numerically significant. The public faculties of Catholic theology were actually suppressed in 1885, the Protestant ones in 1906, though both were revived in 1921. Baccalaureates in the field were awarded at an average rate of less than 50, *licences* and doctorates at less than 5 per year during the nineteenth century, and no theology degrees at all were separately reported after 1900. In law, a *certificat de capacité* and a baccalaureate functioned as intermediate degrees. Baccalaureates were generally a bit more numerous than *licences* before they ceased being reported in 1900. *Capacités* did not reach 200 per year until 1887, or 400 until 1931, but have since been more numerous, at around 700, 900, 1000, 1000, and 500 in 1936, 1946, 1951, 1956, and 1961, respectively. Nonetheless, the *licence* has always been the clear goal of most law students. The numerical range of state doctorates in the field was 100–200 through 1896, 300–600 ca. 1901–1911, and 200–400 ca. 1921–61, with the exception of a high 500 in 1946. In medicine, degrees of *officier de santé* (until 1892 only, with geographically limited accreditation) and *chirurgien-dentiste* were

awarded at a joint yearly rate of 100–200 through 1906, 200–400 ca. 1911–26, and 400–600 ca. 1931–61, with the exception of a high around 900 in 1951. A *diplôme d'état de sage-femme* (range 200–700) clearly had less academic standing than other medical degrees during the nineteenth century; it has been awarded with decreasing frequency since the 1930s. The same is true of a degree of *herboriste* in pharmacy (average rate 100), which ceased being reported in 1900. In letters and sciences, university-level students tended to prepare either for the secondary teaching *licence* or (much more rarely) for the difficult *agrégation*. The yearly rate of sciences doctorates was less than 20 until the late 1870s, around 20–40 until the 1920s, just over 100 in the late 1930s and again in the late 1940s, and still below 300 in 1956 and 1961. The even rarer doctorates in letters did not surpass a yearly 20 until the 1890s, averaged some 30–50 per year until the late 1940s, and around 40–80 since then. A preliminary certificate in the natural sciences required of medical students was the only other degree reported, at least until recently. Beginning in 1959, however, a much more complex pattern of degree awards is described in the source. The most important of the new certificates may be divided into three classes. The first comprises a new set

of introductory diplomas, awarded after an initial year of preparatory study: the *diplôme d'études juridiques générales*, the *certificat d'études supérieures préparatoires* in science, and the *certificat d'études littéraires générales*, earned in 1961 by 2.3, 8.3, and 8.8 thousand students, respectively. A second set of new degrees was made up of *licences* in sciences and letters that, unlike those previously reported, were explicitly not teaching *licences*. Some 0.6 and 3.6 of these degrees in letters and sciences, respectively, are included for the first time in the tabulated figures for 1961. Finally, the source for 1961 reports in detail on a group of certificates that lie between the level of the *licence* and that of the traditional "state" doctorate. These include the *diplômes d'études supérieures*, the *doctorat du troisième cycle*, less demanding than the state doctorate, and various "university diplomas," including the *doctorat d'université*, often awarded to foreign students. None of these is treated in the main table. The most important among them is the *doctorat de troisième cycle*, earned in 1961 by 358 students in the sciences and by 64 in letters.

Women, Foreign Students, and Special Students: The number of female students at French public universities was about 0.9

thousand (3 percent of all students) in 1901, 4 thousand (10 percent) in 1911, 7.3 thousand (14 percent) in 1921, 20.3 thousand (27 percent) by 1936, and 85.9 thousand (40 percent) by 1961. Women have been particularly well represented in the faculty of letters and, more recently, in pharmacy. Foreign students, including those from French colonial territories through 1936, numbered as follows, in thousands (and in percentages of total enrollments): 1.5 (7 percent) in 1891, 1.5 (6 percent) in 1896, 1.8 (6 percent) in 1901, 2.9 (8 percent) in 1906, 5.4 (13 percent) in 1911, 6.5 (13 percent) in 1921, 12.0 (21 percent) in 1926, 17.3 (22 percent) in 1931, 9.0 (12 percent) in 1936, 3.4 (3 percent) in 1946, 9.9 (7 percent) in 1951, 8.8 (6 percent) in 1956, and 14.6 (7 percent) in 1961. Thus noteworthy increases in the relative weight of foreign students among all students occurred between 1906 and 1911 and between 1921 and 1926. Marked decreases in their share took place between 1931 and 1946. The figures do not suggest that a change in the number of foreign students was ever a cause of significant fluctuations in the ratio of total enrollments to the age group. On the other hand, women and foreigners together did account for a substantial part of the enrollment growth at the French universities between 1901 and

1931. As of 1901, total enrollments at the university faculties also included various students in special categories. Thus 154 students in Medicine were in fact working toward the certificat d'études physiques, chimiques et naturelles (PCN), which was a prerequisite for admission to medical studies. In Letters, 595 students were "following courses but not seeking degrees." In the Sciences, 1,389 students were working for the certificate PCN, 163 were attending courses without seeking degrees, and 251 were registered in the so-called écoles spéciales de chimie industrielle and de physique industrielle. Apparently, these special schools were practice-oriented offerings by science faculties who sought contact with local industries. Many of those who attended these courses may not have completed their secondary studies, and this may have been true also of some of those preparing for the less demanding professional certificates in medicine and pharmacy.

Private and Religious Higher Education: Though they did not exist until 1875, a group of "free" faculties and institutes grew up during the 1880s that were both helped and hindered by the repressive policies of the state. Little is known about these institutions, the most famous of which was and is the

Institut Catholique in Paris. There were no students of theology at these schools, but the official statistics reported enrollments of about 0.7 and 1.3 thousand in the other fields as of 1881 and 1896, respectively. This amounts to some 5–6 percent of students in the public faculties, a proportion very similar to their estimated 6.5 percent of all French university-level students reported by Halls for the early 1960s. We also know that higher seminaries (grands séminaires) trained priests and theologians during the nineteenth century, though nothing about them appears in the official sources. This must certainly be kept in mind when interpreting the data for the public faculties.

The grandes écoles: From the official reports on secondary education in 1842, 1865, 1876, and 1887 (see notes to IX) and from sources cited above, one can construct the following summary account of these institutions. École Polytechnique: Students preparing for its entrance examination at public lycées and collèges were 583 in 1865, 773 in 1876, and 990 in 1887. Numbers of entrants (and percentages of entrants having prepared at public lycées and collèges) were 176 (93 percent) in 1839–42 (three-year average), 133 (77 percent) in 1865, 271 (79 percent) in 1876, 220 (70 percent) in 1887. Total enrollments

lic" and "various" *grandes écoles* (the term is used) in 1942–43 and for "public and private *grandes écoles*" (by major fields) in 1960–61.

The large group of 'Other engineering and technical' *grandes écoles* includes the *écoles nationales supérieures d'ingénieurs* (ENSI) in such fields as chemistry and electricity and the now so-called *écoles nationales d'ingénieurs arts et métiers*. Some 14.1 of the 48.2 thousand students listed for all the nonuniversity higher schools in 1961 attended private institutions.

Altogether, the 1961 pattern scarcely resembles that of the nineteenth century. Some 6.2 thousand engineering diplomas were awarded in 1961, in addition to the traditional university degrees. Still, there is a certain continuity in the ratio of *grande école* to faculty enrollments. As of the late 1880s, somewhere near 3 thousand students must have attended *Normale, Chartes, Langues Orientales, Polytechnique, Mines, Ponts et Chaussées, Centrale, Saint-Cyr,* and *Navale*. Many of these students were probably also matriculated for degrees at the public faculties. In 1955, according to a UNESCO estimate, this was true for no less than 40 percent of students at the *grandes écoles*. But if one applies that rate of double enrollment to the estimated total for the late

may be estimated at ca. 300–450 from 1801 to 1870 (apart from lows ca. 1814–20 and ca. 1850), then 600–800 right up to 1954. *Ecole des Ponts et Chaussées* and *Ecole des Mines*: Combined enrollments were in the range of 300–500 from 1888 to 1950. *Ecole Normale* (Rue d'Ulm): Students preparing for its entrance examinations at public *lycées* and *collèges* were 193 in 1865, 280 in 1876, and 461 in 1887. Yearly numbers of entrants (they came almost exclusively from the public secondary schools) averaged 26 ca. 1809–1842, 31–32 ca. 1843–74, and 41 ca. 1875–85. Total enrollments may be estimated in the range of 60–100 from 1809 to 1875, then 110–40 until the late 1880s (range 113–35 confirmed for 1878–88). Graduates of the school were 1,759 of 6,556 aspirants and 561 of 1,018 successful candidates for the *agrégation* in the period 1843–65; they were 414 of 8,251 aspirants and 302 among 1,319 successes in 1875–85. *Saint-Cyr*: Numbers of entrants (and percentages of entrants having prepared at public *lycées* and *collèges*) were 331 (51 percent) in 1839–42 (three-year average), 260 (78 percent) in 1865, 395 (52 percent) in 1876, and 449 (58 percent) in 1887. *Ecole Centrale*: According to Artz, *Development of Technical Education*, pp. 251–52, about 300 students were enrolled in the three-year course by 1840. The *Annuaire* shows that enrollments stood near 700 ca. 1898–1913, moved erratically from about 900 in 1919 to around 2,200 in 1921 and back to 800 by 1924, then settled in the range 700–900 until 1950. *Ecole des langues Orientales*: 129 and 537 students (excluding auditors) in 1888 and 1898, respectively. *Ecole des Chartes*: 46 and 49 students in 1888 and 1898, respectively.

Ecoles nationales d'arts et métiers (ENAM): Day, "Transformation of Technical Education," mentions about 300 students in each of the two existing schools during the late 1830s and comparable enrollments per school (yearly classes of 100, with 75 completing the course) around 1903, when four ENAM's existed. The *Annuaire* shows total ENAM enrollments moving from about 1,100 in 1898 to 1,400–1,500 on the eve of the First World War, 2,000–2,200 in the 1920s and early 30s, and back to ca. 1,400 by 1950. *Ecoles supérieures de commerce*: Total enrollments, again from the *Annuaire*, were about 1,100 in 1898, 2,000 just before 1914, 2,600–3,200 ca. 1928–33, and 1,600 in 1950.

Since the interwar period, the newer commercial and technical "*grandes écoles*" have far outstripped the traditional institutions in size. Table XI.1 lists the officially reported enrollments (thousands) for selected "pub-

Table XI.1

	1943	1961
Normale Supérieure, Paris and Sèvres	0.3	}
Normale Supérieure, St.-Cloud and Fontenay		1.2
Other higher normal	0.1	2.0
Langues Orientales	0.3	1.7
Chartes	0.1	}
Others: humanities		0.3
Total: Academic and higher normal		5.2
Arts, architecture	2.4	4.1
Agriculture, forestry, veterinary science	1.4	2.4
Dentistry		4.2
Ecole des Hautes Etudes Commerciales	0.6	0.9
Ecoles Supérieures de Commerce		
Other commercial	0.2	3.0 / 1.4
Total: Commercial studies		5.3
Polytechnique		0.6
Centrale	0.4	0.8
Other engineering and technical	0.7	19.4
Total: Technology and industry		20.8
Saint-Cyr		0.7
Navale		0.2
Other military		1.1
Total: Military		2.0
Colonial Affairs	0.3	
Instituts d'Etudes Politiques		3.3
Other "juridical sciences"		0.8
Total: Political affairs		4.1
Overall Total		48.2

1880s as well as to the overall figure for 1961, one is left in both cases with *additional* grande école enrollments that are roughly 10–15 percent of university enrollments.

Duration and Age of University Study: The official statistics for 1878–88 and 1889–99 divide matriculated law students into four groups, labeled first through fourth year. Enrollments (thousands) in 1890–91, for example, were 2.6, 1.9, 1.6, and 0.8 in the four successive years. This suggests that in the numerically important faculty of law, three years was the minimum length of study for the *licence*. Liard, *L'enseignement supérieur*, vol. 2, p. 45, seems to refer to the nineteenth century generally in reporting four years in medicine, three in pharmacy, and three for the *licence* in law. In the other fields and for the more recent period, the evidence is more occasional. Medical studies have apparently taken five or more years to complete, while the course in pharmacy lasted four years around 1925. The *licence* in letters or sciences could be earned in two years during the interwar period; but three years in letters and up to five in the sciences have recently been reported as more typical (e.g., by Halls). There is no doubt that the duration of university study has been generally lengthened since the Second World War. In 1954 the minimal program in law was extended from three to four years. The introduction of the preparatory year (*année propédeutique*) in 1948 also meant a delay for most students. On the other hand, it has been estimated that up to 40 percent of students have been forced to leave the universities at the end of this first year.

One great difficulty in the interpretation of such scattered information is that French students have been able to matriculate in more than one faculty. This was particularly true during the nineteenth century, when even attendance and study at a *lycée* could be combined with the taking of faculty "inscriptions" on the way to a degree that was almost a formality. Further, the science faculty began during the late nineteenth century to prepare and certify candidates for entry into the medical faculty, on the basis of introductory courses in physics, chemistry, and biology. Among those matriculated in public science faculties in 1891, 83 were described as students in medicine, 42 as students in pharmacy, and 395 as neither of these but also not candidates for the *licence* or *agrégation* in the sciences. In the faculty of letters during the same year, there were 103 law students and 498 not specifically assigned either to law or to the *license* or *agrégation* in letters. Under the circumstances, the division of total enrollments by a four-year age group is no more than a reasonable convention.

Some relevant distributions in BUS, *Recueil*, and in *Informations statistiques* do suggest that age years 19 through 22 are the most representative four years to choose, at

least for the recent period. It is puzzling at first, however, that *Informations statistiques* obtains 7.3 percent of age 20 as the highest share of any age-year in attendance at public university faculties as late as 1964–65. This is considerably below the 9.6 percent suggested by the ratio tabulated above for 1961. The figure would be 8.9 percent if foreign students were excluded, as was done in *Informations*. A contemporary average duration of study in excess of four years could account for some of the remaining difference. But above all, *Informations* shows students spread over a wide age range, from 18 to

over 30, and that is the most likely source of the discrepancy. The results tabulated above certainly come closer than *Informations* to the proportion of French youths in any age year who received a university education sometime before reaching age 30. Still, the issues raised in this paragraph, together with the problems posed by enrollments in Algerian faculties, private faculties, and *grandes écoles*, do tend to make the tabulated ratio to age 19–22 a somewhat abstract quantity, though surely an indicative one.

Table XII

France: Social Origins of University Students, 1939–1956
(Percentages of Fathers in Stated Occupations)

Father's Occupation	1939	1941	1943	1946	1948	1950	1953	1956
1. Liberal professions	18.8	18.0	20.3	16.5	18.0	17.4	14.6	11.8
2. Officials	25.7	22.6	26.3	26.8	27.4	28.1	27.6	28.6
3. Rentiers, etc.	9.8	15.6	13.1	7.5	6.8	6.2	6.0	3.9
4. Farmers	4.0	0.8	0.6	4.8	5.0	5.1	4.9	5.2
5. Agricult. workers	0.9			0.7	0.5	0.9	0.4	0.8
6. Entrepreneurs	16.0	15.8	16.4	16.2	16.3	} 15.4	9.6	7.5
7. Shopkeepers							12.0	12.5
8. Artisans	3.8	4.4	3.9	5.1	7.1	5.1		
9. Employees	12.6	12.2	11.0	12.6	9.6	12.1	14.6	15.0
10. Workers	1.6	1.4	1.9	1.7	1.5	1.9	2.5	3.4
11. Unknown	6.8	9.2	6.5	8.1	7.8	7.8	7.8	11.3
Absolute totals (100%)	52,014	70,945	97,746	102,499	118,585	122,003	127,246	135,197

1941 by Faculties

Father's Occupation	Law	Med.	Letters	Sciences
1. Liberal professions	18.1	18.8	15.1	20.7
2. Officials	26.9	19.9	21.6	21.3
3. Rentiers, etc. }	16.9	13.7	19.0	12.1
4. Farmers }				
5. Agricult. workers	0.3	0.4	1.6	0.9

1950 by Faculties

Father's Occupation	Law	Med.	Letters	Sciences
1. Liberal professions	14.4	26.1	11.8	18.5
2. Officials	26.9	21.0	39.5	24.1
3. Rentiers, etc.	6.2	7.4	6.5	4.0
4. Farmers	4.5	4.6	6.3	5.0
5. Agricult. workers	1.3	0.7	0.9	0.5

Father's Occupation	1941 by Faculties				1950 by Faculties			
	Law	Med.	Letters	Sciences	Law	Med.	Letters	Sciences
6. Entrepreneurs } 7. Shopkeepers }	15.3	16.3	12.4	20.0	16.3	18.1	10.9	16.6
8. Artisans	3.2	5.7	5.2	3.6	5.0	3.6	5.3	7.0
9. Employees	12.3	11.4	12.6	12.9	14.3	11.0	9.2	13.9
10. Workers	0.5	1.6	1.9	2.0	1.5	1.3	2.1	3.0
11. Unknown	6.5	12.2	10.6	6.5	9.6	6.2	7.5	7.4
Absolute totals (100%)	20,103	19,323	17,776	13,743	38,038	29,578	31,485	22,902

TERMS: The figures pertain to French students in public university faculties, but absolute totals indicate those surveyed rather than total enrollments. The faculties of medicine and pharmacy are combined under 'Medicine' in the lower half of the table. Occupational categories are literal translations of the sources, except that 'Officials' includes military as well as civil government employees of all ranks; 'Rentiers, etc.' are property-owners (propriétaires), rentiers, and those without profession; 'Farmers' are owners in agriculture; 'Entrepreneurs' are heads (chefs) of commercial and industrial enterprises; 'Shopkeepers' are petty merchants (petits commerçants), separated from the "heads of enterprises" and combined with artisans after 1950; 'Artisans' includes small-scale independents in industry; 'Employees' (employés) covers all ranks in industry and commerce; and 'Workers' are further described as "industrial," i.e., not in agriculture or public service.

SOURCES: BUS, Recueil 1949–1951, for 1941, 1943, and 1950 breakdown by faculty; Informations statistiques, no. 22 (1960), for all faculties 1939 and 1946–56.

343

Table XIII

France: Social Origins of University Students, 1959–1963
(Percentages of Fathers in Stated Occupations, Absolute Totals in Thousands)

Father's Occupation and % of 1954 Census	1954 Census	1959 by Faculties						1963 by Faculties					
		Law	Med.	Pharm.	Letters	Sci.	All	Law	Med.	Pharm.	Letters	Sci.	All
1. Professions:	0.6	12.0	29.0	24.9	7.5	8.2	12.8	11.1	19.8	27.1	6.6	7.0	10.1
2. Professors:	0.4	2.0	3.3	3.3	8.5	3.1	4.5	2.6	3.7	3.5	4.1	4.1	3.8
3. High officials:	0.9	7.0	7.2	7.5	5.9	3.9	5.7	6.4	8.2	8.1	5.5	6.6	6.5
1–3. Sum	1.9	21.0	39.5	35.7	21.9	15.2	23.0	20.1	31.7	38.7	16.2	17.7	20.4
4. Teachers:	2.0	2.1	3.4	3.3	8.4	5.2	5.2	3.2	3.2	3.8	6.3	5.8	5.1
5. Mid. officials:	1.1	8.8	4.9	5.6	8.1	5.8	6.8	6.8	5.5	5.1	6.8	7.1	6.7
6. Low officials:	4.1[a]	6.3	2.9	2.5	8.1	6.6	6.1	a	a	a	a	a	a
7. Farmers:	20.8	4.0	3.0	5.1	6.2	5.2	4.9	5.2	3.3	5.5	7.2	8.2	6.5
8. Agricult. workers:	6.0	0.9	0.4	0.4	0.7	1.1	0.8	0.4	0.1	0.1	0.6	0.7	0.5
9. Industrialists:	0.4	{ 7.2	7.4	10.0	6.9	4.2	6.3	4.8	4.0	5.2	2.3	2.9	3.2
10. Merchants:	1.0	(⎫ with 9)						{ 7.6	9.2	12.7	9.8	8.9	9.2
11. Shopkeepers:	6.7	{ 11.5	10.5	15.2	11.6	14.4	12.5	(⎫ with 10)					
12. Artisans:	3.9	(⎫ with 11)						3.1	3.2	3.4	4.5	5.1	4.2
13. High white collar:	1.0	5.6	6.7	6.8	3.1	5.8	5.3	6.9	6.0	7.1	4.9	5.5	5.7
14. Mid. white collar:	2.8	7.0	5.0	4.8	4.0	7.7	5.9	5.6	4.2	4.9	6.5	5.5	5.6
15. Low white collar:	6.8[a]	6.6	3.9	3.0	5.2	8.6	6.2	6.9	6.6	4.5	7.5	8.1	7.4
16. Workers:	33.8[a]	2.3	1.6	1.3	3.0	4.4	3.0	4.2	3.0	1.6	10.4	10.1	7.9
17. Domestics:	5.1	—	—	—	—	—	—	0.6	0.5	0.2	1.1	1.3	1.0

Father's Occupation and % of 1954 Census		1959 by Faculties						1963 by Faculties					
		Law	Med.	Pharm.	Letters	Sci.	All	Law	Med.	Pharm.	Letters	Sci.	All
18. Rentiers:	(−)	6.3	2.3	2.4	6.1	3.3	4.5	8.2	6.8	4.4	9.5	7.3	8.0
19. Others:	2.6	–	–	–	–	–	–	15.8[b]	2.9	2.8	6.4	5.8	7.1
20. Unknown:	(−)	10.4	8.5	3.9	6.7	12.5	9.5	0.6	9.8	–	–	–	1.5
Absolute totals (100%)		29.6	27.6	7.7	47.9	56.7	169.6	41.1	36.9	9.5	82.0	83.1	252.6

TERMS: The table describes surveys of French students in public universities (including Algeria) as of June 1959 and June 1963. In general, occupational categories used in these reports follow the terminology of the census (1954 sample of working population), though the correspondence is somewhat closer in the 1963 than in the 1959 survey. 'Liberal professions' may include artists and clergy in 1959. 'Professors' includes secondary teachers (along with "literary and scientific professions" in the census), and both 'Professors' and 'Teachers' (*instituteurs*), i.e., primary level, combined with middle-level employees in medical and social services in the census) encompass a few individuals in private institutions. 'High officials' and 'Middle officials' are high-level and middle-level employees (*cadres supérieurs, cadres moyens*) in the public sector. For 'Low officials', see note *a* below. 'Farmers' (*culti-vateurs*) include agricultural tenants, share-croppers, and supervisory personnel (*régisseurs, cadres*). Under "owners" or "directors" (*patrons*) in industry and commerce, the census lists industrialists, artisans, fishery owners (*patrons pêcheurs*, 0.1 percent), large merchants (*gros commerçants*, 0.9 percent) and shopkeepers (*petits commerçants*); but the 1959 survey distinguishes only between "heads of industrial and commercial enterprises" and "artisans and shopkeepers," while the 1963 figures list "industrialists," "artisans," and "those in commerce" (*commerçants*). In the census, 'High white collar' covers engineers as well as administrative *cadres supérieurs* in the private sector, though the engineers are not separately mentioned in the surveys of students. This is true also of "technicians" among *cadres moyens* in the private sector. For 'Low white collar (*employés subalternes* in 1959 survey), see note *a* below. Under 'Workers', census distinctions include those among foremen and skilled (*qualifiés*) workers in the public sector (1.5 percent), foremen in the private sector (0.7 percent), skilled and semi-skilled workers in the private sector (21.3 percent), miners, sailors, and fishermen (1.5 percent), apprentice workers (1.1 percent), and unskilled workers (*manoeuvres*, 5.8 percent). But the 1959 survey mentions only "workers in industry," presumably as distinct from agriculture and public service, while the 1963 report (all faculties) itemizes foremen (1.8 percent), "workers" (5.5 percent), and *manoeuvres* (0.6 percent). 'Domestics' translates *personnel de service*; this category was probably subsumed under 'Workers' in the 1959 survey, and it really covers only butlers, maids, and similar occupations. As usual, the 1959 and 1963 surveys carry a rubric for "rentiers, without profession, and [1959 only] property-owners." 'Others' (*autres catégories* in the 1963 report and in the census) is further described in the census as encompassing artists (0.2 percent), clergy (0.8 percent), and the military and police (1.6 percent); these groups are presumably included with the liberal professions and officials in the 1959 survey.

a Census indicates 4.1 percent office clerks (*employés de bureau*) in the public sector and 4.5 percent in the private sector plus 2.3 percent commercial clerks (*employés de commerce*); it also assigns 3.4 percent among the 33.8 percent for workers to the public sector. Data for 1959 include a single rubric of lower officials (*fonctionnaires subalternes*) that clearly comprises blue-collar workers as well as clerks in public employment (and presumably some military as well); the 1963 survey includes blue-collar government with other workers and does not distinguish between public and private office clerks, which are therefore grouped with the commercial clerks under 'Low white collar'.

b Source actually lists 0.6 percent; but calculations from totals indicate 15.8 percent, which is only a little more surprising than the 7.1 percent for all faculties in this category.

SOURCES: *Informations statistiques*, no. 22 (1960), no. 69 (1965). INSEE, *Recensement général 1954, Population active*, I: *Structure professionnelle*.

346

Table XIV

France: Social Origins of Students at Selected Grandes Ecoles, 1961-1962
(Percentages of Fathers in Stated Occupations)

Father's Occupation and % of 1954 Census		University 1963	Normale Paris	Inst. d'Et. Polit.	Polytechnique	Ecole des Mines	Ecole Centrale	Sup. Commerce	ENSI Chem. Eng.	Arts et Métiers	Nat. Agronom.	Other Normale Sup.
1. Lib. professions:	0.6	10.1	7	15	16	9[a]	7	8	7	3	4	—
2. Professors:	0.4	3.8	33	3	8	10[a]	4	1	3	2	3	9
3. High officials:	0.9	6.5	7	11	19	11	16	8	10	6	7	6
1–3. Sum	1.9	20.4	47	29	43	30	27	17	20	11	14	15
4. Teachers:	2.0	5.1	14	3	9	4	5	2	5	5	4	14
5. Mid. officials:	1.1	6.7	5	7	3	8	6[b]	6	7	6	6	6
6. Farmers:	20.8	6.5	1	8	1	5	2	4	5	5	28	7
7. Agricult. workers:	6.0	0.5	—	—	—	—	—	—	—	1	—	1
8. Industrialists:	0.4	3.2	2	8	5	4	3	12	5	4	3	—
9. Merchants and shopkeepers:	7.7	9.2	5	8	6	6	7	17	10	6	10	7
10. Artisans:	3.9	4.2	2	3	2	3	2	3	4	9	2	7
8–10. Sum	12.0	16.6	9	19	13	13	12	32	19	19	15	14
11. High white collar:	1.0	5.7	4	15	14	11	20	17	10	8	8	3
12. Mid. white collar:	2.8	5.6	7	3	3	6	7[b]	6	7	8	8	4
13. Office clerks:	8.6	4.7	3	5	5	11	9	3	7	7	3	7
14. Commercial clerks:	2.3	2.7	2	3	3	1		2	4	3	1	3
11–14. Sum	14.7	18.7	16	26	25	29	36	28	28	26	20	17

347

Table XIV continued

France: Social Origins of Students at Selected Grandes Ecoles, 1961–1962

Father's Occupation and % of 1954 Census	University 1963	Normale Paris	Inst. d'Et. Polit.	Poly-technique	Ecole des Mines	Ecole Centrale	Sup. Commerce	ENSI Chem. Eng.	Arts et Métiers	Nat. Agronom.	Other Normale Sup.
15. Workers: 33.8	7.9	3	2	2	5	2	5	7	17	5	15
16. Domestics: 5.1	1.0	–	1	–	–	–	–	1	2	1	2
17. Rentiers: –	8.0	4	3	1	5	6	5	5	5	5	5
18. Others: 2.6	7.1	1	2	3	1	4	1	3	3	2	4
1–18. Totals: 100.0	98.5[c]	100	100	100	100	100	100	100	100	100	100
1–3, 8, 11 Sum: 3.3	29.3	53	52	62	45	50	46	35	23	25	18

[a] Professors at private institutions counted with the liberal professions.

[b] Estimates based on a figure of 13 percent *cadres moyens* in the public and private sectors.

[c] 1.5 percent of university students' fathers were in unknown occupations.

SOURCE: *Conditions de développement des grandes écoles.*

TERMS: 'University 1963' repeats the distribution for all public university faculties from Table XIII. Occupational and census categories are used exactly as in the 1963 survey described and annotated in that table, except that the unworkable 'Low officials' is here dropped altogether, while 'Low white collar' is divided into office and commercial clerks. See note *a* to Table XIII. The schools, in order of listing (with the number of institutions sampled in each group) are: *Ecoles Normales Supérieures*, Paris and Sèvres; *Institutes d'Etudes Politiques* (five, including what is still informally called "Sciences Po"); *Ecole Polytechnique; Ecole des Mines* (three, not one); *Ecole Centrale des Arts et Manufactures; Ecoles Supérieures de Commerce* (twelve); *Ecoles Nationales d'Ingénieurs* for chemistry (fourteen); *Ecoles Nationales d'Ingénieurs Arts et Métiers; Ecoles Nationales Agronomiques* (three); *Ecoles Normales Supérieures,* Saint-Cloud and Fontenay.

BIBLIOGRAPHY

Citations of government publications, the main primary sources used, begin with the notations Bavaria, France, Germany, Great Britain, and Prussia, but they are otherwise integrated into this single alphabetical list. A few anthologized articles are cited in full even though the anthologies themselves are separately listed. This is to facilitate the identification of convenient short titles used in the footnotes. Which items contain important statistical data should be clear from the notes to the tables, especially to those in the Appendix [I–XIV]. Other works mentioned are of interest for the analyses they offer, as useful general accounts, or as up-to-date clarifications of relatively narrow issues or subjects. Every effort was made to prune this list; it includes only the best and most essential titles in the field. The list excludes works that have appeared since the spring of 1977, when the manuscript for this book was completed.

Anderson, C. Arnold. "Access to Higher Education and Economic Development." In *Education, Economy and Society*, edited by A. H. Halsey, Jean Floud, and C. Arnold Anderson. New York: Macmillan, 1961.

——. "A Skeptical Note on Education and Mobility." In *Education, Economy and Society*, edited by A. H. Halsey, Jean Floud, and C. Arnold Anderson. New York: Macmillan, 1961.

——, and Miriam Schnaper. *School and Society in England: Social Backgrounds of Oxford and Cambridge Students.* Washington: Public Affairs Press, 1952.

Anderson, Robert. "The Conflict in Education: Catholic Secondary Schools (1850–1870): A Reappraisal." In *Conflicts in French Society: Anticlericalism, Education and Morals in the Nineteenth Century*, edited by Theodore Zeldin. London: Allen and Unwin, 1970.

——. "Secondary Education in Mid Nineteenth-Century France: Some Social Aspects." *Past and Present*, 1971, pp. 121–46.

Archer, Margaret Scotford, and Salvador Giner. "Social Stratification in Europe." In *Contemporary Europe: Class, Status and Power*, edited by Margaret Scotford Archer and Salvador Giner. New York: St. Martins, 1971.

Armytage, W. H. G. *Four Hundred Years of English Education.* Cambridge: Cambridge University Press, 1964.

Artz, Frederick B. *The Development of Technical Education in France, 1500–1850.* Cambridge, Mass.: MIT Press, 1966.

Ashby, Sir Eric. *Technology and the Academics: An Essay on Universities and the Scientific Revolution.* London: Macmillan, 1959.

Bamford, T. W. "Public Schools and Social Class, 1801–1850." *British Journal of Sociology,* 12 (1961): 224–35.

Banks, Olive. *Parity and Prestige in English Secondary Education.* London: Routledge & Kegan Paul, 1955.

Barnard, H. C. *A Short History of English Education: From 1760 to 1944.* London: University of London Press, 1949.

Bavaria, Statistisches Landesamt. *Sozialer Auf- und Abstieg im Deutschen Volk: Statistische Methoden und Ergebnisse (Beiträge zur Statistik Bayerns, 117).* München, 1930.

Beier, Adolf, ed. *Die höheren Schulen in Preussen (für die männliche Jugend) und ihre Lehre.* 3rd ed. Halle, 1909.

Blau, Peter, and Otis Dudley Duncan. *The American Occupational Structure.* New York: Wiley, 1967.

Boudon, Raymond. *Education, Opportunity, and Social Inequality: Changing Prospects in Western Society.* New York: Wiley, 1973.

Bourdieu, Pierre, and Jean Claude Passeron. *Les Etudiants et leurs études.* Paris: Mouton, 1964.

———. *Les Héritiers: Les étudiants et la culture.* Paris: Editions de Minuit, 1964.

———. *La Réproduction: Eléments pour une théorie du système d'enseignement.* Paris: Editions de Minuit, 1970.

BUS, *Recueil:* see France, Ministère de l'Education Nationale, Bureau Universitaire de Statistique.

Busch, Alexander. *Die Geschichte des Privatdozenten.* Stuttgart: Ferdinand Enke, 1959.

Bush, John W. "Education and Social Status: The Jesuit Collège in the Early Third Republic." *French Historical Studies* 9(1975):125–40.

Cameron, Rondo E. "Economic Growth and Stagnation in France, 1815–1914." *The Journal of Modern History* 30(1958). Bobbs-Merrill Reprint.

Chapoulie, Jean-Michel. "Le corps professoral dans la structure de classe." *Revue française de sociologie* 15(1974):155–200.

Collins, Randall. "Functional and Conflict Theories of Educational Stratification." *American Sociological Review* 36(1971):1002–19.

Commission Carnegie, *Enquêtes:* see France, Commission française pour l'enquête Carnegie.

Conditions de développement des grandes écoles: see France.

Conrad, Johannes. *Das Universitätsstudium in Deutschland während der letzten 50 Jahre.* Jena, 1884.

————. "Einige Ergebnisse der deutschen Universitätsstatistik." *Jahrbücher für Nationalökonomie und Statistik.* Third Series 32:433–92. Jena, 1906.

Cotgrove, Stephen F. *Technical Education and Social Change.* London: Allen & Unwin, 1958.

Crew, David. "Definitions of Modernity: Social Mobility in a German Town, 1880–1901." *Journal of Social History* 7(1973):51–74.

Dahrendorf, Ralf. *Society and Democracy in Germany.* Garden City, New York, 1967.

Daumard, Adeline. "Les élèves de l'Ecole Polytechnique de 1815 à 1848." *Revue d'histoire moderne et contemporaine* 5(1958):226–34.

Day, C. R. "Technical and Professional Education in France: The Rise and Fall of *L'enseignement secondaire spécial,* 1865–1902." *Journal of Social History,* 6(1972–73):177–201.

————. "The Transformation of Technical Education in France: The Ecoles d'Arts et Métiers 1806–1914." Mimeographed. Simon Fraser University, 1974.

Dieterici, Wilhelm. *Geschichtliche und statistische Nachrichten·über die Universitäten im preussischen Staate.* Berlin, 1836.

D'Ocagne, Mortimer. *Les grandes écoles de France.* Paris, 1873.

Dreyfuss, Carl. *Occupation and Ideology of the Salaried Employee.* Translated by E. Abramovitch. New York: Works Progress Administration and Department of Social Science, Columbia University, 1938.

Eulenburg, Franz. *Die Entwicklung der Universität Leipzig in den letzten hundert Jahren.* Leipzig: Hirzel, 1909.

————. *Die Frequenz der deutschen Universitäten von ihrer Gründung bis zur Gegenwart. Abhandlungen der philologisch-historischen Klasse der königlich-sächsischen Akademie der Wissenschaften,* vol. 24, no. 2. Leipzig: Teubner, 1904.

Farrington, Frederic Ernest. *French Secondary Schools.* London, 1910.

Fischer, Aloys. "Die Entwicklung der deutschen Schulgesetzgebung seit 1918." Münchener Lehrerverein, *Pädagogische Kongressblätter* I(1925): 132–87.

Floud, Jean E. "The Educational Experience of the Adult Population of England and Wales as at July 1949." In *Social Mobility in Britain,* edited by David V. Glass. London: Routledge & Kegan Paul, 1954.

————, and A. H. Halsey. "Social Class, Intelligence Tests, and Selection for Secondary Schools." In *Education, Economy and Society,* edited by A. H. Halsey, Jean Floud, and C. Arnold Anderson. New York: Macmillan, 1961.

————, ed., A. H. Halsey, and F. M. Martin. *Social Class and Educational Opportunity.* London: Heinemann, 1957.

Folger, John K., Helen S. Astin, and Alan E. Bayer. *Human Resources and Higher Education.* Staff Report of the Commission on Human Resources and Advanced Education. New York: Russell Sage Foundation, 1970.

Fortoul, "Rapport": see France, Ministère de l'Instruction Publique.

France. *Les Conditions de développement, de recrutement, de fonctionnement et de localisation des grandes écoles en France.* Rapport du Groupe d'Etudes au Premier Ministre, 26 Septembre 1963. La Documentation Française, 1964.

————, Assemblée Nationale, Chambre des Députés, Session de 1899. *Enquête sur l'enseignement secondaire.* Paris, 1899.

————, Bureau de la Statistique Générale. *Annuaire statistique de la France.* Paris.

————, Commission française pour l'enquête Carnegie. *Atlas de l'enseignement en France.* Paris, 1933.

————, Commission française pour l'enquête Carnegie. *Enquêtes sur le baccalauréat. Recherches statistiques sur les origines scolaires et sociales des candidats au baccalauréat dans l'académie de Paris.* Paris, 1935.

————, Institut National de la Statistique et des Etudes Economiques. *Population par sexe, age et état matrimonial de 1851 à 1962.* Etudes et documents, 10. Paris, Imprimerie Nationale, 1968.

————, Institut National de la Statistique et des Etudes Economiques. *Recensement général de la population de mai 1954. Résultats du sondage au 1/20eme, Population active, I: Structure professionnelle.*

————, Ministère de l'Education Nationale, Bureau Universitaire de Statistique et de Documentation Scolaires et Professionnelles. *Recueil de statistiques scolaires et professionnelles.* 1949, 1950, 1951.

————, Ministère de l'Education Nationale, Service Central des Statistiques et de la Conjoncture. *Informations statistiques.* 1–86 (1957–1966).

————, Ministère de l'Instruction Publique (et des Cultes). *Bulletin Administratif de l'Instruction Publique.* No. 52 (April 1854). Contains H. Fortoul, "Rapport à l'Empereur sur les établissements particuliers d'enseignement secondaire."

————, Ministère de l'Instruction Publique. *Bulletin Administratif du Ministère de l'Instruction Publique.* Vol. 69 (1901).

————, Ministère de l'Instruction Publique. *Rapport au Roi par . . . (Villemain) . . . sur l'instruction secondaire.* Paris, 1843.

————, Ministère de l'Instruction Publique (des Cultes et des Beaux-Arts). *Statistique de l'enseignement secondaire en 1865.* Paris, 1866.

————, Ministère de l'Instruction Publique (des Cultes et des Beaux-Arts). *Statistique de l'enseignement secondaire en 1876.* Paris, 1878.

————, Ministère de l'Instruction Publique (des Cultes et des Beaux-Arts). *Statistique de l'enseignement secondaire en 1887.* Paris, 1889.

————, Ministère de l'Instruction Publique (et des Beaux-Arts). *Statistique de l'enseignement supérieur.* 4 vols. Paris, 1868–1900.

————, Statistique de la France. *Résultats généraux du dénombrement de 1872.* Nancy, 1874.

Fraser, W. R. *Education and Society in Modern France.* London: Routledge & Kegan Paul, 1963.

Frijhoff, Willem, and Dominique Julia. *Ecole et société dans la France d'ancien régime.* Paris: Colin, 1975.

Furneaux, W. D. *The Chosen Few: An Examination of Some Aspects of University Selection in Britain.* London: Oxford University Press, 1961.

Gerbod, Paul. *La Condition universitaire en France au XIXe siècle.* Paris: Presses Universitaires, 1965.

Germany, *Deutsche Hochschulstatistik.* "Herausgegeben von den Hochschulverwaltungen" until 1933, then transferred to Reichsministerium für Wissenschaft, Erziehung und Volksbildung. Berlin, 1928–1936.

——, Federal Republic, Statistisches Bundesamt. *Statistik der Bundesrepublik Deutschland.*

——, Federal Republic, Statistisches Bundesamt. *Statistisches Jahrbuch für die Bundesrepublik Deutschland.* Wiesbaden.

——, Reichsministerium des Innern. *Jahrbuch für das höhere Schulwesen: Statistischer Bericht über den Gesamtstand des höheren Schulwesens im Deutschen Reich.* Vol. 1 (1931–32). Leipzig: Quelle & Meyer, 1933.

——, Statistisches Reichsamt. *Statistisches Jahrbuch für das Deutsche Reich.* Berlin.

——. *Wirtschaft und Statistik.* Vol. for 1967, p. 606: table published as appendix to "Soziale Herkunft der Gymnasiasten," an article elsewhere in the same number of this journal.

Gillis, John R. *The Prussian Bureaucracy in Crisis, 1840–1860: Origins of an Administrative Ethos.* Stanford, 1971.

Girard, Alain. "Enquête nationale sur la sélection et l'orientation des enfants d'age scolaire." *Population,* 1954, pp. 597–634.

——. *La Réussite sociale en France: Ses caractères—ses lois—ses effets.* INED, Travaux et Documents, 38. Paris: Presses Universitaires de France, 1961. Part II: "Les anciens élèves de quatre grandes écoles."

——, and Roger Pressat. "Deux études sur la démocratisation de l'enseignement, I: L'origine sociale des élèves des classes de 6e." *Population,* 1962, pp. 9–24.

Glass D. V. "Education and Social Change in Modern England." In *Education, Economy and Society,* edited by A. H. Halsey, Jean Floud, and C. Arnold Anderson. New York: Macmillan, 1961.

——, ed. *Social Mobility in Britain.* Glencoe, Ill.: The Free Press, 1954.

Gréard, Octave. *Education et instruction. Enseignement secondaire.* 2 vols. Paris: Hachette, 1887.

Great Britain, Committee on Higher Education. *Higher Education: Report of the Committee . . . under the Chairmanship of Lord Robbins 1961–63.* London: HMSO, 1961–63.

Halls, W. D. *Society, Schools and Progress in France.* London: Pergamon Press, 1965.

Halsey, A. H. "British Universities and Intellectual Life." In *Education, Economy and Society,* edited by A. H. Halsey, Jean Floud, and C. Arnold Anderson. New York: Macmillan, 1961.

————. "The Changing Functions of Universities." In *Education, Economy and Society*, edited by A. H. Halsey, Jean Floud, and C. Arnold Anderson. New York: Macmillan, 1961.

————, Jean Floud, and C. Arnold Anderson, eds. *Education, Economy and Society*. Glencoe, Illinois: The Free Press, 1961.

Hans, Nicholas. *New Trends in Education in the 18th Century*. London: Routledge & Kegan Paul, 1951.

Harrigan, Patrick J. "Secondary Education and the Professions in France during the Second Empire." *Comparative Studies in Society and History* 17(1975):349–71.

————. "The Social Origins, Ambitions and Occupations of Secondary Students in France during the Second Empire." In *Schooling and Society: Studies in the History of Education*, edited by L. Stone, pp. 206–35. Baltimore: Johns Hopkins, 1976.

Hartshorne, Edward Yarnall Jr. *The German Universities and National Socialism*. Cambridge, Mass.: Harvard University Press, 1937.

Harvard Educational Review 43:(Feb. 1973). Issue on Jencks et al.

Herrlitz, Hans-Georg, and Hartmut Titze, "Überfüllung als bildungspolitische Strategie." *Die deutsche Schule* 68(1976):348–70.

Hess, Gerhard. *Die deutsche Universität, 1930–1970*. Bad Godesberg: Inter Nationes, 1968.

Hoffman, Johann Gottfried. *Sammlung kleiner Schriften staatswissenschaftlichen Inhalts*. Berlin, 1843.

Horvath, Sandra Ann. "Victor Duruy and the Controversy over Secondary Education for Girls." *French Historical Studies* 9(1975):83–104.

Information statistiques: see France, Ministère de l'Education Nationale, Service Centrale des Statistiques.

INSEE: see France, Institut National de la Statistique et des Etudes Economiques.

Jahrbuch für das höhere Schulwesen: see Germany, Reichsministerium des Innern.

Jaubert, Louis. *La Gratuité de l'enseignement secondaire*. Bordeaux, 1938.

Jeismann, K. E. *Das preussische Gymnasium in Staat und Gesellschaft . . . 1787–1817*. Stuttgart: Klett, 1975.

Jencks, Christopher, et al. *Inequality: A Reassessment of the Effect of Family and Schooling in America*. New York: Basic Books, 1972.

————, and David Riesman. *The Academic Revolution*. New York: Doubleday, 1969.

Jenkins, Hester, and D. Caradog Jones. "Social Class of Cambridge University Alumni of the 18th and 19th Centuries." *British Journal of Sociology* 1(1950):93–116.

Julia, Dominique, and Paul Pressly, "La population scolaire en 1789: Les extravagances du Ministère Villemain." *Annales: Economies, Sociétés, Civilisations*, Nov.-Dec. 1975, pp. 1516–61.

Kaelble, Hartmut. "Chancenungleichheit und akademische Ausbildung in Deutschland 1910–1960." *Geschichte und Gesellschaft,* 1(1975): 121–49.

——. "Sozialer Aufstieg in den USA und Deutschland, 1900–1960." In *Sozialgeschichte heute,* edited by Hans-Ulrich Wehler. Göttingen: Vandenhoeck & Ruprecht, 1974.

Kagan, Richard L. "Universities in Castile 1500–1810." In *The University in Society,* edited by Lawrence Stone; vol. 2, *Europe, Scotland, and the United States from the 16th to the 20th Centuries.* Princeton: Princeton University Press, 1974.

Karady, Victor. "L'expansion universitaire et l'évolution des inégalités devant la carrière d'enseignant au début de la IIIe République." *Revue française de sociologie* 14(1973):443–70.

——. "Normaliens et autres enseignants à la Belle Epoque." *Revue française de sociologie* 13(1972):35–58.

Kath, Gerhard, ed. *Das soziale Bild der Studentenschaft in Westdeutschland und Berlin, Sommersemester 1963.* Deutsches Studentenwerk. Berlin: Colloquium, 1964.

Landes, David S. *The Unbound Prometheus: Technological Change and Industrial Development in Western Europe from 1750 to the Present.* Cambridge: Cambridge University Press, 1970.

Lasch, Christopher. "Inequality and Education." *New York Review of Books,* May 17, 1973.

Lenz, Max. *Geschichte der Königlichen Friedrich-Wilhelms-Universität Berlin.* vol. 3. Halle, 1910.

Lexis, Wilhelm H. *Die Reform des höheren Schulwesens in Preussen.* Halle, 1902.

——, ed. *Die deutschen Universitäten.* 2 vols. Berlin: Asher, 1893.

——, ed. *Das Unterrichtswesen im Deutschen Reich.* 4 vols. in 6. Berlin: Asher, 1904.

Liard, Louis. *L'enseignement supérieur en France, 1789–1889.* 2 vols. Paris, 1888–94.

Lindsay, Kenneth. *Social Progress and Educational Waste.* Studies in Economics and Political Science, London School of Economics. London, 1926.

Lipset, Seymour Martin, and Reinhard Bendix. *Social Mobility in Industrial Society.* Berkeley: University of California Press, 1966.

Little, Alan, and John Westergaard. "The Trend of Class Differentials in Educational Opportunity in England and Wales." *British Journal of Sociology* 15 (1964):301–16.

Lundgreen, Peter. *Bildung und Wirtschaftswachstum im Industrialisierungsprozess des 19. Jahrhunderts.* Berlin: Colloquium, 1973.

——. "Industrialization and the Educational Formation of Manpower in Germany." *Journal of Social History,* 9(1975–76):64–80.

MacLeod, Roy. "Resources of Science in Victorian England: The Endowment of Science Movement, 1861–1900." In *Science and Society, 1600–1900*, edited by Peter Mathias. Cambridge: Cambridge University Press, 1972.

Maillet, J. "L'Evolution des effectifs de l'enseignement secondaire de 1809 à 1961." In *La scolarisation en France depuis un siècle*, edited by Pierre Chevallier. Paris: Mouton, 1974.

Manegold, Karl-Heinz. *Universität, Technische Hochschule und Industrie.* Berlin: Duncker & Humblot, 1970.

Marsh, David C. *The Changing Social Structure of England and Wales, 1871–1961.* London: Routledge & Kegan Paul, 1965.

Metzger, Walter P. *Academic Freedom in the Age of the University.* New York: Columbia University Press, 1955.

Meyer, Ruth. "Das Berechtigungswesen in seiner Bedeutung für Schule und Gesellschaft im 19. Jahrhundert." *Zeitschrift für die gesamte Staatswissenschaft* 124(1958):763–75.

Miller, S. M. "Comparative Social Mobility." *Current Sociology* 9(1960).

Mitchell, B. R., ed. *Abstract of British Historical Statistics.* Cambridge: Cambridge University Press, 1962.

Mountford, Sir James. *British Universities.* London: Oxford University Press, 1966.

Mouton, Marie-Renée. "L'Enseignement supérieur en France de 1890 à nos jours (étude statistique). In *La scolarisation en France depuis un siècle*, edited by Pierre Chevallier. Paris: Mouton, 1974.

Musgrave, P. W. "A Model for the Analysis of the Development of the English Educational System from 1860." In *Sociology, History and Education: A Reader*, edited by P. W. Musgrave. London: Methuen, 1970.

———. "Constant Factors in the Demand for Technical Education, 1860–1960." In *Sociology, History and Education: A Reader*, edited by P. W. Musgrave. London: Methuen, 1970.

———. "The Definition of Technical Education, 1860–1910." In *Sociology, History and Education: A Reader*, edited by P. W. Musgrave. London: Methuen, 1970.

O'Boyle, Lenore. "Klassische Bildung und soziale Struktur in Deutschland zwischen 1800 und 1848." *Historische Zeitschrift* 207 (1968):584–608.

———. "The Problem of an Excess of Educated Men in Western Europe, 1800–1850." *The Journal of Modern History* 42(1970):471–95.

Palmer, R. R. "Free Secondary Education in France before and after the Revolution." *History of Education Quarterly*, 1974, pp. 437–52.

———, ed. *The School of the French Revolution: A Documentary History of the College Louis-le Grand . . . 1762–1814.* Princeton: Princeton University Press, 1975.

Paquier, J.-B. *L'enseignement professionnel en France: Son histoire, ses différentes formes, ses résultats.* Paris, 1908.

Paulsen, Friedrich. *Geschichte des gelehrten Unterrichts auf den deutschen Schulen und Universitäten vom Ausgang des Mittelalters bis zur Gegenwart.* 3rd ed. Edited by Rudolf Lehmann. Vol. 2. Berlin, 1921.

Peyre, Christiane. "L'Origine sociale de élèves de l'enseignement secondaire en France." In *Ecole et société,* edited by Pierre Naville. Recherches de sociologie du travail, 5. Paris: Rivière, 1959.

Pfetsch, Frank R. *Zur Entwicklung der Wissenschaftspolitik in Deutschland 1750–1914.* Berlin: Duncker & Humblot, 1974.

Piobetta, J.-B. *Le Baccalauréat.* Paris: Ballière, 1937.

Ponteil, Félix. *Histoire de l'enseignement en France: Les grandes étapes, 1789–1964.* Paris, 1966.

Prost, Antoine. *Historie de l'enseignement en France 1800–1967.* Paris: Armand Colin "Collection U," 1969.

Prussia, Ministerium der geistlichen, Unterrichts- und Medizinalangelegenheiten. *Statistische Mitteilungen über das höhere Unterrichtswesen im Königreich Preussen.* Berlin.

———, Statistisches Landesamt. *Preussische Statistik (amtliches Quellenwerk).* Berlin.

———, Statistisches Landesamt. *Statistisches Handbuch für den Preussischen Staat.* Berlin.

———, Statistisches Landesamt. *Statistisches Jahrbuch für den Preussischen Staat.* Berlin.

Reynolds, Edgar O. *The Social and Economic Status of College Students.* New York: Teachers College, 1927.

Ribot, *Enquête:* see France, Assemblée Nationale.

Richard, Camille. *L'Enseignement en France.* Paris, 1925.

Rienhardt, Albert. *Das Universitätsstudium der Württemberger seit der Reichsgründung.* Tübingen: Mohr, 1918.

Ringer, Fritz K. *The Decline of the German Mandarins: The German Academic Community, 1890–1933.* Cambridge, Mass.: Harvard University Press, 1969.

———. "Higher Education in Germany in the Nineteenth Century." *Journal of Contemporary History* 2(1967):123–38.

———. "Problems in the History of Higher Education," *Comparative Studies in Society and History* 19(1977):239–258.

Robbins Report: see Great Britain, Committee on Higher Education.

Rogoff, Natalie. "Social Stratification in France and in the United States." In *Class, Status and Power: Social Stratification in Comparative Perspective,* edited by Reinhard Bendix and S. M. Lipset. 2nd ed. New York: Free Press, 1966.

Rosenberg, Hans. *Grosse Depression und Bismarckzeit.* Berlin: Gruyter, 1967.

Rothblatt, Sheldon. *The Revolution of the Dons: Cambridge and Society in Victorian England.* London: Faber & Faber, 1968.

Runciman, W. B. "Class, Status, and Power?" In *Social Stratification*, edited by J. A. Jackson. Cambridge, 1968.

Ruppel, Wilhelm. *Über die Berufswahl der Abiturienten Preussens in den Jahren 1875–1899.* Fulda, 1904.

Sampson, Anthony. *The Anatomy of Britain Today.* New York: Harper & Row, 1965.

Samuel, Richard H., and R. Hinton Thomas. *Education and Society in Modern Germany.* London: Routledge & Kegan Paul, 1949.

Sanderson, Michael. *The Universities and British Industry, 1850–1970.* London: Routledge & Kegan Paul, 1972.

Sauvy, Alfred, and Alain Girard. "Les diverses classes sociales devant l'enseignement." *Population,* 1965, pp. 205–32.

Schoenbaum, David. *Hitler's Social Revolution: Class and Status in Nazi Germany, 1933–1939.* Garden City: Doubleday, 1966.

Schumpeter, Joseph A. *Imperialism and Social Classes.* Translated by Heinz Norden. New York: A. M. Kelley, 1951.

Schwartz, Benjamin J. "The Limits of 'Tradition versus Modernity' as Categories of Explanation: The Case of the Chinese Intellectuals." *Daedalus,* Spring 1972, pp. 71–88.

Schwartz, Paul. *Die Gelehrtenschulen Preussens unter dem Oberschulkollegium (1787–1806) und das Abiturientenexamen.* Vol. 1. Berlin, 1910.

Seabold, Richard. "*Normalien* Alumni in the *Facultés* and *Lycées* of France from 1871 to 1910: Promotions 1831 to 1869." Ph.D. dissertation, UCLA, 1970.

Shinn, Terry. *The Dawning of a Bourgeois Elite; The Ecole Polytechnique and the Polytechnician Circle.* Unpublished manuscript, scheduled for publication in French under the title *Savoir scientifique et pouvoir social: l'école polytechnique et les polytechniciens.*

Simon, Brian. *Education and the Labour Movement, 1870–1920.* London: Lawrence & Wishart, 1965.

————. *Studies in the History of Education, 1780–1870.* London: Lawrence & Wishart, 1960.

Smith, Robert J. "L'Atmosphère politique à l'école normale supérieure à la fin du XIXe siècle." *Revue d'histoire moderne et contemporaine* 20 (1973):248–68.

————. Manuscript on the Ecole Normale, to be published shortly.

Sozialer Auf- und Abstieg: see Bavaria, Statistisches Landesamt.

Statistische Mitteilungen: see Prussia, Ministerium der geistlichen, Unterrichts- und Medizinalangelegenheiten.

Stephenson, Jill. "Girls' Higher Education in Germany in the 1930's." *Journal of Contemporary History* 10(1975):41–69.

Stone, Lawrence. "The Size and Composition of the Oxford Student Body 1580–1909." In *The University in Society,* edited by Lawrence Stone. vol. 1, *Oxford and Cambridge from the 14th to the Early 19th Century.* Princeton: Princeton University Press, 1974.

Sutter, Jean, R. Izac, and T. N. Toan. "L'Evolution de la taille des polytechniciens, 1801–1954." *Population,* 1958, pp. 373–406.

Talbott, John E. *The Politics of Educational Reform in France, 1918–1940.* Princeton: Princeton University Press, 1969.

Taton, René, ed. *Enseignement et diffusion des sciences en France au XVIIIe siècle.* Paris: Hermann, 1964.

Thernstrom, Stephen. *The Other Bostonians: Poverty and Progress in the American Metropolis, 1880–1970.* Cambridge, Mass.: Harvard University Press, 1973.

UNESCO. *World Survey of Education.* vol. 3, Paris, 1961.

Vaizey, John E. *The Costs of Education.* London: Allen & Unwin, 1958.

Vaughan, Michalina. "The *Grandes Ecoles.*" In *Governing Elites: Studies in Training and Selection,* edited by Rupert Wilkinson. New York: Oxford, 1969.

Veysey, Laurence R. *The Emergence of the American University.* Chicago: University of Chicago Press, 1965.

Villemain, *Rapport:* see France, Ministère de l'Instruction Publique.

Vincent, Gérard. "Les professeurs du second degré au début du XXe siècle." *Le Mouvement social* 55(1966):47–73.

Weber, Max. *From Max Weber: Essays in Sociology.* Translated and edited by H. H. Gerth and C. Wright Mills. New York: Oxford, 1958.

———. *Gesammelte politische Schriften.* 3rd ed. Edited by Johannes Winckelmann. Tübingen: Mohr/Siebeck, 1971.

Weill, Georges. *Histoire de l'enseignement secondaire en France, 1802–1920.* Paris, 1921.

Weiss, John H. "The Origins of a Technological Elite: Recruitment of Students to the Ecole Centrale des Arts et Manufactures in the Nineteenth Century." Mimeographed. Ithaca, N.Y.: Cornell University, 1974.

Weisz, George. "The Politics of the Medical Profession in France 1815–1848. Mimeographed.

Wirtschaft und Statistik: see Germany.

Young, Michael. *The Rise of the Meritocracy, 1870–2033: An Essay on Education and Equality.* Harmondsworth: Penguin, 1961.

Zeldin, Theodore. "Higher Education in France, 1848–1940." *Journal of Contemporary History* 2(1967):53–80.

Zorn, Wolfgang. "Hochschule und höhere Schule in der deutschen Sozialgeschichte der Neuzeit." In *Spiegel der Geschichte: Festgabe für Max Braubach,* edited by Konrad Repgen and Stephen Skalweit. Münster: Aschendorff, 1964.

Index

The index is meant to cover only major institutions and concepts. For details on specific German and French institutions, the reader should consult the Appendix, particularly the full notes to Tables I, V, IX, and XI.